SOUTHWEST SHUFFLE

SOUTHWEST SHUFFLE

PIONEERS OF HONKY-TONK, WESTERN SWING, AND COUNTRY JAZZ

RICH KIENZLE

Routledge

New York and London

Published in 2003 by
Routledge
29 West 35th Street
New York, NY 10001
www.routledge-ny.com

Published in Great Britain by
Routledge
11 New Fetter Lane
London EC4P 4EE
www.routledge.co.uk

Printed in the United States of America on acid-free paper.
Design and typesetting: Jack Donner

10 9 8 7 6 5 4 3 2 1

Cataloging-in-Publication Data is available from the Library of Congress.

ISBN 0-415-94102-4 — 0-415-94103-2 (pbk.)

CONTENTS

PREFACE

If country music's deepest roots lie in the rural South, much of its color, vitality, and style originated in a vast arc from Texas and Oklahoma to California—the Southwest. What you'll find here are portraits of southwestern-based singers, songs, instrumentalists, and producers whose accomplishments had a profound influence on country music and, in a few cases, on American popular music. Some are acknowledged legends; others, behind-the-scenes players or unknowns. Each made unique and meaningful contributions.

Country music in the Southeast, Southwest, and Midwest possessed distinctive traits in tone, instrumentation, and repertoire, though traditional tunes and old-time fiddling were common to all. As each region grew and matured, its particular form of rural music took on characteristics indigenous to that region.

The rural Southeast drew deeply from traditional ballads, folk tunes handed from generation to generation along with fiddle tunes from the British Isles and antebellum and postbellum parlor tunes. Some songs were variants of the old "broadsides" describing current events and often spiced with moral messages. Though southern cities like Atlanta and Nashville were more urbane, the rural Southeast, a hotbed of religious fundamentalism, had many "dry" areas where alcohol sales were banned. Some preachers and like-minded politicians discouraged dancing except, in most cases, square dancing.

After the advent of radio, musical presentations typically took place in theaters, auditoriums, and schoolhouses, to sit-down audiences. As the automobile, railroad, radio, telephone, and air travel created greater mobility, a certain nostalgia grew for the "good old days" of rural isolation and simpler lifestyles.

In the 1920s, record companies and others bent on playing to that nostalgia created an illusion of "pure" rural music after seeing strong sales of records like Fiddlin John Carson's "Little Old Log Cabin in the Lane" and

Vernon Dalhart's "Wreck of the Old 97." These were the first manifestations of artifice in what came to be known as country music, conjuring up idyllic images of mountain folk playing rural songs of home and mother.

George Dewey Hay, the former Memphis newspaper reporter who conceived both the WLS *National Barn Dance* in Chicago and the *Grand Ole Opry* in Nashville, was a prime mover in this effort. As historian Charles Wolfe points out, Hay created a virtual rural fantasyland from the time the show began as the WSM *Barn Dance* in 1925. Hay put performers who normally wore suits into overalls to give them rural appeal, and he fabricated colorful names for the show's string bands.

As Hay defined this idealized rural ethos, it had no place for music or instruments (horns, drums, or accordion) that didn't seem "country" or were associated more with pop or jazz. A few renegades like fiddler Clayton McMichen openly incorporated jazz and pop into their repertoire, but they were exceptions to the rule.

Things differed in the Midwest. The traditional songs and fiddle tunes were there, but with Chicago, Cincinnati, and St. Louis and surrounding regions boasting huge numbers of German, Polish, and Italian immigrants, the idea of incorporating accordions, clarinets, and even drums into country bands was far less alien than in the Southeast. Parlor tunes were popular there, giving the music a more noticeably Victorian edge.

Midwestern country bands playing popular songs of the day, polkas, and even the occasional jazz tune raised few eyebrows there in the 1930s or 1940s. Protestant religious fundamentalism was certainly present, but dancing was far less alien a concept there, particularly in the larger cities. Many among Midwest's immigrant population were members of the Catholic Church, generally less doctrinaire on matters of drinking and even gambling. Both the WLS *National Barn Dance* and the WLW *Boone County Jamboree* epitomized this slightly more liberalized stance.

The Southwest stood apart from either of those regions. This was America's last continental frontier, settled by a tougher, hardier crew, many of whom left those other regions. Individuality held sway, and the idea of church-imposed morality or constraints of any sort were alien to the very fiber of those living there.

Its audacity manifested itself in many ways, from the Old West culture of the nineteenth century to the twentieth century's cheeky roadside attractions along the legendary Route 66 and Hollywood's glitz and glamor. More than the South or Midwest, the Southwest was multicultural, mixing not only whites and blacks but Mexicans and Indians. That didn't necessarily connote racial enlightenment, evidenced by wholesale killings of blacks in cities like Tulsa and overt racism in Los Angeles before and after World War II.

Texas was a melting pot for white southerners, Cajuns, Mexicans, Germans, Poles, Irish, and blacks, and the cowboy traditions and culture mixing blues, jazz, pop, Mexican, hillbilly, and polkas were part of daily life. In that looser, less-absolutist atmosphere, Bob Wills, Milton Brown, Tommy Duncan, and jazzmen like Jack Teagarden and Charlie Christian grew up surrounded by musical riches. Each assimilated all that they heard and melded it into something far greater than the sum of its parts. Dancing was commonplace, an outgrowth of Old West ranch dances. Dance halls were common. Jimmie Rodgers, whose music mixed pop, blues, old-timey, and jazz, based himself in Texas.

In the 1930s, a new type of "fiddle band" music came to be. This new, eclectic sound epitomized the diversity of Texas, mixing all styles of music for dancers. Bob Wills, Herman Arnspiger, and Milton Brown, working as the Light Crust Doughboys, pioneered this style. From 1932 until his death in 1936, Milton Brown and his groundbreaking band, the Musical Brownies, went even further in defining it. Starting in 1934, Wills, based in Tulsa, created his own legend leading his Texas Playboys, mixing everything from "El Rancho Grande" to "Empty Bed Blues."

At the same time, with Prohibition ended, blue-collar Texas taverns long known as "honky-tonks" became common. In the 1930s, a few Texas singers, Floyd Tillman, Al Dexter, and Ernest Tubb (inspired, in part by Rodgers), created plain-talking, hard-hitting songs dealing with romantic woes and fast living for these blue-collar patrons. That style, a pillar of country music, became known as honky-tonk, and the idea of spicing this music with amplified guitars and drums caused little controversy.

California was a sparsely settled rural state in the 1920s. Its early performers drew on a westernized version of the southeastern string band sound. As the area morphed into the entertainment center known as Hollywood by the 1930s, with the growing film industry and the popularity of singing cowboys, the region's country music took on a decidedly different tone. It wasn't just groups like the Sons of the Pioneers that brought a new polish and style to cowboy tunes, but also singers like Stuart Hamblen, who used trumpet and clarinet in his bands.

The Great Depression and the drought that strangled Texas and Oklahoma in the 1930s brought the first seeds of a population shift. As rural Texans and Oklahomans abandoned their parched farmland and headed west they brought along the "fiddle band" music of Bob Wills and others (not yet called "western swing").

World War II turned that flow of newcomers into a veritable tidal wave of immigrants from not only Texas, Oklahoma, and the Midwest but also the Southeast. California was not only a major military center for the Pacific Theater of War but a hotbed of defense manufacturing. The vast rural area surrounding a small coastal city became a newly sown metropolis teeming with new country music dance halls and bars to accommodate these new arrivals. From 1930 to 1950, the Depression and the war doubled California's population from 5 million to 10 million.

No one worried about musical purity or adding showbiz artifice to country music in Hollywood, where style and cutting-edge ideas were the lifeblood of the industry. That flashy sense of style, epitomized by flamboyant western outfits inspired by the movie garb of Gene Autry and others, even set the sartorial standard in country music and was de rigueur for Nashville performers by the 1940s. The pool of gifted, versatile musicians who worked on movie soundstages, in Hollywood radio and recording studios, routinely played with country bands.

Southern California was also fertile technological ground for electric instrument innovators like Adolph Rickenbacker, Leo Fender, and Paul Bigsby. Fender routinely road-tested his legendary Telecaster and Stratocaster electric guitars (as well as his early steel guitars and amps) on southwestern musicians. In 1948, Speedy West became country music's first pedal steel guitarist, playing an instrument custom-built for him by Paul Bigsby.

From 1944 to 1949, according to Joel Whitburn's *Top Country Singles: 1944–1997*, 15 of the 25 top-selling artists in that five-year period were southwestern. After Nashville's rise in the late 1940s, things changed permanently. From 1950 to 1959, only two of the top 25, not including Ray Price (who moved to Nashville in 1951), were Southwest-based: Hank Thompson and Tennessee Ernie Ford.

Southwestern music left an impact on country music everywhere. As the acoustic string band sound slipped into obscurity, sidemen in Nashville, Cincinnati, and at radio stations throughout the Southeast (and Northeast) grabbed musical ideas from records by Bob Wills, Spade Cooley, and others. Hot, jazz-influenced fiddle, stinging lead guitar, and blazing steel guitar breaks began appearing even on the Opry and on records by Nashville acts. A few brave Nashville singers like Carl Smith added drums to their bands in the 1950s, when the Opry still discouraged them.

George Hay didn't like it, but the Opry had to accept the change when Ernest Tubb left Texas to join the show in 1942, bringing with him electric lead guitar as part of his sound. Tubb's influence on Alabama-born Hank Williams was undeniable, and Hank's growing fame, with the popularity of southwestern singers Al Dexter, Floyd Tillman, and Hank Thompson, made honky-tonk a vital part of Nashville. Hank's style influenced his Texas protégé Ray Price, who was still seeking his voice, in 1951. Once Price found his own voice by turning to his Lone Star roots, as he did in the 1950s, his sound and shuffle rhythms became a bedrock country style. They remain so today, decades after his controversial move to an orchestrated country-pop sound.

It may seem unusual that such a large portion of this book focuses on artists and producers for one label: Capitol Records. In fact, Capitol became the great postwar catalyst for southwestern and particularly West Coast country, and continued in that role through the 1960s. When the label began in 1942, singing cowboy Tex Ritter was its first country artist. It was a vital incubator for the spin-off West Coast style known as Bakersfield Sound, which Buck Owens, Merle Haggard, and Wynn Stewart helped transform into a phenomenon with repercussions far beyond the West.

Capitol epitomized California's progressive country ethos. No one there cared about playing it safe. Lee Gillette, the label's first country producer, carted early portable tape equipment from California to Texas to record Hank Thompson in 1947. In the conservative postwar years when certain subjects were taboo, Capitol had no problem allowing Jimmy Wakely to record not one but *two* songs about adultery. The label's country successes helped it through some tough financial times.

Today Nashville is the acknowledged home base for country music. But that status didn't come until the late 1940s as the Opry grew dominant and a new recording scene blossomed there. Country music today would not be what it is without the contributions of singers, songwriters, instrumentalists, and music created in the Southwest. This is not a definitive history of country music in the Southwest. It's a look at some of those who made a difference.

ACKNOWLEDGMENTS

Interviews for these profiles took place over the past quarter century; many of the musicians interviewed then are long gone. They reflect my own experiences over that time, starting with the Spade Cooley and Hank Penny interviews, the first serious work I did in this field, up through the Speedy West–Jimmy Bryant and Willie Nelson interviews done over the past several years. Hank Penny became my guide to West Coast country, and explained much of the ebb and flow to me. I'm glad to tell his story again here, perhaps with a bit more candor than it's been told in the past.

Most of these chapters and sidebars originally appeared in substantially different form elsewhere. The pieces on Ray Price, Luke Wills, Bob Wills, Tommy Duncan, Hank Thompson, Speedy West–Jimmy Bryant, and Willie Nelson were originally written to accompany Bear Family Records collections. All have been considerably altered and updated.

Richard Weize began Bear Family in Germany in 1975 as a folk music label and eventually turned it into the preeminent country-music reissue label in the world. It's safe to say that, although his comprehensive, encyclopedic box sets may be too costly for many average budgets, along the way, he has spearheaded not only musical preservationism but major-league research into the music and careers of many country legends. It's ironic that no American historical or cultural institution (including the National Endowment for the Arts) has ever come close to matching what Weize has accomplished on his own. He has reissued a good chunk of the important country music of the past eight decades, and shows no signs of slowing down. Working with him is sometimes a challenge, but it's largely been a pleasure, and I appreciate his support. To get an idea of the massive scope of his undertaking (including his reissues of European pop music), check out www.bear-family.de. I'm also grateful to his associate R. A. Andreas for the generous offering of photos.

The stories on the *Hometown Jamboree*, Lee Gillette, Wade Ray, Ken Nelson, Tennessee Ernie Ford, "Smoke! Smoke! Smoke!" and "Slippin' Around" all ran in different form in the *Journal for the Preservation of Old-*

Time Country Music. Russ Barnard, the editor and publisher of *Country Music Magazine* since 1983, founded this sister publication in 1990. I was its senior editor, and for its first seven years the *Journal* was a stand-alone publication. With capable assistance from Managing Editor George Fletcher and Assistant Editor Helen Barnard, we published a remarkable number of articles, many featuring rare photographs and new research. With worthy contributions from the likes of, among others, Charles Wolfe, Nolan Porterfield, Wayne Daniel, Ken Griffis, Kevin Coffey, Charlie Seemann, and Dave Samuelson, the *Journal* was a valuable resource, and I remain deeply proud of the work we accomplished. Although a Spade Cooley piece I wrote ran in the July 1977 *Country Music Magazine*, the longer piece that appears in this book was essentially written from scratch with considerable new information added, including a more in-depth look at Cooley's music. I'll always be grateful to Russ in particular for allowing me the freedom to explore all aspects of country's history, as well as the unparalleled editorial freedom he gave me and my colleagues at *Country Music Magazine* during his stewardship, which ended with the magazine's sale in 1999.

The Jimmy Wyble piece originally appeared in a much shorter form in the November 1982 *Guitar World* magazine. Though I interviewed Roy Lanham for a 1987 *Guitar Player* magazine article and annotated a 1996 Lanham album for Bear Family, the piece here is essentially brand new. A portion of the Hank Thompson piece was adapted from an interview I did for an article that ran on amazon.com in 2000.

A number of people deserve special mention for their assistance. Dave Samuelson was always ready with insight, advice, or clippings from his substantial library of information. Kevin Coffey, the foremost western swing researcher of a new generation, graciously read over the Tommy Duncan and Luke Wills chapters and offered suggestions. Speedy West was always available to answer questions, as were the late Hank Penny until his death in 1992 and Cliffie Stone, until he passed on in 1998. Glenn White, the dean of Bob Wills collectors, is someone I got to know in the 1970s. His generosity with facts and memorabilia is as sincere as his love of Wills's music.

Charles Wolfe's friendship and knowledge have been tremendous assets over the past 22 years. Ronnie Pugh and Bob Pinson have been equally helpful. The Country Music Foundation is poorer for Ronnie's absence. Long before he became Elvis's definitive biographer, Peter Guralnick was a source of encouragement and inspiration to me, and he has been a friend for more than two decades. A newer friend, Chrissie Dickinson, former editor of the *Journal of Country Music* and a first-rate journalist with integrity to burn, has steadily lent support. It's likewise been a pleasure to know John Morthland, who goes back to *Country Music* days. I'll always be grateful to Ed

Ward and Nick Tosches. Without their help in the early days, I wouldn't have been doing this for 27 years.

Friends like Rochelle Friedman, Rob Santos, George Fletcher, John Johnson, Bob Irwin, the late Keith Kolby, Hank Thompson, D. D. Bray, Buck Ford, Dave Stewart, and the late Merle Travis all played roles in this book. Closer to home, Mary Kiley, Helen Adisey, Jim Albert, Sue and Denny Cavanaugh, Karen and Bob Stepanovich, and Randy and Jeannie Heffelfinger helped without even realizing it.

Thanks also to my editor, Richard Carlin, Robert Byrne, Lisa Vecchione, and the gang at Routledge, who showed infinite patience through the year this book's preparation time consumed.

My late parents, Dick and Nootie Kienzle, were never less than encouraging. I first heard "Sixteen Tons" on a jukebox at the old William Penn Club in Greensburg, where we were having dinner. Their forcing me to take guitar lessons in 1964 kicked open the door that led to what you're holding in your hands right now. Anything I know about swing music I got from Nootie, a hard-core Benny Goodman fanatic of the mid-1930s who appreciated everyone from Bob Wills to Muddy Waters and Lyle Lovett.

The America of 2002 is far different than the country was during the days covered in this book. It changed during and after World War II, and it changed again on September 11, 2001. Given those newer, more ominous realities, I believe that preserving these and other aspects of America's historical and cultural heritage—both the known and the obscure—is more important now than ever.

Rich Kienzle

1
Western
Swingers

Grit meets Glitz—Bob Wills and Spade Cooley: mid- to late 1940s.
(Courtesy Glenn White)

Jekyll and Hyde
Spade Cooley

Anyone who's read James Ellroy's *L.A. Confidential* or his novella *Dick Contino's Blues* has noticed the name Spade Cooley strung through the fictional text. Ellroy's vivid, mostly fictionalized characterization may have given readers pause. In fact, the noir master had good reason to seed Cooley throughout his dark backstreet world, for the fiddler-bandleader paved the way for the celebrity murder suspects of recent years.

In 1961, 34 years before O. J. Simpson and 41 years before Robert Blake faced charges of murdering their spouses, Cooley was arrested for fatally beating his wife, Ella May, part of the beating committed in front of the couple's 14-year-old daughter. Following his conviction, he spent the last eight years of his life in prison and in 1969, on the eve of parole, shortly after telling a reporter, "Today is the first day of the rest of my life," a fatal heart attack abbreviated that day.

Long before his lurid side emerged, Cooley redefined western swing as it existed on the West Coast. He expanded its parameters to encompass both the music's Texas blues-jazz-country-pop-Latin roots and strong elements of classical music, and the non-jazz, non-swinging pop "sweet band" dance music in vogue before and during World War II. His most significant music came during a three-year period extending from 1944 through 1947. Innovative, polished, and harmonically sophisticated, Cooley's band mixed smoothly arranged fiddle sections with daring electric guitar and steel guitar fireworks, a classical harp, and a sense of urbane dynamics that surpassed that of Bob Wills. Those achievements reflected the glitzy sophistication of Hollywood, its musical community, tied to the film and broadcasting industries, as well as the melting pot that the L.A. basin became as millions of southwesterners relocated there during the war, bringing their musical preferences with them from the plains and prairies.

Yet for all his impact on the West Coast, and six songs on *Billboard*'s charts from 1945 to 1947, Cooley's overall musical impact beyond the West Coast was negligible aside from the influential instrumental work of certain of his sidemen. Except for one cross-country tour to the East Coast, he largely confined himself to working from San Diego to Seattle, rarely going further east than Nevada. His greatest fame came from hosting a local TV variety show never seen beyond Southern California.

One-quarter Cherokee, Donnell Clyde Cooley was born on a ranch near Grand, Oklahoma, on February 22, 1910. His early life is largely a blur, though he lived in Oregon in 1925 and attended an Indian school where he learned violin and classical cello. His love of the classics was complicated by the realities of the Depression, and he turned to playing hoedown fiddle. By 1931, he'd relocated to Modesto, California. He cultivated formidable poker skills. In one game, he managed three straight flush hands, all in spades, earning himself his nickname.

Married by 1937, he and wife Ann had a son. To pay bills, Spade fiddled at square dances and, seeking greater opportunities, he hopped a train to Hollywood that year. Given the local musical industry, it wasn't a bad place for a classically trained musician to settle, but Cooley didn't head for the soundstages where reading musicians were welcomed. His physical resemblance to Roy Rogers, including similar slit eyes and smooth facial features, helped him land stunt work in many of Rogers's films for $17 a day. The two became close friends.

He made additional money fiddling in local clubs with cowboy groups like the Rhythm Rangers and the popular new western vocal group the Sons of the Pioneers, although that group had an eminently qualified fiddler in Hugh Farr. With the Rangers, he proved himself capable of accompanying others on upbeat cowboy tunes like "Dusty and Dry." His playing with guitarist Gene Haas on instrumentals like "Haas Stomp" evoked the swinging, jazzy guitar-fiddle instrumentals that Hugh Farr and his guitarist brother Karl played with the Pioneers. Later Cooley favorites like "Topeka Polka" first took shape during his days with the Rangers. He later acknowledged drawing inspiration from Clayton McMichen, the progressive-minded, jazz-loving southeastern fiddler whose 1930s band, the Georgia Wildcats, played ample amounts of Dixieland and swing-oriented music. He was particularly inspired by the fiddle arrangement on their recording of "Farewell Blues."

Illinois-born bass player Jack Williams worked with him in the band. "I was with the Rhythm Rangers when I first met him in 1939," Williams said in 1976. "His fiddle playin' and his ability to entertain [impressed me]. We played with everybody. We were doing more country and western." Spade's local reputation grew as the '40s began. Singer-guitarist-banjoist Smokey Rogers, who began his career working in Detroit radio at age 13 with Texas Jim Lewis and came to California in the 1930s, remembered Spade's status in those days. "Spade was the first fiddle player that was called," Rogers said in 1976. "Even with some of the smaller groups he worked with before, he was always a leader. You could call him if you needed a trio, quartet, or whatever. He could take a mediocre two or three guys and make 'em look like a million dollars."

Bob Wills's 1940 trip to Hollywood with part of the Texas Playboys to make the film *Take Me Back to Oklahoma* introduced his music to the West Coast. His return in 1941 with the full Playboys band for more movies led to an engagement at the Venice Pier ballroom in Santa Monica, where local country disc jockey Bert "Foreman" Phillips ran what he called the "County Barn Dances," bringing in talent from the *Grand Ole Opry* and the WLS *National Barn Dance*.

Phillips presented Wills at Venice Pier, where he and the Playboys, a full orchestra at the time, played to overflow crowds. In the audiences, Wills found many longtime fans from Texas, Oklahoma, and Arkansas who'd listened to his KVOO radio show in Tulsa before moving west. Phillips booked more local western talent into Venice Pier, including the Jimmy Wakely Trio—Wakely, singer-songwriter Johnny Bond, and Dick Reinhardt—who'd arrived from Oklahoma two years earlier and joined cowboy star Gene Autry's organization. In an interview in 1976, Bond said that Phillips was happy to have the Trio at Venice Pier, but wanted to attract dancers as well as listeners. "[Foreman] said you'll have to get some more pickers. And we hired Spade Cooley as one of them. And it was at that point that we noticed Spade had the ability to stand out and attract attention, and we noticed it and the crowd noticed it and everything was fine. Then, of course, Foreman Phillips noticed it." The Wakely Trio's engagement at Venice Pier lasted only three weeks. Bond remembered what happened when their engagement ended, and Phillips retained a house band at the ballroom.

> We had to leave, and when we left, Foreman put Spade Cooley in charge of the band. [Cooley] was an energetic character. He was always eager to work, eager to please. He had that drive about him that showed that he wanted to get ahead. He wanted to be more than just a fiddle player. In other words, on the bandstand prior to his having his own band, he had the ability to stand out. He had a thing that a lot of musicians didn't have, and it was called showmanship. He got a lot of that from Bob Wills. I'm sure that he copied Bob Wills's movements on the stage. It was his showmanship that put him across, a little like [Roy] Acuff—personality first and the fiddle second.

The Venice Pier house band was evolving into a Cooley-led entity unto itself by the first half of 1942. The band drew dancers to Venice Pier, headlining there (except when Phillips brought in the southeastern acts he favored, like Roy Acuff) for a record 18 months. He had first-rate musicians including Gene Haas, Smokey Rogers, Jack Williams on vocals, and fiddler Rocky Stone. Smokey Rogers remembered Phillips telling Cooley, "you're always showing up leadin' the band for other guys, so how about gettin' a band of your own?"

In 1943, Cooley hired pianist Eddie Bennett as a last-minute replacement at a Venice Pier show. As the two became acquainted, he met Bennett's wife, Barbara, an attorney known as "Bobbie." At some point that year, Cooley asked Bobbie to manage him. She never forgot the conversation. "I hadn't known anything about western music or anything like that," she recalled in 1976. "Spade came to see me and said he wanted to get away from just being another fiddle player and leading the band with other musicians. It wasn't his own band. And then he started his own band, and he asked me if I would take him over and handle him. I said, 'Well, I'll think about it.' He said, 'Well, I have $2,000 left, and that's all the money I have in the world. What can you do with me?"

Cooley expanded the group into an organization mixing the best of the Wills style with some decidedly more cosmopolitan elements. He hired gifted instrumentalist Larry DePaul, a Cleveland native who came to California with singer Texas Jim Lewis. DePaul, who played accordion, violin, and trombone, became the band's principal arranger. He built a fiddle section of musicians able to handle written arrangements, including Rex Call and Andrew Soldi. Later, he added Paul "Spike" Featherstone, surely the first classical harpist ever to play in a western swing band. Johnny Weis joined as lead guitarist; Smokey Rogers played banjo and guitar. Soldi and Rogers, also part of Texas Jim Lewis's band, were recruited for the Cooley band by DePaul. Dick Roberts was the band's first steel guitarist.

Bobbie Bennett negotiated a recording contract with Columbia, signed in September, 1943. Recording anything was a moot point at the time because of a "recording ban," a labor dispute between the Musicians Union and U.S. record companies that barred all musicians from recording anything except the V Discs shipped to the armed forces. The band personnel would change considerably during that time as Rocky Stone and others moved on.

Phillips was well aware that the wartime migration of southern, southwestern, and midwestern natives to the region that began in the 1930s had mushroomed. He realized that he could exploit their need for music from home. To manufacture connections between his dance patrons and musicians, Phillips dubbed Illinois native Jack Williams "Tex." Smokey Rogers, a native of Tennessee, became "Smoky Okie." Wyoming native Dean Eacker became "Arkie." Italian-American DePaul became "Pedro." Soldi became "Cactus." George Braunsdorf, the band's second bassist, became "Deuce Spriggens." He created a local ballroom network to accommodate workers coming off each of the three shifts around Los Angeles defense factories. Cooley's rising popularity soon brought him more job offers than he had time to handle. To handle these second-string engagements, he built a second band, around singer Happy Perryman.

"Spade wanted to build another band," explained Smokey Rogers. "Foreman had two or three dances going: one in Compton, one in Baldwin Park, Venice Pier, and the Riverside Rancho at that time. So Spade wanted a second band that could play when he wanted to go do bigger and better things and somehow keep this connection with Foreman going. So we had auditions for musicians to build this band."

At the auditions, Cooley and his musicians stumbled on an unknown who became another key member of the band: Earl Murphey, Jr., whom Phillips later dubbed "Joaquin" in honor of California's San Joaquin Valley. Depending on whom one interviews, either Smokey Rogers or Dean Eacker discovered the young musician. In 1976, Rogers explained:

> Joaquin, I guess, must have been about 18 or 19 years old. And we had different members of the [Cooley] band in different areas of the Riverside Rancho. I was out on the patio, listenin' to people play out there, and Deuce would be somewhere else, Pedro somewhere else . . . listening to them individually, what they could do.
>
> Well, I heard Joaquin. I was the first one that ever heard him. He played one tune on this little old six-string, a National or some little old student-type guitar, and he just knocked me plumb out. I run and got Cooley right away and said "Hey, come and look at this. Listen to what we got!" And he hired him right then, but not for no second band. He put him in *our* band immediately.

Dick Roberts, a player of limited abilities, moved over to Perryman's band, and soon Cooley's enthused cries of "Joaquin-o!" onstage were all that were required to turn Murphey loose on wild, freewheeling improvisations.

As Cooley's sound coalesced, he began recording an amazing set of transcriptions for Standard Radio Transcription Services in 1944 (transcription recordings weren't affected by the recording ban) demonstrating the band's depth and sense of adventure. Dynamic, swinging arrangements of venerable pop tunes like "Charmaine" showcased the tight fiddle section and Murphey's flawlessly articulated steel playing. A revisionist approach to jazz tunes like "South" and "Copenhagen" reflected the band's more visionary elements. While his sound owed much to Wills, the execution, split-second timing, and harmonic sophistication stood out from Wills or from anything else. Closer to home, Johnny Bond, a part of that era's history and an erudite observer of it, recalled the impact those discs had on that era and the entire West Coast:

It seems like everything we were doing at the time, everything that was being done in country music, there was a sameness involved, a pattern. If you listen to all of the records, we used the same musicians, and it pretty much sounded alike. And then one day, we learned that Spade was making some electrical transcriptions for Standard, and we thought nothing particular about that until they played 'em on the radio. And overnight, everybody's ears perked up with kind of a new sound. His arrangements had taken a giant step forward.

Hank Penny, working at Cincinnati's WLW, was floored when he heard the Cooley transcriptions. Penny had been bucking trends for nearly a decade, playing western swing in the Southeast. Well versed in jazz, he immediately grasped Spade's sophisticated ideas and his influences:

The best thing that he could do was pattern [himself] after Bob Wills, because Bob was the most important thing in the business at that time. And how could he do this without saying that he was copying Bob? There's no way that he could do it.

So what he had to do was take the idea of western swing and dress it up a la Benny Goodman, only go all with strings. Now we had the idea jelling and all of a sudden someone came up with the idea Here's the king of *western* swing, because Benny Goodman was the king of Swing. Bob Wills hadn't heard of the word "western swing." Bob was known as a Texas fiddle band. That's what they called him.

The recording ban ended. Columbia signed a new contract with the Musicians Union. Spade was free to record. He finally went into the studio on December 4, 1944, under the guidance of Uncle Art Satherley, who produced Bob Wills, Roy Acuff, Johnny Bond, and Gene Autry. The standout recording from that session was "Shame On You," one of those catchy tunes in the nexus between country and pop. Enhanced by Tex Williams's plangent vocal, Smokey Rogers harmonized on the chorus. Spade wrote the song at the Bennetts' home at 3 A.M., just a few hours before the session. Songwriter Fred Rose, who was visiting L.A. at the time, gave them another ballad, "A Pair of Broken Hearts."

Released on Columbia's OKeh label, "Shame" stood out from the pack and apart from the more raucous, direct music of Wills. It topped *Billboard*'s Folk Music Charts for nine weeks in the spring of 1945. "Broken Hearts," the flip side, also did well. "Shame" became so popular that Red Foley covered it for Decca, accompanied by Lawrence Welk's orchestra, in an obvious attempt to bridge the country and pop markets.

Early in 1945, Hank Penny was vacationing in L.A. on leave from WLW when he heard the Cooley band at the Sunset Rancho on Sunset Boulevard. If the Standards had blown him away in Cincy, seeing the band in person did it twice over. "I flipped," he said. "I couldn't *believe* this! He had a real flair for flash." Some of that flash, originally heard on the Standards, reappeared on the band's Columbia recordings in the form of numbers like "Swingin' the Devil's Dream," which transformed the shopworn fiddle favorite into hip, sophisticated jazz. Even on more conventional country tunes, the band's dynamics added exciting new dimensions. A surviving Riverside Rancho broadcast of the band, featuring Roy Acuff's "Fireball Mail" sung by Smokey, revealed a zestful Rogers vocal amid a relentlessly swinging arrangement, the arranged fiddles riffing away behind him like a horn section.

Not all Cooley band members read music. With gifted arrangers like DePaul assembling complex musical interactions, the band's readers taught the non-readers their parts by rote, until they'd polished and rehearsed them enough to play them from memory. That's what they did as they learned material for the Standard Transcriptions. As Tex Williams recalled, "After a couple years with the western swing–type band, most everything was arranged. It was memorized. He didn't use music on the stand but most of it was arranged." Rogers explained the arranging this way: "Most all of the choruses played in harmony [by the fiddle section] were written out. Sometimes he'd write [guitar parts]. Joaquin couldn't read a lick of music. Everything he played was strictly what he heard or what we told him, what harmony to play."

Early in 1945, Cooley and the band landed a national outlet on NBC by replacing Spike Jones on the wartime show *A Furlough of Fun*. During the April 12 broadcast, an announcer rushed into the studio to announce Franklin D. Roosevelt's death. Bobbie Bennett was there. "We switched the show completely around, and did all of the numbers that Roosevelt liked, like 'Home on the Range.' He was quite a western fan. Eddie Dean happened to be a guest star on the show that night. And Eddie did a tremendous job on 'Ave Maria,' which I have never heard as beautifully done."

With the war ending late that summer, Spade continued pressing ahead. He had a second hit that fall with "I've Taken All I'm Gonna Take from You." By then, Bobbie Bennett had so many local offers for the band that she revisited the Perryman idea and recruited Hank Penny, Ray Whitley, Tex Ritter, and Merle Travis to lead bands and play jobs that Cooley couldn't handle. "We had so many places to play that Spade wasn't able to play all of these," she said. "So it was Spade Cooley band number 1, 2, 3, 4 . . ."

The Columbia sessions continued yielding amazing pieces like Murphey's dynamic and audacious instrumental, "Oklahoma Stomp." Originally titled "Riverside Drive" in honor of the Rancho's address, a dramatic Featherstone harp flourish, followed by drummer Muddy Berry's pounding tom-toms, introduce a Murphey tour-de-force that's lost none of his power in the nearly six decades since he recorded it. Even with Pedro DePaul spending most of 1945 in the service (replaced on accordion by the gifted George Bamby), creativity continued flowing from the Cooley band.

Murphey's soaring arrangement of "Steel Guitar Rag" places the song in a more cosmopolitan context than Leon McAuliffe's original version with Bob Wills, while enhancing the song's sense of excitement. The guitarist's ability to mix complex harmonic ideas, shivery chord melodies, and dazzling single-string work, became one of the band's great assets. Johnny Weis's blazing, arcing lead guitar, in the tradition of Charlie Christian, enhanced the band's cutting-edge sound as he and Murphey played against the smoothly arranged fiddles.

Although Pedro was the principal arranger, Spade's classical training stood him in good stead. "He was an excellent musician," Bobbie Bennett remembered. "He could tell if any note was wrong. He could read [music] beautifully. He was educated as a concert cellist, originally. He went to the Indian school, and then he went to the violin. His father before him was just a hoedown country fiddler."

Spade divorced his first wife, Ann, and married Ella May Evans, who sang in his band between six months and a year. Looks, not musical prowess, most likely spurred her hiring. "She had no voice," Bobbie Bennett remarked. Yodeler Carolina Cotten brought her vivacity to the band until Spade's continued success brought more bookings than either the first or second band could handle. In June 1945, he built yet another spin-off band around Deuce Spriggens, Eddie Bennett, and Cotten. Eventually Ossie Godson replaced Bennett on piano (Godson also doubled on vibraharp) in the main band.

Cooley never ignored the visual aspects. He and his musicians wore flamboyant western outfits made by L.A. tailor Nathan Turk (Nudie's distinguished predecessor), who also crafted rainbowlike western duds for the Maddox Brothers and Rose. Onstage, the bandleader was a dynamo. Speedy West, who worked for Cooley a few months in 1948, never forgot the man's onstage charisma: "He was outstanding, I believe, as good a showman as I ever saw hit a stage as a bandleader. He was not comical or anything. He had spirit, he had poise. He had lots of enthusiasm, a big smile on his face, and he jumped from one side of that stage to the other, constantly waving that fiddle bow and then pointin' it at the audience and wavin' it at the band as a baton."

Fidoodlin': Spade, Ginny Jackson, Hank Penny in the early 1950s.

It may have looked spontaneous, but all of Cooley's sliding and dancing came from meticulous planning. Bobbie Bennett watched him rehearse those onstage moves in front of a mirror for hours until he had them right. "He was a Nijinsky. He was all over the stage. He was a forerunner of Elvis Presley." Merle Travis never forgot it. He recalled that Spade "had the footwork of Muhammad Ali. He'd simply glide from one side of that stage to the other. His band was perfection, and his costumes were elaborate." For audiences, his charisma was irresistible. Bobbie Bennett's and Spade's flair for promotion continued as Spade, reveling in his "King of Western Swing" title, sponsored a "Queen of Western Swing" contest.

Pedro DePaul returned in January 1946. That spring, Cooley enjoyed another hit single with Paul Westmoreland's ballad "Detour," sung by Tex with Rogers and Eacker (who left the band shortly afterward) on harmony, and the successful B-side "You Can't Break My Heart." Murphey left to join Andy Parker and the Plainsmen, a group that included George Bamby. His replacement, Noel Boggs, formerly with Bob Wills and Hank Penny, made his mark on instrumentals like Cooley's minor-key, Middle Eastern–toned "Spadella," likely named for the bandleader and his new wife. A version featuring Murphey is preserved on a 1946 radio transcription, but Boggs's trademark, his brittle, astringent tone, stood out on the Columbia recording, as did his rich harmonic sensibilities, different yet every bit as exciting as Joaquin's. The growing sophistication of the guitar section was apparent on "Three Way Boogie," a whirlwind instrumental built around the standard guitars of Weis and Rogers, Boggs's steel guitar, the fiddle section, and DePaul's awesome accordion. This doesn't mean that the original band always batted a thousand. At times it literally drowned in schmaltzy or blatantly cornball fare tilting to gimmicky fluff. Certain performances on the Standard Transcriptions substitute cuteness and excess embellishment for substance, particularly on trite instrumentals like "Blonde Fiddle Blues."

Handling the music was one thing. For Spade, handling success was quite another matter, an affliction that extended to Tex Williams. Spade could throw tantrums that were aggravated and amplified when he drank. But even sober, his insecurity grew alongside his success. Tension blossomed after Capitol Records, impressed by Tex's vocals, offered Tex his own contract with the label. Bobbie Bennett said that as his fame grew, "Spade wanted to expand, and the boys wanted a little more recognition. By that time, Spade was getting a little conceited, and Tex was getting a little conceited." Spade's egomania blinded him to events and situations that didn't suit his increasingly swelled head. "He thought he was God," said Bobbie Bennett.

Tex's ego, buoyed by the Capitol offer, stemmed from a tangible truth both he and Cooley knew all too well: his warm baritone played a pivotal role in the band's success, especially on records. Interviewed in 1976, Tex, known throughout his life as a gentleman and diplomat, was highly guarded as he discussed Cooley, though his careful, deliberate choice of words left little doubt of his underlying contempt for his former boss. Discussing money, he dropped that restraint ever so slightly. "I thought I was paid adequately—up until a point. And when I had the contract from Capitol, money entered into it," he said. Tex proposed staying with the band, singing on Cooley's records as a guest. Cooley and the band would back him on his solo Capitol discs. " 'I'll share billing on your records with you, and [I'll get] a little more money and share in a little more royalties.' I think at that time it was $85 for a singer to do a three-hour session. And he just couldn't see it," Tex said.

As tensions grew between Spade and Tex, Cooley's temper explosions around the band, exacerbated by his heavy drinking, began disillusioning many of his key musicians. Smokey Rogers, equally close to Spade and to Tex, noted the growing chasm between the two:

> Tex and I had heard that Spade wanted to make some changes in the band. He primarily wanted to get rid of Tex because Tex was getting to the point where he was a star, the vocalist of the band and was gettin' notoriety and so naturally [Tex wanted] more money. But every time Tex asked for more money, Spade gave *me* a raise automatically. He was tryin' to get rid of Tex, and Tex and I were buddies, so we said months before the split came that if either one of us got fired, the other would quit and we'd do our own thing.

The band recorded "Spadella" and other material for Columbia at a June 6 session. It would be their final session for the label. Events moved quickly after that, as Smokey Rogers remembered:

> On this particular night, I think it was a frame-up job, I don't know for sure. Spade never let me in on it. He booked a thing in San Diego either at the Navy hospital or Navy base to do a show down there. We had a television show [in Hollywood] that night. So it's go to San Diego, do that show and drive back and do this television show in a matter of no time in between to spare. And [the] fact is, it was practically impossible to do it. You had to be a magician in order to make it. Spade had promised Tex that we would fly.
>
> Last-minute changes were made, and there was no flight. And so Tex just flat refused to go. And when he came back, the notice was handed to Tex on the stage by Spade. At the intermission, Tex told me, and I gave Spade my notice. That was really the only people involved in the whole

plot or plan of anybody quittin'. But being such a hassle of getting the band to San Diego and back, everybody was kind of peeved and mad anyway. So before the night's out, 11 of his 13 men quit.

When I relayed Rogers's account to Tex in 1976, "That I don't recall" was his only terse comment. Otherwise, he declined to discuss any details of his departure.

Within weeks, the core of Cooley's band, including Weis, Godson, Pedro, Featherstone, and Soldi, walked out. Cooley was particularly enraged at Pedro's defection. They and eventually a good part of the Cooley spin-off band led by Deuce Spriggens, including Spriggens himself, joined Tex in what became Tex Williams and the Western Caravan. "We started a co-op band when we left, [jointly owned by] Tex, Pedro, Cactus [Soldi], and I," said Smokey. The Cooley sidemen "preferred to go with us." Each of the four handled specific duties. Tex was the leader, Pedro the arranger, and Cactus handled the finances. Tex and the Caravan continued and actually *improved* upon the "classic" Cooley sound on Williams's million-seller "Smoke! Smoke! Smoke! (That Cigarette)" and other hits until 1951. A goodly amount of Cooley material like "You Can't Break My Heart" became the core of Tex's solo repertoire. Pedro took the original Cooley sound even further with the Western Caravan, adapting complex numbers like Stan Kenton's "Artistry in Rhythm" into the Caravan's Capitol recording "Artistry in Western Swing," with Kenton's approval.

Cooley left Venice Pier for the Santa Monica Ballroom and settled on a drastic reorganization. Bob Wills led a big band in Tulsa from 1936 through 1942, then revived it for one 1944 West Coast tour. From his start in Texas in 1933, Wills played pop tunes but also emphasized hard-driving swing and fiddle numbers. Spade's new vision, perhaps a result of his classical training, differed.

The new Cooley sound could be heard on the new, four-hour *Spade Cooley Time* show on L.A.'s KFVD Radio. Boggs remained on steel guitar. Red Egner became the band's new vocalist. Spade revived one aspect of the 1945 Wills sound by hiring Boggs's old Texas Playboys bandmates Jimmy Wyble and Cameron Hill to re-create their twin guitar sound along with their old bandmate, former Playboys drummer Monte Mountjoy. Wyble, Hill, Mountjoy, and the fiddlers provided most of the creative sparks. Cooley then added full brass and reed sections along with the fiddlers to create a western swing orchestra far smoother than any Wills big band.

Early in 1947, *Billboard* reported that Spade wanted out of his Columbia contract. Though Columbia had an option for another year, the label released Cooley for reasons not totally clear. He signed a considerably better deal with RCA Victor that, according to the February 1, 1947, *Billboard*, guaranteed him four releases a year to Columbia's three and a royalty deal 50 percent higher than Columbia's. If that sounds like so much hype, it may well be, because the magazine also erroneously characterized him as Victor's "only western swing band," a questionable declaration given the fact RCA had had Bill Boyd under contract for more than a decade and had just signed Pee Wee King and His Golden West Cowboys in 1946. Cooley's loss didn't come at the best time for Columbia, which had lost both of its top swing bands, Count Basie and Benny Goodman, in late '46.

Given those big-name defections, it's unclear why Columbia so readily granted Cooley's release, but his move to a big band had to be a major factor. It was no secret that Art Satherley preferred the smaller "fiddle band" version of the Texas Playboys to the big band version; Wills's horn-laden hit version of "New San Antonio Rose" notwithstanding. Satherley deliberately left many of the Playboys' outstanding 1940–42 big-band recordings unreleased. Given Cooley's new orchestra sound, Satherley probably had few qualms about letting him go.

The Victor contract began with some promising recordings like the big band "Boggs Boogie" and "Texas Playboy Rag," both showcases for Wyble and Boggs. The band varied between 18 and 23 pieces over the next five years, with definite strengths and weaknesses. Radio transcriptions reveal outstanding versions of jazz favorites like "South." The be-boppish 1947 instrumental "Diggin' with Spade," centered on Wyble and Hill, was among the first western swing acknowledgments of the modern jazz of that day. It's preserved only on a 1947 Standard Transcription and tapes of live radio performances.

Cooley hired gifted pianist Freddie Haynes, whose playing possessed undeniable modern jazz elements. The new band did uncredited backup work for other labels, backing other singers, such as Red Egner on his solo recordings for King. Egner's contract didn't seem to threaten Cooley's ego, probably because Egner was no Tex Williams. While Cooley briefly abandoned the horns in late 1947, in 1948, he expanded again into a full-fledged orchestra.

Although Steve Sholes, RCA's country A&R man, had handled Cooley's signing, most of the actual RCA sessions were handled by West Coast rep Walt Heebner, who produced many of RCA's Hollywood-based pop acts. It was no coincidence, given the cushy relationship between Hill and Range Music and Sholes, that nearly all the 1947 Victor vocal recordings, including asinine throwaways like "Big Chief Boogie," were Hill and Range copyrights.

Spade's new sound fueled a debate on the West Coast. Some fans, including many partial to Wills, or the original Cooley band, decried its slickness. Cooley partisans partial to the sweet sound of the bigger band, and to pop music in general, felt Wills was too earthy, raw, and basic. With the Western

Caravan continuing the original Cooley sound, everyone certainly had plenty to choose from. As before, Cooley's band also served as a backup unit. They backed various RCA artists ranging from Dinah Shore to the Sons of the Pioneers. No matter. Satherley's instincts were vindicated in the end. Cooley never had a nationwide hit after "Crazy 'Cause I Love You," a 1946 Columbia recording featuring Tex, in the spring of 1947.

Understandably self-satisfied, in 1976 Williams said: "When [the] guys left with me . . . I think [Spade] was almost forced to change his style. Of course, he admired Lawrence Welk, and Lawrence was down the Pier from him and maybe Spade aped Lawrence just a little bit. I don't think he had a hit with that particular band."

Early in 1947, bandleader Woody Herman decided to get off the road awhile. Renowned for his 1939 hit instrumental "Woodchopper's Ball," Herman's legendary First Herd orchestra became one of the first well-known white bands to embrace bebop. While much was made of Herman's disbanding as a sign of the decline of the big bands, he actually disbanded to assist his wife, Charlotte, in her struggle with alcoholism. To keep busy, he opened an office in Hollywood to handle business projects. Spade Cooley became one of those projects. Woody decided to handle his bookings while Bobbie managed Cooley and the band.

Woody convinced Spade to undertake short tours, but he understood the band's limitations. Writing in his autobiography, published after his death, Woody recalled telling his staff: "Take [Cooley] up and down the West Coast and back again, and don't go any further east than Nevada. Anywhere else, they're not going to know him." The gambit worked. The band made money playing venues within that zone. Acting on their own, Woody's staff foolishly chose to headline Spade on a full-blown western show and scheduled a tour of locales well east of Nevada. They booked Cooley and the band into Cain's, Bob Wills's old haunt in downtown Tulsa. In the heart of Wills country, Cooley drew a pitifully puny audience of 400. "Nobody knew him, or cared," Woody wrote. "And I started to get phone calls at four in the morning. It was Spade Cooley, making soulful, moaning sounds such as 'Like, man, I'm ruined.' It was a terrible fiasco."

Sticking closer to home, the Santa Monica Ballroom became his new venue. Cooley took a seven-year lease on the place in the spring of 1947. To mark the release of his first Victor single, "Red Hair and Green Eyes," sung by new vocalist Red Egner, Cooley sponsored a beauty contest to select the girl who had those attributes. There's little doubt Spade's roving eye had a few other things in mind with certain contestants.

Cooley's orchestra paid well enough that jazzmen in need of a few bucks occasionally joined the group, wearing the flashy Turk-created show outfits with a huge spade on the front. Among them were innovative jazz arranger

Jimmy Giuffre, who as a member of Woody Herman's Second Herd penned the now-classic Herman sax instrumental "Four Brothers." "Spade was able to take men from the various pop bands in the country because he was paying more than the rest of them were. And this I know, because I paid the salaries," Bobbie Bennett said.

Lack of hits notwithstanding, 1948 became a banner year. "I went to Channel 5 [KTLA-TV] and I talked with them," Bennett said. "I'd been trying to sell Spade, because we were starting to move up." That June, he became host of a new Saturday night variety show, the *Hoffman Hayride*, sponsored by a TV manufacturer. Broadcast live from the Santa Monica Ballroom, Spade, billed as "your fiddlin' friend," made the *Hayride* a mainstay of Southern California TV with a variety format much like Ed Sullivan's, featuring acrobats, comics, singers, actors, and celebrities. Frank Sinatra, Bob Wills, Bob Hope, and other major-league stars who lived in the region routinely stopped by. Everyone expected the volatile bandleader to clash with short-fused Klaus Landsberg, KTLA's German-born producer. A TV innovator who also helped invent live on-the-spot news coverage, Landsberg also launched Lawrence Welk's weekly KTLA broadcasts, which evolved into his popular Saturday night ABC show. To everyone's amazement, Spade and Landsberg hit it off.

Spade's friend Hank Penny, convinced that his own comedic strengths outweighed his vocal talents, joined the *Hayride* as a rube comic around 1950. Of his boss and friend, Penny said, "He was a fabulous straight man for me to bounce off of as a comic. I went on his television show, and this did more for me than anything in my career. I could walk around Hollywood and, man, I was a *star!* I was on that show when it was getting a 51 percent rating!"

Top athletes also appeared on the *Hayride*. Penny remembered Cooley infusing his perverse sense of humor into the proceedings when legendary boxer Max Baer was to appear on the show. In 1935, Baer lost the heavyweight title to Joe Louis, amid rumors that Baer's carousing cost him the title:

> We always had a break-in about 5:30 or 6 every Saturday evening and Spade would come on camera and say "Hi, folks! We're rehearsing the Spade Cooley show down at the Santa Monica Ballroom and tonight we have so-and-so! Don't forget! Come on down tonight and join us. If you can't join us be sure to watch right here on Channel 5!"
>
> We got notice from KTLA they were running short on time and wouldn't put this break-in. Spade says, "Okay, don't tell nobody." Spade ordered the band to keep quiet. The teaser had been canceled, but he decided he was bringing Baer out unaware, assuming he was appearing live. He only told Baer that he'd ask him a couple questions as part of the teaser.

The engineer gave Spade the signal. They threw on the red light which of course [wasn't for real]; Baer walked onstage in his boxing trunks. [Spade] said, "Max, tell me. There's been a lot of talk about why you screwed up the championship." And Max looked at him kinda funny and Spade said, "Yeah. You know, people said you was runnin' around, drinkin', sleepin' with broads, and screwin' around. *You really loused it up, man!*"

Baer didn't know whether to run or wind his watch or scream. And Cooley said, "Were you runnin' around and shackin' up and everything like that?" Spade looked in the camera and said, "Well, friends, obviously Max don't wanna say anything about it but why don't you come down tonight, and we'll really talk about it and see if we can get some answers out of him?"

They turned the red light off, and I thought Baer was gonna die. The guys in the band were just splittin' their sides. And this completely flipped him. That was one of the highlights of the Cooley show that the audience never saw.

Publicly at least, Spade strove to live up to the Fiddlin' Friend image. "He didn't ever want to displease anyone," Bobbie Bennett remembered. "No matter what [the public] asked, he answered, 'That's a deal, son!'" It seemed that he applied "Son" to every male he came in contact with, the same way Benny Goodman called nearly everyone "Pops."

Although Penny never denied the darker moments, his views of Cooley were far more charitable than most. Asked about the complaints of Cooley sidemen, he defended Cooley, explaining their criticisms away as jealousy or other petty animosities. One example of Cooley at his best, Penny recalled, happened one day when fiddler Billy Hill, who also played in Penny's band, was involved in a serious traffic accident. A truck sideswiped his car and Hill's wife, riding with him, lost an arm.

"You would have thought it was Spade's own child," said Penny, who witnessed Cooley's reaction. "He just about fainted. He cried, called [Billy] into his office, gave him money and got some of his staff and told him to take him home and help him any way they could." Bennett, told of that incident, replied, "This was Spade, and he would extend himself over his allowance that I would give him. Anybody that came up to him and say, 'You know, Spade, I'm really broke; I need a buck.' Spade would give it to them."

JIMMIE WIDENER, *announcing Spade's absence from the airwaves*: Spade's a pretty sick man up there with that sore leg he got up there from the baseball game with Woody Herman. Incidentally, we got beat. Tonight, we thought a more appropriate tune would be "Diggin' with Spade."

UNKNOWN SIDEMAN: You mean Spade's *dead*? He's *dead*? *Oh noooo!*
WIDENER: No! I said, he's *not dead!*
SIDEMAN: *Then, let's kill him!*

That may have been a joke to the audience, but as with the first band, more than a few band members probably entertained the idea. Even Bobbie Bennett called her former client a "Jekyll and Hyde, and a bastard most of the time." On rare occasions, his wrath had a modicum of wit. He fired one pianist who insisted that his contract was unbreakable. Spade agreed and retained him. The musician's new assignment: playing in the "M" room at the Santa Monica Ballroom. The musician soon discovered he was playing in the Men's restroom and had to honor the agreement.

Smokey Rogers saw Spade's demons during his days with the first band: "Cooley had a tendency of getting mad for no particular reason and maybe fired from six to a dozen people in his band in an hour's time and called 'em back the next day and begged 'em to go back to work for him." Speedy West agreed with the Jekyll-and-Hyde description: "Spade had a terrible temper off-stage at times, under drinkin' conditions. He was good to the guys normally."

Speedy joined the band in the spring of 1948 at a time Noel Boggs was out of the band. While Spade had another steel player in vocalist Les "Carrot Top" Anderson, a former Texas Playboys steel guitarist, Speedy clearly had potential. One Friday night, wanting to quit his day job at a dry-cleaning plant, Speedy asked his boss how he was doing, hoping that he'd hear the right words. He did:

Spade said, "Son, you're doin' fantastic! You're gonna make more money than you ever *dreamed* of makin'. Everything just looks wonderful. Just go right ahead and quit your job."

I went in [to work] the next morning, turned in my resignation at the cleaners, and the next night Spade fired me and 12 other people for no reason whatsoever. He called me repeatedly for a year after that and begged me to go back to work with him. I said, "Cooley, let's just be friends when we see each other." We worked shows together after, but I never would return to work for him.

Speedy never had a chance to record with Cooley because of the Musicians Union's second recording ban. This dispute with record companies kept everyone out of the studio for nearly all of 1948. The promise of the '47 band wasn't fulfilled when it returned to the RCA studios in 1949. The 1947 band's cutting edge gave way to stifling, vanilla blandness, with Cooley's overall sound now a syrupy orchestral melange of fiddles and bland, mediocre Welkish big-band fare. Except for the occasional

Wyble-Boggs instrumental excursion, the band played flawless versions of rococo instrumentals, stuffy covers of pop or country hits, or embarrassing, stupid novelties.

It wasn't that the band was musically inferior. For the most part, Cooley maintained a highly competent pop band staffed by proficient musicians, as good as or better than any number of other middle-of-the-road (or in big-band lexicon, "Mickey Mouse") bands. Whether it played country or pop, only the presence of the fiddle sections, Boggs, and Wyble set the Cooley band apart from the lifeless mediocrity of Lawrence Welk's or Ralph Flanagan's orchestras. Even Penny, the closest Cooley had to an apologist, took a far dimmer view of his friend's RCA material, much of it musically inferior to Penny's own swinging RCA recordings. "Spade's later releases for RCA were very bad, very ersatz," he said. "They weren't country, and they weren't pop. They didn't swing. It wasn't good enough for jazz, and it wasn't plaintive enough for country, so it just didn't fit." Tex Williams continued to succeed with the early Cooley sound, which still sounded fresh and witty by comparison. His continued success may have exacted a measure of revenge on his old boss.

Occasionally, creative sparks re-emerged. By 1951 a tiny Dixieland ensemble existed within the band, often popping up to wail away behind the vocalists. Nonetheless, the bulk of the music was simply dull. Ginny Jackson's renditions of contemporary country hits were often unlistenable, with silly rural affectations reminiscent of then-popular New York pop singer Dorothy Shay, who billed herself as "the Park Avenue Hill-Billie." Jackson's snorting rendition of Hank Williams's "Honky-Tonkin'" was particularly vile and mocking.

The only real jazz or western swing content in the Cooley big band came, not surprisingly, in spurts onstage. There'd be a hot version of "Perdido" or a swinging Billy Hill fiddle break, a Haynes piano interlude, or Wyble's fleet solos on numbers like "Bach Boogie" or Boggs's showcase numbers "Steel Guitar Rag" or "Texas Playboy Rag." Wyble's and Boggs's presence also allowed Spade to adapt some of the original band's numbers like "Three Way Boogie" to the bigger band.

Nonetheless, Cooley faced another challenge. By the early '50s, both western swing and the big-band era were sinking like the western sun. Solo vocalists were taking over in both pop and country. Nashville's power grew nationwide, the Southwest included. Television, Cooley's new outlet, now kept dancers out of ballrooms. Nor was the *Hoffman Hayride* a stepping-stone to network TV success. New York was still the epicenter of the new television industry; Ed Sullivan and Milton Berle ruled the airwaves from Manhattan. KTLA had no network affiliation, and more than ever, Cooley's music didn't translate well to a national audience.

Nonetheless he enjoyed material successes. He owned a 56-foot yacht and a home in Encino, an exclusive L.A. suburb. It also became clear that he was pushing himself physically. In 1950, while working on the film *Everybody's Dancin'*, he suffered his first serious heart attack. Unable to finish the picture, the physically diminutive Noel Boggs had to wear Spade's uniform to complete the films. "They just photographed Noel from the back," Bobbie Bennett remembered.

RCA parted ways with Cooley that year, most likely because of his abysmal record sales. Signing with Decca in 1951, Spade reverted to the small-band sound of the Columbia years, minus the flash and sophistication. Indeed, he sounded more like Wills than ever before. Del Porter, renowned for his work with Spike Jones's City Slickers, sang on the first two Decca sessions. The material remained trite or cloying, even with the return of Joaquin Murphey to the fold. KTLA strengthened its position by persuading Cliffie Stone to move *Hometown Jamboree* from KCOP to KTLA as a lead-in for the *Hayride,* which won local Emmy Awards in 1952 and 1953.

Spade himself didn't mellow. Stories circulated that when Ginny Jackson gave him notice, he tried to throw her off the Santa Monica Pier. Since he had no more commercial success with Decca (where some records billed his band as "The Buckle Busters") than he had with RCA, it was hardly shocking the Decca contract ended in 1955. One oddly prescient number recorded at the last session featured Betsy Gay cheerfully warbling the jaunty novelty "You Clobbered Me."

Things were changing across the board. Network TV grew stronger. At the suggestion of his friend Spike Jones, Spade organized an all-female orchestra that even Bobbie Bennett acknowledged "wasn't too hot." He'd taken an interest in lapidary (gem cutting and finishing), and became active with other like-minded hobbyists in Hollywood. As his TV *Hayride*'s ratings slipped, he abandoned the show and Los Angeles in favor of semi-retirement at his Willow Springs ranch in the Mojave Desert between L.A. and Bakersfield.

Real estate development became his new focus, according to Bobbie Bennett. "He was very much interested in building this dynasty up in the desert called Water Wonderland. He was going to build a ballroom, and recreation, similar to Disneyland, only not quite a Disneyland." Bobbie Bennett was arranging for a national TV broadcast link.

He reorganized a small band around 1958, briefly returned to TV, and recorded a final album with studio musicians for tiny Raynote Records in 1959; in 1960, he played Vegas. Still drinking heavily, he suffered another coronary. His final public performance came December 31, 1960. Shortly afterward, a serious fall hospitalized him, but he was soon back working on plans for Water Wonderland. The ranch at Willow Springs surrounded a lavish home, described in a local newspaper story that painted a portrait of wealth and family values all the way.

Beneath the façade, Cooley remained the consummate hypocrite. Of Ella May, Bobbie Bennett said, "He virtually kept her a prisoner. He was very jealous of her. Of course he was with another woman, or two or three, every night." Spade and Ella May had been battling for years, and their private war headed for an inexorable conclusion. She planned to file for divorce in March 1961, citing incompatibility, only to relent, reportedly (and futilely) hoping for reconciliation.

It proved a fatal mistake. On the afternoon of April 3, 1961, Cooley drank heavily during a Water Wonderland business meeting that ended abruptly when he lashed out at one of the participants. Sometime after 6 P.M., his and Ella's 14-year-old daughter, Melody, returned home after staying with friends to find her mother nude and unconscious, and her dad with bloody clothes. In the teenager's presence, Spade, babbling irrationally, made "attempts" to wake Ella May, burning her breasts with a lit cigarette. He brandished a rifle, and then ordered Melody to put her mother to bed. Terrified, she fled the house as Spade threatened to kill her if she told anyone.

Bobbie Bennett arrived a couple hours later and eventually found Ella May's body. When she suggested Spade call an ambulance, he refused, then summoned a family friend who called for help. The ambulance driver testified when he arrived at the Cooley home, Spade was dazed and largely uncommunicative, stammering an explanation that Ella May had fallen. She was pronounced dead at a Tehachapi Valley Hospital at 12:20 A.M. on April 4.

The bruises and burns on her body and Spade's bruised, swollen hands set off alarms with Kern County Sheriff's investigators. A sergeant arrived at the hospital and interrogated Spade, who claimed Ella May had attempted to jump from a moving car a couple days earlier and fell in the shower that night. He finally admitted to roughing her up. Investigators scouring the home found bloodstains in several rooms. Spade had changed his clothes, but in his haste, he left bloody clothing in easy reach of investigators. The blood type was later found to be Ella May's. It was a no-brainer for the local lawmen.

Cooley's arrest made national headlines, though few East of the Mississippi knew who he was. He was charged with murder and later indicted by a coroner's jury. He entered a plea of not guilty by reason of insanity in an attempt to avoid trial. Psychiatrists appointed by the court determined he was fit to stand trial, set for July 10, 1961, in Bakersfield.

Bobbie Bennett maintained that the killing resulted from an argument that got out of hand: "It was an accident. He never intended to kill her." Public reaction was swift and varied, she continued. "We had thousands of letters from all over the country and most of them felt that because of the pleasure he had brought to them and so forth, they didn't feel he was particularly guilty. But I must say as far as the particular *entertainers* in the field, they were very harsh as far as he was concerned."

Not surprisingly, Hank Penny saw it as a crime of passion. Shortly after his arrest Cooley scrawled an anguished letter to Hank, then living in Las Vegas, that ended with "You know how much I loved her." Even Tex Williams dropped his guard a bit when asked about the industrywide lack of support for his ex-boss. "I think a lot of the people in show business were contacted and told how brutal this thing was," he said. Did he think it was a crime of passion? "I can't agree, because the Deputy District Attorney from Bakersfield came down and spent two or three hours with me and he was on the scene. There's no way I could say it was an accident. It went on for so long."

Smokey Rogers was equally blunt while discussing the deafening silence from the industry. "Personally," he admitted, "I don't think Spade had many friends, I mean *friends*. He had lots of people who used him and he used them and it's kind of a toss-up over who used who the most."

The Kern County Coroner listed the primary cause of death as internal bleeding from a ruptured aorta, caused by a punch or a kick, and noted trauma to the neck and pelvic area. At the trial, which began on July 10, prosecutors presented evidence of the Cooleys' marital woes. They offered details of an attempted strangulation and vaginal and anal abuse so graphic that Presiding Judge William Bradshaw banned children from the courtroom. One child not banned was Melody Cooley, who tearfully testified to her dad's actions, including his demand that "You're going to watch me kill her."

Spade's rambling, incoherent testimony undercut what little defense he had. He admitted hitting Ella May, explaining that that he lost control after she told him she was part of a "sex cult." It was a tenuous explanation given his psychotic possessiveness. He claimed she burned her own breasts and reiterated the fantasy that she'd fallen in the shower. He claimed Melody wanted to date adult men, then vaporized his 24-year friendship with Roy Rogers by accusing him of having an affair with Ella May.

Prosecutors easily ran roughshod over all this. When the trial ended in August, a jury found Donnell Clyde Cooley guilty of murder in the first degree. Because of Cooley's ongoing cardiac problems, Judge Bradshaw sentenced him to life in prison, to be served at the California Medical Facility at Vacaville. Two appeals were rejected. A discouraged, heartsick Bobbie Bennett, named Spade's legal conservator, walked away from the music business. "It was such a shock to me that I just closed my office, and I went back into law." For eighteen years she'd nutured, packaged, tolerated, and advanced Cooley despite his volatile personality. *This* was just too much.

Spade found a measure of peace at Vacaville. By all accounts, he became a model prisoner. Bobbie Bennett sent up his gem machinery as a donation to the facility so Spade could use them, along with a tape recorder. He continued gem polishing, built violins, and for a time led a band of inmate musicians. Bobbie recalled, "He did very fine paintings, fine jewelry. He adapted himself quite well. While he was in Vacaville he gave a couple of concerts for the townspeople."

Officials noted his exemplary behavior. Among the handful of performers who stood by Spade was Opry star Hank Snow, who played Vacaville more than once. In the late '60s, Snow interceded with California governor Ronald Reagan, presenting a petition for clemency and enlisting support from two southern governors he knew. Spade's parole was approved in 1969, effective February 22, 1970. Bennett recalled: "He had gotten in touch with me and thought he would like to do something . . . sort of a Billy Graham–type thing, religious and so forth. But he also felt he would like to go back into music. I had three or four offers for him from Las Vegas."

As Spade's parole application moved through channels in 1969, Hank Penny visited him:

> Not long before his death, Spade had said to me, "Son, do you think that I would be able to get out of prison and get back into show business?" I said, "Spade, I have no doubt about it . . . everything would be great. People love you." I was kidding . . . because I knew that people would give him a hard time and make his life extremely unhappy. I couldn't say that, even though I knew that *he* knew it.

Asked if Cooley could have made a comeback, Johnny Bond was blunt: "Not a chance," he replied. "No way." In addition, California's country scene now centered on Bakersfield and the stripped-down honky-tonk of Buck Owens and Merle Haggard. Western swing was moribund in 1969. Bob Wills lay bedfast in Fort Worth, his fiddling days ended by a massive stroke earlier that year. Leon McAuliffe spent much of his time running his radio station in Rogers, Arkansas.

Cooley received a furlough to play fiddle at a benefit show for the Alameda County Sheriff's Department in Oakland, California, on November 23, 1969. He went onstage, played three songs, including "San Antonio Rose," dedicated to his ailing former rival Wills. After receiving a standing ovation, he walked backstage and dropped dead of a massive heart attack.

Writing in his 1999 autobiography, Hank Snow could hardly contain his fury over the way Spade died, blaming a Nashville booking agent's insensitivity to Spade's fragile emotional state. "He was driven that same Sunday afternoon to Oakland to perform during the matinee. The person who set up this appearance didn't have brains enough to give Spade at least a week to adjust to the outside world after being locked up . . . for years." Snow had a point. Cooley was undoubtedly euphoric, yet being on the outside for the first time in eight years could have been predicted to be stressful.

A *Rolling Stone* obituary in its Random Notes section dripped with sarcasm, citing Cooley's "terrible C & W" music (an obvious reference to the music of the *Hoffman Hayride* era). Cooley's legendary status is assured through his best music, but his dark, violent side, a leitmotif throughout his career, left the mystique James Ellroy and so many others found irresistible. Talk about a movie circulated in the mid-1970s but came to naught. In the end, Spade Cooley's crime will define him for posterity, very likely overshadowing his importance in adding a new dimension to Western swing. In the mid-'40s, he left behind music with vision and class, even if the man himself is destined to occupy a place alongside other celebrity murderers.

What? No dancers? The Radio Cowboys: Louis Dumont, Sheldon Bennett, Noel Boggs, Carl Stewart, Boudleaux Bryant, Hank Penny, Atlanta, 1939.

2

Insurgency in Ascendance

Hank Penny

Cincinnati, Ohio: Late 1946

A typical day at King Records headquarters on Brewster Avenue in Cincinnati. Nothing was out of the ordinary. Syd Nathan, King's penurious and mercurial founder, was in his office, screaming in his asthmatic wheeze over a 2,000-mile connection with Hank Penny in Los Angeles.

Nathan began the conversation by posing a philosophical question: *What the hell are you trying to do?*

"I'm only tryin' to be fair, Syd. Don't try to take advantage of those people. I hired 'em and you're gonna pay 'em!"

I will like hell!

For the next 15 minutes, Nathan ranted about $860 in assessed charges against the company. These were musicians' overtime costs for five recent recording sessions, three of them Hank's. When Nathan wouldn't pay, Hank filed charges against him with the Musicians Union.

Nathan had traveled to L.A. in September to produce sessions on several King artists. At one of Hank's sessions, he and the band stood by as Nathan ran the session into overtime while he sweet-talked a female companion he brought along from Cincinnati. Hank's complaint didn't go unheeded. American Federation of Musicians President James C. Petrillo agreed with him, and on March 12, 1947, Nathan paid in full.

Such conflicts were all too common in Hank Penny's career: a mixture of episodic turmoil and prodigious talent that left behind dashed hopes and opportunities. Some battles reflected high artistic principle; others resulted from an obstreperous nature forged in a traumatic childhood, aggravated by a formidable temper. It all undermined a career that could have achieved far greater success. Standing his ground against all comers regardless of the issue gave him an aura of nobility to some; failing to better pick and choose those battles cost him dearly in the end.

*   *   *

Penny swam against the tide from the start, playing Texas dance music in Southeastern regions where more conventional country string-band music held sway. On radio, at fairs, theaters, and schoolhouses, he offered audi-   ·
ences their first taste of Milton Brown and his Musical Brownies, the Light Crust Doughboys and Bob Wills. From the beginning, he set a high musical standard permeating nearly every band he led.

"I've never been satisfied with the psychology that three chords were enough," he declared in 1980. "And I don't think that any of my musicians were satisfied with that feeling. When I had an opening in one of my groups, I hired the best that I could find."

That may have been part of the problem. For Hank Penny, the music was an end in itself. Along with the Texas and Oklahoma musicians he admired, Benny Goodman, Count Basie, and Django Reinhardt were among his heroes. He freely mixed Goodman and Basie into his repertoire and made a fearless stab at bebop in 1949. It all reflected the unparalleled freedom he afforded his sidemen to create music that satisfied them and himself.

He had only three national hits during western swing's heyday, and over time, he relied more on the baggy pants comedic alter ego he developed in the 1930s. By the early 1950s, he was as well known around Hollywood for his comedy on Spade Cooley's local TV show as his music. Though he had major-label recording contracts stretching over two decades, Penny battled two of those labels over everything from choice of material to producers' interference to simple personality clashes. Paradoxically, he made the best records of his career for the man he battled most bitterly—Syd Nathan.

Surely his boyhood didn't help matters. Herbert Clayton Penny, born September 18, 1918, outside Birmingham, Alabama, was second to last of 11 children (two died at birth) in a family with ample problems. His birth certificate read "Boy" Penny and his parents, William and Inez Penny, never quite got around to filling in his given name (something Hank didn't discover until he applied for a passport in 1966). Not long before Hank's birth, Will Penny, a coal miner, barely survived a mine explosion. Originally presumed dead, rescuers recovered him two days later. His injuries were horrific. Many shards of slate from the mine remained embedded in his body, one in his brain. He was never the same.

The Pennys lived in Wylam, a tiny mining community just west of Birmingham, where Will Penny's disability left them in poverty. At one point, Herbert counted a Coca-Cola bottle and a wooden block as his only toys. Will's avocations included an amateur hypnotist act with Inez, carpentry, guitar playing, and writing poetry. All those brought solace; another post-injury "hobby" did anything but that. Will embraced a religious fanaticism replete with hellfire-and-brimstone preaching that left young Herbert terrified. It may explain why anyone—a promoter, producer, or authority figure—who ever preached at him in later years faced a ferocious response. The boy maintained a phobia about all religion that remained for years. Years later, he'd blame his dad's obsessions for many of his problems.

Herbert found solace in music. Brother Clarence Penny bought a Hawaiian guitar Herbert tried adapting to standard guitar use. Herbert's interest in music pleased his mother and his brother-in-law, local musician Albert Stracener, who sang in a duo with his brother. Albert encouraged Herbert to do an impromptu blackface comedy routine at a Stracener Brothers show. The kid went over well enough that he landed his first glimpse of the rewards of entertaining. Inez Penny encouraged her son, and as 15-year-old Herbert worked odd jobs to bring in money and save for a guitar, his mother splurged to buy him an Epiphone acoustic guitar at Forbes Music in Birmingham. At the same time, his brothers pushed him to find some real employment. Get a job with Hal Burns, said his brother. *That* would be something.

Hal Burns was a big dog in Birmingham in 1933. He and his Tune Wranglers performed over Birmingham's WAPI radio. Herbert Penny decided to give it a shot. Toting his Epiphone, he strolled into WAPI's studios one day and watched Burns's daily broadcast. After it ended, he caught the older man's eye.

"Mr. Burns, you don't need a guitar player do you?" "That's right. I don't," the performer replied. But, he added, he did need a four-string tenor banjoist. Stretching the truth, Herbert Penny assured Burns he indeed fit the bill, and then hustled back to the music store to swap the guitar for a tenor banjo. Tuning it like a guitar's first four strings, he headed back, auditioned and, to his surprise, landed the job. He later took tenor banjo lessons so he wouldn't have to fake it. Burns remained a friend for the rest of his life.

"Hal worked diligently to teach me show business. He tried to develop me as a comic in the early years. He worked real hard to help me learn stage presentation and personality projection. And he was always talking to me about staging things. What I learned from Hal was a valuable lesson: there is more to show business than just playing three chords and getting a record contract." On the air, Burns nicknamed the teenager "Hanky-Dank," shortened to "Hank." He inhaled every rudiment Burns could teach him. He embraced a conviction in those days that never left him. An older musician at the station named Asa White enjoyed his booze. He tried to get Hank to join him. The kid refused and remained a teetotaler for the rest of his life. At times his lectures on the subject would have pleased a prohibitionist.

In the mid-1930s, Burns suddenly disbanded. Hank, who had enjoyed listening to WWL in New Orleans, left Birmingham bent on landing a staff job there. He succeeded and soon met steel guitarist Noel Boggs, an Oklahoma native enthralled with jazz trombone great Jack Teagarden. When Boggs lost his clothes in a burglary, he and Hank became roommates and shared Hank's wardrobe. Hank also got a chance to play guitar on a recording session with singer and future Louisiana governor Jimmie Davis. He spent two brief periods working in New Orleans, a total of about six months.

At some point in the mid-1930s, he heard records by Milton Brown and his Musical Brownies, Bob Wills and his Texas Playboys, and the Light Crust Doughboys. These groups, often called "Texas fiddle bands" (the term "western swing" was nearly a decade away), doled out a cutting-edge goulash of fiddle tunes, jazz, blues, pop, and jug-band fare. The Fort Worth–based Brownies particularly captured Hank's imagination as he collected their records. It was also the swing era and, like millions of other American teenagers, Hank absorbed Benny Goodman's music.

On a brief trip back to New Orleans, Hank was listening to WWL when he heard a new musician at the station: fiddler Sheldon Bennett. A Port Arthur, Texas, native, Bennett was well versed in the new music from that region. Back in the Crescent City, he met the fiddler and his friend, banjoist Louis Dumont. Back in Birmingham, he set to forming his own Texas-style band with Bennett, Dumont, and Boggs. A better-paying job took Boggs out of the picture, so when Bennett and Dumont arrived, Hank hired Julian Akins, an old friend from WAPI, to play bass, along with Sammy Forsmark, who played Hawaiian steel guitar locally.

He named the band the Radio Cowboys, not terribly original but a name that made sense since the airwaves, not dancehalls, would be the band's main outlet. With a repertoire largely culled from Milton Brown, the Cowboys landed a spot at 100-watt Birmingham station WKBC, amid straight hillbilly string bands. It didn't take long for them to find their music put them way out of their element. At one point, they played a local restaurant just to earn a meal. Akins left, replaced by fiddler-bassist Carl Stewart, a talented multi-instrumentalist who'd work with Hank for most of the next decade.

Actually, the Cowboys weren't alone. Fiddler Clayton McMichen, renowned for his work as a member of Gid Tanner and his Skillet Lickers in Atlanta, went a similar direction with his Georgia Wildcats. In the end, their success was no more than moderate. Such music had only a limited appeal, often in more urban areas of the South.

In 1937, the Cowboys relocated to Chattanooga's WDOD *Chattanooga Playhouse*, one of the many live country radio shows on larger Southern radio stations. On this daily show, the band introduced Tennessee audiences to Milton Brown favorites like "Four or Five Times," "Hesitation Blues," and pop tunes like "When I Take My Sugar to Tea." Shows in theaters, grange halls, and schoolhouses provided a substantial part of the band's income and raised money for organizations sponsoring the shows.

WDOD also had the Stringdusters, a group featuring guitarist Homer Haynes, mandolinist Jethro Burns, his brother Aychie Burns on bass, and guitarist Charlie Hagaman, who played a similar mix of swing music. On occasion, talent from Knoxville's WNOX visited Chattanooga, and Hank heard a Stringdusters-like group called the Fidgety Four. In it were Roy Lanham on guitar, bassist Red Wooten, and mandolinist Doug Dalton, three future members of the Whippoorwills.

Realistically, the Cowboys only held its own in Chattanooga. The band remained there through the summer of 1938 before aiming at an even bigger southeastern venue: Atlanta's 50,000-watt WSB and the station's Opry clone, the daily *Crossroads Follies*. On September 18, Hank's twentieth birthday, his band debuted in Atlanta. It was a more cosmopolitan milieu, where the Cowboys' jazzy sound, combined with WSB's high wattage, seemed to do better. They weren't there long when Hank recorded transcription discs of the band at WSB. Hoping to land a recording contract, he packed them and addressed them to one he knew would understand his sound: Arthur E. Satherley of the American Recording Company (ARC).

Traveling the country recording rural acts for ARC in the 1920s, the British-born Satherley discovered a strong affinity for American vernacular music, particularly blues and jazz. He produced countless country and western artists for ARC (later purchased by Columbia Records); Bob Wills, the Light Crust Doughboys, Gene Autry, and Roy Acuff were but a few. Bob Wills nicknamed the urbane Brit "Uncle Art."

What happened next was one of those serendipitous events that still seems astounding more than a half century later. Hank had his package of discs ready to mail to Satherley in New York. He parked his vehicle, emblazoned with the band's name, on a downtown Atlanta street and ran to the barbershop. Returning to his car, he encountered a tall, dignified individual who asked if he knew how to find Hank Penny. Asked who wanted to know, Satherley identified himself and stated his purpose: to meet Penny about recording his band. Hank nonchalantly reached into the car and handed Satherley the parcel. "Here's your mail," he said.

That November, Satherley recorded the band in Columbia, South Carolina. Even after two years, the band was looser and rougher sounding than any of the Texas acts. With no piano, Hank's Martin D-18 guitar and Stewart's bass propelled the rhythm. Hank's vocals were appealing and lively as they blended Milton Brown favorites like "Hesitation Blues" and "Cowboy's Swing," the group's retitled arrangement of the fiddle favorite "Draggin' the Bow."

Satherley proved to be the only record producer Hank truly respected. "Uncle Art would bring talent in and let them do what they damn well pleased. The only thing he would do is try to help you with anything you wanted to do. There were numbers of times in speaking with Uncle Art that I would ask him, 'Do you think I ought to do it this way?' And, he'd say, 'M'lad, don't ask me. You have to work to your fans.'"

On the *Follies,* which began daily at 12:30 P.M. and ran until 2 or 3 P.M. (each act performed from 15 to 30 minutes), Hank and the band worked alongside some of the South's top non-Opry talent, including the Coon Creek Girls, the Pine Ridge Boys, Pop Eckler and His Young'Uns, Harpo Kidwell, and Uncle Ned and His Kinfolks. The show's blind singer, Pete Cassell, one of the first smooth-voiced country crooners, became one of Hank's close friends. Privately, while Hank appreciated many of the artists, he dismissed some of the rawest acts as "shitkickin'" music, an epithet he'd use for the rest of his life to describe anything more country than he could stand.

It was no small irony that, musical opinions notwithstanding, Hank's comic persona was pure, unadulterated "shitkicker" all the way. Even at WSB he did comic routines, wearing bumpkin-like outfits and acting, like most comics of the time, in an almost stereotypic approximation of a backwoods rube. While his alter ego grew hipper over time, the image remained much the same: flopped-over hat, vest, loud shirt, and baggy pants.

When the Cowboys wasn't on the air, it worked jobs throughout the region, playing its mixture of dance music and comedy at schoolhouses, theaters, and grange halls throughout rural Georgia and surrounding states. Competition from more established, acceptable country acts proved tough for Hank to handle.

We would book 75 percent [of the gate] for the Cowboys and 25 percent for sponsors like the Future Farmers of America or whatever. But it seemed like we were constantly watched by the booking offices out of WSM [the Nashville radio station that was home to the Grand Ole Opry]. The first thing we knew, the Artists' Service from the Grand Ole Opry would send down a tent with 97 stars, and they would get into that area and give the [show] sponsors 50 percent. That would kill us for the future, because no more could we go in and get 60–75 percent when the Opry was givin' 'em 50 percent. It was a scorched-earth policy, assuring that we would never play it again, that [the area would] become WSM property.

That particular story is difficult to refute or confirm. Whatever happened, however, was simple business, nothing as personal as Hank chose to take it. Nonetheless, even when recounting the story four decades later, he found it tough to not take it personally. "I don't want to sound bitter," he added. "I'm just relating what was extremely hard for us to contend with in the formative years. I was 19 or 20. What person that age has the wherewithal, the ability to understand, to reason things out? We just felt we were being taken advantage of because we didn't have any way to fight WSM." Whatever damage might have been done to the personal appearances, it spawned a certain wariness of Nashville and the Opry.

When Sammy Forsmark returned to Birmingham, Hank found Noel Boggs was available at last. Boggs's sophisticated musical finesse was just one factor elevating the Radio Cowboys to a higher musical level. The band's new fiddler played a role as well. Boudleaux Bryant was 19. He'd grown up in Shellman, Georgia, and started his classical violin studies at age six. He proudly played violin with the Atlanta Civic Symphony and, to pay his bills, reluctantly worked at WSB with Uncle Ned and His Kinfolks. Bryant's playing impressed Sheldon Bennett, and Hank brought him into the Cowboys. Bryant took awhile to adjust.

The Cowboys were less corny than Uncle Ned, yet hearing Hank write songs gave the fiddler a profound culture shock. "Boudleaux," Hank said, "used to say, 'You're not writin' songs, you're writing SHIT! Music is written by the masters: Beethoven and Bach!' That was his evaluation of country music in those days."

That evaluation soon changed. Bryant, with Bennett's help, began challenging himself by writing instrumentals like "Mississippi Muddle" and developed into a polished, swinging fiddler. It set him on a path to becoming one of country's greatest songwriters (with his wife, Felice), creator of such country standards "Hey, Joe!" "Bye, Bye Love," "Rocky Top," and "Midnight." In the '60s, a now-prosperous Bryant picked up his phone in Nashville only to find Hank on the other end, teasing, "How does it feel to be a millionaire writin' *shit*?"

Married and with a new daughter, Hank and his wife, Helen, achieved a certain amount of security. Things seemed on the upswing. The Cowboys did a second session with Satherley on a blistering July 4, 1939, in Memphis. At the session at Memphis's Peabody Hotel, the band members stripped to their underwear to fight the heat. Songs like the driving, intense instrumental "Mississippi Muddle," a showcase for Boggs and the fiddles of Bryant and Bennett, reflected the marked improvement in their sound. Boggs shined on the aggressive "Chill Tonic." Hank sang "Won't You Ride in My Little Red Wagon," penned by his friend, the brilliant, alcoholic Alabama singer-songwriter Rex Griffin, composer of the country standard

"The Last Letter." Inspired by watching a boy and girl play with a coaster wagon, Griffin wrote "Red Wagon" for his parents' wedding anniversary. Griffin played it for Hank and left town; when he returned, he'd totally forgotten the song. Hank, who remembered the lyrics and melody, had to refresh the composer's memory.

WSB's broadcast signal and the Cowboys' Vocalion and OKeh releases spread the band's exposure. While nothing on records approached hit status, Hank claimed he received an offer to front the Light Crust Doughboys, a move he seriously considered. He even considered relocating the Cowboys to Texas. Soon after the Memphis session, the Opry invited the Cowboys to Nashville to audition. Things hit a snag. Opry founder George D. Hay's ban on any music or instruments that didn't fit his narrow criteria of that which was pure and rural applied to electrically amplified instruments, horns, and drums (he initially had problems accepting Pee Wee King's accordion). The officials who auditioned Hank told him Boggs would have to play an acoustic steel or a Dobro, which used metal resonators to amplify the sound acoustically. Asked to think it over, the Cowboys opted to keep the amplifier and stay in Atlanta.

Hank had justified the band's staying thusly: "In Oklahoma City, you had the Hi-Flyers; in Shreveport, you had Bob and Joe Shelton and the Sunshine Boys. In Dallas, you had Bill Boyd and his Cowboy Ramblers. Of course Bob Wills was in Tulsa and the Swift Jewel Cowboys—not really western swing—were in Memphis. We felt there were two things we had to do: stay out of the Oklahoma/Texas area and stay out of Nashville, which in those days was rank-and-file hillbilly."

The Memphis session was Boggs's swan song. He returned to Oklahoma, where he hooked up with his childhood friend, singer (and future movie cowboy) Jimmy Wakely. Bennett, newly married, also headed to Oklahoma, where he joined the Hi-Flyers. Hank replaced Boggs with Eddie Duncan, who played steel guitar in the Texas band the Tune Wranglers in 1936 and 1937. One of the more eccentric Radio Cowboys, Duncan, Penny recalled, "had a bad tooth one day, and pulled it with a nail file." The $15-a-week guitarist's brash, aggressive style came off beautifully on numbers like "Tobacco State Swing," and his showcase, "Peach Tree Shuffle," recorded at a June 1940 session in Chicago with Satherley.

That fall, with the pre–World War II draft pulling in musicians, the Cowboys, facing uncertain futures, disbanded. Hank's resonant voice and faultless enunciation landed him a job as a WSB staff announcer, disc jockey, and newscaster at a respectable $35 a week. He worked for Alabama native Douglas Edwards, WSB's news director, later a member of Edward R. Murrow's legendary team of World War II radio reporters and Walter Cronkite's CBS-TV evening news predecessor. Still involved on the musical side, Hank met a WSB newcomer: singer-guitarist-bassist Louis Todd Innis, who became his closest friend until Innis's death in 1982.

Itching to play music, Hank and Innis left Atlanta for KXEL in Waterloo, Iowa. Hired as backup musicians, they found themselves in a no-win situation. The station manager surreptitiously struck a deal with the local musicians union officials allowing sidemen to work non-stop for hours on end without any of the mandatory breaks, while new singers were shuffled on for 15-minute sets. Hank put up with two weeks of it before he walked. "[The station manager] was a bastard. I quit him without givin' him notice, and he filed charges against me through the union and beat me." Fined for violating union rules, he recalled, "I asked the union guy, 'If I give you some more money, can I do it again?'" Over the next 15 years such conflicts landed him in hot water time and again.

For the next eight or nine months, he happily returned to behind-the-mike chores at WSB and played the Saturday night WSB *Barn Dance*. Contractually, he owed Satherley and Columbia one more Radio Cowboys session. In June 1941 he did one final session in Charlotte, North Carolina, with a pickup band that included three Atlanta players—ex-Radio Cowboy Carl Stewart, and accordionist Kelland Clark and harmonica player Eddie Smith, both from WSB—and Charlotte-area steel guitarist Jimmy Colvard. The music lacked the edge of the Memphis and Chicago sessions. Even Hank's vocals sounded perfunctory.

In 1941 Hank spent a few months reunited with Hal Burns in Memphis until Burns joined the Army. WSB's door remained open to him. He stayed in Atlanta until 1942, when he decided to relocate to the Midwest. The WLS *National Barn Dance* was his first choice. It may have lost some of its luster to the Opry's rising stature, but it remained an important showcase. He'd already met Red Foley, the show's star, on a brief visit a year earlier. Cincinnati's WLW was his second choice, and that's where he settled. The high-wattage station, owned by the Crosley Corporation, had cultivated an audience through the South and Midwest for its various country and pop music shows and its own barn dance program, the weekly *Boone County Jamboree,* on the air since 1937. The station's day began at 4:45 A.M. with its Monday through Friday "Top of the Morning" show, featuring live country music aimed at the huge midwestern farm audience.

At WLW, he combined comedy with a new Radio Cowboys–style band dubbed the Plantation Boys who were every bit the musical equal of the Bryant-Boggs Radio Cowboys. He summoned Carl Stewart to play fiddle and Louis Innis to handle bass. He hired ex–Fidgety Four guitarist Roy Lanham from a job in Florida. Springfield, Missouri, swing fiddler Zed Tennis later arrived. Lanham, who played a mixture of chord melodies and single-string licks a la Chicago jazzman George Barnes, gave them as strong

Big Balls at Cowtown: Harold Hensley, Hank Penny, Speedy West, Hank Caldwell, Al Tonkins, 1949.

or stronger a swing content than the Cowboys. Tennis further enhanced the sound.

WLW attracted a mix of country and pop talent few other stations could match. Hank fell in with fellow *Boone County* artists Grandpa and Ramona Jones, singer-guitarist Merle Travis, the Delmore Brothers, Rome Johnson, Bradley Kincaid, Smiley Burnette and, later, guitarist Joe Maphis. The Plantation Boys' swing did well on the daily shows and the Saturday night *Jamboree* broadcast. Hank and the entire cast appeared throughout the region at theaters, schoolhouses, and, in the summer, at fairs. As in Atlanta, Hank mixed baggy-pants country comedy with his music and seemed satisfied.

Travis, who became a particularly close friend, nicknamed Hank "Hardrock," a play on the fact that Alabama singer Sidney "Hardrock" Gunter, later renowned for his proto-rockabilly tunes like "Birmingham Bounce," auditioned at WLW doing Hank's material (he didn't get the job). The Williams Brothers (featuring Andy Williams), bandleader Bert Farber, the Clooney Sisters (Rosemary and Betty), and Doris Day were among the pop talents who learned their craft there. Hank's rhythm guitar skills were sophisticated enough to land him extra work at the station as a sideman backing Day on various shows.

Sydney Nathan came into the picture around 1943. Over the years, the cigar-smoking Cincinnati native proved himself a consummate huckster. He ran a local carnival-style shooting gallery, a photo-finishing business, and a used-furniture store. In that store, he branched into selling used 78s. WLW performers hung out at Nathan's seeking old country, jazz, gospel, and blues records. Despite the war raging across Europe and the Pacific, Nathan decided that with WLW present, the region had enough talent he could record, though station policy barred staff musicians from recording.

In October 1943, Nathan squired Travis and Jones to Dayton for their first low-budget record on his new King label. He issued it under the pseudonym of the "Sheppard Brothers" to shield them from the station's wrath. It didn't matter. Management soon found out about the record, and all the station's performers received a memo reminding them of the no-recording policy, which was supported by the local Musicians Union, still uneasy over the entire idea of records costing musicians jobs.

It was inevitable that Hank and Nathan connected. In 1944, Hank, the Plantation Boys, and a local trumpeter named Richard (last name lost to history) recorded four songs in a makeshift studio, including an aggressive version of the song "Last Night" and the Milton Brown favorite "Talkin' About You." Tennis swung with fire and passion, and Lanham's guitar crackled with George Barnes–style leads, but the room wasn't acoustically suitable for recording music. The muffled sound hurt the finished recordings. "I bet the bass notes are still rollin' around that room," Hank quipped years later.

Nathan issued the disc under Hank's name, and when WLW management called him on the carpet, Hank had a comeback ready and waiting. "I will record for whom I want to record for," he told his bosses. "There is no way you're gonna tell me that I can't. I fulfill my duties to this station. You hired me for one thing, and when I get through with these programs, I can do what I want to do. I just won't adhere to that restriction at all!" "From then on our situation deteriorated," he added. "And maybe it was for the best."

WLW had already started losing talent to the West. Smiley Burnette moved to Hollywood, as did other secondary acts like Margie and Charlie, the Fiddlin' Linvilles. In March 1944, Hank drove Merle Travis, escaping a failing marriage, to the train station for his own move west. Within months, Hank started getting a steady stream of letters from Travis extolling both California's wonders and the work available there for entertainers. He read those letters with growing interest.

Meanwhile, another letter arrived in Cincinnati for Hank: orders to report to Georgia for his Army physical. When he told an examining officer he was an entertainer, the officer, apparently leery of entertainers in uniform, rejected him. He wound up classed as 4-F, in other words, undraftable.

Wanting to help the war effort and avoid the increasingly testy atmosphere at WLW, he volunteered the Plantation Boys for a USO tour through the South. Lanham stayed behind, but Hank, Tennis, Stewart, and Innis did so well that USO officials offered them a tour entertaining the troops in Europe; they declined.

Late that year, Hank met Bob Wills at a late-1944 show in Indianapolis during the same ill-fated vaudeville tour that took the Playboys to the Opry. They became fast friends. Meeting Wills—who'd moved to California only a year earlier—further whetted Hank's curiosity about the West Coast. Travis's letters continued arriving, and as Hank's marriage grew rocky, he took a vacation in California early in 1945.

WLW had received subscription copies of Spade Cooley's lavish, ultra-sophisticated Standard Transcriptions. But hearing Cooley and his band live at Hollywood's Sunset Rancho left him in awe of the band's combination of flash and West Coast sophistication. Hank also met Bert "Foreman" Phillips, the Hollywood disc jockey and dance promoter, who gave Cooley his first venue. Phillips ran a network of ballrooms that ran 24 hours a day to serve World War II defense-plant workers coming off three shifts. Having heard some Radio Cowboys discs, Phillips offered Hank a band-leader's job, leading the house band at one of his ballrooms, if he decided to move to Hollywood.

In April 1945, Hank gave WLW his notice, dropped his wife and daughter off in Birmingham and drove to Los Angeles. To him, the West Coast represented freedom, sophistication, and a break from a style of radio he'd been doing for 12 years. A decade of playing early-morning shows aimed at farmers, hawking patent medicines and similar nostrums, had left him with a deep-seated contempt for that entire style of radio: "There wasn't any-body [in California] saying that I had to get up at 4:30 A.M. to play on a radio station. Everything was done at a decent hour: noon or after. I had had my share of (patent-medicine sponsors like) Peruna, Colorback and those 4 A.M. radio programs."

Travis helped him over the rough spots, and Foreman Phillips made good on his offer. At Phillips's Venice Pier Ballroom, where Cooley got his start, Hank set to forming a new band built around three stellar swing soloists: fiddler Harold Hensley and two former Texas Playboys. One was Noel Boggs, who'd only recently left Wills. The other was guitarist Jimmy Wyble, who with his Texas buddy Cameron Hill was half of Bob's famous 1944–45 "twin guitar" team heard on hits like "Roly Poly." Despite a weak rhythm section, Penny's new band often played sizzling jazz instrumentals allowing Boggs, Wyble, and Hensley to swing away. With tens of thousands of trans-plants from Texas, Oklahoma, Kansas, and other Prairie and Plains states this was a place where audiences appreciated Hank's Wills-like dance fare.

Phillips seemed supportive when he recruited Hank. Over time, the promoter proved to be an unpleasant surprise. Despite the fact that he'd played Radio Cowboys records as a disc jockey, his heart was with southeastern fare of the Ernest Tubb–Roy Acuff variety: simple lyrics, vanilla chords, and melodic instrumental accompaniment. Cooley was his own man with a growing following, and Phillips wouldn't have dared tell a "name" act like Wills what to play. But Penny's band was a salaried house act, and Phillips started carping about the band's jazz content. Within months, he summoned Hank to his office and ordered him to fire Boggs, Wyble, and Hensley because "they just don't play the melody." "Now there's a helluva note," Penny remembered thinking. "I'm gonna fire a guy because he's *too good? No way!!*" Though he asked Phillips why, he already knew the answer.

"They just don't play what I want to hear," Phillips explained.

"When in the hell are we supposed to be playin' for *you?* You just hire us! We play for the *public!*"

"Well, I'm payin' your check, and you'll play what I want!"

"Really? And just what is it you *want?*"

"I want to hear the *melody!* When those guys play, I don't *hear* the melody."

"You'll hear the melody *when I sing it,* and outside of that, you're not gonna *hear* any melody!"

Phillips told him to think about it, adding, "don't be hasty." Hank thought about it long enough to meet with the band, who voted to "tell Foreman Phillips to go to hell." When he returned to Phillips's office, he directed him, "Write out their notices. Then write out a fourth one and put my name on it. Thank you very much." He turned and walked out, leaving behind an enraged Phillips.

As V-J Day came and World War II ended late in the summer of 1945, months after turning his back on the 4:30 A.M. radio shows of Cincinnati, Hank Penny was out of work and flat on his ass. He pawned the Martin D-18 guitar he'd used since the Radio Cowboys days and fronted an all-female band for a while. His friendship with Spade Cooley pulled him out of the chute. Barbara "Bobbie" Bennett, Cooley's personal manager and wife of Cooley pianist Eddie Bennett, recruited Hank to form a small band to appear in a Charles Starrett western. Bennett also had an overflow of job offers for the Cooley band in the wake of his national hit recording of "Shame on You." With more dates available than the band could handle, she organized several swing bands to handle the overflow engagements. Merle Travis and singing cowboy film stars Tex Ritter and Ray Whitley each fronted a swing band, as did Hank. Free to play what he wanted, it got him back on his feet and cemented relations with the Cooley organization.

Booked into Hoot Gibson's L.A. club, the Painted Post, he formed a new band with drummer Jack Peltier, guitarist Dick Morgan, and bassist Johnny Morgan, Dick's brother. Two former Cooley sidemen, pianist Joe Bardelli and steel guitarist Dick Roberts, rounded out the new group, which worked four nights a week. At $150 a week for Hank and $100 a week for each sideman, it was a cushy job in postwar L.A. Their repertoire would have driven Phillips bonkers, but the crowd had no problems. They not only played requests, but tore into Count Basie's "One O'clock Jump" or the Benny Goodman Sextet favorite "Soft Winds."

Meanwhile, Syd Nathan hired Merle Travis as King's West Coast talent scout and A&R man. Travis set to signing local talent. Some were old WLW buddies like the Fiddlin' Linvilles, others were local unknowns like Jimmy Thomason and Curt Barrett. On October 8, Travis produced and played on a 12-song Penny session that included Boggs, Hensley, and bassist Allen Reinhart from the Phillips band. Two accordionists were present: former Spade Cooley sideman Frank Buckley and Stan Ellison. Except for Kelland Clark's accordion on his 1941 post–Radio Cowboys session, Hank had never used an accordion. "But when I got out here," he explained, "I used an accordion mainly [to give the music] body."

Two significant instrumental numbers emerged from the largely vocal session, held at Universal Studios in Pasadena, the home of KXLA Radio. The first was "Steel Guitar Stomp," a remake of the Radio Cowboys' coy 1939 instrumental "Steel Guitar Hula." This band recast it as a propulsive showcase for Boggs, driven by Travis's blazing, syncopated fingerstyle electric guitar, his ever-reliable right thumb maintaining the beat alongside Allan Reinhart's bass. As the song's featured instrumentalist, Boggs played with a chilling, intense abandon equaled by Hensley and Travis. The session also yielded "Merle's Buck Dance," Travis's first recorded instrumental (known around his Muhlenberg County, Kentucky, birthplace as "Buck and Wing").

Numbers like the playful "Now Ain't You Glad, Dear" and the plaintive "When You Cry, You Cry Alone" were far removed from the jazz material Hank played at the Painted Post, and he realized it. His vocals were animated and vibrant, if not terribly passionate. "Those were some of the most commercial things I ever recorded," he said of those recordings. "Everything on those 12 songs had a real good, strong beat, mainly because of Travis and his ability to give everything a good SWACK!" In 1946, "Stomp" became Penny's first nationwide hit.

Hank's 1946 recordings included "Get Yourself a Red Head," a raw 12-bar blues with a down–and-dirty vocal, double-entendre lyrics ("she's at home in bed all right, but brother, she ain't asleep"), and tough low-register clarinet from Slim Duncan. At the same session, the group finished two of the most raucous California western swing performances of all time: the ferocious "These Wild, Wild Women" and "I'm Gonna Change Things," marked by Duncan's forceful clarinet and Truman Quigley's wailing trumpet. Lascivious lyrics notwithstanding, "Red Head" became his second chart hit.

In the summer of 1946 Hank inherited a new band. Spade Cooley's bassist Deuce Spriggens had left Cooley to form his own band. In the latter half of 1946, Spriggens left his band and joined his former Cooley band-mates in Tex Williams's Western Caravan. Hank took over Spriggens's band, a group that by design emulated Cooley's smooth sophistication.

Syd Nathan showed up in September to record his West Coast acts and, as usual, behaved like a bespectacled cigar-chewing bull in a china shop. As Hank and the band recorded an unnamed boogie-woogie instrumental on September 23 at Radio Recorders, steel guitarist Ralph Miele kept blowing his solo. An enraged Nathan bounded from his chair toward the studio to ream some butt. "Nathan was known for blowin' his stack," Hank said.

> He'd come in and yell and scream and push musicians around. We were tryin' to get this thing done and Syd came rushing out of the control room to go and overhaul [Miele]. I stepped right in front of him, and I said, "Hold it just a minute. There's *one* area where you're boss here, and it's in that control room. Now get back in that control room and pay attention to what we're doing and work with me as I'm trying to work with you, and we'll get a take on this thing! Now, get your ass back in that control room where you belong! These musicians don't work for you. They work for *ME!*" And he turned, never said one word, went back in, and we started a take.

Still seething after the session ended, Hank was packing his guitar when a hand touched his shoulder. It was Nathan, wheezing, "I like you when you're mad. You work better. You get things done." Hank snapped back. "One of these days, man, I'm gonna hit you right in the mouth, because you really get to me with that eatin' on musicians." Nathan would remember this, as he would the overtime pay issue.

Hank faced another problem that year. He'd gotten his first regular network exposure doing comedy on ABC Radio's *Roundup Time,* a show that also featured his band's clarinet player, Slim Duncan. While doing the show, Hank began receiving threatening letters addressed from Cain, New Hampshire, pertaining to his being sued for divorce. Since he'd never set foot in New Hampshire, he pitched the letters. ABC began receiving letters accusing Hank of abandoning a wife and three kids and failing to pay support, requesting the network garnishee his wages. When the network asked Hank for an explanation, he explained that he'd never been in the state and in fact had just been divorced from his first wife in Long Beach.

That satisfied the network, but soon a process server appeared at his hotel room with a summons to New Hampshire. Hank brought in his lawyer, who finally determined Herbert Clayton Penny would have been six years old when the other Penny's first child was born. The authorities were convinced, and the culprit was apparently a Maine performer who recorded old-time music as "Old Hank Penny" for Columbia's 15000-D series in June of 1932.

Hank soon married Philomena Rickiewicz and began using "Phil Rickey" as his new pseudonym for songwriting. With two hit singles ("Steel Guitar Stomp" and "Red Head") under his belt in 1946, he dissolved his band in late November and embarked on an eight-week Texas tour with yodeler Carolina Cotten and Merle Travis, a hitmaker in his own right for Capitol and no longer producing for Nathan. The tour sputtered, but Hank, with his hit singles, got invited by the Opry to perform on the show's network segment, sponsored by Prince Albert Tobacco and hosted by Red Foley. In late January 1947 he returned to Cincinnati for the first time since leaving in 1945. Nathan wanted another recording session.

Two years of success with country and rhythm and blues releases had made a substantial difference in the fortunes of King Records, now housed in a converted icehouse complex at 1540 Brewster Street. Crosley had sold WLW to another company after Hank had left. The station no longer barred staff musicians from recording. On January 29, 1947, Hank reunited with Roy Lanham and his old friends Homer Haynes and Jethro Burns. The duo, who recorded exaggerated hillbilly versions of pop standards for King were, like Hank, enamored of Django Reinhardt. Homer's driving rhythm guitar and Jethro's intense mandolin leads easily captured the Django spirit. For Hank's session, pianist Eddie Wallace and bassist Larry Downing handled rhythm.

Hank brought along his bluesy original novelty "Locked Out." Nathan wanted a cover of one of the day's biggest hits: R&B saxophonist Jack McVea's nationwide hit novelty "Open the Door Richard." Poised to exact revenge for Hank's previous intransigence with the union, the producer handed him "The Freckle Song," a 1946 double-entendre ditty written and recorded by "party song" specialist Larry Vincent, and bluesman Tampa Red's explicit "Let Me Play With Your Poodle."

Hank voiced his displeasure but knew Syd had him by the short hairs. "I did not want to record these. Nathan insisted that I record 'em," he complained in 1980. "I felt they were too risqué, and I recorded 'em under the condition they would release 'em under the name the Freckle Faced Boys." Syd twisted the knife. King 606 paired "Freckle" and "Poodle." The artist? Hank Penny. The Opry retracted its invitation to the Prince Albert segment.

"I feel that this was the thing that caused Syd and I to eventually just split up." Nathan later withdrew the disc.

Why Hank returned to the Midwest, a region he seemed so weary of in 1944, isn't clear. Nor is it certain his divorce played a role. He spent the better part of 1947 exploiting his two hits and, for a time, signed on at WLW, where new management welcomed him back. In 1945, *Boone County* had been renamed the *Midwestern Hayride,* and under new ownership the era of high salaries for artists was history. Hank tried to adapt but discovered "it wasn't like it used to be. It's like they say: you can't go back."

In Arlington, Virginia, Connie B. Gay had brought full-blown live country radio to the Washington, D.C., area, at WARL radio. Hank relocated

Goofin' at the Riverside Rancho, 1949: Speedy jumps Hank, Caldwell trumps Billy Hill.

there and reunited with old Atlanta friend Pete Cassell. As before, they joked offstage about Cassell's blindness and neither minded joking about it onstage. One night, Hank came up behind Cassell as he sang onstage, chiding him for playing a wrong chord. While Cassell fell apart laughing, offstage, WARL official Bob Stirewald was not amused. He accosted Hank and bluntly reprimanded and preached to him for "ridiculing a blind man." The preaching sent Hank into full confrontation mode. Cassell rose to Hank's defense, but when the smoke cleared, Hank stormed out of WARL after persuading a furious Cassell not to quit with him.

Nathan wanted Hank in Nashville again. With a Musicians Union recording ban set to begin in January 1948, record companies recorded and stockpiled new material. Arriving at Nashville's newly opened Castle Studios, Hank found Red Foley's band waiting for him. Zeke Turner played lead guitar; Louis Innis handled bass, and Bob Foster played steel guitar. Joe Ross was the accordionist, and local dance band trumpeter Malcolm Crain rounded out the lineup. The visceral, percussive rhythm guitar came from Foley himself. Hank recalled with amusement what sparked Foley's musical gusto: "One of them silly musicians slipped some bennies in the Coke bottle Red was drinkin' from. Later, Red says, 'Man, I didn't sleep for a week!'" Penny, still a hardline teetotaler whose friends nonetheless included notorious boozers like Travis, was often bewildered by such antics.

The mixed bag of novelties, blues, and ballads included "Kentucky," one of those fanciful, clichéd homages to a southern state. "Politics," a satirical talking blues Hank wrote under his Phil Rickey pseudonym, featured the sly, acerbic wit seldom far away from Penny's private persona. The music here was commercial country, yet Hank's vocals and the loose instrumentation made the performances rollicking and wry.

Those months in the Southeast may have given Hank a heads-up on a reality many of his West Coast peers had yet to comprehend. True, he disdained Nashville and "shitkickin'" music, but as an astute observer, Hank couldn't help see the shift in the musical winds. From 1944 to 1946, Bob Wills, Tex Ritter, Merle Travis, and other West Coast acts generated a substantial portion of the nation's country record sales. Eddy Arnold's success, along with that of Foley, Ernest Tubb, and other Nashville-based solo singers, heralded a new era. It weighed on him.

When Penny returned to Hollywood late in 1947, the dancehall business was in a temporary slump as the country slipped into a postwar recession. For a time, musical work proved scarce, so he returned to radio, hosting the daily *Penny Serenade* show at KGIL in the San Fernando Valley. Sitting behind a mike didn't mellow him. Decca initially declined to provide new releases for airplay. Hank took the bait, calling for a listener boycott of Decca and making a point to play Johnny Bond's Columbia cover of Red

Foley's hit Decca single "Tennessee Saturday Night." It was blatantly unprofessional, but Hank got results. Decca added KGIL to its mailing lists.

As the recession eased, he formed a new band, dubbed the Penny Serenaders in honor of his radio show. Over the next two years, the Serenaders evolved into the finest band of his career. Cooley fiddler Billy Hill worked with him, as did Tex Williams's former guitarist Benny Garcia, and Speedy West. "Speedy was brave," Hank said. "He had distinctive ideas of his own. He was very good at tone and dynamics, young and full of vinegar. He would come in like a storm and did one hell of a job." West returned the compliment. "Hank and his band encouraged me to get off of the mainstream and try to reach out. He wanted you to play all you could play and then some. Hank could turn you on."

Having played clubs throughout the area, Hank decided that he wanted a club of his own. When he saw Pop's Willow Lake, a local swimming hole in the Sunland/Tujunga area of the San Fernando Valley, he met with its owner, Amand Gautier. Discussing dancehalls, Gautier offered him the chance to "put one here if you want." Gautier, Penny, and most of his musicians built a place in 28 days. The new hall accommodated 600. Bob Wills and His Texas Playboys opened the place.

Hank's first post–recording ban King session in March 1949 yielded the plaintive "I Was Satisfied" and his best-known number, "Bloodshot Eyes." Hank wrote "Bloodshot's" lyrics. His friend Harold Hensley wrote the melody. Penny gave him half the song under Hensley's wife's maiden name, Ruth Hall. In 1950, it became Hank's final hit single. Nathan handed it to King blues shouter Wynonie Harris, whose explosive version became an immense R&B hit that year. Syd wasn't striking blows for musical cross-pollination with this move. His own Lois Music published the song. He'd do it again a year later with another tune from a Penny session.

"Hillbilly Be-Bop" was the first western swing instrumental to embrace that era's cutting-edge modern jazz. The alternate take, an early try, reveals that bop harmonies and flatted fifths proved daunting even to such capable sidemen as guitarist Dick Morgan and accordionist Billy Liebert, while Speedy, Slim Duncan, and Joe Bardelli's Earl Hines–style swing piano breezed through the piece. But Morgan and Liebert got the idea, making the final, finished version an incendiary gem. Speedy's flamboyant solo provoked Nathan. Unaccustomed to hearing such dazzling pyrotechnics on Cowboy Copas, Hawkshaw Hawkins, or Clyde Moody sessions, the King owner demanded Speedy tone it down. Yet again, Hank angrily ordered Nathan to back off.

Then, late in '49, Hank, driving down Lankershim Boulevard in the San Fernando Valley, noticed an old, broken-down beer joint called the Mule Kick Club. An idea flashed; he bounced it off Amand Gautier. They tracked down and found the building's owner, an elderly woman who wanted $250 a month rent. After signing the papers, they renovated, installing a new kitchen and restaurant furnishings, and obtained a beer and wine license.

The club lacked a name, and Hank stumbled onto one by happenstance one day when he and Gautier were downtown. Hank picked up a sport shirt at a nearby men's clothing store. Riding along with Gautier, Hank looked at the shirt's label, which depicted a horse rearing; it read "The Palomino." The club struggled, but slowly built a regular following. Hank reached out beyond the country music crowd with "jazz nights" that were pure jam sessions, attracting such luminaries as jazz violin master Joe Venuti and bebop guitar master Barney Kessel, who became a friend.

Speedy eventually joined Cliffie Stone's organization. Hill, fiddler Billy Wright, Garcia, and pianist Jo Ella Wright remained, along with bassist Hank Caldwell and various drummers, plus the band's latest addition: 19-year-old vocalist Mary Morgan, the sister of Penny sidemen Charlie, John, and Dick Morgan. They continued without a steel guitarist for a while. A surviving live recording of "Steel Guitar Rag" reveals that Benny Garcia capably played the steel parts.

Released in 1950, "Bloodshot Eyes" attracted the attention of CBS daytime radio and TV talk maven Arthur Godfrey, renowned for his laid-back style and his penchant for kidding sponsors and commenting on the day's events. Godfrey would pick up his ever-present ukulele, sing a bit of the song, then laconically comment, "Wonder who'd write a song as *stupid* as that?" Hank was delighted by Godfrey's cheekiness; "I just said, 'Go, Arthur!' Didn't make any difference to me. It got an awful lot of publicity, and every time he sang it there were [performance] royalties."

Around that same time, Hank heard that Herb Remington, who'd just left Bob Wills, was in L.A. seeking studio work. He offered Remington a job and never forgot their first rehearsal as Remington tuned up: "When I heard Herb's tuning, I thought anybody who can even *tune* like that must be able to play well!" Soon Remington and Garcia were working out ensemble pieces of their own. Both appreciated Hank's confidence. "He'd let the guys work (arrangements) out," Remington said. Garcia agreed. "I loved those guys," he said in 2000. "Hank was always on the ball. I liked his ideas, and if somebody else had an idea he'd always listen to you."

With Remington's hiring, the Serenaders hit its musical peak. "Out of all the records I made," Penny reflected, "some of the most interesting were with Herb and Benny Garcia. On my last King sessions, Benny did double guitar ensemble things with Herb . . . some of the best stuff I ever cut. He really kicked the band along."

This was a western swing band like no other, one that melded the sophisticated textures and voicings of the Cooley/Tex Williams sound with Wills's intense drive, creating a unique blend of sophistication and swing. Pianist Jo Ella Wright clearly knew her way around modern jazz. Hank Caldwell and drummer Pee Wee Adams created a light, agile rhythm section. Within the band, a second ensemble counterpointed Garcia and Remington. This one blended Hill's fluent, swinging fiddle with Stan Ellison's robust accordion. Their full-bodied, unison voicings sometimes evoked a full brass section and at others, accordionist Joe Mooney's 1946–49 "chamber jazz" quartet.

Three sessions, one on March 31 and two on April 3, fulfilled Hank's King obligations. While Penny shrugged off Syd's bellowing after six years, it thoroughly irritated Remington: "I couldn't stand that old fart. I was looking at him through the window in the studio. I never even knew him personally—his voice and the things he demanded. [He was] obnoxious all the way around."

"We did a bunch of Charlie Christian tunes," Garcia recalled. "We didn't record any of that stuff." A tornadic demo acetate of the 1939 Benny Goodman–Charlie Christian instrumental "Shivers," discovered years later, proved Garcia's point and then some. Hank's vocal on his reworked version of "You're So Different," a ricky-ticky 1929 ballad from orchestra leader Blue Steele, is more distinctive than he himself might have concluded, conveying an emotional depth seldom present on his more upbeat material. Hill and Ellison provided a second thrill in the midst of the record: a breathtakingly complex accordion-viola ensemble passage with the feel of French bistro music.

Remington made another lasting contribution: an untitled instrumental he'd written during his days with Bob Wills. "Hank wanted to know if I had written any instrumentals in the past," he remembered. "I said, 'Well, I had one that Bob [Wills] didn't like.' I played it for him. And they liked it immediately, and we [recorded] it before we even named it. Then we said, 'What are we gonna call it?' Syd named it 'Remington Ride.' " It wasn't strictly swing, yet it reflected a number of interesting harmonic ideas and became a steel-guitar standard. Nathan, who published it, had various King artists cover it, from organist Bob Kames to blues guitarist Freddie King, who years later created a remarkable blues performance that remains one of his finest moments on King Records.

That third session brought down the curtain on Hank's five tumultuous years with King—and on the Penny Serenaders themselves. Remington moved to Houston, where he remained into the twenty-first century. Hank had stayed close to Spade Cooley and appeared on Cooley's Saturday night *Hoffman Hayride* TV program on KTLA one night in 1950 to promote "Bloodshot Eyes." He wound up joining the *Hayride* as the show's comedian.

His reasons for doing so aren't quite clear, but the new paradigms from Nashville almost surely played a role. For that and other reasons, he finally concluded that his own singing voice simply wasn't distinctive enough in a new era of vocal stylists like Hank Williams, Ernest Tubb, and, more locally, Tennessee Ernie Ford:

> I went on Cooley's show strictly as a standup comic. I sang once in a while, I'd do "Little Red Wagon" or [later], "Bloodshot Eyes" and that was it. I never attempted anything serious and I didn't want to. Spade and I had many conversations about it and he'd say, "Son, what do you want to do?" I told him, "Look, I don't have an identifiable Ernest Tubb–Roy Acuff–Al Dexter sound, and that's good, fine for them, but for me it poses a problem. So if I'm gonna spend six minutes entertaining before the camera, let me do something I *know* I can entertain them with, and that's comedy."

And so, at the *Hayride,* he focused on his role as the "Plain Ol' Country Boy" from "Rimlap, Alabama" (a real hamlet outside Birmingham), often using Cooley as his straight man. On the surface, the paradox of a sophisticated bandleader who scorned all things hillbilly performing every week as a dimwitted rustic in a bent-up hat and too-small vest was lost on Hank. With Cooley's writer Paul Conlon creating new material for him, Hank happily carved himself another niche.

During the week, Hank focused on his radio show, which moved from KGIL to KWIK in Burbank, and on his weekly Cooley broadcasts. That summer he reorganized a new and smaller band and signed with Cooley's label: RCA Victor. A major-label deal should have been a godsend, affording Hank professionalism and budgets beyond Nathan's capability.

That wasn't to be. He quickly found himself up against Steve Sholes, RCA's country A&R man, who had sweetheart deals with the music publisher Hill and Range. Though the records had fiery musical moments from Noel Boggs and others, the overload of throwaway ditties by writers like Cy Coben, composer of such forgettable pop fare as "The Old Piano Roll Blues," gave Hank nothing even approaching a hit. Hank's contentious side undoubtedly complicated matters. Vocally, he'd begun infusing more of his comic persona into the music, which helped the novelties a bit, but not enough to enhance their anemic sales.

Discussing the RCA contract, he castigated the venerable Sholes and his associate, Henri Rene. "I don't know of many people with less to offer than Steve Sholes," he griped. "I was constantly hurried in the studio. There was no one to produce anything. They were timekeepers." The material was certainly a mixed bag of inane novelties, their sharp, intense arrangements often their only saving grace. A silly number like "Taxes, Taxes" worked only because of Boggs's explosive steel guitar work. "Hadacillin Boogie," a half-baked attempt to exploit the fame of the patent medicine Hadacol and the antibiotic penicillin, was a song Hank despised because the song's lyrics forced him to have the band break meter. He and Morgan kicked an arrangement of the old blues number "Fan It" through the wall with a cacophonous, pile-driving boogie arrangement, but turned treacly on the 1920s pop throwaway "That's My Weakness Now." As with "You're So Different," the more reflective "I Want to Live a Little" reflected the depth his vocals had when he put his mind to it.

He had a second recording operation going by 1951 when he recorded a series of transcriptions for Standard Radio Transcription Services. He used the same musicians he had used on the RCA tracks, including Noel Boggs. Standard required a varied repertoire for its radio clients (each song carefully categorized by tempo and key). The mix of pop standards, remakes of past recordings, new originals, instrumentals (some of them renamed or reconfigured jazz favorites), and covers of current hits had its strong and weak points, instrumental excellence being the sole constant.

The early 1950s were loaded with other transitions. He'd divorced Philomena, letting her have the couple's North Hollywood home while Hank took his clothes, guitar, record collection, and little else. While he still played clubs, western swing was losing its grip in the region. He was out of Pop's Willow Lake, and the TV phenomenon that brought him into tens of thousands of L.A. homes every Saturday night had an inverse and lasting effect on dance crowds. People who once danced now stayed home, many of them with their new families. Hank and Gautier brought in a third partner at the Palomino before they sold to the Thomas Brothers, who developed it into the West Coast's preeminent country nightclub until it closed for good in 1995. "The only regret I have is that I was not given credit for having the foresight to open that club," he complained in 1980.

In 1952, Cliffie Stone approached him about joining *Hometown Jamboree,* as Tennessee Ernie Ford's singing success began moving him away from his comedic duties on the show. When Hank demanded more money and insisted that Cliffie hire Conlon to write his skits, Cliffie backed away.

Meanwhile, L.A. singer Dude Martin, seeing the success of the *Hayride* and *Hometown,* was about to begin his own broadcast, sponsored by Sears, and he approached Hank's manager, Eames Bishop. Making $400 a week with Cooley, Penny was less than enthused about leaving. Martin asked what it would take to change his mind. The response was $100 more a week, full production for his comedy skits, and his own writer. Martin agreed, and Hank amicably left Cooley for the Martin TV show. At the same time, he worked as a comic on the new *Town Hall Party* TV show in Compton for $200 a night.

The problems started within months. Problem one: Hank, divorced three times, met Martin's wife, singer Sue Thompson, and the two became friendly. Problem two: Martin and Hank shared a manager, who maneuvered Hank off *Town Hall* and into Martin's nightclub show for a mere $100 a night. Hank then discovered that Martin's guarantee of a yearlong contract for the TV show rested on his landing Penny, a measure of the *Hoffman Hayride*'s status in the early '50s. Problem one led to problem three: Hank and Sue's blossoming romance. When local gossipmeisters picked it up, Hank, typically blunt, confirmed it. By 1953, Hank and Sue, who was divorcing Martin, were off Martin's show. They married that year.

As he signed with old nemesis, Decca Records, in 1954, Hank surveyed the turmoil he and Sue had endured in the past two years. In 1955, *The Hank Penny Show,* a half-hour weekly TV show, debuted over KHJ in Los Angeles, sponsored by Bill Murphy Buick of Culver City. The concept had promise. Sue was part of the cast; Jimmy Wyble served as bandleader. The mix of comedy and music attracted guests like Tex Ritter; jazz trombone great Jack Teagarden; Hank's old friend, swing fiddle pioneer Joe Venuti; and jazz guitar master Barney Kessel, a regular at the Palomino Jam sessions. For reasons never made clear, Murphy canceled the show after seven weeks, provoking Hank to sue and tie up the car dealer's bank accounts. Hank lost that suit as well as a countersuit Murphy filed to recover his lost bank interest.

Given all this and the reality that western swing was fading into nostalgia, the couple made a risky move. With a new son, Greg, born on Columbus Day, 1955, the Pennys spent a bit more time in Los Angeles. Hank appeared in a short film with Webb Pierce, one of Nashville's biggest stars. The two did not get along, furthering Hank's alienation from Nashville. Finally the couple headed for Las Vegas. The odds weren't great. Hank Williams tanked there two years earlier, although country entertainer Sunny Joe Wolverton had based himself there and made some inroads.

Could Hank have done better staying put in Hollywood? With his local visibility, it's not hard to imagine him and his "hip hick" persona showing up on *I Love Lucy* as Tennessee Ernie Ford did in 1954, on Red Skelton's or Jack Benny's network TV shows, or any network variety show filmed in or broadcast live from Hollywood. Unfortunately, in a town with as few secrets as Hollywood, Hank's intractability, demonstrated by the very recent battles with Martin and Murphy, might well have put off network producers. He did appear on one episode of the *Colgate Comedy Hour* alongside the hip, bizarre comedy of a young Jonathan Winters. But it led nowhere else.

Vegas realities dictated a different type of Hank Penny band: a rhythm section augmented by a tenor sax and trumpet. He drilled them in pop, jazz, and country, accentuating the jazz: "I felt that the best place for me to get musicians was out of the pop field, or to go to the Musicians Union and get musicians that didn't know one thing about country music." He insisted that they stay true to themselves onstage:

> I always said as long as I'm on the front of this band, that's all the coun-
> try I need. I don't want some yahoo up there who'll lay claim to a musi-
> cian just because he's recorded with Webb Pierce. I'd tell the guys, "Don't
> you ever play down your nose at me or at the audience. You play the best
> [that] your ass can play. I'll sell it. I can sell it to the people. So don't you
> ever play down. I don't want you to be commercial. *I'll* be commercial!"

At the Golden Nugget from 1955 to 1961, Hank's and Sue's popularity soared as they freely mixed jazz and pop with country. Hank often sang country hits tongue-in-cheek, interjecting double entendre wherever it felt right. With the exception of his comic monologue "A Letter from Home," little of this surfaced on his Decca recordings, produced by Paul Cohen and Charles "Bud" Dant. Though some of the earliest Deccas had their moments, most sounded tired and dull. The Vegas band appeared only on the last Decca session. A 1961 jazz instrumental album for Atlanta-based NRC had little going for it, except the presence of ex–Radio Cowboy Shel-don Bennett on guitar. One rare thrill came when Hank and his band were pressed at a Vegas USO show to back Ella Fitzgerald. Hank, flattered and giddy with the experience, recalled with awe how saxophonist-arranger Glenn Blair created impromptu arrangements for Ella on the spot. Clearly, his insistence on maintaining the band's jazz content paid off.

Over time, other old friends appeared in Vegas. Hank hired his old friend Wade Ray, who'd also left California, to sing and play his driving swing fiddle. He also added Curly Chalker, Hank Thompson's former pedal steel guitarist, and Roy Clark, Wanda Jackson's former lead guitarist. When Clark moved on, he took along comedic ideas from Hank that would influ-ence his own comedy style. Sue's career revved up after Nashville's Hickory Records signed her in 1961. That year, she had two Top 10 pop hits with "Sad Movies (Make Me Cry)" and "Norman" and several lesser successes. As Hank and Sue realized they were growing apart, they amicably divorced in 1963.

Now based in Carson City, Nevada, Hank was briefly married to a cock-tail waitress named Sherry before divorcing her. He performed solo for a time and recorded mediocre musical and comedy fare for Seattle-based Wasp Records. He relocated to California and organized a new band with a new vocalist named Shari Bayne. He added an even younger talent: teenage singer-guitarist Thom Bresh, the biological son of Merle Travis. Bresh had hung around the Riverside Rancho as a kid and developed into a formidable entertainer (and guitarist) in his own right. The new group worked an area encompassing California, Lake Tahoe, Reno, and Vegas, with one European tour for the USO, doing a fairly standard lounge show that featured Bresh on guitar and singing various pop hits of the moment. Shari Bayne had been married when she joined Hank's band, but was divorced from her husband by 1967. Hank married her that year.

They were doing a local TV show in Reno in 1969 when Hank got a phone call from Merle Travis. Travis was living in Nashville, writing special material for his old hunting and pill-popping buddy Johnny Cash's new ABC-TV variety show. Merle pitched Hank's name around as a possible regular cast member. After turning the band over to Bresh, the Pennys moved to the town Hank had avoided all his life. It didn't take long for him to shoot himself in the foot. Hank's agent asked for $2,500 a week; Cash's producers offered $250. It was an insulting, condescending offer, and with no middle ground, it left Hank justifiably offended. At the same time, the national exposure the Cash show offered could have led to other things. Neither side would bend, and Cash's producers rescinded their offer. The Pennys went back to California.

Still, Hank had other friends with connections, including longtime admirer Archie Campbell, a veteran country comic who was gaining a national reputation as a regular on *Hee-Haw*. The show seemed a perfect match for someone with Hank's comedic skills. Campbell made a pitch to producer Sam Lovullo, touting his friend's experience and the seminal nature of his nearly three decades doing country comedy. Lovullo, who probably already knew about Hank's attitude (and the very recent demands made on Cash's producers), explained that the show had enough comics, including Roy Clark. "I don't think Roy could fill the bill as a full-time comic," Hank said years later. "He's a fabulous entertainer. But I have Sam Lovullo tell me he has all the comics he needs because he's got *Roy Clark*? To me, it was an insult to *Archie Campbell.*"

This rejection was different. It sent Hank into a spiral of resentment and depression that didn't lift for several years; traces of bitterness remained even after that. With the help of Louis Innis, who lived in Nashville, Hank bought a farm outside town and scraped by doing occasional TV shows over the next two years and a radio show in Franklin, Tennessee. In 1971, the Pennys' daughter, Sydney, was born. She was named for his old nemesis, Syd Nathan, who'd died in 1968.

By 1972, Hank had connected with Mack Sanders. A Birmingham native who grew up idolizing Penny, Sanders was a western swing bandleader based in Wichita, Kansas. He also owned several radio stations, including KFRM in Salina, Kansas, and he hired Hank as a disc jockey. He kept his band musicians working for him at his stations and played occasional shows. Sanders allowed Hank to program any music he wanted on his show.

Despite that, angst hung above Hank Penny like a prairie storm cloud. So what was the problem? Some health problems surfaced, but he dealt with them routinely. Though he had a brief love affair with playing horses in California, he had few other vices. He avoided drugs. He'd never been a drinker. He'd forgiven Cooley's alcoholism and looked compassionately on Cooley even after his old friend went to prison in 1961 for stomping his wife to death in a drunken rage. But those old hang-ups over religion, the memories of Will Penny's preaching, remained at the heart of many of his problems. He battled anyone who preached at him, be it Foreman Phillips, Syd Nathan, WLW management, or anyone else. He couldn't overcome it, and it cost him dearly. In the '50s he once avoided a chance meeting with evangelist Billy Graham. The anger over Clark's success and his own failures bore deep into his soul.

"This bitterness was working on me," he admitted. "And I felt bad that I wasn't able to give Mack Sanders my best. I did the job and got by." He was supporting Shari and Sydney but simply went through the motions. He stayed until late 1975. He and Shari occasionally worked casual music jobs in the Wichita area. As time went on, he decided that he needed to go home to a place he'd only visited in the past 20 years: Southern California and the San Fernando Valley.

It was a very different L.A. The music business he knew was gone, and for a time, he sold air conditioning to pay the bills. He and Shari continued to travel the country playing corporate shows and soon found that young Sydney had a flair for the stage that neither parent ever expected. He'd read some self-improvement books that seemed to dim many of his old inhibitions, even those about religion. At the same time, he and Shari tried moving Sydney toward show business.

Hank soon faced another battle, this time with Local 47, the L.A. local of the Musicians Union. Two years from receiving his lifetime membership card, officials decreed he'd have to start from scratch. A newsletter that pictured Hank as participating in a September 1976 union benefit show also listed him as "removed from membership." "I said, 'The hell with it. I don't care. I won't be union.'"

While the "Freckle Song" fiasco and the other clashes left a bad taste, succeeding decades mellowed his views. Hank realized he did his best recordings, despite the tensions, with Syd Nathan at the helm, and years before the King founder's 1997 induction into the Rock and Roll Hall of Fame, he advocated Nathan's induction into the Country Music Hall of Fame, an unlikely event even in 2003.

Save one appearance as an incestuous country-music patriarch on the Norman Lear talk show satire *America 2-Nite* with Martin Mull and Fred Willard, Hank sang and did comedy in non-union clubs and at private parties. It wasn't enough. For a time, he worked for Amtrak as a laborer, a rude and abrupt transition. Vowing to put the past behind him, he wrote Roy Clark a letter of apology that seemed to bury that hatchet. They later met when Clark played the old Knott's Berry Farm amusement complex. Despite the new amity, Clark's autobiography mentioned nothing about Penny's influence.

The western swing revival that began in the 1970s afforded him few chances to return to the stage. With support from some old friends from the Vegas days, the Pennys spent much of their time developing Sydney as a successful child actress and, where appropriate, accompanying her to location shoots. She made numerous appearances in commercials, films, and on TV. Later she became a longtime regular on the soap *General Hospital*.

Aside from an early '80s appearance reuniting him with several Radio Cowboys at the San Diego Folk Festival, Hank Penny's active career was over. While he was at peace with that, his edge hadn't dulled as he talked about his career and its travails. He remained close to old friends from the past like Eddie Dean, Roy Lanham, Speedy West, Joe Maphis, and Leo Fender. He'd played Fender guitars (all finished in Hank's trademark color of Heliotrope Purple) from the first Broadcaster solid-body Fender gave him in 1950. He also maintained a huge record and tape collection heavy on jazz and western swing. He wound up inducted into the Atlanta Country Music Hall of Fame, a reminder of the WSB years.

In the late 1980s he and Shari hosted annual "pickin' parties" at their San Fernando Valley home, often inviting other surviving musicians like Speedy West. Younger singers and fans who attended had discovered Hank's old records, and they peppered him with questions, paying him long-overdue homage. The timing couldn't have been better. It became a much-needed coda. He'd moved to Simi, California, by then, and while raking leaves in his backyard on April 17, 1992, he suffered a fatal heart attack.

Age and maturity gave Hank Penny sufficient wisdom to realize that, at least some of the time, he'd allowed his childhood demons to undermine him. Still, pride left him certain that he'd been right much of the time when he defended his principles. In the end, he seemed satisfied with what he did achieve, having lived long enough to enjoy the sort of respect from younger generations he'd given Milton Brown and Bob Wills. Perhaps, for him, that was enough.

Walk Softly

Wade Ray

Wade Ray, early 1950s.
(Courtesy Rob Santos)

Each year, the Sparta, Illinois, Lions Club sponsors the Wade "Pappy" Ray Fiddle Contest and Bluegrass Show. The highlight: presenting the "Pappy's Choice" award. Teenage fiddlers competing for the award have to meet several criteria. Musical ability counts, but no less than their enthusiasm and zest for performing. These standards epitomize the man whose name graces the festivities: a local personality, a retired fiddler who started as a child prodigy and never played a lick of country music until his teen years.

A Sparta resident since 1979, Wade Ray started the contest in the early 1990s. After his death in 1998 following years of ill health, Sparta continues the tradition. Residents considered him one of their own, yet it's unlikely that even today, many realize the full breadth and depth of Wade Ray's remarkable career. There are no Wade Ray box sets, not even a truly comprehensive compilation of his work. He was interviewed only rarely during his life, although his story is fascinating.

He began in the days before radio and was a veteran performer before 1920. And yet once he focused on country and, later, on western swing, he never went back. His instrumental verve and enthusiasm were matched only by his outstanding vocals and impeccable musical standards. His health wasn't the best when I interviewed him in 1994, yet his mind, particularly as he reminisced about the old days, was crystal-clear.

Wade was born in Griffin, Indiana, not far from Evansville, on April 6, 1913. He and his folks moved to Arkansas that fall. Wade was three when he got his first fiddle, a primitive "cigar box" instrument, for Christmas in 1916. The tyke became obsessed with the toy and played it constantly. By age five, he'd gotten good enough to play a real violin on vaudeville stage. He spent several years touring various theater chains (or "circuits," as they were called), billed everywhere as the "World's Youngest Violin Player" and playing popular tunes of the day.

Vaudeville finally came to a crashing halt in the 1920s, trounced by the new silent movies that now dominated the theaters. Home entertainment grew popular as cheap phonograph records and players became available, joining the new medium of radio. Wade adapted. He played traveling tent shows, medicine shows, circuses, and carnivals. By the late 1920s, he was in his teens, "too big to cry and too little to cuss," as he put it. He did some amateur boxing for a time. The pounding left him pug nosed, hence his longtime nickname "Pug." He quit when "it got to interfering with my hands."

The Jazz Age of the '20s wasn't lost on him. He worked to mimic jazz clarinetists on his fiddle, then found his ultimate role model in Joe Venuti, the father of jazz fiddle. Venuti, who made his name playing with Paul Whiteman's orchestra, dueting with jazz guitar innovator Eddie Lang and leading his own band, also became a fountainhead for western swing fiddlers.

But Wade didn't pursue a jazz career. Instead, in 1934 he joined Pappy Cheshire's National Champion Hillbillies on KMOX radio in St. Louis. "[The music] was strictly country," he remembered. He made his first records with Cheshire in 1936 on the local Town and Country label and stayed with the group until the Army grabbed him in January 1942. He spent the next two years as an Army MP in Harrisburg, Pennsylvania. Off duty, he led a country band of other MPs. He returned to Cheshire after his 1944 discharge, but he didn't stay long. In 1945, Wade joined the Prairie Ramblers, who since 1932 had been a fixture at Chicago's WLS *National Barn Dance*. The group, originally a Kentucky quartet whose aggressive music influenced Bill Monroe, evolved into a band heavy on western, pop, and jazz influences. The band backed Patsy Montana on her 1935 recording of "I Wanna Be a Cowboy's Sweetheart." He wasn't stepping into a tranquil situation, since he replaced Ramblers fiddler Alan Crockett, who'd only recently committed suicide. "Everybody loved Crockett," he said. "There was nobody gonna take his place."

Cheshire's music demanded country fiddling. He loved the Ramblers's jazzier focus as they played daily 15-minute morning WLS radio programs and the Saturday night *Barn Dance*. "They were the most versatile group I ever worked with," he said. "They had the largest repertoire of old folk songs that we did on the air that I never heard before or since." The band also recorded extensive transcriptions and some discs for Mercury.

WLS dropped the Ramblers in January 1949. Wade's good friend, singing Cowboy Rex Allen, who'd replaced Red Foley as *National Barn Dance* star in 1946 after Foley joined the Grand Ole Opry, also quit. Both of them headed to California and arrived on January 20. That night, a few of Rex's friends threw a party welcoming the newcomers. Wade met Capitol A&R man Lee Gillette, along with two of Capitol's stars: Hank Thompson and Merle Travis. Gillette invited the fiddler to play on a Tennessee Ernie Ford session the next night. On January 21, he and Harold Hensley played the twin fiddles on Ernie's hit recording of "Smoky Mountain Boogie." That quick initiation into the Hollywood recording scene couldn't obviate one big hurdle: the mandatory six-month waiting period imposed by Local 47 of the Musicians Union. Any new arrival from another Union Local (in Wade's case, Chicago) could only record and do one-night gigs. Wade landed bit parts in Rex's western films and played sessions and one-nighters until the period ended.

More important, Wade formed his own band at the L.A. nightclub Cow Town. His residency there turned into part ownership of the club, and for a time, a Cow Town record label that released four 78 discs of Wade with his band. Wade's band was a first-rate unit with bassist Bob Morgan and his guitarist brother Dick, ubiquitous figures on the California western swing scene. Steel guitarist Freddie Tavares was the native Hawaiian who later helped Leo Fender design several of his groundbreaking electric guitars. Former Bob Wills and Spade Cooley drummer Monte Mountjoy completed the lineup. For a while, the brilliant Joaquin Murphey played steel with Wade at Cow Town. Murphey's rich, lyrical style and chord work were equaled only by his grating eccentricities. With the band setup and ready to go at the club one Sunday, Murphey suddenly decided on a whim to disassemble his instrument onstage. It was too much for Wade's professionalism; he sacked Murphey on the spot.

Western swing was in decline, which was one reason Ray wasn't snatched up by a major label. Through his Capitol connections, he recorded "Cuddle Bug," a flaccid performance vocally and instrumentally, distinguished only for his overdubbing all the instruments along with the fiddle and vocal. Things got more serious when RCA Victor signed him in 1951. His first single, "Walk Softly," showcased his dynamic pop and jazz-flavored vocal style. Other RCA releases paired him with Noel Boggs's dynamic steel guitar (Boggs received billing on the records). The pair created magic in the studio. Wade's fiddle wasn't all of the show. He'd developed a powerful, pop-influenced singing voice. The band was often blazing on swing instrumentals like the big-band favorite "Dipsy Doodle" and "Sentimental Journey." "Boggs was my boy," Wade said. "I loved him dearly."

"Walk Softly" earned Wade an invitation to the Opry in 1952, and he took Boggs, Mountjoy, and bassist Stan Puls along. With Steve Sholes producing, they recorded four songs for RCA at Brown Radio Transcriptions, one of Nashville's early studios. Sholes augmented the band with guitarist Chet Atkins, rhythm guitarist Velma Williams, and Owen Bradley on piano. From the session came a blazing rendition of "It's All Your Fault," the Cindy Walker tune that Bob Wills first recorded in 1941. Everyone yanked out the stops. Wade's vocal was powerful as Boggs slid in chords beneath him. Atkins played what for him was an unusual, single-string jazz solo, and Boggs, as always, shoved out his chords in typhoon-like waves. The ballad "The Things I Might Have Been" became one of Wade's best-selling singles. As his passionate vocal threw sparks, Boggs complemented every line. Given the amount of raw country the jazz-loving Nashville guys played on sessions, letting loose behind a true western swing vocalist had to have been a lark for Bradley and Atkins.

Not everyone in clique-happy Nashville felt the same way. Speedy West took his share of shit from the union when he played there with Tennessee Ernie Ford and Kay Starr in 1950. Wade remembered that Noel received similar shabby treatment. "Poor Boggs was treated pretty roughly because they wanted Nashville guys on the session," he said. At the Opry, sidemen marveled at Boggs's four-neck Fender Stringmaster steel, an instrument Boggs helped design. The three necks accommodated his penchant for switching between necks even during one solo; the fourth was all bass strings for special effects. A few wiseasses assumed it was an electric zither.

Around 1954, Wade picked up a song previously recorded by Chuck Miller. With a swinging arrangement propelling it, he made "Idaho Red" one of the great underrated country trucker songs of all time. Though Wade occasionally toured to promote a record, California remained home until 1956, when he moved to Las Vegas and formed a jazz-country band that over its lifespan featured such gifted sidemen as country-jazz guitarist Thumbs Carlille and steel guitarist Curly Chalker.

In Vegas, versatility was the key, and Ray knew it. "We were sharing the bandstand with Louis Prima, the Mary Kaye Trio, things like that," he explained. "Sharing the bill with those people, you'd better come up with something. It was marvelous to have Curly and Thumbs on the bandstand together. I can't describe it. People just couldn't believe what they were hearin'. It was just unreal." Later, he spent some time working with Hank Penny's equally dazzling band.

He left Vegas in the early '60s to join both the Sons of the Pioneers and Roy Rogers for tours and TV work. He moved in 1964 to Nashville, where he spent a year with Ray Price's Cherokee Cowboys, fiddling alongside former Bob Wills sideman and swing virtuoso Keith Coleman, which gave him a chance to do a lot of swinging behind Price, a diehard western swing fan. Wade was particularly outstanding on the Cowboys' solo LP *Western Strings*.

Wade played six months with Ferlin Husky's band, then made some RCA sessions with a studio instrumental group known as the Country Fiddlers, which included Homer and Jethro, pianist Pig Robbins, bassist Henry Strzelecki, and others, playing instrumental renditions of bluegrass and country standards. RCA released one album by the group on its Camden budget subsidiary. Around 1965, Ernest Tubb brought him into the cast of his syndicated TV show, something Wade called "an experience I'll treasure the rest of my life. To know him was to love him."

Meeting Willie Nelson, another regular on the show, was a thrill for Willie as well. For years, he'd cited Ray as a vocal influence, and he covered "The Things I Might Have Been" during his days recording for Liberty. "Willie says he borrowed some from me and some from Floyd Tillman," Wade explained. Wade, along with the Texas Troubadours, added his fiddle and voice to Willie's honky-tonk LP *Country Favorites Willie Nelson Style*, recorded in 1965 and released in 1966.

Wade joined Willie's road band as bass player in 1965, the two traveling together for a time, picking up musicians in each town. Wade left in 1967 and wound up at the Kentucky's revered Renfro Valley Barn Dance: "I became manager over there. I managed the whole complex from '67 along there until '70." A return to Nashville followed, where he did sessions and worked for Fender guitars as the company's Nashville Artist Relations representative.

But there were rough times. He never seemed to connect with the western swing revival that began during the '70s. For a time, he even worked as a security guard. In 1979 he moved to Sparta with his wife, Gracie, played in bluegrass festivals around the area, and became a regular performer at DeWitt Scott's annual International Steel Guitar Convention in St. Louis until failing health slowed him down. Willie Nelson never forgot his old friend. In 1996, he brought Wade and Gracie to St. Louis, where he was doing a show, so Wade could sit in.

Wade was clear on his vocal influences: largely jazz and pop, specifically Ella Fitzgerald, Perry Como, Nat King Cole, and Frank Sinatra. In an interview in 1994, he scorned the radio-driven, producer-controlled country music of the era compared to the relative freedom he had in his day. Back then, he says, "You had a style that you were proud of, had principles you were proud of. You did it for the love of it. I never done nothin' I wasn't proud of, or I wouldn't do it. I think today kids are doin' things because the producer says do it. I think it's become too commercial."

He was proud of the Fiddle Contest and Bluegrass Show. He had the chance to present the first Pappy's Choice Award to 14-year-old Jennifer Herzig in 1992. His health was precarious throughout the 1990s, however, and he died November 18, 1998. Though the man himself is gone, the presence remains. Every year in Sparta, they remember. On that stage, and the jam sessions around the Lions Club, Wade Ray lives on.

Tommy leaps in: the original 1948 Western All-Stars. Top row: Davie Coleman, Glynn Duncan. Middle row: Noel Boggs, Jimmy Wyble, Cameron Hill, Joe Holley. Front row: Ocie Stockard, Tommy, Millard Kelso. (Courtesy Glenn White)

3

Wrong Road Home
Tommy Duncan

Tommy Duncan had everything going for him when Bob Wills fired him from the Texas Playboys in the late summer of 1948. He had one of the highest profiles of any western swing performer, built on 16 years of visibility with the top band in the country. He organized a new band with some of the best sidemen in the business and within a year had a national Top 10 record. And it all went downhill from there.

Duncan's decline came gradually, but come it did. Changing times and tastes, bad luck beyond his control, and, to some extent, his own short-sightedness were all to blame. While his talent was undeniable, he failed to accentuate his strengths, too often tried becoming something he wasn't, and ignored changing musical trends. It was tragic, given the distance he'd traveled from his humble beginnings.

Between Dallas–Fort Worth and Waco lies Hill County, Texas. Southwest of the county seat of Hillsboro is the small town of Whitney, where Thomas Elmer Duncan was born on January 11, 1911, the eighth of 14 children born to Jack and Edna Duncan. The Duncans farmed in the area. "I was never around Tommy much whenever we were younger," admits Glynn Duncan, Tommy's younger brother (born in 1923) and future sideman. He recalls that Tommy left home around age 17 for West Texas, settling near the town of Hedley.

Like the young Bob Wills, Tommy spent much of his youth farming West Texas soil and, also like Wills, frequented country dances. He lived with cousins who sharecropped and attended school. Glynn recalled, "When he was out there in West Texas, we had some other cousins that worked as country musicians, played the country dances. Tommy ran around with them, so that's probably when he got interested in the music business, out there with those guys." Somewhere he learned to play a four-string tenor guitar and dabbled—a charitable term at best—with piano. Finding little success at farming, he headed for Fort Worth. By 1932, Tommy, whose musical heroes included Jimmie Rodgers, Bing Crosby, and the gifted white minstrel singer Emmett Miller, was working at a dry cleaners. For amusement (and tips) he sang and played tenor guitar at Fort Worth's Ace High Root Beer stand.

Bob Wills was enjoying his first shot at fame with vocalist Milton Brown in the original Light Crust Doughboys, which included guitarists Derwood Brown and Herman Arnspiger. Sponsored by the Burrus Mill and Elevator Company, makers of Light Crust Flour, the Doughboys became a sensation on local radio after being embraced by officious Burrus Mill sales manager W. Lee O'Daniel. The executive despised the music and the musicians while using them to expand Light Crust's market (and his own personal power). O'Daniel became the show's emcee even as he did his best to stick it to the musicians. That September, he continued his penurious ways by giving the Doughboys a token raise with the proviso they cease playing the dance-hall jobs that provided added income. Already planning his own band, Milton Brown found in O'Daniel's edict the perfect excuse to quit. The Doughboys needed a new singer—fast.

On September 21, 1932, after auditioning 67 singers, according to Glynn Duncan, Herman Arnspiger told Bob about the kid singing at the root beer stand. Bob asked Tommy if he could sing "I Ain't Got Nobody," a 1920s pop tune song recorded by several singers, including Bob's and Tommy's mutual idol, Emmett Miller. Duncan auditioned, and the Doughboys had a new vocalist.

In April 1933, Bob, who'd endured countless scrapes with O'Daniel in the past two years, went on another of his occasional booze binges. This time he missed a broadcast; O'Daniel fired him. Bob made no attempt to beg for his job, as he'd done before. Tommy, citing the fact that Bob, not O'Daniel, had hired him, left with him. Bob quickly formed a new band, the Playboys, configured similarly to Milton's new group, the Musical Brownies. They relocated to Waco, where they joined local station WACO.

The band's sound was ragged in comparison with the more sophisticated Brownies, yet Bob's relentless showmanship and Tommy's vocals helped it to develop a local following. Nonetheless, with the Doughboys and the Brownies dominating the region, Wills needed a less cluttered market. Noting the amount of fan mail he received from Oklahoma, the Playboys moved there in January 1934.

Following an abortive start in Oklahoma City, the newly renamed Texas Playboys found a permanent home at KVOO in Tulsa. As time passed, the band became an entertainment phenomenon in the region with a regular circuit of dances and a following that grew over time.

Tommy became an enormous musical asset both for his vocal stylings and his phenomenal memory for song lyrics. He and Bob created a magical combination onstage. Their rapport brought out the best in both. Tommy occasionally wrote material for the band, including the jazzy "Get with It," a pastiche of jivey lyrics the band recorded at its first session in 1935. Three years later, he co-wrote the ballad "I Wonder If You Feel the Way I Do" with Wills just hours before a recording session. "Tommy was pretty versatile. He liked all kinds of music and he could sing most any kind of song," said Glynn. "[His memory for lyrics] was unbelievable. He could hear a tune a couple of times and he knew it." Still growing up in Texas, Glynn remembered the family having to "pour water on the [radio's] ground wire" so the family radio could pick up Wills's KVOO broadcasts down there.

Tommy's vocalizing for the first few years with the Playboys had an enigmatic quality. He seldom took time to probe the depths of a lyric, preferring a straightforward approach to laying out a number rather than actual interpretation. Even with the Emmett Miller and Jimmie Rodgers material he loved, he used their lyrics as an actor might use a mask, rarely seeking any emotional connection or revealing anything of himself. While it allowed him to sing the hell out of nearly anything he tackled, his detachment often left a dimension missing. Over time, he found maturity, mastery, and eventually, songs that would reveal his cowboy's soul. By the time he recorded "I Wonder If You Feel the Way I Do" in 1938 and "Dusty Skies" in 1941, he'd found that emotional connection.

He also found no small element of grief in dealing with Bob, whose rollercoaster personal life included five marriages and divorces during the Tulsa years. When Bob, a binge drinker, got himself on a tear, he was often out of commission for days, leaving Tommy to front the band both on the air and in the dance halls. These periods came and went, but when Bob was indisposed, Tommy often had to take the heat from disappointed fans at dances. Those pressures planted the seeds of dissatisfaction in him even before World War II.

Tommy was married by then, living in Tulsa with his wife, Willie May. Despite war clouds and increasing draft calls, the good times rolled in Tulsa even after the December 7, 1941, Japanese attack on Pearl Harbor. The Playboys continued with their dances, recording, and Hollywood filmmaking even as the draft and defense plant work took musicians from the band. In February 1942, Willie May died; on May 9, Tommy said his goodbyes to the KVOO audience and headed for the Army. Bob replaced him with singer Leon Huff, who'd replaced Tommy in the Doughboys in 1933.

After basic training, the Army moved Tommy to California's Fort Ord before a kidney problem led to a 1943 medical discharge. Bob's Army hitch proved more disastrous. He was unable to adjust to buck private status, so the Army honorably discharged him in July 1943 after seven drunken and insubordinate months. He and Tommy reorganized the Playboys in Tulsa, then moved to Los Angeles that fall. Bob knew a lot of his old fans were now living there, working in defense plants.

When the Playboys resumed recording for Columbia early in 1945, Tommy's vocals dominated hit singles like "Smoke on the Water," "Roly Poly," and "New Spanish Two-Step," the biggest hit singles Wills and the Playboys ever had. On the West Coast circuit, they made money hand over fist playing to the transplanted folks from Texas, Oklahoma, and surrounding states. Wills moved the Playboys to Fresno in 1946, then to Sacramento in 1947, where the band broadcast daily over 50,000-watt KFBK. To create a local venue similar to Cain's in Tulsa, Bob bought the Aragon Ballroom outside Sacramento, renamed it Wills Point, and spent vast sums turning it into an entertainment complex, hoping to cut back on the extended tours. That was fine with the band, including Tommy and his new wife, Marie. However, in the end, the touring continued.

The intermittent drinking binges that had incapacitated Bob in Tulsa surfaced yet again and worsened during 1947–48. Stress may have been a factor. Bob's expenditures for Wills Point, plus supporting his family and the band, left him strapped for cash. As in Tulsa, Tommy fronted the band when Bob was in his cups, and the situation gradually grew to annoy him just as it had in Tulsa. When it flared yet again in Sacramento, Tommy grew more disgusted. Standing at a radio mike filling in was one thing. It was quite another to face angry, disappointed crowds and to reap severely diminished wages because Wills was a no-show. Many dance promoters considered their contracts void when they'd contracted for Bob Wills and His Texas Playboys and had gotten only the Playboys. That often meant the band made union-scale wages, far less than they earned with Bob present.

Apprised of Bob's tight finances, the Playboys had no problem jumping back in their bus for a six-week tour starting in Southern California in the fall of 1948, assuming Bob would be along. It turned out to be a bad assumption. Hitting the bottle hard back home, Bob never showed once; he literally left the band on its own. Glynn Duncan remembered the account that Tommy gave him: "They started out, and the first job they played was in Fresno. Bob didn't make it. They only got paid union scale. Next night was in Los Angeles. Bob didn't make it. All they got was scale. Next night they were in San Bernardino. Bob don't show, [the band gets] nothin' but scale. Next night . . . San Diego. And he don't show . . . nothin' but scale. Tommy got a lot of booing."

With everyone frustrated and underpaid, Tommy made a furious phone call to Wills Point. Guitarist Eldon Shamblin, sitting out this tour, was taking care of business matters. Tommy angrily laid out the situation to Shamblin, a Wills loyalist who was no fan of Duncan's. Tommy complained of the financial woes Bob cited to justify the tour, then, according to Glynn, ticked off the scorecard of their earnings: "Tommy said, 'We played Fresno, we played Los Angeles, we played San Bernardino, now we played San Diego.

That's four jobs we only made scale. If we're just gonna get scale for this whole trip, we might as well just turn around and go home now, because we can't make it on just scale. You tell Bob that!'"

Shamblin did as Duncan asked. A few days after the band returned, Bob called a rehearsal at Wills Point. Duncan, talking to the band, openly questioned "if he'll be here tonight." Herb Remington, present at the rehearsal, confirmed that remark. As Duncan asked the question, a sober Wills walked in, overheard the remark and answered the question with a sarcastic, "He's here. What did you expect?" The fabric of the 16-year Wills-Duncan partnership had unraveled completely.

The conflict had corroded the partnership even beyond drinking. Bob had complained to Shamblin that Tommy wanted more of a share in the band's profits while insisting Bob alone pay all expenses. Shamblin himself complained that Duncan, who handled band publicity on the road, plastered his own publicity photos everywhere while barely distributing photos of Bob, perhaps as a subtle form of protest. Shamblin referred to Tommy as someone who "kept the band upset just a little" and an "agitator."

Shamblin followed the boss's orders. He intercepted Tommy before the daily KFBK broadcast, took him to a nearby diner for a cup of coffee and gave him two weeks' notice. Glynn Duncan remembered his brother's understandable reaction to the firing: "The thing that hurt Tommy more than anything was that Bob didn't have enough guts to [fire him] himself, that he had to send somebody else to do it."

The precise ratio of Duncan-to-Wills photos at dances long ago passed into history, but it's not difficult to reconcile these divergent accounts. It's true, and understandable that Duncan had an ego and in fact may well have been the irritant that Shamblin described. Nonetheless, Tommy would have had no grounds to agitate had Bob's binges not wreaked financial and psychological havoc on the entire band's psyches and wallets. It's a mark against Wills, a decent and generous man in many ways and one who rarely avoided confrontations, that he wouldn't fire Duncan face to face.

Over the next several weeks, Tommy began his transition to solo singer in Los Angeles. He and Marie settled outside L.A. in Pacoima, in the nearby San Fernando Valley. Songwriter Nat Vincent, who composed the pop standard "When the Bloom is on the Sage" and headed Peer International Music's Folk division, became his manager. He signed Tommy to Peer as a songwriter and in mid-October landed him a Capitol recording contract that at that moment wasn't worth any more than scratch paper. For the entire year of 1948, a contract dispute between the American Federation of Musicians and U.S. record companies kept musicians out of the studios. Initially, the October 23, 1948, *Billboard* speculated Duncan would record, backed by what the magazine called "foreign background soundtracks." That could

Sittin' in with Hank Thompson's Brazos Valley Boys. (Courtesy Glenn White)

have been achieved only with instrumental tracks recorded in Mexico, some-thing other singers had done. In Duncan's case, it never happened.

Meanwhile, Tommy was busy organizing his new band, the Western All-Stars. Glynn, who was 25 by then, had already played bass with Bob's brother Luke Wills's band the Rhythm Busters, and he joined Tommy after the All-Stars' bassman, Stan Puls of Spade Cooley's band, pulled out. Tommy also hired the nucleus of the 1944–45 Texas Playboys, by any stan-dards one of the all-time great incarnations. From that group came fiddlers Joe Holley and Ocie Stockard, pianist Millard Kelso, lead guitarists Jimmy Wyble and Cameron Hill, and steel guitarist Noel Boggs. Wyble, Hill, and Boggs all left Spade Cooley to join Tommy. Stockard, Holley, and Kelso had been with the Playboys at the time of Tommy's firing. It's not inconceivable that after Bob's no-shows hurt their wallets enough times, they were as ready as Tommy to move on. Dave Coleman was the band's drummer.

Tommy and the All-Stars debuted at the 97th Street Corral in Los Ange-les on October 11, 1948. The recording ban ended in December, and Duncan finally went into the studio in January. Despite months of working together in the studio, the band turned out results that were underwhelm-ing. Tommy remade three songs he'd done with the Playboys along with the lifelessly sung "Worried Over You."

It was a given that against Tommy, these musicians could generate instru-mental fireworks. They didn't. All this talent wound up functioning as an Ernest Tubb–style backup band with few of the explosive moments that characterized their work with the Playboys or, in the case of Wyble, Hill, and Boggs, their later efforts with Spade Cooley. This musical punch-pulling was deliberate—and Tommy's doing. "He didn't want the band to sound exactly like Bob," explained Glynn Duncan.

One tune taken from the Playboys' repertoire, Jimmie Rodgers's "Gam-blin' Polka Dot Blues," became his first and only hit single. It reached number 8 on the *Billboard* charts in 1949.

Another reality dogged Tommy. Western swing's popularity was in a state of constant erosion as times changed and solo vocalists rose in popularity. As he was now a solo vocalist, that fact should have worked in his favor. Again, his style got in the way. He interpreted some songs but simply did a good job singing others. His emotional range emerged only intermittently. When he sang the lyrics, he needed strong instrumental soloists to avoid sounding utterly ordinary. By relegating sidemen of the stature of Wyble, Hill, Boggs, Kelso, and Holley to perfunctory accompanists, he wasted their talents and hurt himself as well.

The band spent the spring of 1949 touring the South and Southwest in its 1941 Chevrolet stretch bus, never going east of Arkansas. "Gamblin' Polka Dot" provided a boost, albeit a brief one. Even Glynn noted that "the bookings were reasonably good, but it was beginning to cool down a little bit." Wyble, Hill, and Boggs were gone by October, all three returning to Spade Cooley. Duncan hired a new steel guitarist, Sherwood R. Ball, nick-named "Ernie," who later parlayed his experience as a musician into becoming a major guitar string manufacturer.

Tommy continued recording for Capitol. Trying to ride the success of using Jimmie Rodgers material as he did on "Gamblin' Polka Dot Blues," he laid down versions of "In the Jailhouse Now" and "Never No Mo' Blues." Two weeks before Red Foley recorded his hit version, Tommy took a stab at "Chattanoogie Shoe Shine Boy," with a performance so flat and lifeless it only ratified the excellence of Foley's. Capitol dropped Tommy in 1950. It was hardly surprising.

That wasn't the only career brushfire he faced that year. Western swing's fading popularity was by then obvious to everyone in the Southwest. TV cut into dance-hall business, and the baby boom kept many onetime dance-hall denizens at home with kids. Nashville-based singers like Hank Williams, Eddy Arnold, and Lefty Frizzell became dominant. These trends affected everyone, even someone of Bob Wills's stature.

Tommy started a record company he dubbed Natural Records, and its sole release, a rendition of the western tune "High Country," became one of his finest ballad performances. With no distribution to speak of, few heard the release, and Natural quickly faded. He hired honky-tonk pianist Bill Woods of Bakersfield, hoping Woods's playing would enhance his sound. It didn't, and late in 1950 Tommy dissolved the All-Stars for good. Glynn and Ocie Stockard took the remnants of the band to Lubbock, Texas, then worked around Texas and Oklahoma. Glynn joined popular bandleader Merl Lindsey before abandoning music, an option more western Swing musicians began exercising as musical opportunities continued drying up.

Tommy began appearing as a solo act at clubs and ballrooms, backed by local musicians or house bands. With no major labels kicking down his door, he signed with the independent Intro Records of Beverly Hills early in 1951. The material vacillated between outstanding and vile at Intro; the mediocre middle was rare. "Some of the songs he did," Glynn said, "he didn't have any business even thinkin' about doin' them."

The earliest Intros were in many ways the best ones. Backed in the studio by Ole Rasmussen's Nebraska Cornhuskers, a band developed as a virtual Texas Playboys clone, one can hear what might have been at Capitol. This time, the instrumentalists are unleashed and—given the fact that the Cornhuskers included powerful soloists like guitarist Earl Finley, pianist Austin Strode, fiddler Woody Applewhite, and the Stone brothers, Virgil on bass and Rocky on fiddle—the performances were exhilarating. Each soloist got ample space to play between Tommy's vocals.

Backed by a rip-roaring band allowed to be themselves, Tommy sounded revitalized on "There Ain't a Cow in Texas" and on his covers of Jimmie Rodgers's "Mississippi River Blues" and Johnny Bond's "Sick, Sober, and Sorry." The latter two made up his debut Intro single. He did nearly as well with "Wrong Road Home Blues," a reworking of Kokomo Arnold's "Milk Cow Blues" (which Bob Wills reworked into "Brain Cloudy Blues").

With a little luck and better distribution of Intro's releases, Tommy could have wound up on top, using a formula similar to that of Hank Thompson: combining robust honky-tonk vocals with blazing western swing accompaniment. A November 1951 recording date with a vocal group dubbed the Ranger Trio, along with some Texas musicians and former Texas Playboys trumpeter Alex Brashear, also yielded quality performances, among them Cindy Walker's "I Was Just Walking Out the Door," a remake of "Nancy Jane" (the song Wills and Milton Brown recorded in 1932 for Victor as the Fort Worth Doughboys), and Whitey Simpson's witty, dry-humored novelty "Relax and Take It Easy."

Nonetheless, even first-rate musicians couldn't save rotten material, and that quickly became an issue as Tommy recorded utter throwaways like the 1952 loser "Who Drank My Beer (While I Was in the Rear)." "Tomato Can," a painful pun song (co-written by Duncan), uses "tomato," the 1950s slang equivalent of "babe" or "hottie," in various contexts. Muddy Berry's drumming on what sounds like a metal garbage can only made matters worse. That this marked the nadir of his recording career is a point Glynn Duncan doesn't argue, laughing as he comments, "I hate that. I won't even play it."

One 1953 Intro recording, however, was a benchmark. Backed by the Texas-based Miller Brothers, Tommy covered a then-current R&B hit: Big Mama Thornton's "Hound Dog," making him the first white vocalist to cover it three years before Elvis turned it into rockabilly hellfire. Duncan's intense vocal, which accentuated the song's original blues content, surpassed even his best blues singing with the Playboys.

Though he didn't succeed at Intro, Tommy's 1954–1955 Coral recordings, including a stunning "Time Changes Everything" and "Walkin' in the Shadow of the Blues," were among the finest moments of his solo career, equal to his high points with the Playboys and sadly underexposed. It was his final major-label excursion as a solo act. From then on, Tommy recorded sporadically for small labels. Occasionally, one of his records stood out, like his tough, blues-drenched 1957 recording of "I Want My Gal" with Smokey Rogers's band on Rogers's Caravan label. Recording for tiny Challenger Records label in the late '50s, Tommy revived "Frankie Jean," a Memphis Minnie blues number he'd been singing for years (a fragment exists from a 1945 Playboys session). Tommy improvised his vocal with a tape machine running as guitarist Jimmie Rivers played blues vamps behind him on acoustic guitar.

It's quite likely that both Tommy Duncan and Bob Wills were delighted to see the '50s ending. It had been no picnic for Tommy's former boss. He'd bounced from California to Oklahoma City to Dallas, where a disastrous venture into the dance-hall business devastated his finances. His dance crowds throughout the Southwest continued to dwindle and age.

Late in 1959, 11 years after he ordered Shamblin to do the deed in Sacramento, Bob broke the impasse and phoned Tommy. They soon agreed to reunite.

Things got off to a promising start. Bob, Tommy, and the Playboys drew crowds throughout the Southwest, including Las Vegas, as fans relived old times. Things looked promising. Liberty Records signed them in 1960, and they landed the perfect producer: Tommy Allsup, who had played guitar for Johnnie Lee Wills and backed Buddy Holly on his ill-fated 1959 tour. Allsup produced Wills and Duncan's *Together Again!* debut LP. Tommy's passionate vocal on the honky-tonk ballad "Heart to Heart Talk," a song light years from their earlier work, gave the pair (billed as Bob Wills and Tommy Duncan) a Top 10 single in 1960. A year later "The Image of Me," another barroom weeper, scored in the Top 30.

They continued recording and performing together, but by 1962, the partnership had dissolved for pretty much the same reason it shattered in 1948: Bob's boozing. "Bob got to pullin' the same old stuff, not showin' up and everything," said Glynn Duncan. "Tommy said, 'I just ain't gonna put up with it.'" Bob also suffered a serious heart attack that year, the beginning of a physical decline that eventually let to his crippling 1969 stroke. By 1964 he, like Tommy, was working as a solo act.

Tommy, who lived on a 260-acre ranch near Mariposa, in Northern California, with Marie, raised cattle and kept horses. On the road, he worked lower-level jobs and made an occasional record. Unfortunately, his common ground with Bob extended to failing health. By the mid-'60s he was suffering his own cardiac problems yet stayed on the road. After a show in Imperial Beach, California, he died of a heart attack on July 24, 1967, in San Diego.

When the word spread, Bob immediately called Marie Duncan. Tommy was buried in nearby Merced, but the underwhelming response of his many old friends and former colleagues left Glynn Duncan puzzled and understandably bitter:

It's a funny thing. The musicians right there in Fresno that worked with Tommy for years and years, like Joe Holley and Alex Brashear and all those guys, were only about 60 miles from where Tommy's funeral was in

Merced. Not a one of them came. The only musicians that came were Noel
Boggs, Fred Maddox [of the Maddox Brothers and Rose], and [former
Playboys steel guitarist] Roy Honeycutt. If they lived across the country, I
could understand, but he hired Joe and Alex for sessions and stuff.

The massive stroke that ended Bob Wills's career came two years later.
But unlike Tommy, Bob, despite paralysis, recovered sufficiently to enjoy a
bit of adulation as the western swing revival began in the early 1970s.
Tommy died a few years too early. The "what ifs" are interesting. What if
Tommy, still alive and well, had been able to sing on Merle Haggard's salute
to Wills, *A Tribute to the Best Damn Fiddle Player: Or, My Salute to Bob
Wills*, or at the final Bob Wills–led Playboys recording session in 1973 that
produced the *For the Last Time* album? Somehow, it might have been a more
fitting end.

The Rhythm Buster

Luke Wills

Luke Wills, late 1940s.
(Courtesy Glenn White)

It happened sometime in 1935, probably within a year of Bob Wills and His Texas Playboys setting up shop in Tulsa. Bob and younger brother Johnnie Lee, the Playboys' tenor banjoist, went to see the Paul Whiteman Orchestra. Much to their amazement, Whiteman, whose size and mustache made him instantly recognizable, was nowhere to be seen onstage. Bob later discovered that this Whiteman band was actually a spin-off unit, one Whiteman organized to play secondary venues like Tulsa. That allowed him to concentrate on America's major metropolitan areas and top venues while maintaining his franchise (and raking in the money) on a wider level.

From a business standpoint, the principle made perfect sense to Bob and his manager, O. W. Mayo. In the fall of 1935, Bob considered setting up a dance band in Tulsa to be led by his father, "Uncle John" Wills, a Texas fiddle master who'd been Bob's primary mentor on the instrument. Dubbed Uncle John and His Lone Star Rangers, the band would play jobs in the smaller Oklahoma towns that the Playboys, who by then had a full calendar of regular dance engagements in the region, couldn't handle. That band didn't materialize for a couple years, but the idea stuck. For most of his career, Bob used second-string bands as "farm clubs" to nurture talent for future use in the Texas Playboys.

Of all the performing Wills brothers, Bob was the most famous, and his legendary status needs little explanation. It's a well-known fact that Johnnie Lee kept the Wills presence in Tulsa—both for dances and the noontime broadcasts over Tulsa's KVOO—after Bob left for California in 1943. By the time Johnnie Lee ended the daily KVOO show in 1958, Bob had returned to join forces with Johnnie, there at the end as he was at the start.

Billy Jack Wills was the least-known Wills brother until a group of his transcribed radio shows was released commercially in the 1980s. Recorded at KFBK in Sacramento from 1950 to 1954, they revealed a driving, progressive sound with R&B and jump blues overtones that strongly hinted at rock and roll. Even though he'd recorded for 4-Star and MGM, the transcriptions made his contributions more visible than they had been.

That leaves the second-youngest Wills brother: bass-playing Luke Wills who, like Billy Jack, spent most of his performing life as one of the Texas Playboys. Luke was a Texas Playboy longer than any other Wills brother, playing in the band steadily, aside from brief periods when Bob set him up with his own band in 1946 and in the early 1950s. With two first-rate role models, Luke had no problem leading a band. Nonetheless, running a secondary band in Bob's shadow had its difficulties, not so much in performing but in the recording end of things.

Bob was 15 when Luther Jay Wills was born in Memphis, Texas, on September 10, 1920. Bob and Johnnie Lee, who was eight years younger than Luke, both learned to fiddle. Luke, like younger brother Billy Jack, focused on playing rhythm instruments. Luke and Billy both lived with their parents, "Uncle John" and "Aunt Emma" Wills, as they lived on farms throughout West Texas. According to Kevin Coffey's research, Luke's first musical experience may well have come playing tenor banjo for a band that Uncle John led in the Clovis, New Mexico, area. Around 1937, Bob, who'd prospered in Tulsa, moved his family there from Texas. He assumed all expenses, a generosity sometimes tested by Uncle John's fiscal irresponsibility.

At that point, Uncle John and His Lone Star Rangers began in Tulsa, occasionally hosting Bob's daily KVOO broadcasts if Bob and the Playboys were on the road or otherwise indisposed. In 1938, Bob launched Johnnie Lee as the leader of the short-lived Rhythmairs. Luke got his first actual performing experience as that band's tenor banjoist when he was 18. When the Rhythmairs disbanded, Johnnie Lee returned to the Playboys. Coffey's research indicates Luke worked part of that time with a band that Uncle John led.

For a time in 1940, Bob and a few Texas Playboys hosted an early-morning show on KVOO devoted strictly to old-time fiddle music. Late that year, Bob set Johnnie Lee up as leader of a band called Johnnie Lee Wills and His Boys, with Luke playing bass fiddle in the band. When doing two broadcasts a day finally became too overwhelming for Bob, he turned the morning slot over to Johnnie Lee's band. It may have been a second-string outfit, but it evolved into a formidable band featuring Junior Barnard's raw, screaming amplified guitar, fiddler-vocalist Cotton Thompson, and pianist Millard Kelso. In 1941, the band had a hit with "Milk Cow Blues" on Decca.

Bob's Army induction in late 1942 effectively bequeathed both Tulsa and the daily KVOO broadcasts to Johnnie Lee. Even after Bob's discharge in late July 1943, Luke remained busy with Johnnie Lee. Bob relocated to California that fall. Luke stayed in Tulsa until he joined the Navy in 1944, then returned to Tulsa after his 1946 discharge. By then, Bob and the Texas Playboys had moved from Hollywood to a new home base in Fresno.

One day, probably in mid-1946, Luke got a long-distance phone call from his brother. "Bob wanted me to come to Fresno," Luke recalled in 1987. Luke made the move. "We were still workin' pretty close to the southern part of California," he said. "So Bob got into the touring area again, and we had a live show [over KMJ], and the idea began to form in Bob's mind about having [another] band to handle the circuit."

That summer, Luke Wills and the Texas Playboys No. 2 was born. Bob himself auditioned the musicians. After hearing the remarkable playing of youthful Indiana-born steel guitarist Herb Remington, Bob moved him into the Playboys and gave Luke the Playboys' current steel player, Roy Honeycutt.

Bob obviously didn't consider the reality that two bands with nearly identical names was an invitation to confusion. His wife, Betty, did, and suggested Bob rename Luke's band the Rhythm Busters. With Bob busy touring up and down the West Coast and occasional jaunts back to Texas and Oklahoma, Luke and the band created a dance-hall circuit in Northern and central California, with regular jobs in Richmond, Oakland, Bakersfield, Stockton, and Modesto.

The early Rhythm Busters were excellent, in part because Bob continued importing good musicians from Johnnie Lee's band for the Texas Playboys. Among these was Junior Barnard. He became a Texas Playboys, having left Johnnie Lee late in 1945 after a fatal hit-and-run accident in Tulsa for which he barely escaped prosecution. Junior joined Luke, as did Fiddler Joe Holley, who'd worked with both the Playboys and Johnnie Lee, pianist Mancel Tierney, and Johnnie Lee's former fiddler-vocalist Cotton Thompson. Shorty Welker played second guitar; Tommy Duncan's younger brother Glynn played bass; Roy Honeycutt, formerly of the Texas Playboys, handled steel guitar, and Oklahoma musician Richard Prine handled drums.

King Records president Syd Nathan, aggressively signing artists on the West Coast, wanted a Wills presence on King Records. Luke recalled, "Syd Nathan contacted me, and we had a couple—I thought—pretty good tunes. Cotton had a contract with King and [Syd and I] haggled a little bit about him bein' on my records. So I said, 'Well, just forget the whole damn thing.' So they worked something out." Actually, as Kevin Coffey has pointed out, Thompson also sang on some of Moon Mullican's King releases. It may well have been that presence that made Syd uneasy about using Thompson on Luke's records. In any case Nathan finally backed down.

On February 19, 1947, Luke and the band recorded four songs at Broadcast Recorders in L.A. Cotton Thompson excelled on a propulsive version of Johnny Bond's "Those Gone and Left Me Blues." A brilliant blues singer, Thompson put forth his grittier side on the blues-drenched "Sweet Moments" and "Four or Five Times," the romping big-band favorite that was a staple of the Texas Playboys' repertoire from the beginning. Glynn Duncan, Thompson, and Holley each took a chorus of "Bring It on Down to My House." Thompson's and Holley's dazzling fiddles and Junior's gut-ripping guitar made the entire session special.

There's no question that Luke's King discs weren't strong sellers, but Bob in that day was a greater national presence than ever. He now enjoyed immense hits like "Smoke On the Water," "Hang Your Head in Shame," and "New Spanish Two-Step" that took his music beyond the Southwest to country music fans across the country.

It wasn't surprising, then, that a few months after the King session, RCA Victor approached Luke. The company had already signed Spade Cooley that year. While Bob was in his last year with Columbia (his managers were already steering him toward the new MGM label), Luke seemed a viable alternative. RCA's country A&R man Steve Sholes signed the band, but as with Cooley, Walt Heebner, the label's Hollywood producer, would oversee Luke's sessions.

Like other country A&R men of that time, Sholes had a cozy relationship with various song publishers but particularly Hill and Range, a publishing company founded in New York in 1944 by two brothers, Austrian immigrants Jean and Julian Aberbach. Hill and Range published a number of country hits including two early Spade Cooley hits: Cooley's own "Shame on You" and "Detour" (a Paul Westmoreland composition). The firm gradually developed its own stable of writers. Some were great; others were merely prolific hacks able to write ditties virtually on demand.

Bob loaned Luke four current Playboys musicians for the first Rhythm Busters RCA session that July. Playboys guitarist/arranger Eldon Shamblin, fiddler Ocie Stockard, pianist Millard Kelso, and drummer Johnny Cuviello strengthened the band's instrumental end. Tulsa-era Playboys Darrell Jones played bass. Tommy "Spike" Doss was also part of the lineup. Doss, a cowboy singer in the style of the Sons of the Pioneers' Bob Nolan, had a vocal style way too stiff for any western swing band despite working briefly with the Texas Playboys. His shivery, rigid vocal phrasing on "Shut Up and Drink Your Beer," "High Voltage Gal," "Gotta Get to Oklahoma City," and the unissued "Long Train Blues" reaffirmed Doss's utter incompatibility with western swing.

Only the tough, aggressive instrumental sound, led by Junior's lead guitar, saved the day. The July instrumentals fared better, although they hardly reflected original thinking. "Louisiana Blues" was a melody Bob learned as a kid in Texas from the blacks he picked cotton with. He'd already used it in the 1938 Playboys instrumental "Steel Guitar Stomp" and again in 1940 as the basis of the classic Playboys instrumental "Big Beaver." The little-known melody of "Bob Wills Two-Step" allowed Junior and Honeycutt, along with the twin fiddles of Holley and Stockard, some room to stretch.

The unissued "Uncle Tom Wills Schottische" was named for Luke's grandfather Tom Wills, Uncle John's father and a brilliant fiddler who also taught Bob to play. The song became better known when Bob and the Playboys recorded it for MGM in November 1947 as "Hop, Skip and Jump (Over Texas)." "Cain's Stomp" was actually "Osage Stomp," the first song Bob recorded with the Texas Playboys at his first session in 1935. Luke's version renamed it for Bob's and Johnnie Lee's Tulsa home base, Cain's Dancing Academy.

Barely a week after the first session, Sholes, likely not present at the actual session, listened to Doss's vocals and immediately fired off a memo to Claire Menai and several others at RCA's Camden production studios. In it, he stated, "With respect to the Luke Wills Rhythm Busters recording sessions of July 23rd, please make certain that under no conditions the names of the vocalists appear on any record labels or release information."

What was going on here isn't exactly clear. Sholes had already nixed other vocalists' names appearing on western swing records because the singers involved had solo contracts elsewhere (Spade Cooley vocalist Red Egner, for example, had a solo deal with King). RCA omitted Doss's name from the labels of Rhythm Busters releases, and Luke resented it. He explained Sholes's discomfiture in a way that makes sense: "At the time, the Sons of the Pioneers were a hot item with RCA. Spike Doss had such strong [resemblance] to Bob Nolan's voice and I didn't have any pull strong enough to say, 'I want this or that,' and stick to my guns, because I was just beginning." Clearly, Luke had turned a blind eye to how badly Doss's style clashed with the band.

At the October and November 1947 sessions, the Rhythm Busters presented a different lineup. Joe Holley and Darrell Jones were the only former Playboys still with the band. Luke hired two new sidemen: Los Angeles–based lead guitarist Dick Morgan and fiddler Bobby Bruce, whose hard-driving style made him nearly Holley's equal. Two new vocalists also appeared on the sessions. On the October and the first November session was Johnny Tyler, composer of the Jack Guthrie hit "Oakie Boogie." At the second November date, Luke's final session, Billy Hughes, composer of "Tennessee Saturday Night" and "Cocaine Blues," handled vocals with the little-known Curt Dunn.

Luke deeply resented the song publisher's continuing interference: "Julian Aberbach, he's the one that brought in the other two singers who had nothin' to do with my band. Bob and I had a long talk, and he said since we were tryin' to make it with Victor, try to go along with 'em, so we went ahead with it, but it wasn't what I wanted." In this case, Luke's resentment was understandable. Still, in fairness to Aberbach's judgment, Tyler and Hughes were far more compatible with Luke's style than was Doss.

At the October session, the band laid down a smoking remake of "High Voltage Gal," a song they'd recorded with Doss at the first session. Luke admitted he hadn't cared for the results with Doss, and Tyler's obvious comfort with rhythm tunes made it one of Luke's best performances for RCA. The quality of the remaining songs, however, left much to be desired, especially on the two November sessions. Even with Tyler's and Hughes's vocals, trite throwaways like "Never Turn Your Back to a Woman," "I'm a Married Man," "Honky Tonkin' Sal," "Corn Fed Arkansas Gal," and "Is It True What They Say" weren't worth the paper their sheet music was printed on.

Nine of the 12 songs recorded at Luke's final three RCA sessions came from Hill and Range. Interviewed in 1987, four decades hadn't diminished Luke's disgust over the matter. "Aberbach was Hill and Range," Luke complained. "That's all his cotton-pickin' songs . . . not one of my selection. I wouldn't have had it if I had any choice at all!" Luke wasn't alone; Spade Cooley also had Hill and Range material shoved down his throat.

Luke later discovered that some or all those songs had crossed someone else's path at roughly the same time: "Billy Jack was recording with Bob in Chicago [at their final Columbia sessions before joining MGM]. And when we met in Fresno after the session, and I started namin' the songs [we recorded], Billy said, 'Hell, Bob threw all that crap on the floor in Chicago.'" Bob had his own favored songwriter for that session: Fred Rose, an old friend who worked in Tulsa and who now co-owned Acuff-Rose song publishing and produced Hank Williams. With Rose producing Bob's final Chicago sessions for Columbia, he and the Playboys recorded six Rose compositions, including the now-classic ballad "Deep Water."

Oddly enough, after Luke's final sessions, Sholes sent out another memo instructing that label credits omit Hughes and Dunn's names from Rhythm Busters releases, presumably because they, too, had contracts with other labels.

It was a moot point; the Rhythm Busters disbanded early in 1948 as Bob pulled up stakes in Fresno. "When Bob decided to cancel the [Fresno] radio show and bought the Wills Point Ballroom in Sacramento, that was the deciding point," Luke said. Luke rejoined the Playboys and worked with the band until June 1950, when he revived the Rhythm Busters in Oklahoma City as a secondary band. The new band's fiddle section alone was awesome, consisting as it did of ex-Playboys Keith Coleman and Bob White along with another swing fiddle giant: Roddy Bristol, formerly of Paul Howard's Arkansas Cotton Pickers. Sleepy Summers, brother of Colleen Summers (a.k.a. Mary Ford), played bass. Buster Van Houser played drums. Playing piano and singing was a true wildman of the prewar western swing years: John T. "Smoky" Wood, renowned for his pot-smoking and his brilliant work with the prewar band the Modern Mountaineers. This version of Luke's band never recorded.

"That was a time that Bob moved out of Oklahoma City [in November 1950] and [opened the Bob Wills Ranch House] in Dallas," Luke said. "I stayed in Oklahoma City at the Trianon Ballroom and did the broadcast [on KBYE radio] and toured the Oklahoma areas." By then, he was sharing the Trianon with the new headliner: Hank Thompson, who'd decided to aim for the dance-hall crowd.

Luke felt this newer band far superior to his 1947 groups. With sidemen of Coleman's, White's, Bristol's, and Wood's caliber, it's understandable. "I was just a little better organized there," he said. By 1951 he was back with the Playboys and by year's end was managing the Ranch House—which by then was heading toward total financial collapse—into 1952. At various times afterward, Luke assembled other groups until resuming his role in the Playboys, playing bass fiddle, then electric bass, and singing his signature tune "Little Star of Heaven" until the Playboys disbanded in 1964.

Luke moved to Las Vegas, a place he'd often worked as one of the Playboys in the '50s and '60s, and he worked in non-musical jobs there until he retired, although he occasionally played with former Texas Playboys at reunion shows. Despite a mild stroke suffered in the 1980s, he remained the most visible surviving Wills brother. Johnnie Lee died in 1984. Billy Jack, who worked menial jobs in Oklahoma, died in 1991. After a second, massive stroke, Luke Wills, the last surviving Wills brother, died in Las Vegas on October 20, 2000.

II
Capitol
Chronicles

The Kid from Chicago

Lee Gillette

"Even in the country field, he never got the credit he deserved," said legendary Capitol country producer Ken Nelson. "He did so many great things at the beginning there, like 'Smoke! Smoke! Smoke! (That Cigarette)'.... I'll never forget when I first came out to California, Lee took me in the office and played it for me, and he was so proud of it."

Nelson should know. Lee Gillette was his best friend and Capitol's first formally hired producer. Today, Gillette's name shows up only on reissues of Capitol material and only then when individuals realize he was the man behind the original music. It's understandable that his name is inexorably linked with Nat "King" Cole, the best known of all the stars he produced at Capitol. But that encompasses only part of the larger portrait. No single man (except for Nelson, his hand-picked successor) played a more vital role in establishing Capitol's credibility in the country field. Assisted by Cliffie Stone, Gillette gave Capitol and its artists an unmistakable style during his six years as head of country A&R. His work may have helped the company through some difficult times.

Like Nelson, the first music Leland James Gillette embraced was not country. Born in Indianapolis, Indiana, October 30, 1912, he grew up in Peoria, Illinois, until his family settled in Chicago in the 1920s. A singer and drummer, Gillette performed with local orchestras, which is how he met Kenneth F. Nelson, an orphaned teenager who'd worked for singer–song publisher Gene Austin. The two and another singer formed the Campus Kids, a vocal trio affiliated with the Harry Sosnik Orchestra, who performed over KOYW Radio in Chicago. The two became close friends; Nelson boarded with the Gillettes for a time.

After the Campus Kids dissolved, Gillette played drums in Chicago-area nightclubs, eventually moving to staff musician slots at WAAF and WJJD. Then he joined the band for the radio comedy *Fibber McGee & Molly*, broadcast on a nationwide hookup from Chicago. The show was a hit, and the orchestra became so important to the show that, when the entire cast moved to Hollywood, the Chicago musicians went with them.

In Hollywood, the show was recorded on transcription discs by Glenn Wallichs, who worked for his father's downtown record store, Wallichs' Music City. Young Wallichs became friendly with Gillette, who'd quit the *Fibber McGee* band to join the Buddy Rogers Orchestra before returning to Chicago in the early '40s. When he returned, Ken Nelson said, Gillette made a career change out of music: "He always wanted to be in radio. He was a radio nut. In fact, he used to write a radio column when he was a kid for a newspaper in Chicago. His big ambition was to become an announcer."

When Nelson moved to WAAF in Chicago to host a program and announce, his old announcing position became open also. Nelson helped Gillette land the job. He held it until the day Glenn Wallichs called. Two years earlier, Wallichs, singer-songwriter Johnny Mercer, and theatrical producer Buddy DaSylva founded the new Capitol Records in Hollywood. Tex Ritter was one of the first country artists they signed. Mercer did some of the early production work but with a growing artist roster, Capitol needed an A&R man. Gillette accepted the job and headed West.

After settling in, he began producing sessions in Los Angeles and traveled through the South in 1943, recording local acts with portable equipment. (Capitol was actually first to record Chet Atkins, then a sideman at WNOX in Knoxville, when Atkins played fiddle behind WNOX artist Pappy Beaver at his Capitol session.)

Gillette hired local radio personality and bass player Cliffie Stone, renowned for his work with Stuart Hamblin, as his A&R assistant. Together, they signed some of Capitol's greatest postwar country acts. Behind Ritter came Woody Guthrie's cousin Jack, whose "Oklahoma Hills" became a hit in 1945, the same year that Capitol signed Wesley Tuttle. In 1946 they signed Merle Travis, whom Gillette and Stone quickly turned into a hit artist. Impressed by Spade Cooley's vocalist, Gillette had Cliffie approach Tex Williams. When Cooley fired Tex, the singer founded his Western Caravan, which languished on Capitol until Tex and Travis wrote "Smoke! Smoke! Smoke! (That Cigarette)," the label's first million-seller.

Gillette's musical background aided his production skills. He had no inhibitions about using horns, reeds, or drums, and he seemed quite happy to focus on finding the right songs for single releases. He never allowed himself to favor a specific "sound," which gave the label's country division a diversity of sound and style that couldn't help but have broad appeal. He used pop musicians on country dates and vice versa. Pop and jazz pianist Buddy Cole frequently showed up on Capitol country sessions as did big-band drummer Ted Romersa. Except for his field trips to the Southeast, Gillette wasn't overly focused on music from that region, though his production of duets by Merle Travis and Wesley Tuttle (who also recorded Capitol Transcriptions under the name of The Coonhunters) reflected that style. Whether he was producing the stripped down honky-tonk and swing of Jack Guthrie, Ritter's more stately ballads, Travis's rollicking ditties, the Western Caravan's complex western swing, or Cliffie Stone's novelty tunes, Gillette focused on getting the artist's best work down without micromanaging, while still focusing on the hits the label desperately needed.

That would become all-important by 1949. After a record year for profits a year earlier, things became so tight at Capitol that the company netted only $60,000 after taxes, the result of vast expenditures aimed at establishing the label nationally and the fact that virtually no records were made in 1948 due to the musicians union strike known as the recording ban. By '49, with its pop sales stagnant and its jazz sales limited, Capitol had certain profit in only one area: the country division. Pianist-accordionist Billy Liebert, who worked hundreds of Capitol sessions in the '40s and '50s, remembered the story Gillette told him:

Capitol overextended themselves. They were a new company, they were growing, spending all this money in the pop field, and they were having success, and all of a sudden that dried up. And the only people that were selling any records—Merle Travis had three or four songs on the charts at one time, and it didn't cost anything to do a country date. . . . I think union scale was $33 to do a record date for four songs. And the Country Music department at Capitol saved their ass.

Gillette signed Tennessee Ernie Ford in 1949 and produced several of his early hits, including "Tennessee Border," "Smokey Mountain Boogie," and "Shot Gun Boogie," as well as "I'll Never Be Free," his hit duet with Kay Starr. Those and other records helped, and by the end of 1950 Capitol had turned the corner. It was now a solid success both artistically and financially. Wallichs asked Gillette to take over pop and jazz production. Ken Nelson succeeded him as head of country A&R, where he'd make his own mark. Gillette kept only one country artist—Tennessee Ernie— producing his 1955 multimillion-seller "Sixteen Tons."

He now concentrated on the pop and jazz fields. Peggy Lee and Dean Martin, bandleaders Stan Kenton, Billy May, Paul Weston, and Nelson Riddle, Dixieland clarinetist Pee Wee Hunt, and ragtime pianist Joe "Fingers" Carr were all under his direction. He, Cliffie, and Ken Nelson had another profitable enterprise. Together, they'd founded the publishing company Century Songs in 1946. Eventually renamed Central Songs, it published a good bit of the material written by Capitol artists and became one of the main suppliers of material to the label, a conflict of interest that was routine in those days.

As Gillette continued his string of hit records, he found a special creative bond with another Capitol act, creating musical nirvana with his friend Nat King Cole. The producer helped him make the transition from jazz piano virtuoso to stagger- ingly successful pop singer. Along the way, Gillette helped organize the National Academy of Recording Arts and Sciences (NARAS), which created the Grammys to promote excellence in recorded music. Gillette's pop music career at Capitol would (and should) be a full-length study.

Capitol's sale to EMI in 1955 didn't diminish Gillette's success as he happily pro- duced Cole. Eventually times and fortunes changed. By 1964, Capitol, previously weak in rock music, was home of the Beatles and the Beach Boys, making room for a new generation. Then that same year, Nat Cole's doctors discovered lung cancer, the price of years of smoking. His death in 1965 shattered Gillette's spirit beyond repair, to the point that he took early retirement from Capitol and sold his interest in Central Songs for a tidy profit. Depression seemed to wrack his spirit. Twenty years after the fact, Ken Nelson still found the memory of his friend's disintegration painful: "I cannot, to this day, figure out why in God's name that when Nat died, Lee threw in the sponge. He gave up. There was no reason for it. My God, sure he and Nat were very close, but he just . . . quit. Lee was one of those guys who could drink and never show it—the same with Tex Ritter. When Nat died, Lee quit Capitol and just stayed home and did nothing but sleep all day."

He didn't drink all the time. Lee and his wife, Edith, a former singer, were the parents of two sons. The family traveled extensively. He never liked flying, so they frequently boarded trains and boats for their trips. He produced few records, except for projects with orchestra leader and steel guitarist (and former Capitol artist) Alvino Rey in 1981.

In early August of that year, a serious fall at his California home left Gillette comatose. Though he briefly rallied, he deteriorated and died on August 20, 1981. At his memorial service at Emanuel Lutheran Church in North Hollywood, his virtues were extolled by old friends, including Nelson, Alvino Rey, and former Capitol orchestra leader Paul Weston. Surprisingly, none of the performers in the country acts he produced were known to have attended. He was cremated, and his ashes spread at sea.

Perhaps it's understandable that Lee Gillette's name has been forgotten in the context of Capitol's country division. After all, he worked only six years in his country A&R position. Ken Nelson became Capitol's answer to Owen Bradley. Nonetheless, in those brief years, Lee Gillette set in motion a direction that produced innovative country material in the 1940s. He set the stage for his friend Nelson's later triumphs—including the Bakersfield sound. For that alone, Lee Gillette deserves far more recognition than he has received.

Capitol Tower Twins and friends. Left to right: Lyle Reid, Lee Gillette, Hank Thompson, Don Larkin, Ken Nelson. (Courtesy R. A. Andreas ... and more bears)

"Fate Just Puts Everything Together"

Ken Nelson

"I never came up to Owen Bradley or Chet Atkins as far as producing records, in my mind. I just never thought of myself as a great producer. So, you know, that's just the way I feel, and I'm thankful. I'm grateful I was able to have the career I did have."

In the fall of 2002, Ken Nelson was inducted into the Country Music Hall of Fame. At 91, he was healthy enough to appear at the induction ceremony, still plain-spoken, still looking, as writer John Grissim described him more than 30 years earlier, "like an amiable Midwestern dry goods dealer." There's no question that Nelson's plaque should have graced the Hall of Fame a couple decades earlier. For a remarkable quarter-century, Nelson *was* country music at Capitol, as identified with the label as Don Law was at Columbia or Owen Bradley at Decca.

It's a staggering legacy. Producing the label's Southwest and West Coast artists, he molded and nurtured the greatest work by Merle Haggard, Buck Owens, Hank Thompson, Jean Shepard, Tommy Collins, Rose Maddox, and Ferlin Husky. He was responsible for Nashville classics by Faron Young, Sonny James, and Wanda Jackson. Nor did he stop at country. He was in the producer's chair when Gene Vincent recorded his gut-ripping rockabilly and when Stan Freberg created his legendary 1950s musical satires.

Ample parallels exist between Nelson and his friend Owen Bradley. Both began their careers as urban pop musicians. They accumulated extensive experience working in radio. Neither planned to become a country producer, but literally fell into it only to find the studio his true calling. There, the resemblance ends. While Bradley used his arranging skills to mold a record, Nelson's style was just the inverse. He sat in the control room of whichever Capitol studio he was using, seemingly preoccupied with doodling on a notepad. All the while he listened, jumping on a bad note or fluffed lyric like a dog on a bone. If he felt a suggestion might help, he made it. Otherwise, he left the artists to create and helped them achieve their goals.

Buck Owens, with whom Nelson had an almost magical rapport, marveled at that style of production. "Ken signed people that knew what they wanted in the studio," he explained. "The Wynn Stewarts, Hank Thompsons, Merles, Bucks, all those people, Ferlin Husky, knew what they wanted and most of the time they'd bring in the musicians and the songs. He understood that, especially about Merle and I and Wynn Stewart. In his nice, easygoin', doodlin' style, he always was listening and always was workin' and always tryin' to stay out of our way except to be of assistance . . . the best damn producer Merle Haggard and I could ever have."

Nelson described his production philosphy this way.

My theory always has been if you have to tell an artist what to do, if you have to show them how to sing, they're not real artists. I always hired an artist for what they could do. A lot of artists, you have to help them pick songs and so forth but you don't tell them how to sing. Buck was always well prepared when he came in the studio. He had his own band, and they always rehearsed before they got to the date. Buck always had the ability to pick the right material for himself and he was very easy to get along with, never had any problems. As far as creating the sound, that was just a matter of the engineers and the studio.

Kenneth F. Nelson's own life experience reflected struggle, serendipity, and ample hard work. Born January 19, 1911, in Caledonia, Minnesota, his mother, who had separated from his father, took the baby to a Chicago orphanage when he was just six months old. He spent nearly the first decade of his life there. The idea that he had musical talent didn't hit him until he was 11, when he visited a Chicago amusement park:

When I was 11 years old, there was an amusement park in Chicago called White City. And one day I had on a pair of overalls. I'd been helping somebody. And I went to this amusement park and there was a stand there where they were selling sheet music, kazoos, and ukuleles. And they had a piano in there, and they were playing, and I leaned over the counter, and I started to sing. And this fellow Marty Bloom, he turned around and said, "Hey, kid, you've got a pretty good voice. Come in here."

So I went in there and he sat down. He wrote some lyrics to what was a big hit at the time called "The Sheik of Araby." It drew the crowd and I had this megaphone and this broom and I stood on the piano stool and I got a job there every night. When school started, Walter Melrose, who was the owner of the stand, had a music store across the street from a theater in Chicago called the Tuvalu Theater. He said, "Hey, kid, how would you like to work in the store after school and on Saturdays?" I said, "Great." So I did.

And I used to sing in a [movie] house. They used to have slides with the words on it that you were supposed to sing. I was paid 50 cents a night to sit in the theater and sing and get other people involved in it. Then for some reason or other I took up the banjo and started to play banjo and then I just evolved from there. I worked for Melrose Brothers Music Company for quite a few years, and one day I went in and asked Walter for a raise, and he said, "Well, kid, if you can do better, go someplace else."

At 17, Nelson joined a Chicago song-publishing firm co-owned by pop singing star Gene Austin. That job evaporated when the Great Depression began. He fell back on his musical skills and soon found a kindred spirit in singer-drummer Lee Gillette: "I still, to this day, cannot remember how I met Lee Gillette, I have racked and racked my brain, and I cannot member how we met. But we formed an orchestra. And we called ourselves the Campus Kids. And Lee and I and a fellow by the name of Jim Crotty, we formed a vocal trio."

KOYW Radio hired them, and Nelson paid $4 a week to room with Gillette and his parents. The trio sang in local clubs and at one, Nelson met a country songsmith of the future: "We kept singing at KOYW, and there was a singer there at the same time named Fred Rose. Lee and I used to play in a nightclub there. And there was a hat-check boy by the name of Wesley Rose [Fred's son]. So I mean, somehow or another, fate just puts everything together."

Gillette, who played with the orchestra for the Chicago-based network radio comedy *Fibber McGee & Molly,* stayed with the show when it relocated to Hollywood. There, Gillette met Glenn Wallichs, whose father owned the downtown Los Angeles record store, Wallichs' Music City. Meanwhile in Chicago, Nelson continued his radio career, singing at WAAF and moving into announcing before signing on at WJJD, where he'd gain his first experience with country music.

WJJD was home to the country program the *Suppertime Frolics.* Nelson quickly got his feet wet buying the station's country records (free disc-jockey copies were a few years away, a Capitol Records innovation). He also worked with WJJD staff country acts like singer Bob Atcher and Uncle Henry's Original Kentucky Mountaineers until the pre–World War II draft caught up with him. After his hitch, he settled back in at WJJD and reunited with Gillette, who had returned to town and now worked as an announcer, until Capitol offered him a job as its first A&R man. Nelson and Gillette, however, maintained close contact.

"Lee came back periodically to Chicago to record some of the country artists," Nelson said. "One time he came back and set up a recording session with Uncle Henry." At the last minute, Gillette couldn't get back for the session and asked Nelson to step in and produce the records. By 1946, Gillette used Nelson as Capitol's de facto Chicago talent scout.

It took Nelson awhile to develop the instincts. That same year Karl Davis (half of the legendary old-time singing duo Karl and Harty), who worked at WJJD at the time, had a house guest. He brought the guest, a gangly 22-year-old guitarist—a fiery thumbpicker—to see Nelson. "Karl said, 'Ken, this guy is a great guitar player. He oughta be on a record label.' I said, 'Okay, Karl. I'll write Gillette and see what he has to say.' So I write Lee, and Lee wrote back and said, 'Well, that's great, but we've got a guitar player: Merle Travis.' The kid's name was Chester Atkins." A little over a year later, RCA's Steve Sholes signed Atkins, now known as "Chet," as the label's answer to Travis.

In 1947, Nelson got his feet wet recording a Capitol pop act: the Chicago-based Dinning Sisters. He recorded their version of the pop hit "Buttons and Bows," with local jazz accordionist Art Van Damme's quartet. As 1947 went on and the 1948 Musicians Union recording ban loomed, Capitol had all its artists recording to stockpile material, and Nelson began learning about the vagaries of dealing with recording artists. It would help him immensely later on:

> During this period when the record companies were worried about recording, I made an album with Art [Van Damme]. At that time we had to get out of the studio in three hours come hell or high water, because they were booked up so solid. You didn't dare go overtime. If you weren't through—out! That was it. I was recording Art Van Damme, and he faints. I called his wife. She said, "Just give him some brandy. He'll be all right." I gave him some brandy, and by God, he was! He did the session without any problem!

"Capitol decided they wanted Lee strictly in the country department," Nelson continued. "So Lee talked Glenn into bringing me to California to take over [Capitol's] transcriptions [department]. I took a cut in salary." He started at $600 a month and oversaw the label's growing transcriptions division, which produced recordings for radio airplay. A change of mind at Capitol in 1951, as the company continued expanding, changed the destinies of both. "They decided they wanted Lee to go into the pop department. When he took over pop, I took over country." Cowboy singer Eddie Dean was Nelson's first signing. "The guy had a fantastic voice, beautiful voice. But you couldn't give his records away," he laughed. "He was too good. He was too smooth. He was just a great singer."

Cliffie Stone, the creator of the popular Southern California TV show *Hometown Jamboree*, brought a local comedian from the show to Nelson, one renowned for his voice-over work and wicked flair for satire. Stan Freberg had an idea. He wanted to satirize radio soap operas on a record he would call "John and Marsha." For his part, Nelson was amenable to the idea:

> I said, "Oh, what the hell, let's take a chance on it. What can we lose?" And we did it at the end of a session. And we only used Billy Liebert, who played organ, and Harold Hensley, who played fiddle, and Stan did his thing.
>
> So anyway, when the record was finished, I took it to [Capitol executive] Alan Livingston—and I think Jim Conkling was still there. I think Jim was head of A&R at that time; anyway, I took it to them and they thought it was great! And we decided to put it out, and so I went to our head salesman, the guy who was head of the sales department. I went in his office, and he was standing up, and I played the record for him, and he sat down on the couch, and he said, "What the *hell* are ya throwin' the company's money away for?"

"John and Marsha" became a huge hit for Freberg, who followed with satirical versions of "I've Got You under My Skin," Johnny Ray's pop hit "Cry" (rewritten as "Try"), and his famous satire "St. George and the Dragonet," spoofing the TV cop show *Dragnet*. Nelson enjoyed working with Freberg, but he was quick to add a couple of caveats:

> It was a lot of fun doing it except it was very nerve-wracking, because the other thing that used to be so aggravating was that Stan would say, "Well, now, call the session for 8 o'clock," and he'd show up maybe at 10 sometimes, and we'd have to pay the musicians for all that time. The thing about Freberg that used to drive me nuts was that without question, every time I had my wedding anniversary, he wanted to record. And we'd start in about 8 at night and wind up at about 2, 3, 4 in the morning, sometimes all night, sometimes end at 5 in the morning, but he was very meticulous and used to drive me nuts because the costs were fantastic, but I guess it worked out all right.

Nelson spent most of his time producing Capitol's country artists except Tennessee Ernie, whom Gillette retained. Merle Travis, Tex Ritter, Hank Thompson, Jimmy Wakely, and Tex Williams were among the label's core acts. His and Gillette's Central Songs business partner, Cliffie Stone, brought singer Terry Preston to Nelson. Preston, who sang on *Hometown*, previously recorded for Four Star. Hank Thompson brought him a teenage Jean Shepard, an Oklahoma native who'd been working in a California club.

Thompson liked her voice, and Nelson signed her to Capitol, although she brought some baggage with her. As a minor, she had to be under a guardian's care, complicating things for everyone, including Nelson. Neither Preston nor Shepard got anywhere until Nelson teamed them on the ballad "A Dear John Letter," which made both of them stars.

He pushed Terry Preston to drop his stage name and use his given name, Ferlin Husky. "I thought, 'Oh, my god, Terry Preston, my goodness' sake'— it sounded too sweet for a country singer. So I said, 'Ferlin, why don't you use your *right name?* It's a good masculine name, and it's an *unusual* name.' And he didn't want to do it. One day, he and his father and I were riding in the car, and I mentioned it to his father, and his father said 'Ferlin, you're never gonna be a success until you use your right name.' "

Early on, Nelson took an approach to recording diametrically opposed to the producer-driven music of today's Nashville. He involved himself in recordings and (as we'll see later) selection of material. But he never believed in relying upon artifice to get results. "I always felt that the main thing is to let a musician or an artist be themselves. Naturally, I would guide them, and if something was wrong, I'd rectify it, but I never was a really dominant guy in the booth. I never really raised my voice or told them how to sing, like some producers do. Maybe I was wrong, but you hire a person for what they can do. If you infuse yourself into every record, they're all gonna be the same."

Nelson's instincts occasionally failed him. On a trip to Shreveport, Louisiana, around 1951, he heard and turned down Kitty Wells before Decca signed her. There, she became country's first enduring female star. In 1956, his pop background sowed the seeds of what became the Nashville Sound when he recorded Ferlin Husky singing western swing vocalist Smokey Rogers's ballad "Gone." Husky, still going by the name Terry Preston, first recorded the song for Capitol in 1952, backed by, among others, Jimmy Bryant and Speedy West. That version stiffed. In 1956, they tried it again, this time in Nashville, with a drastically different style of accompaniment.

Nelson produced the revised "Gone." There was no Jimmy Bryant or Speedy West in the backup band—no steel guitar at all. He used a simple rhythm section, the Jordanaires' voices, and Millie Kirkham's high soprano behind Husky's vocal. He sang it similarly to the 1952 original, but this new, dramatic accompaniment set it apart, to the point that as Husky recalled years later, some traditional country disc jockeys, considering the record overwhelmingly pop, would not play it.

In truth, the record's timing was providential. Nashville was in turmoil as rock and roll cut deeply into country record sales and concert attendance, leaving the future up in the air. By early 1957, "Gone" was number 1 and stayed there 10 weeks. By reaching number 4 on the pop charts, it demonstrated what became the ultimate goal for Nashville producers: creating country hits configured to cross over to pop success. Some view "Gone" as the first actual Nashville Sound hit, although Nelson never made that claim. As for the neutral accompaniment, he explained, "The song didn't call for a real country background, country fiddles and things of that type; it called for what we put on it." Whatever the case, similar-sounding records soon began appearing on other labels, among them Jim Reeves's 1957 smash "Four Walls," produced by Chet Atkins.

Though rockabilly might have seemed alien to a producer with Nelson's Roaring '20s musical background, he was probably among the first major label producers, aside from Steve Sholes at RCA, to discern the changing times. "I saw rock and roll was the coming thing, and at first, Capitol refused to recognize that," he said. "But I went ahead and signed Gene Vincent, which proved that I was right."

He never forgot the first session with Vincent in Nashville. "[Country disc jockey] Sheriff Tex Davis sent Gene to me. I said, 'Hey, if you get him here on such and such a date I'll record him.'" When Vincent and the Blue Caps showed up at the session, Nelson said, "I thought, have I made a mistake? Of course, when they got in the studio, I realized I was okay. Gene was another sad case. He was emotionally immature. He could have been a big star, but he was just unmanageable."

Signing Esquerita, the flamboyant, piano-pounding wildman whose style deeply influenced Little Richard, was also Nelson's idea: "I signed him, and of course, the problem was that Capitol's sales force couldn't see it. So Esquerita never sold. He was so queer, and he didn't care who knew it. He had to have an audience. That's the first time I ever let a whole group of people in the studio. He just had a ball."

While Capitol recorded a respectable number of rock artists, as well as country artists jumping on the bandwagon (like Hank Thompson's "Rockin' in the Congo"), the label's successes in early rock and roll were modest at best. They did better with veteran country singer Sonny James, who enjoyed country success and a 1957 teen pop smash covering Ric Cartey's ballad "Young Love." "The only time I ever had an argument with an artist in the studio was with Sonny James, recording 'Young Love,'" Nelson said. "He wanted to do it over and over, and I said 'Sonny, we've got it! *That's it!*' That's the record that's gonna be released."

After Hank Thompson brought Wanda Jackson to Nelson, the producer, recalling the legal red tape that complicated Jean Shepard's signing, waxed skeptical. "Hank suggested I sign her," he said. "I was reluctant because of her age." After she recorded briefly for Decca, Nelson changed his mind. She became rockabilly's preeminent female star with such masterpieces as "Fujiyama Mama" and "Hot Dog! That Made Him Mad." From there, in 1961, she moved to more conventional country with her hit single "Right or Wrong" including the Jordanaires and Millie Kirkham.

"I used the Jordanaires on practically everything, with Wanda, Jean Shepard. . . . I didn't use 'em with the Louvin Brothers," Nelson laughed, thinking of the earthy, close harmony duo. "It's a funny thing. Everybody tells me what a temper Ira [Louvin] had, but I never had one single bit of trouble with him—*never!*"

He was not only present at the dawn of the Bakersfield sound, he helped define it. He'd discovered Buck Owens when the young picker came to L.A. to accompany Bakersfield singer Tommy Collins on the 1953 session that produced his novelty hit "You Better Not Do That." Bakersfield, teeming with Texans and Okies who poured into the region during the Depression-era dust storms of the 1930s, had a thriving country music scene by the early '50s, one whose rhythmically aggressive but austere sound echoed a stronger Texas/Oklahoma identity. Compared to Bakersfield, the wild sophistication of Hollywood country seemed almost overkill.

Nelson implicitly understood those differences. "It was much different from Los Angeles," he said. "It was more Okie. It was so many of the people out there came from Oklahoma. Buck came from Texas. I got a lot of talent out there. Joe and Rose Maphis, Ferlin and Tommy Collins, Rose Maddox, and several others. We recorded what was there."

Nelson didn't hesitate to push Central Songs material on his artists. Around 1956, he got irritated at Buck, whom he'd frequently used as a session guitarist since the Tommy Collins hit. Nelson had signed the Farmer Boys, a Northern California duo. The pair came to a Capitol session armed with some of Buck's songs they wanted to record. Before the session they'd asked Buck for some original material. Nelson, expecting to give the act Central material, was incensed. He chewed out Buck, who had no idea that he'd tramped on toes. Nelson relented after realizing that Buck's songs had no publisher. The songs became Central's and the duo recorded the tunes. He never forgot Buck's ambition:

> Buck kept bugging me. He wanted an audition. He said, "Why don't you listen to me? I want to be a singer." He kept bugging me and said, "Well, I'll go to Columbia Records," or made some kind of a threat [in fact, Columbia's Don Law fully intended to sign Buck in 1957]. And I thought 'Oh hell, audition this guy and get it over with.' One day after a session, [I] took him in the studio and said, 'Okay, and he started to sing. He sang 16 bars and I said, "That's enough." He thought I turned him down, but I heard something there and . . . I signed him.

That happened in 1957, and their collaboration got off to a rocky start. Given Buck's youth, Nelson decided Buck might hit the same crowd who bought Sonny James and mistakenly recorded him in a teen-pop setting. As Buck recalled in 1992, he "recorded with little doo-wahs . . . kinda pop country [with] this big choral group and I thought, *'Eeeee, God!'* But that's what they was lookin' for. They wanted to make the biggest hillbilly in Bakersfield into somethin' he wasn't!"

Buck's early records sputtered and died, and Nelson soon found himself battling corporate higher-ups over Buck's future. With the label now owned by EMI, a corporate mind-set began crowding the collegial, experimental atmosphere at the label. "Every six months, the finance department would come in and we would review how an artist stood," he said. "The artist used to be charged for the session, and if an artist was not at least breaking even, they asked you to drop him."

"Some people I dropped, and others I wouldn't. As a matter of fact [after] the first few records of Buck Owens, they asked me to drop him. And I said, 'You're sick!' Voyle Gilmore, who was the head of A&R at the time, asked me to drop him and I said, 'No. No way!'" Buck's success with the 1958 honky-tonk hit "Second Fiddle" and a year later with "Under Your Spell Again" ended Gilmore's requests.

With Buck's career rising fast, Nelson stood in the vortex of a West Coast honky-tonk cyclone as unstoppable as the dust storms that drove Texans and Okies to California in the first place. One day in 1963, Nelson was in Bakersfield to produce a live album, a salute to local radio and TV personality Cousin Herb Henson. The producer met a new singer on the bill: Merle Haggard. Until recently, Haggard had played bass for Buck's new band the Buckaroos (which Haggard had named). At the time,

> Merle was on the show, and I couldn't use him on the album because he wasn't signed to Capitol. But I was very impressed with his singing, and so after he got through, I went to him and said, "Merle, would you like to sign with Capitol?" He said no. I said, "Oh? Well, why not?" He said, "Fuzzy Owen and Lew Talley [of Bakersfield-based Tally Records] gave me my first break on records and I'm gonna stick with them." So, okay, that was how he wanted it.

A few weeks later, Nelson went right to Fuzzy Owen, Merle's manager at the time:

> I kept seeing Merle's single "Strangers" on Tally Records, on *Billboard*'s charts, and I said, "For Christ's sake, Fuzzy, come down here and cut out this baloney! You're not gonna sell any records, you have no distribution,

no nothing!" So he came down here, and I bought all of his masters and signed Merle. One of the problems I had recording Merle was I liked his voice so much that sometimes I didn't know what was going on. I was just listening to his voice.

He remembered in those days the misperceptions within the industry about music from Nashville as opposed to music from California. What might have been obvious to dedicated listeners wasn't so apparent to those who perceived music not as art but as a commodity. "I went to a symposium; I was on the dais, [with] people from the recording industry, promotion, A&R, and so forth. As a test I took two records, one [recorded] in Nashville, one made in California. And I played them and asked the audience to decide which was made where and of course, they picked the wrong ones," he laughed.

As head of country A&R, Nelson managed two operations: Capitol's West Coast and Nashville offices. He had to hire and manage local staff producers, with all the attendant frustrations. For a time, former Opry official Dee Kilpatrick produced Capitol material. Nelson then hired veteran session pianist Marvin Hughes.

(Marvin was) another guy that broke my heart. I never had a successful producer in Nashville. Marvin was really a terrific producer. He did Faron Young's "Hello Walls" and quite a few records. On every one, he was a hell of a producer, but his problem was drinking. And I had a couple of artists complain about it, and they said they couldn't work with him because he was drunk. So I had to let him go. He begged me, and I said, "What can I do?" And he said, "I won't drink anymore."

I had George Richey for awhile, and then [in the 1970s] Frank Jones, the guy that used to be with Columbia. Frank just . . . didn't seem to have the talent necessary to be a producer or an A&R man. [He was] a real sweet guy.

Whatever Nelson concluded, Jones was a capable executive who worked for various Nashville labels into the 1970s.

For a time Nelson employed Nashville A&R man Joe Allison at Capitol. He remembered that Allison, who went on to bigger and better things at Liberty Records, had problems with his philosophy. "The problem with Joe was he was too—it had to be his way or nothing. That doesn't work, I don't think. He never made a hit record for us. He signed a couple of people, and he was too dogmatic—you *can't do that* with an artist. An artist has got to be *themselves!*"

He handled Buck's and Merle's sessions himself, producing all Buck's hits, including "Act Naturally," "Love's Gonna Live Here," "(I've Got A) Tiger by the Tail," "Together Again," "Buckaroo," and the rest. Nelson saw the dynamic between Buck and his bandleader, guitarist and harmony singer Don Rich, closeup: "Don was a helluva guy. I signed him to sing, but he couldn't sing, as a soloist. I don't know how he got with Buck, but Don was a real fine guy, and he ran the whole band, rehearsed the band and did all the work, and Buck really missed him when he was killed." (Rich died in a 1974 motorcycle accident; Buck was devastated by the loss.)

Buck's attempts at more progressive music in the late '60s left Nelson less impressed: "He got off on the deep end a little later on. He wanted to do that rock stuff and I didn't dig it, and in fact I didn't record any of his rock stuff." Nonetheless the two remained close friends, and the deep moral center that seemed to sustain the orphan kid from Chicago inspired the poor kid from Sherman, Texas. Buck almost saw Nelson as a father figure. In 1992, he said, "He kept us in tune, he kept me singing, he helped me grow immensely. He was a huge influence on doin' the right thing, bein' at the right place; he wanted that from me. He was a very silent influence on me, as far as growing, being a good citizen and learning how to live. Ken Nelson was a very great man."

For a time, Nelson produced a number of artists that Buck signed to management contracts, whose releases wound up on Capitol. The gamble left both Buck and Nelson frustrated. Buck found many of his discoveries lacked initiative. "I wanted it for these people a hell of a lot worse than they wanted it," he admitted in 1992. Nelson saw the problem differently. "The problem with that was that Buck was insisting on recording people that had no talent . . . and he wanted to sign people who had no talent."

"I retired from Capitol when I was 65," Nelson said. He continued producing Haggard independently for a time. "I left Capitol, and didn't produce anybody else but Merle. I didn't do anything outside of Merle. I guess I got lazy." But he left Capitol with ample memories of the company's more innocent days, though pained over the decline of the man who had brought him there, his old friend Lee Gillette. He thought back to the days when the company had its own identity and spirit before the 1955 EMI takeover. Though EMI, who spent $8 million to buy Capitol's controlling interests, denied there were changes, a new corporate culture evolved even though Capitol co-founder Wallichs stayed on into the '60s:

When Glenn Wallichs was still there and alive it was just—oh, God, what a wonderful company. We used to go on sales meetings, we'd have picnics—just a great company. And then when Glenn left, all of that camaraderie kind of left. The A&R department used to get together once a week and play each others' records, and that was a panic. They'd play everybody's record all the way through. I was left till last. And they'd play my record, put on about eight bars and say "That's enough!" It would get me so darn mad, and then I'd finally begin to laugh about it.

Nelson, living in Northern California, remains in good health. In 1995, he talked about his lengthy post-Capitol life:

Ever since I was a kid, I wanted to play piano. And I said, when I retire, before I kick the bucket, I'm going to learn to play piano. So I take lessons and I practice piano three, four hours a day. I play golf, and of course take care of business, so on, so forth, keep busy. I have three wonderful grand-children I'm giving piano lessons to. My daughter comes over twice a week, and we go out to dinner. My son, an attorney, passed away. His wife was a terrific woman, remarried, to a wonderful guy, and the kids love him, he loves the kids, takes them to ball games. I'm very lucky in all respects.

That sanguine feeling didn't translate into admiration for the state of country music circa 1995:

I never listen to music today. I don't know what's going on, and I tried to listen to Garth Brooks, and all you hear is the goddamned drums, the musical background, you can't tell what the singer is singing. Last night the same damn thing happened. You had three girl singers on there, and you couldn't hear them. The damn drums were so loud, and the [instrumental] background. I didn't know what they were doing. I said, "Well, if that's the way it is, maybe it's progress. I don't know. At least you should be able to hear what they're singing." That was one thing I always insisted on, was by God that voice was always the important thing on a vocal record. I want to hear every word, I want to hear what they're saying. That's the way I felt, I still do.

But I'm out of the business, so it doesn't make any difference what I think.

"The One We Have Been Looking For"

"Smoke! Smoke! Smoke! (That Cigarette)"

Tex Williams, late 1940s.

"Smoke! Smoke! Smoke! (That Cigarette)"
Written by Merle Travis and Tex Williams
Capitol 40001 (Americana Series)
Recorded at Radio Recorders, Hollywood, March 27, 1947
Produced by Lee Gillette
Tex Williams, vocal; Deuce Spriggens, bass fiddle, harmony vocal; Larry "Pedro" DePaul, accordion; Johnny Weis, lead guitar; Cactus Soldi, Rex Call, Harry Sims, fiddler; Ossie Godson, piano; Spike Featherstone, harp; Earl "Joaquin" Murphey, steel guitar; Manny Klein, trumpet; Smokey Rogers, guitar, harmony vocal; Muddy Berry, drums

San Fernando Valley: March 26, 1947

As he drove through the Valley north of Los Angeles, Tex Williams knew he was in trouble.

He'd done half a dozen Capitol recording sessions since July of 1946. Just a month before, in June, Spade Cooley fired him, and most of Cooley's band, fed up with Cooley's alcohol-driven tyranny, formed the Western Caravan with Tex as leader. The Capitol sessions resulted in only one hit: the mediocre "California Polka." The lack of continuing success, combined with Capitol's financial woes, led producer Lee Gillette to declare that Tex had to find a real hit soon or risk being dropped. Gillette was a musician, but he also worked for a label that five years after it began was still struggling. Tex had a session the next evening: March 27. Two of the four songs to be recorded were polkas. Given his track record with such material, Tex was not optimistic.

He pulled in at his pal Merle Travis's home in the Valley. The master guitarist and songwriter was Capitol's fair-haired boy at that moment, propelled by rollicking Top 10 honky-tonk hits like "Cincinnati Lou" and "Divorce Me C.O.D." Tex found the hit-maker painting a fence in his yard and explained his situation. Merle gave it some thought. He'd heard Tex perform the old talking blues "The Darktown Poker Club," onstage. The song, originally recorded by black singer-songwriter Bert Williams in 1914, became a 1946 hit for jive-talking singer-bandleader-comic Phil Harris, known for his work on Jack Benny's radio show.

Travis thought back to a source of frequent inspiration: the Muhlenberg County, Kentucky, coal country of his boyhood. He recalled his dad's boss at the local coal mine, who'd say, "Wait a minute till I roll another cigarette." Recalling that line, Merle, a smoker himself, blended it with the talking blues format and satirical view of smoking to create "Smoke! Smoke! Smoke! (That Cigarette)."

Tex loved it, expressing concern about only one verse about a lover's lane dalliance he feared would get the record knocked off radio. He rewrote the verse, and at Merle's insistence, took a co-writer's credit. He and the Caravan, given their years together as Spade Cooley's original band, had no trouble working up an arrangement, and Lee Gillette came to attention when he heard the song. "This," he declared, "is the one that we've been waiting for."

They recorded three other songs that day: an excellent version of Bob Wills's "Miss Molly" (a song Tex had sung with Cooley) and the two polkas, before tackling "Smoke!" Deuce Spriggens opened with one of his characteristically aggressive walking bass fiddle lines before Tex started the first verse and chorus, with Spriggens and Smokey Rogers joining him on the chorus, singing the same vocal trio harmonies they'd used with Cooley. Manny Klein, a veteran New York pop and jazz studio trumpeter who'd moved to L.A., let fly with a feral, sassy muted trumpet break before Tex picked up the second verse.

Tex wasn't the only one showcased. The amazing instrumental skills of the Western Caravan, especially Johnny Weis's piercing lead guitar and Klein's aggressive work, received ample exposure on the disc. Having played for years under Cooley's leadership, the Caravan's musical sophistication placed them at the cutting edge of West Coast western swing acts.

"Smoke!" became a quintessential country crossover hit of the '40s, not only topping the country charts for 16 weeks in mid-1947, but also spending six weeks at number 1 on *Billboard*'s pop record charts. Its sales of two million copies gave Capitol Records, a label only five years old at the time, greater credibility. Phil Harris, whose vocals inspired the entire idea for the song, had a hit with his own version. Whereas few of the West Coast's western swing bands toured nationally, Tex and the Caravan did, although the West Coast, specifically Los Angeles' Riverside Rancho, remained their main stomping grounds.

Tex followed up with other talking blues hits like "That's What I Like About the West" and "Suspicion," and recorded a series of remarkable transcriptions for Capitol that revealed the unbelievable sophistication of the Caravan. Still, he never replicated "Smoke's" success. The problem was obvious. Tex's singing talent notwithstanding, the very talking blues that made his name ultimately stereotyped him as a novelty singer, a bit of typecasting that would make it difficult for any performer to maintain a long shelf life.

It wasn't surprising that in the fall of 1951, after two years without a hit, Capitol dropped him, though he continued recording Capitol Transcriptions for another year.

A brief stint with RCA proved unrewarding, as he made fruitless attempts at more insipid novelties and, in an even a bigger stretch, tried recording the pop hit "Shrimp Boats," a major misfire. Carrying a band that large at a time when such groups were losing popularity to Nashville solo singers, forced Tex to disband the Caravan in 1951. Smokey Rogers took over the band, which relocated to the Bostonia Ballroom in San Diego. They hosted a local TV variety show through most of the 1950s.

Tex, fronting a smaller band, spent five years (1953–1958) with Decca that, despite some excellent singles like "Sidetracked," brought no success. A 1960 return to Capitol produced one mediocre LP remaking his old hits with a clumsily arranged big band. He eventually opened a new club, the Tex Williams Village, in Newhall, California, and retained a band for touring.

With western swing music moribund, Tex sold his club in the mid-'60s and disbanded his touring group. Like Bob Wills and Tommy Duncan, he performed as a solo act from then on. He recorded for tiny labels like Boone (which released *another* remake of "Smoke! Smoke! Smoke!") and Denim. He made one last jump to the Top 30 in 1971 with the overly cute whorehouse novelty "The Night Miss Nancy Ann's Hotel for Single Girls Burned Down," on Monument Records. Things weren't even that good when he made the mistake of covering Nat King Cole's pop hit "Those Lazy, Hazy, Crazy Days of Summer," for Cliffie Stone's Granite Records, which charted at number 70 in 1974. His last LP came in 1981 with the little-known country rock band Country Express. Meanwhile, Commander Cody and His Lost Planet Airmen covered "Smoke!," closely following the Caravan's original, in 1973 on their *Country Casanova* album. It remained a staple of their onstage repertoire, ably performed by Cody himself.

Burdened by health problems, Tex gradually wound down his career in the 1980s to the point that he retired. In 1985, he died of pancreatic cancer (not lung cancer, as was widely reported). Today Asleep at the Wheel's Ray Benson often does the song during the band's shows, and "Smoke! Smoke! Smoke!," the song that legitimized both Tex Williams and Capitol Records, has become an American standard beyond musical category.

Hometown Jamboree cast, early 1950s. Back row: Roy Harte, Billy Liebert, Les Anderson, Herman the Hermit (Cliffie's dad), Billy Strange, Speedy West, Les Taylor, Al Williams. Middle row: Jimmy Bryant, Bucky Tibbs, Cliffie Stone flanked by the McQuaig twins, unknown, Harold Hensley. Front row: Tennessee Ernie, Molly Bee, Gene O'Quinn.

5

A Happy Hello

Cliffie Stone and
the *Hometown Jamboree*

As Cliffie Stone and Tennessee Ernie Ford sang the 1920s pop hit "Flamin' Mamie," stagehands at the El Monte Legion Stadium set off the smoke bombs right on schedule. Searing pain suddenly engulfed Cliffie's legs. One of the smoke bombs contained too much gunpowder and ignited his pants in full view of a packed auditorium and a TV audience of hundreds of thousands. For the next four weeks, Ernie hosted the show until the burns on Cliffie's thighs and calves healed.

Hometown Jamboree wasn't the first Southern California TV show hosted by a country music star. Spade Cooley's *Hoffman Hayride* bore that distinction. Nor was *Hometown* a network entity. During the decade it spent on the air, from late 1949 to the fall of 1959, its audience was limited to the L.A. Basin. It didn't mark the start of Southern California's country scene, which began decades earlier. Another live Southern California TV show, *Town Hall Party,* which started in 1952, gained greater fame because segments were filmed and syndicated nationwide. *Hometown* was, however, the West Coast's first regularly televised "barn dance" show (as opposed to the earlier *Hollywood Barn Dance,* which was radio-only). Its music and performers had far-reaching influence.

So, for that matter, did Cliffie Stone, the West Coast's first true country music impresario. He followed a straight generational lineage that began in 1929 with Stuart Hamblen. Cliffie learned his craft by literally working his way through the music business under Hamblen's tutelage, in many ways becoming the older singer's protégé. His experience as a working musician led him into record production, songwriting, and song publishing. It placed him in a formidable position to help define West Coast country when he became an A&R assistant and talent scout at Capitol Records, the label that defined West Coast country. His radio experience afforded him an entrée to TV production and, later, managing his most important discovery, Tennessee Ernie Ford, and producing Ford's hit NBC variety show.

As the Opry sprang from the mind of George D. Hay, *Hometown* blossomed from Cliffie, a native Californian who'd spent his entire adult life performing. He was born Clifford Gilpin Snyder in Stockton, California, in 1917 and grew up in Burbank. His dad, Herman, whose long hair and full beard set him apart in the '30s, was part of Hamblen's morning KFVD *Covered Wagon Jubilee*. Known as "Herman the Hermit" on the air, he sang and played banjo, bass, or piano. The *Jubilee*'s music was freewheeling and far beyond the set standards for country or western music that dominated the Southeast. Hamblen's band, for example, included clarinetist Darol Rice. Newly graduated from Burbank High, Cliff joined the show in the spring of 1935 playing bass and doing comedy. Hamblen soon dubbed him "Cliffie Stonehead."

It was a textbook case of being at the right place at the right time. In 1932—before radio personalities had exclusive contracts—Hamblen, while working on KFVD, started hosting *Lucky Stars,* an afternoon program on KFWB. The Hamblen cast members were on that show, along with singer-guitarist Eddie Kirk, who later became an integral part of Cliffie's organization. When Hamblen divested himself of some of his shows in the early '40s, Cliff, now calling himself Cliffie Stone, inherited them, even while remaining part of Hamblen's organization.

Cliffie played bass in clubs with pop dance bands and on records. For a time, he even ran his own Bel-Tone label, recording artists like Merle Travis, newly arrived from Cincinnati. In 1944, while hosting a show titled *Radio Ranch* at KFWB, Pasadena's KPAS hired Cliffie. He hosted *Harmony Homestead*, a morning show broadcast from Wallichs Music City, the popular Hollywood record store owned by the father of Glenn Wallichs, who co-founded Capitol Records in 1942. He also played bass on Capitol sessions. Pedal steel guitar pioneer Speedy West, who worked with Cliffie starting in the early 1950s had high regard for his bass playing: "Cliffie wasn't the best, legitimate [formally schooled] bass player in the world, but he had the great feelin' that you just don't find with the legit bass players. I'm not the greatest steel player in the world, but I'd rather work with Cliffie playin' bass behind me because of the feeling he got. He just set me afire when I'd hear that bass."

At KPAS, Cliffie also began hosting the noontime *Dinner Bell Round-Up*. To focus on that show, he quit the other two shows. *Dinner Bell* continued after the station's call sign changed to KXLA. Back then, he recalled, "I had a microphone in front of me each day more than I didn't have one." He gained considerable weight during the war years, so much that the draft board bypassed him.

Around 1945, Lee Gillette, impressed with the quality of Cliffie's Bel-Tone productions, hired him as a talent scout, session bass player, and assistant A&R man at Capitol. He played on and helped produce records by Tex Ritter, Jack Guthrie, Merle Travis, and Wesley Tuttle. The latter two became part of Cliffie's early radio family. In addition Cliffie and Travis formed a songwriting partnership. They co-wrote several hits, including Travis's "Divorce Me C.O.D." Over the next five years, Cliffie's vision, congenial nature, and creative energy made him a catalyst for the new postwar country scene around Los Angeles, which had far-reaching implications. He played a pivotal role in establishing Capitol as a force in country music. By 1946, he was a partner in a music-publishing company called Central Songs. Formerly Century Songs, the company was co-owned by him, Lee Gillette, and Gillette's friend Ken Nelson, still working in Chicago radio.

Like Hamblen, Cliffie (who still appeared on Hamblen's shows) had other irons in the fire. He ran a Saturday night dance featuring the *Dinner Bell* cast at an American Legion hall amid the orange groves near Placentia, California. With World War II ended, the Southern California dance hall scene was booming as returning soldiers looked for places to blow off steam, along with the defense plant workers who'd made up the bulk of the crowds. That same year, preparing for a *Dinner Bell* broadcast at the studio, Cliffie met newly hired KXLA announcer Ernest Jennings Ford, who doubled as disc jockey "Tennessee Ernie," hosting the station's *Bar Nothin' Ranch Time.* Ford soon joined the *Dinner Bell* cast.

Dinner Bell continued prospering at KXLA in 1948. The Placentia dances became so popular that they were overcrowded. Ernie, who lived in Monterey Park, knew about the huge American Legion Stadium in the community of El Monte. Cliffie arranged to relocate the dances there late that year. Thinking about postwar Southern California's changing population, a concept for a new type of show in a new medium occurred to Cliffie, who started fleshing it out:

> I began to feel we needed a group name, like the Grand Ole Opry [or] Renfro Valley [Barn Dance]. We were sitting around, Ernie, Merle Travis [who penned the show's theme song], myself, and a couple of other people tryin' to come up with names. Somebody came up with "Hometown" and then "Jamboree." When I was with Stuart Hamblen, we worked the Texas State Picnic in Long Beach. Any Texan in California could come. There was an Oklahoma picnic and one for Missouri, so I was aware that everybody in California was from some other state. You rarely met a native Californian. I was aware of the importance to people of their hometown. This could only happen in Southern California at this time in history.

During the war, California's population underwent an exponential increase. Tens of thousands of these newcomers came there from the South and the Midwest to work in the defense plants, from Arkansas, Missouri, Texas, and Oklahoma and surrounding states. Cliff recalled, "A record [based on the names of Spade Cooley band members] came out in 1948 by Doye O'Dell called 'Dear Oakie' (with lyrics): 'Dear Oakie, if you see Arkie, tell him Tex has got a job for him in Californy.' The Hometown idea would only have worked out here, so we came up with *Hometown Jamboree*."

His wife, Dorothy, suggested he try bringing the *Hometown* idea to TV. He phoned Don Fedderson, manager of KCOP (and later producer of the '60s sitcom *My Three Sons*). He quoted Cliffie $700 for one hour of live, two-camera remote TV from El Monte. Stone raided his $1,400 savings for two one-hour shows from 7 to 8 P.M. on KLAC-TV channel 13 (now KCOP).

Hometown's first live broadcast from El Monte Legion Stadium took place on December 18, 1949. A local ad agency contacted Cliffie the following Monday, and he soon had his first sponsor: the Gold's Furniture store chain. Other sponsors followed. Crowds packed El Monte. After the broadcast, the *Hometown* band played for an hour of dancing before the cast took to the air again, this time for a second, 10–11 P.M. radio-only *Hometown Jamboree* over KXLA. By then, the daily *Dinner Bell Round-Up* was renamed *Hometown Jamboree*.

With a regular cast, formidable band, and a musical focus embracing country and pop, Cliffie created a family atmosphere among cast and fans alike. Looking back 45 years later, he saw it in more contemporary terms. "*Hometown* was kind of like Garrison Keillor's Lake Wobegon," recalling the hamlet at the center of Keillor's storytelling on Public Radio's *Prairie Home Companion*. "It was kind of a little fantasy place." The decor wasn't as hillbilly as other shows, he adds. "We didn't use bales of hay or any of that. The bandstand was decorated in real modern western stuff."

ERNIE: Do you know what one carrot said to the other carrot?
CLIFFIE: What DID one carrot say to the other carrot?
ERNIE: Nothin'. Carrots cain't talk, Cliffie . . .
                    —*Hometown Jamboree*, February 10, 1951

The *Hometown* cast emphasized variety. Herman the Hermit was on hand for comic numbers. Eddie Kirk played rhythm guitar in the band and sang ballads (he had a brief run of hits on Capitol). The show also featured the energetic teenager Bucky Tibbs, a sort of West Coast Brenda Lee. Much of the singing and clowning came from the show's biggest star, Tennessee Ernie, who had gained national prominence thanks to his hit singles for Capitol. There were costumed production numbers, brief segments that featured most of the cast singing bits of old and new songs. The Maddox Brothers and Rose and Tommy Duncan were frequent visitors. The show had two pre-teen singers. Molly Bee remained for the show's entire run. Her male counterpart, young singer Dallas Frazier, later composed such classics as "Mohair Sam" and "There Goes My Everything."

The roster of guests and talent was impressive. "I had over 300 people [guests and regulars] on the show at one time or another," Cliffie said. "Lefty Frizzell and Freddie Hart had become almost regulars." Ferlin Husky, calling himself Terry Preston, was a regular. The show was a stop-off for such stars as Eddy Arnold, Bob Wills, Chet Atkins, Johnny Cash, and others who performed and promoted local appearances. Cliffie ended each show with a gospel song.

The *Hometown* band, which doubled as Capitol's country studio band, included keyboard player/musical director Billy Liebert, pedal-steel wizard Speedy West, drummer Roy Harte, bassist Al Williams, pianist Les Taylor, and fiddler Harold Hensley. In 1950, Stone replaced guitarist Charlie Aldrich with Jimmy Bryant. Later, singer-guitarist Billy Strange replaced Eddie Kirk. The TV show also had a gifted producer in Milt Hoffman.

By the early '50s, *Hometown* had dented the ratings of Spade Cooley's *Hoffman Hayride*, which shared the same time slot. In 1953, KTLA approached Cliffie about moving *Hometown* there from KCOP as a lead-in for Cooley, affording both shows a potential benefit. Cliffie hesitated at first, until KTLA offered double the money he was then making. On the same station, both shows soared in popularity.

Cliffie couldn't do much the night his pants caught fire, but throughout the show's history, he turned other adversities into assets. The Santa Fe Railroad tracks sat 20 feet from the El Monte Stadium. At 7:25, like clockwork, a train rumbled through, the noise carrying onto the broadcast. Cliffie made the train's arrival a regular feature. One night when it didn't show at the specified time, viewers actually complained. Cue cards and Teleprompters didn't yet exist, so singers had to memorize their song lyrics. One night Molly Bee, who normally knew all her songs, went blank on camera. Terrified, she ran in tears to her buddy Speedy West, who treated her like a daughter. After Speedy calmed her, she returned, her trouper's instincts intact, and sang the song note-perfect.

Backstage problems occurred as well. The normally mild-mannered Merle Travis went ballistic when Cliffie, in the prudish early '50s, wouldn't let him sing the moonshine anthem "Mountain Dew," popularized by his old friend Grandpa Jones. Though barring such a song might seem ridiculous by the standards of later decades, Cliffie had problems with the song, popular or not, in an era in which the Opry barred onstage mentions of booze: "I had a real family show with a gospel thing at the end. At that time I didn't consider that to be proper fare for my listeners. I let Merle always pick whatever he wanted. So he showed up one Saturday and wanted to do 'Mountain

Dew' and I said, 'Travis, let's just do something else.' Well, he really got burned up at me—*really*. And it was really difficult."

Success brought other headaches. At El Monte, Cliffie sold food and soft drinks inside. Audiences, allowed "pass outs" to go in and out, had tailgate parties with booze outside. After two rival high schools brawled in the stadium parking lot, El Monte's City Council banned pass outs. "The crowd dropped by about a third," Stone said. Moving the show to Anaheim's Harmony Park Ballroom didn't help. By 1957, *Hometown* was the longest continuous local program in Southern California to keep the same sponsor, yet the show's audience had eroded. The show moved to the Valley Garden Arena in North Hollywood where crowds dropped to 500. The show finally moved into KTLA's studios.

Part of the problem was changing trends and the rise of network TV, which cut into local prime-time schedules. A second factor was the other hat Cliffie began wearing in 1951: Tennessee Ernie's personal manager. With Ernie's career skyrocketing as his TV exposure grew and his 1956 hit recording of "Sixteen Tons" boosted him to national superstar with a weekly network TV series, Cliffie's schedule turned into gridlock. He also became producer of Ernie's show, using some of *Hometown*'s ideas on NBC.

Something clearly had to give. Cliffie's and Ernie's success became *Hometown*'s death knell. The show not only lost its biggest star but was practically abandoned by its creator, who was now strapped for time. "Ernie had gotten so big, that slowly I began to let *Hometown* slide," he admitted. When he couldn't make a broadcast, Los Angeles country disc jockey Dick Haynes, known as "Haynes at the Reins," often substituted. Cliffie's absence simply accelerated the decline.

The end came, almost anticlimactically, in September of 1959 when Cliffie was in a Detroit hotel, meeting with Ford Motor executives regarding *The Ford Show*: "The phone rang in my room, and it was the program director of KTLA. He said, 'Cliffie, we're gonna take your show off because we can run movies, or that kind of thing and you're not on it too much anymore.' I didn't like [being put on the spot] because I was making a career decision. I was makin' a lot of money with Ernie; we were riding the crest of the wave. So I taped a closing announcement, and we closed down *Hometown*." The final show took place September 12, 1959. By late 1960, the competing *Town Hall Party* was gone as well.

Cliffie managed Ernie until the *Ford Show* ended in 1961. By the time Ernie moved to Central California, Cliffie had managed Ford for 10 years and was thoroughly stressed out. He turned his friend's affairs over to longtime assistant Jim Loakes, the former *Hometown* stagehand who'd been Ernie's road manager. Still a bankable Southern California radio personality, Cliffie continued on the air for a while and owned three music publishing companies until he, Gillette, and Nelson sold Central Songs in 1969. He later managed Gene Autry's song-publishing concerns.

By the late 1970s Cliffie missed performing. He reorganized a stage show he called *Cliffie Stone's Country Showdown,* which did well locally until Disneyland and other area parks began booking big-name country stars. Despite long-standing animus between many West Coast artists and Nashville, Cliffie's ability to politic stood him in good stead and led to his 1989 induction into the Country Music Hall of Fame. Though no longer tied professionally to Ernie, their friendship remained a constant until Ernie died in 1991.

Even in semi-retirement, he never slowed down. After Dorothy died, he remarried and, with second wife, Joan Carol, a songwriter, he kept busy. He remained active in the Academy of Country Music and became a trusted mentor to son Curtis, original bassist in the popular 1980s West Coast country-rock band Highway 101. His older son, Steve, produced for Capitol in the 1970s.

Cliffie occasionally revived *Hometown* as a stage show, mixing neophyte entertainers with original cast member Molly Bee and octogenarian cowboy singer Eddie Dean. He maintained an extensive archive of *Hometown* audio transcriptions and memorabilia at his Southern California ranch until he sold it. Only two kinescopes of *Hometown* in its prime are known to survive. Though the new *Hometown* bore no resemblance to the original, the nostalgia factor attracted sellout crowds at local performing arts centers and senior citizen venues, where many in the audience remembered the glory days. His desire to perform remained strong. "If I'm not in front of an audience at least once a month, I begin to feel strange. I get depressed," he reflected.

"One thing you can be sure of in show business is *the show will go off.* Not that the audience gets tired—the entertainers get tired of doing it. I wish now, as I look back, that I could have established a bigger Saturday night thing and been on some network. We would have had a thing on the West Coast like the Opry that we could cling to. As it is, we have nothing." But, he adds, "As I look back . . . we were trying to make a living, not history."

Cliffie was correct. The show went off for him on January 16, 1998, when he suffered a massive heart attack at his Saugus, California, home and died at a local hospital. He was 80.

Cliffie and Ernie shake on it: circa 1951.

6

Pea-Pickin'
Tennessee Ernie Ford

I don't like to inject myself into these essays. Peter Guralnick does that sort of thing masterfully, but I consider myself more of a storyteller, and that's the way I've tried to present everything here. There are, of course, exceptions to every rule. So here goes.

In 1956, I was five years old and living in western Pennsylvania. I didn't know what country music was, and I hated playing cowboys and Indians. But I loved Tennessee Ernie's version of "Sixteen Tons" the minute I heard it on the radio. My folks bought me that purple-label Capitol 45 at a local record store called the Trading Post. They weren't country fans either, but we watched *The Ford Show* every Thursday night when it started that fall.

It might have seemed backward, even nerdy, but I always thought Ernie was cool, cornball sayings and all. Later on, I caught his mid-'60s daytime ABC show when I could, but through high school too much was going on in America, and in rock with Hendrix, Clapton, the Stones, and the rest. Then in 1968, while playing records at a friend's house, I found his mother's copy of the *Sixteen Tons* LP. Curious after a dozen years, I pulled Hendrix off the turntable and put Ernie on. "Sixteen Tons" still sounded great, but the "Shot Gun Boogie," recorded a year before I was born, utterly destroyed me. This was an Ernie I never heard before. His sassy vocal, riding atop a boogie beat with juicy fiddle and blazing guitars, reflected what was, for me, a fresh side of the man. It stomped; it swung; it bopped along like early rock and roll. It grabbed me as much as Hendrix did. I'd never heard that kind of country music before, and didn't quite understand what it was except it didn't sound like the garden-variety stuff, or even like Buck Owens, whom I sort of knew about. From then on, I sought this music out, never realizing it would become my life's work. I didn't like everything Ernie recorded after that, but I never forgot that moment. It reaffirmed what I knew years earlier: Ernie *was* cool. It turned out that a lot of my fellow baby boomers agreed.

*   *   *

Set aside the voice, the hits, his membership in the Country Music Hall of Fame, and the many honors and accomplishments in Tennessee Ernie Ford's past. It's a substantial legacy, but one that pales alongside his achievements as an ambassador. His glowing-hot country-boogie records were among the profound harbingers of rock and roll in America. They were so popular in England that John Lennon identified them as an early inspiration of his. In the middle '50s, when the West Coast country scene hit the skids, when Buck Owens was still playing Bakersfield honky-tonks as he dabbled in rockabilly and Merle Haggard still qualified as a troubled teen, Ernie brought country music and Southern gospel to a white bread, split-level, gray-flannel suited America that wouldn't have crossed its suburban streets to see a Grand Ole Opry artist.

On his TV variety shows, particularly his prime-time NBC *Ford Show* from 1956 through 1961, Ford proved a country singer could be as earthy and down home as collard greens while still projecting poise, sophistication, and flawless comedic instincts. His TV success opened the door for every subsequent country singer who found success on the tube. From Jimmy Dean to Johnny Cash, Glen Campbell, and Barbara Mandrell, every country singer who ever landed a steady network TV gig can thank Ernie for the opportunity.

The story began in rural East Tennessee, though it didn't play out there. Clarence and Maude Ford, who'd married in 1914, both hailed from that area. They were a working-class couple, their circumstances modest though not impoverished. Clarence spent two years managing a rural general store. Maude, having grown up in the country, wanted a life away from farming. Their first son, Stanley, came along in 1917.

In 1918, Clarence finally satisfied Maude's desires to leave the hinterlands when he found a job in the state-straddling city of Bristol, its northern half in Virginia, its southern half in Tennessee. In 1927, Ralph Peer would set up portable recording gear there to record rural southern music and return to New York with two profound discoveries: Jimmie Rodgers and the Carter Family. Clarence worked at the local Coca-Cola plant for $5 a week. With another baby on the way, he took a second job to make ends meet.

Ernest Jennings Ford came along on February 13, 1919, born at the family's four-bedroom home on Anderson Street on the Tennessee side of town. As the boys grew, Clarence taught Stan and Ernie to hunt and fish, launching Ernie's lifetime love of the outdoors. Family finances underwent a temporary strain when Clarence landed a job in Bristol's post office in the early 1920s and had to begin as a part-time worker. As Clarence graduated to full-time postal work, the family relocated to a larger house on Windsor Street.

Pop, country, and gospel music all fascinated Ernie, whose public singing debut came in 1922 when he sang "The Old Rugged Cross" for the men's Bible class at the nearby Anderson Street Methodist Church. As he grew into adolescence, he sang there and at other Bristol churches. He sang as part of Clarence Ford's 20-person gospel choir, the Cornfield Canaries. For a time, he and Stan joined their parents in a gospel quartet. They occasionally accompanied local preachers on prison visits, and on at least two occasions they entertained local chain gangs, which left a lasting impression on young Ernie.

Ernie later made rural homilies and stories such a vital part of his onstage persona that most audiences had no trouble believing he had spent years living in the country when in truth he spent most of his time in Bristol or close by. His rural experiences came largely during summer vacations from school when he spent part of his time working at a relative's farm eight miles outside town. Still, putting in 16-hour days with the threshers for 50 cents a day gave him firsthand experience with farmers, with their folkways and idiosyncrasies.

Ernie graduated from Bristol High with the class of 1937. After delivering for a dry cleaners 25 miles away in Kingsport, Tennessee, for a while, he reacquainted himself with Harry Hudson, husband of one of his grade school teachers. A copywriter for Bristol's WOPI radio, Hudson, recalling Ernie's excellent elocution, suggested the kid try for a $10-a-week announcer's position at the station. Even with Clarence's post-office job, the Fords needed every extra cent. Ernie got the job, at first doubling as an announcer and messenger boy.

WOPI had a local advertising deal with the Robert Boswell Insurance Company that took an ingenious approach to breaking news. Whenever Bristol's town fire whistle went off, someone alerted the station to the fire's location. A WOPI announcer immediately broke in on whatever program was in progress to announce the fire, its location—and to advertise the insurance company. Ernie was often the announcer. After calmly providing the information and delivering the commercial, his tagline was always, *"Please do not follow the fire truck."*

By 1939, Ernie had been at WOPI two years and was a full-time announcer. He hosted various shows, read the news, and did whatever else the day's programming required. That behind-the-mike experience would benefit him for nearly a lifetime. He'd managed to save some money. Dreaming of a professional singing career, he committed himself to formal voice training. Friends recommended the highly regarded Cincinnati Conservatory of Music, home of voice instructor Hubert Kockritz. He was accepted, and after a brief summer vacation trip to Atlanta, Ernie left Bristol for Cincinnati that fall.

Living in Bristol was one matter; expenses in the big city crowded his finances. He seized on the idea of making extra cash by singing hillbilly music at Cincinnati's WLW, which two years earlier inaugurated the Opry-like radio and stage show the *Boone County Jamboree*. Station officials rejected him, and the strain on his finances turned critical. Able to afford only three voice lessons a week, he sang in Kockritz's church choir to pay for a fourth weekly lesson. Cheap meals kept him going; unable to pay for a laundry, he mailed his dirty clothes home. Maude Ford washed them, then mailed them back to her son.

Despite the dismal money situation, Ernie returned to Bristol in November for Thanksgiving vacation in high spirits. Just as he readied himself for the trip back to Cincinnati, the phone rang. On the Georgia vacation, he'd left his name at Atlanta station WATL; it needed an announcer for $20 a week. He headed for Atlanta. In January 1941, he found an announcer's job closer to home: WROL in Knoxville, Tennessee. While he was there, he joined Charlie and Danny Bailey, whom he'd met when they performed on WOPI. The Baileys formed the original Happy Valley Quartet in Knoxville. In his off time, Ernie became the quartet's bass singer.

On the afternoon of December 7, Ernie became the first announcer to inform Knoxville of Japan's surprise attack on Pearl Harbor. Expecting to be drafted, he enlisted in the U.S. Army. He aspired to the elite Army Air Corps, predecessor to the Air Force, but realized that it was a long shot because most Air Corps candidates had college degrees. It was only happenstance that an officer at his induction station asked for Air Corps volunteers. With only a high school education, Ernie passed the rigorous entrance test. After basic training in Alabama, he was commissioned a second lieutenant. It wouldn't be the first time that Ernie literally fell into a career.

The Air Corps shipped him to Victorville, California, for bombardier training. There, he met San Bernardino native Betty Heminger while borrowing some carbon paper from one of the base's civilian secretaries. By the time they married on September 18, 1942, Ernie was a bombardier instructor who occasionally appeared on war-related radio programs over KFXM in San Bernardino. The Air Corps sent Lieutenant Ford to New Mexico, where he supervised crews loading bombs onto B-29s. As the war in Europe ended in April 1945, B-29s were bombing Japan in preparation for a mass land, air, and sea invasion. Ernie, still stateside, was preparing to head for the Pacific when the atomic bombs on Hiroshima and Nagasaki forced Japan's surrender. In November 1945, he was discharged as a captain.

The Fords spent a few months in Bristol, where Ernie reprised his job at WOPI. The couple had limited savings and pondered moving to Alaska until they heard that KFXM needed a staff announcer. Already a known quantity from his wartime appearances on the station, Ernie landed the job for $65 a week. The situation was much like Bristol; announcers filled whatever on-air role was required.

Assigned to handle both announcing chores and a morning country disc jockey program, Ernie drew on his East Tennessee roots and his imagination to create the archetype of the image that later made him famous. It forced him—literally—to split his on-air persona. Staff announcer Ernest Jennings Ford was a paragon of dignity, his resonant voice possessing the commanding presence required of 1940s newsmen. Those dulcet tones and impeccable enunciation went out the window when he hosted *Bar-Nothin' Ranch Time* as "Tennessee Ernie," the station's loopy, high-strung hillbilly in residence. He vaporized any semblance of formality, spewing out high-velocity rural patois between records, complete with barnyard sound effects and a cowbell. He often sang along with the hits of the day as they played on the studio turntable. The approach fooled nearly everyone; few in the audience equated the polished announcer with the ridge runner in hyperdrive.

Word of Ernie's novel approach spread. Fifty miles west in Pasadena, just outside Los Angeles, Loyal King, owner of KXLA radio since 1940, heard about the wildman in San Berdoo. King was an old-time radio man, the opposite of the consultant-driven, corporate-owned radio stations of the early twenty-first century. He took a hands-on role in programming. Needing a new personality for KXLA's lineup, he drove east on the legendary Route 66 early one morning until his car radio caught KFXM's signal near Cucamonga, 14 miles east of San Bernardino. He liked what he heard and later drove east again to hear more.

Staff changes at KFXM in 1947 left Ernie, always a child of the Depression, concerned about job security. He took a job as head announcer at KOH in Reno, Nevada, for $75 a week. King tracked him there and offered $80 a week. Ernie wanted to give Reno a chance, but when KOH disillusioned him, he accepted King's offer and brought his clanging cowbell to KXLA. Only the locale changed. "Tennessee Ernie" began *Bar Nothin' Ranch Time* at 9 A.M. on weekdays, carrying on as always, singing along with records. After the show ended, at 11:15, Ernest Jennings Ford, tones resonant and precise, read the news from KXLA's Studio B in the tradition of network newsmen H. V. Kaltenborn and Gabriel Heatter.

At noon, another country show, this one featuring live music, took over: *Dinner Bell Round-Up* was hosted by 30-year-old Cliffie Stone, who'd heard Tennessee Ernie singing along with records and was impressed with his singing voice. He needed a baritone for *Dinner Bell*'s vocal quartet. Spying Ernest Jennings Ford finishing his news broadcast in Studio B, Cliffie asked where he could find "Tennessee Ernie." He was stunned to discover the secret. Cliffie invited Ernie to join the vocal quartet. Ernie savored the idea but not as anything more than a lark. The child of the Great Depression wouldn't dare risk his secure job as disc jockey/announcer. And so "Tennessee Ernie" became part of the *Dinner Bell* family, singing and performing the same baggy-pants hillbilly comedy he did every morning. Fan mail poured in, and he began singing at Cliffie's Saturday night dances in nearby Placentia for $30 a night.

The contrast between the comedic Tennessee Ernie, clad in size 52 bib overalls with a blacked-out tooth, and the effervescent, poised vocalist was astounding, not unlike the difference between Jim Nabors and his comic Gomer Pyle persona. On one 1948 broadcast, Ernie held a yodel on Jimmie Rodgers's "Muleskinner Blues" for an unbelievable 20 seconds, a measure of the radio-trained lung power beneath that baggy denim.

When Lee Gillette at Capitol heard Ernie on *Dinner Bell*, he wanted to sign him. The recording ban, set to begin January 1, 1948, thwarted that idea for the moment, but Ernie continued doing the morning show and *Dinner Bell* for the rest of the year. The ban ended in late December when the union and the record companies, hurt very little by the strike, settled. On January 21, 1949, Ernie signed with Capitol. That same day, he entered the company's new Melrose Avenue studio to record a cover version of the hot country hit of the day: Red Foley's "Tennessee Border." While Foley's easily made the Top Five, Ernie's reached number 8, an impressive beginning for an unknown. "Country Junction," the next single, became the first of the Ernie Ford "boogies." The pianist was Texas honky-tonk and western swing legend Moon Mullican, who was visiting the West Coast at the time.

Moon was one of the pivotal figures in the so-called country boogie movement that started in the Southeast in 1940, when Johnny Barfield recorded the song "Boogie Woogie" (more a 12-bar blues than a boogie) for Bluebird Records. It took off in California during the war with regional hits like guitarist Porky Freeman's West Coast hit "Porky's Boogie Woogie on the Strings." The new style spread nationally after the war. Owen Bradley and a studio group including guitarist Zeb Turner had a best-seller in 1946 with "Zeb's Mountain Boogie," an instrumental featuring horn accompaniment. The Delmore Brothers embraced boogies with the 1946 hit "Freight Train Boogie." Instrumentals like Arthur Smith's "Guitar Boogie" and Bob Wills's "Bob Wills Boogie" sustained the sound, as did Red Foley's "Tennessee Saturday Night" and "Pin Ball Boogie."

Ernie's "Smokey Mountain Boogie" went Top 10 in the fall of '49. Only a couple months later, he earned his first number 1 single by covering Frankie Laine's pop hit "Mule Train." Ernie's version also crossed over to the pop Top 10. The "whip" sounds on the record came from Merle Travis, who created the effect by "wooshing" through his pursed lips and filtering the sound into an echo chamber.

Covering others' hits with nothing of one's own was a dead end for any recording artist. Ernie needed his own style, and both he and Gillette knew it. In December 1949, Betty's pregnancy with the couple's first child inspired "Anticipation Blues," a zany Ernie original. With the postwar baby boom in full swing, it struck a chord that sent it all the way to number 3. The first week of 1950, Ernie, while reluctant to jeopardize his paycheck for *Bar Nothin'*, took two days off to perform on the Grand Ole Opry. While he was away, Betty gave birth to Jeffrey Buckner "Buck" Ford on January 7. Lee Gillette sent Ernie a wire in Nashville bearing the good news.

Hank Thompson had stumbled on a recording of the ballad "I'll Never Be Free," a melodic variant on Mississippi bluesman Sam Chatmon's "Sittin' on Top of the World." Thompson, whose instincts proved solid in his own work, thought "Free" might be a perfect song for Ernie. He gave the record to Gillette, who decided to team Ernie with Capitol pop singer Kay Starr. Starr, who'd had her first hit in 1948, had been leaning toward country in 1950. Her fifth hit covered Pee Wee King's "Bonaparte's Retreat" and the next, Red Foley's novelty "M-I-S-S-I-S-S-I-P-P-I." On "Free," accompanied by the sleek modern sounds of Speedy West and Jimmy Bryant, their duet made both the country and pop Top Five that fall, proving that Ernie's voice had appeal beyond the country crowd.

Gillette built on that in July when he had Ernie record two songs with a vocal group: the Starlighters. Eddie Kirk's ballad "Bright Lights and Blonde Haired Women" bounced along with a natural feeling, but neither Cliffie nor Gillette were satisfied with another song recorded that day: a reading of the pop favorite "It's the Talk of the Town" that they considered too tentative for release. Still, every Monday through Friday morning, Ernie hosted *Bar Nothin'* on KXLA, wary that his nascent singing career could implode tomorrow. The show stayed loose. Greeting his audience one day with, "Hi, you little old pea-pickers!" the term stuck to him.

Barely a month after the session with Kay Starr, Ernie recorded an original inspired by his dove-hunting sojourns into the woods around the railroad tracks near his Monterey Park home. It might never have been recorded but for the fact he'd recorded only three songs at a July session and needed another to round things out. With studio time remaining, Speedy remembered what happened at the studio. "Lee Gillette says 'What else you got, Ernie?' Ernie said, 'I got one thing I did when I was dove huntin' on the railroad: "Shot Gun Boogie."'" Speedy remembered Gillette's reaction: "'"Shot Gun Boogie"? What the hell's that?'" Speedy added, "'Shot Gun Boogie' was not intended to be released." Several months indeed passed before Capitol released it. When it finally did, in November, the song became Ernie's second number 1 country single, topping the charts for 14 weeks and breaking the pop Top 20. When Lee Gillette moved from country to pop A&R in 1950, he kept only one country artist: Ernie.

After four years and phenomenal success on records, Ford finally felt secure enough to close down *Bar Nothin' Ranch* for good. "Shot Gun Boogie" became a huge hit in England, where younger members of the Royal Family, including Princesses Elizabeth and Margaret, quickly became Ernie fans. He enjoyed two more Top 10s in 1951: the rollicking barrelhouse ditty "Tailor Made Woman" featuring Merle Travis and ragtime pianist Lou Busch (a.k.a. Joe "Fingers" Carr) and the ballad "The Strange Little Girl."

Heading home from a hunting trip in Price, Utah, Ernie stopped in Las Vegas to see Kay Starr perform at the Thunderbird Hotel. Hal Braudis, entertainment director for the Thunderbird, offered Ernie an engagement there. When Braudis asked who managed him, the question stopped Ernie in his tracks. Things had been so loose that he'd never considered the idea that he needed a manager. Braudis advised him to find one. Ernie asked Cliffie, who'd never managed anyone, to do the job. A handshake was their sole contract. Ernie debuted at the Thunderbird in May 1951, dressed in white dinner jacket, black slacks, and a black string tie.

Over the next few years, he'd bump into one unexpected opportunity after another. The man who would have been happy to sit behind a radio mike every day took a major step forward when Berle Adams at MCA began booking him. In Ernie, Adams saw potential appeal far beyond country audiences. His bookings began reflecting that. He performed at New York's Copacabana as well as high-end nightclubs in Detroit and Honolulu. Needing more help, Cliffie and Ernie tapped *Hometown*'s Jim Loakes as Ernie's personal assistant. In the fall of 1952, Ernie had another dynamic boogie hit with "Blackberry Boogie," framed yet again by Speedy and Jimmy. Ernie and Betty's second son, Brion, was born that year.

The success of the boogies in England led to a more prestigious offer. In April 1953, Ernie became the first American country singer to play the London Palladium. Even while romping boogies like "Hey! Mr. Cotton Picker" continued to chart, in the summer of '53, Berle Adams landed Ernie his first network TV show. *The Kollege of Musical Knowledge* was a popular 1940s radio quiz show hosted by bandleader Kay Kyser and His Orchestra. This new version, pairing Ernie with Frank DeVol and His Orchestra, lasted only a couple months, but proved his ability to handle more than baggy-pants comedy and news. All that diverse experience on the airwaves in Bristol, Atlanta, Knoxville, and California now paid off.

Nineteen fifty-four saw the start of a new musical direction. Lee Gillette teamed Ernie with Capitol bandleader-arranger Billy May. In April, he recorded the ballad "River of No Return," the theme of the Robert Mitchum–Marilyn Monroe western, with May. That single went Top 10, though his equally explosive collaborations with Capitol pop singer Betty Hutton and May didn't do so well. The wailing "This Must Be the Place" featured the best of both worlds, with backing by May's big band *and* West and Bryant, but it failed to chart.

Most of his comedy so far appeared on *Hometown,* a local show never seen beyond Los Angeles. Ernie's chance to demonstrate his comic alter ego on network TV came in May 1954 when he appeared on a two-part episode of *I Love Lucy* as Lucy's well-meaning but backward country cousin Ernie. It went a long way to proving how well his style transferred to network TV.

While Ernie's musical style was changing, the boogie era got one last hurrah when he, surrounded by many of the *Hometown* sidemen, hosted a series of 15-minute radio programs for Si Siman's RadiOzark, a transcription company in Springfield, Missouri, that produced the *Ozark Jubilee* TV show. Ernie's shows featured a wide range of material: hits and numerous songs he never recorded commercially, including duets with various female singers. Speedy or fiddler Harold Hensley usually threw in an instrumental. Loose and informal, these shows served as a farewell to the sound that made Ernie.

That the *Hometown* era was clearly ending manifested itself in an idea broached by Capitol higher-ups. Why not drop "Tennessee" from Ernie's label credits to avoid stigmatizing him as a "hillbilly" and simply market him as Ernie Ford? He and Cliffie flatly rejected the idea. Ernie's next big break returned him to a turntable, as a network disc jockey for ABC Radio, minus the hillbillyisms of *Bar-Nothin' Ranch Time.* Based in a Hollywood studio looking out onto Vine Street, he spun various kinds of records, which soon led to a radio variety show for CBS. Any ideas anyone had about moving Ernie to CBS-TV, his *Lucy* guest shot notwithstanding, were quickly squelched by autocratic CBS board chairman William S. Paley. He deemed Ernie, "Tennessee" or otherwise, "too bucolic" and too hayseed for the Tiffany Network—the same CBS that a few years later prospered with such rustic fare as *The Andy Griffith Show, The Beverly Hillbillies, Petticoat Junction,* and *Green Acres.*

It didn't make any difference. Late in 1954, Berle Adams arranged Ernie's first half-hour daytime TV variety show for NBC. Adams recruited Chicago bandleader-arranger Jack Fascinato, the former music director for the hip NBC-TV puppet show *Kukla, Fran, and Ollie,* as Ernie's new music director. The show debuted on January 4, 1955, broadcast Monday through Friday. Ernie had one big country and pop hit early in 1955 with "The Ballad of Davy Crockett" and a lesser hit with "His Hands."

A problem soon developed. Ernie's hectic TV and personal appearance schedule left him too busy to record for several months. With Capitol out of material to release, Ernie was technically in breach of contract. He needed a new single, and fast. Two songs immediately came to mind. Around 1951, Ernie and the *Hometown* band filmed several performances for the Snader

Telescriptions: musical short films sold to local TV stations to fill in air time in an era when local schedules were crazy quilts of local shows, network shows, and dead air. One song they filmed was "You Don't Have to Be a Baby to Cry." Another came to mind: Merle Travis's coal-mining ballad "Sixteen Tons," a song he'd heard Travis sing on *Dinner Bell Round-Up* and on *Hometown*.

Its origins were a story in themselves. In August 1946, Cliffie called Merle Travis to discuss recording a 78-rpm album (four discs in a binder) of folk songs. Seeing the success of a Burl Ives album released by Decca, Capitol wanted its own folk album. Merle responded that he assumed that Ives had sung every folk song. Stone suggested Travis write some new songs that sounded like old folk tunes. Whatever he wrote, he had little lead time. The first four-song session was scheduled for the next day.

Travis recalled the traditional mining tune "Nine Pound Hammer" and that night wrote two more songs about life in his native Muhlenberg County, Kentucky, coal mines, where his dad and brothers worked. "Dark as a Dungeon" and "Sixteen Tons." The chorus on the latter came from a letter Merle received from his coal-mining brother John Travis, still living in Kentucky. Both men admired brilliant, eloquent World War II journalist Ernie Pyle, killed while covering combat in the Pacific in 1945. Reflecting on Pyle's death, John Travis wrote, "*It's like working in the coal mines. You load sixteen tons and what do you get? Another day older and deeper in debt.*" Merle also recalled a remark his father, Rob Travis, once made to neighbors asking how he was: "*I can't afford to die. I owe my soul to the company store.*" He was referring to the coal-company-owned stores where miners bought food and supplies with "scrip" money supplied by the coal company.

Having heard Travis perform "Sixteen Tons" on *Dinner Bell Round-Up* over the years, Ernie sang it on the daytime NBC show in early 1955. Viewer response was positive. Later that summer he sang it at the Indiana State Fair, then repeated it on the Labor Day TV show. Favorable viewer mail gushed in to the point that Cliffie brought a box of it to Lee Gillette. They agreed Ernie would record it as the B-side of the single "You Don't Have to Be a Baby to Cry," an excellent performance in its own right with a smooth but, by Fascinato standards, straight-ahead arrangement.

When Gillette asked Ernie to set the tempo at the October 17 session for "Sixteen Tons," he snapped his fingers to kick off the tempo. The producer liked the idea, and Ernie's finger-snapping stayed on the record, giving it a hipness beyond anything in country. Fascinato's unconventional arrangement and orchestration also set the song apart. He used a bass clarinet, trombone, trumpet, and another clarinet (longtime Stuart Hamblen/Cliffie Stone associate Darol Rice) with a rhythm section. The sound wasn't unlike the clever and hip orchestrations the bandleader created in Chicago for jazz guitarist George Barnes's Octet. The blend of arrangement, finger-snapping, Ernie's vocal, and lyrics was magic. To everyone's amazement, when disc jockeys got the rush-released single, "Sixteen Tons" quickly became the hit. It sold 400,000 copies by October 26 and two million by Christmas.

What was it about the record that resonated so deeply in Cold War America? Certainly, some of Travis's lyrics were fantasy or macho posturing. The composer was amused by the meanings others read into the song, because lyrics like *"I was raised in a cane brake by an old mama lion"* were clear fantasy. Nonetheless, the song's impact went beyond coal miners (who deeply appreciated the song). Metaphorically, any blue- or white-collar worker who punched a clock, who owed his soul to a bank or a finance company because of mortgages, car payments, or other debt, could feel connected to the lyrics. "Sixteen Tons" was among the few country songs acceptable in the Soviet Union of that era, where communist broadcasters often played it on the radio to demonstrate how the American government exploited its working class.

The song immortalized Travis, already a legend for his hit songs and for popularizing the fingerpicking guitar style he'd learned as a boy in Kentucky. On July 29, 1956, he returned to his boyhood home in tiny Ebenezer, Kentucky, to a huge celebration, organized to unveil a granite monument the town built to immortalize his accomplishments, including "Sixteen Tons." Travis died in 1983; eight years later, his ashes were interred under that monument.

The hit left Ernie well placed for his next career move. MCA proposed him to the Ford Motor Company as host of a nighttime TV variety show the automaker would sponsor on NBC. While minds there were more open than that of CBS Chairman Paley, it went only so far. Some within Ford and their ad agency were skeptical about a country singer representing such a pillar of American industry, despite founder Henry Ford's high regard for rural music. Cliffie Stone remembers NBC Chairman David Sarnoff's being impressed, but like Capitol, proposing to bill him as "Ernie Ford." Again, artist and manager flatly declined.

The Ford Show debuted on Thursday night, October 4, 1956, as a half-hour program (Ernie continued his NBC daytime show until June 1957). The cast regulars included a 20-member choir known as Walter Schumann's Voices (renamed The Top 20 after Schumann's death). The earliest shows weren't terribly promising. The natural personality Ernie projected and his own comedic instincts were suppressed as he found himself being pushed into standard Hollywood showbiz clichés. The first show included a British straight man (former music hall comic Reginald Gardner), who was then replaced by an equally unsuitable American.

The idea of a straight man gave the entire show a self-conscious air that left Ernie, as he might put it, hogtied. A frustrated Cliffie insisted to NBC that the host they hired wasn't being allowed to be himself, that the network was refining away the very things that attracted them to Ernie, rendering him just another TV host. The need for change was obvious and immediate. Cliffie took over as producer, working with rising young director Bud Yorkin, who later produced *All in the Family* and other classic '70s sitcoms with creator Norman Lear, who at the time was one of *The Ford Show*'s writers.

Cliffie's presence gave the show a country flavor but as with *Hometown*, he handled it in a way that made it accessible to national audiences and comfortable for guest stars who ran the gamut of entertainment. He found ways to present Ernie that made the most of his comedic and musical talents. On occasion, *Hometown* cast members appeared as guests, most frequently Molly Bee. The show gradually found its rhythm, and its popularity rose.

One other feature of the show aided its rising popularity. In the planning stages, Ernie and Cliffie suggested ending each show with a hymn. They'd done that on *Hometown Jamboree* (the WLS *National Barn Dance* did it years before). They tried it on the first shows, but the idea made NBC bigwigs uneasy. For a time, they halted the hymns. Ernie stressed to NBC that the songs were *good music*, emphasizing that he wouldn't perform them, as he later recalled, in "sackcloth and ashes." They'd present them with the same informality that characterized the entire show.

As the show caught on, viewer response to the hymns was phenomenal. Many wrote that, much as they enjoyed everything else on *The Ford Show,* the hymn was what they really waited for. Most of the sacred material on the show wasn't much of a reach. They were Protestant hymns common to most mainstream churches around the country. The difference came when Ernie added spirited southern gospel numbers to the mix; jumping, joyous hymns, many of them from black or white rural churches. To perform this sort of material at all on a network TV show was almost unheard of.

Even in the era of Elvis, Ernie rode high. It was a rare and winning combination for TV success. Handsome enough to attract women viewers, he did it without alienating their husbands or boyfriends who enjoyed his down-to-earth, guy-next-door masculinity. His 16 years as an announcer, his seasoning on previous network radio shows, and vocal versatility made him the ideal country singer to reach the mainstream. He shattered stereotypes, like the views held in white, middle-class America that all country singers were rubes of the sort Ernie portrayed on *Bar Nothin'* and *Hometown Jamboree.*

Many loved the old hymns, and it's likely others heard southern gospel for the first time. The fact that millions heard and loved them led Ernie to record the *Hymns* LP for Capitol. Released in the fall of 1956, just as the show began, *Hymns* remained on *Billboard*'s Top LP Chart an unbelievable 277 weeks, nearly six years, from early 1957 to 1963 and won a Platinum Album award for a million units sold.

A second LP in 1957, *Spirituals,* and *Nearer the Cross* in 1958 were best-sellers for well over a year and earned Gold Records. Ford's 1958 Christmas LP, *The Star Carol,* went platinum and entered the charts every Christmas season through 1962. From then on, the bulk of his Capitol material would be gospel. A few secular oddities surfaced. On his 1957 album *Ol' Rockin' Ern,* an attempt to market Ernie to teenagers, he recorded remakes of his boogie records with clumsy big band accompaniment that rocked far less authentically than the originals.

Ernie's ability to combine folksiness with simple poise allowed him to trade lines and occasionally songs with guest stars that ran the gamut from Spike Jones and Zsa Zsa Gabor, then-current TV stars Spring Byington and Jack Webb's *Dragnet* sidekick Ben Alexander, to Rosemary Clooney, actors Charles Laughton, and Aldo Ray, along with singer Ethel Waters. Cliffie used the show as a platform for other talent he managed, including Molly Bee and teen idol Tommy Sands. The show garnered an Emmy nomination during the first season. TV guest shots on *The Jack Benny Program* and *Make Room for Daddy* followed. On *This Is Your Life,* Ernie's parents, friends, and family sat in a meticulous reproduction of the family's Bristol living room.

Assuming that Ernie's TV stardom became the basis for the 1957 movie *A Face in the Crowd,* a satirical drama starring Andy Griffith, Patricia Neal, and Walter Matthau, is understandable, but a superficial conclusion. The film, written by Budd Schulberg, centered on Larry "Lonesome" Rhodes (Griffith), an unsavory, guitar-picking southern drifter who stumbles into fame on local radio and TV. As he discovers his flair for manipulation, he graduates to hosting an enormously popular network program not unlike *The Ford Show*, millions buying into a wholesome "just plain folks" image that's utterly false. In the end, Lonesome's megalomania, raw political ambitions, and sheer hubris lead him to discard the inner circle who made him. Ultimately, he self-destructs on the air.

None of this had any relevance to Ernie, a solid citizen and family man scrupulously loyal to his own inner circle and not known for scandal. Schulberg most likely based Rhodes on CBS-TV and radio icon Arthur Godfrey, whose warmhearted public image masked a fiery arrogance that eventually surfaced on the air and demolished his popularity. It's nonetheless a mark of Ernie's importance in that era that Schulberg wrapped Rhodes's persona in a down-home TV context almost surely tailored after Ernie's. It would also have been a necessary step to avoid trouble with the notoriously thin-skinned

Godfrey, yet allowed Schulberg to satirize TV, advertising, and TV ratings of that time.

Rock and roll made it rough on network variety shows in the late '50s and early '60s unless those shows were specifically geared to younger audiences. Many mainstream variety-show hosts either held their noses while introducing rock acts or, even worse, patronized them. Ernie again deviated from the norm. Hosting the Everly Brothers in 1961, near the end of *The Ford Show*'s run, Fascinato's band not only learned their arrangements, Ernie sang along with them on their hit single "Bird Dog" and the old blues "Rattlesnakin' Daddy." The Everlys never forgot the red-carpet treatment.

In 1960, Ernie vowed to give up the show, preferring to go out on top and spend more time with his family. That August, he recorded the first live album ever done by a solo country vocalist. *Come to the Fair* largely consists of non-country material, including tired lounge numbers like "Bill Bailey" and "You're Nobody Till Somebody Loves You," with a country medley, closing hymn, and versions of "Sixteen Tons" and "Tennessee Waltz." He used local musicians led by Fascinato. It was hardly a groundbreaking effort.

The final *Ford Show* aired June 29, 1961. Ernie continued recording for Capitol. His 1961 LP *Hymns at Home* took him back to Bristol, where he recorded with local choral singers at his hometown church. In 1961, at the start of the Civil War centennial, he recorded two volumes of *Civil War Songs*: one of Union tunes, another of Confederate music. Both gained wide acclaim.

Uneasy with Hollywood's wilder side, he and Betty wanted their boys to grow up in a different atmosphere, and so they decided to move north to rural Central California. After a decade, Cliffie Stone was burned out. When Ernie relocated around 1962, he and Cliffie turned management reins over to Jim Loakes, who handled Ernie for the remainder of his career, which still included plenty of live shows.

He also continued doing unconventional albums. In 1963, four years before Johnny Cash recorded his famous album at Folsom Prison, Ernie took mobile recording equipment to San Quentin where he and the prison choir recorded a gospel album. *Great Gospel Songs* (1964), his second collaboration with the Jordanaires, won a Grammy for best inspirational performance.

His plans to leave TV were short-lived. He was back on the air in April 1962 hosting *The Tennessee Ernie Ford Show* for ABC, a daytime variety program taped in San Francisco. Jack Fascinato still did the music. The cast included singer-guitarist Billy Strange, who'd worked with Ernie at *Hometown*, the vocal team of Hank and Dean, folksinger Cathy Taylor, and singer Anita Gordon. The ABC show's relaxed taping schedule allowed Ernie to spend more time with his family in addition to keeping fans apprised of his upcoming personal appearances. In 1964, the show inspired one of the finest albums of his career. *Country Hits . . . Feelin' Blue* stemmed from a segment where he'd sing, backed only by Billy Strange's acoustic guitar and John Mosher's bass. Viewer response still influenced Ernie's recording ideas, and as Jim Loakes remembered, "It was just pure Ernie. People loved it, we got mail on it. We decided, let's do an album that way. They rehearsed [each] number a couple times [before recording it]." He sang a dozen country ballads rendered totally intimate by the spare orchestrations. Pure Ernie, indeed.

He'd have only one more secular Top 10 single for Capitol in 1965, the ploddingly mediocre "Hicktown." Lee Gillette left the company on April 1, around the same time the ABC show ended. From then on, Ernie concentrated on TV guest shots, records, and concerts. Gospel continued to dominate his studio time, though he now had Capitol's Dave Cavanaugh producing him. His later secular albums were another matter. They were heavy on predictable renditions of other artists' hits, the very thing he'd quit doing in the '50s.

In trying to demonstrate his depth and versatility with sterile pop albums like *My Favorite Things* and *Tennessee Ernie's World of Pop and Country Hits,* he seemed to be refining himself into nothing. One notable exception was a wailing 1962 version of the jazz favorite "Work Song." His singles barely charted. In 1973 the dreadful "Printers Alley Stars" peaked at number 66. Nonetheless, his TV visibility remained high as he hosted several early Country Music Association awards shows.

Beyond the acclaim and success that TV and records brought was a darker side largely hidden to Ernie's fans. Sober and professional while working, offstage Ernie had fallen into alcoholism that grew worse over time. As the social climate changed through the 1960s, the cultural and moral fabric of America began weighing heavily on Ernie. The ordinary guy found himself alongside the California elite. Long sympathetic to conservative politics, he loathed drugs, rock music, and long hair on men, though he generally kept these deeply-held views to himself. But on one occasion, some of that hostility broke into print. During a 1974 *Country Music Magazine* interview with Editor Patrick Carr, done in Hawaii, where Ernie had a retreat, he spoke forcefully about the virtues of gospel music and lashed out harshly at permissiveness and the "new morality." In retrospect, many of his views might seem valid in the age of AIDS and crack. At the time the article appeared, his substance-abuse issues weren't widely known to the public. Still, his harsh, judgmental attitude given his own problems reflected a staggering irony, even hypocrisy.

He was still considered golden, however. That was apparent in 1974, when the U.S. State Department sent him to the Soviet Union as star of its

Country Music U.S.A. show, heading up a cast of young American singers and dancers. Ironically, he was selected in part because of the continued popularity of "Sixteen Tons" in Russia. The group did 27 concerts in five Russian cities. Meanwhile, the Capitol albums appeared with a predictable mix of bland studio versions of others' hits. Even Cliffie Stone, still a close friend, expressed dismay years after Ernie's death about the sheer mediocrity of much of his later secular work. If he'd sounded tentative on "Talk of the Town" in 1950, hearing him croon the same tired Tin Pan Alley and recent Nashville hits everyone else sang proved painful.

That situation improved at the end when Cliffie's son Steve Stone became Ernie's producer. Ernie and Betty had baby-sat Steve and knew him well. He gave Ernie's final years with the label a more fitting conclusion. In early 1975, Ernie and Steve revisited the *Country Hits ... Feelin' Blue* concept by pairing Ernie with a Capitol star with impeccable guitar credentials: Glen Campbell. Jim Loakes recalls that "Steve and Glen Campbell were good friends, and Ernie and Glen loved one another. We could have had anybody playing guitar, so we had to have Glen make comments so listeners knew Glen was there."

Campbell's love for Ernie led him to happily revert to his pre-stardom role as one of Hollywood's A-team studio guitarists. *Ernie Sings and Glen Picks* was Ernie's final classic album for Capitol. On it, he recorded everything from country classics to traditional blues and did it live, without the overdubbing that Ernie had long loathed in modern recording. In the mid-1990s, Campbell recalled the sessions. He recalled, "I wish we'd have had more time to do it, because I was busier than a two-headed woodpecker at that time. Ernie was, too. But as I listen to it now, it actually sounds pretty raw, pretty good." The results delighted Ernie, who had despaired that his greatest days were past. "You made me want to sing again," he told Steve Stone. One is left to wonder what might have happened had Stone again teamed Ernie with Jimmy and Speedy.

In 1976, with Steve Stone again producing, Ernie recorded his last Capitol album: *For the 83rd Time,* marking exactly that many Capitol albums (new releases and compilation LPs) since he started with the label in 1949. One song he tackled came from a new Texas singer-songwriter, Billy Joe Shaver, whose rough-hewn numbers became popular in the early '70s after Waylon Jennings recorded nearly an entire album of Shaver tunes (the classic *Honky Tonk Heroes*). Ernie recorded Shaver's driving "I Been to Georgia on a Fast Train." The band featured the best West Coast country sidemen of that time. Cliffie's son Curtis, later part of Highway 101, played bass; future Nashville producer Richard Bennett played guitar; and the Desert Rose Band's Jay Dee Maness played pedal steel. Steve Stone remembered Ernie's delight in recording live with the band, and added that Shaver was moved to tears by the fact Ernie, a longtime idol, recorded his song. It became the final Tennessee Ernie Ford single to chart (number 95).

After the Capitol contract ended, Ernie recorded several more gospel LPs for Word Records. The TV appearances continued, and *Hee-Haw* became a frequent stop that played to his strengths. He returned to comedy, sang (including a memorable "Sixteen Tons" with Merle Travis on guitar), and worked with the show's Gospel Quartet. He gradually cut back live personal appearances to spend more time relaxing and hunting. He became a regular on Cable TV's Nashville Network when it debuted in 1983. In 1984 President Ronald Reagan, who'd once appeared on *The Ford Show*, presented him with the Presidential Medal of Freedom.

Betty Ford, who'd long suffered from osteoporosis, died February 27, 1989. The loss devastated Ernie, whose drinking continued unchecked despite warnings from doctors. "It seemed to get somewhat worse after Mom passed away," reflected Buck Ford. "I think he had the ability to stop. I'm not so sure he had the *will*." Ernie remarried a few months later and, that same year, was honored by the TNN special *50 Golden Years*. Produced by Buck Ford and taped at Opryland, it featured Della Reese, Dinah Shore, Roy Clark, Andy Griffith, and a reunion with nearly his entire Top 20 from *The Ford Show*. His boogie records were being rediscovered and reissued in Europe and the United States Asked about that material, he remained as proud of it as he was the day he recorded it.

Meanwhile, his health took an alarming turn. TV appearances in the late '80s showed a robust if pudgy man in his late sixties whose voice remained strong. By 1990, his visage was gaunt, the hair thinning and white, his frame emaciated. He had, tragically, paid the ultimate price for years of ignoring his doctors: severe, irreparable liver disease.

In Nashville for the 1990 Country Music Awards, Ernie was clearly moved when the Oak Ridge Boys announced his induction into the Country Music Hall of Fame. It was also easy to conclude that as much as he deserved the honor (indeed, it was overdue), it was fortunate that they honored him this year. In September 1991, Ernie taped an extended interview in Nashville with his old pal Dinah Shore. As he reflected on his career, the entire presentation had an elegiac quality, and for good reason.

A month later, the Fords attended a state dinner at the White House at President George Bush's invitation. En route to catch a flight back to California, a perforated ulcer aggravated by his liver problems felled him as he traveled to the airport. He lay critically ill and comatose in a Reston, Virginia, hospital. Buck and Brion were summoned. Though he briefly regained consciousness as Brion talked to him about fishing, he died October 17.

That evening as the news spread, rocker Tom Petty interrupted a Nashville concert. Alone with his acoustic guitar, he sang "Sixteen Tons" as a spontaneous tribute, a mark of Ernie's deep impact on boomers. Six hundred attended the funeral service in Palo Alto as a bereaved Cliffie Stone, a Country Music Hall of Fame member himself, eulogized his old friend with great difficulty. Ernie is buried in Alta Mesa Memorial Park in Palo Alto under a simple granite headstone.

By today's country music standards, in an era of far greater achievements, Tennessee Ernie Ford's half-century legacy may not seem terribly noteworthy. View it in the context of its times, and it was staggering. Born when primitive phonographs and radio were cutting-edge technology, he ended his career with TV appearances bounced off satellites and recordings on digital CDs. He came from the Southeast, made his name in the Southwest, and left an impact with far-reaching implications. Not bad for a pea-picker.

III

Honky-Tonkers

Just a 'honky-tonkin' around: Hank, Kermit Baca, Billy Gray, and Billy Stewart in full blow, 1954. (Courtesy R. A. Andreas . . . and more bears)

7

Hey, Mister Bartender

Hank Thompson

Nashville, Summer 1949

You'd have thought that the new kid had committed heresy.

Even in the Southwest, small-time singers busted their asses playing honky-tonks, radio stations, and theaters, hoping against the odds they'd someday succeed in reaching the Grand Ole Opry. Opry membership carried a magical cachet, and any singer who got a shot had better grab it the first time; it likely wouldn't come again.

Now, a week after joining the cast, a young Texas singer who grew up revering the Opry headed home to Texas, disillusioned by the show's stodgy conservatism and his $9 paycheck for a single appearance.

Leaving WSM with his modest check, he ran into Hank Williams, the Opry's recently arrived fair-haired boy riding high with his hit single of "Lovesick Blues," which had propelled him onto the show. They'd met before and got along. Hank was amazed to hear that the Texas newcomer was heading home.

"Somebody said Ernest got you on the Opry and you're LEAVIN'! Man, this is what we all dreamed about, bein' on the Grand Ole Opry."

"Yeah. Me, too," replied Thompson. "Except, I can't live on those dreams. Look at this check," he said, showing Williams the $9 token payment.

Hank Thompson has long been perceived as a singer whose skillful blend of honky-tonk and western swing opened doors for Ray Price, George Strait, Johnny Bush, and other singers who wrapped their vocals in a Texas dance beat. That much is true. It's likewise correct that he paid the western swing side of things little mind even while growing up in Waco. That didn't change when he began his professional career. Several years passed before he infused his Brazos Valley Boys with danceable swing arrangements.

Thompson's timing proved impeccable. He'd always been a convincing vocalist, whether he sang a decades-old country ballad, a more contemporary weeper, or a breezy, irreverent barroom anthem. His unswerving command of inflection drew forth whatever emotion and mood a lyric required, enhancing every record he made. Rarely during his Capitol years did he ever sound less than totally convincing. The robust, swinging sound he adopted in the early fifties did more than satisfy southwestern dance crowds. It gave Hank a clear identity on records. On the radio, the bouncy instrumental intros and steel-guitar licks signaled his identity before Hank sang a word.

An astute talent scout, he discovered both Wanda Jackson and Jean Shepard and helped them get on record. Some of western swing's greatest instrumentalists graced the Brazos Valley Boys, among them steel players Bobbie White, Curly Chalker, Pee Wee Whitewing, and Bobby Garrett, and fiddlers Keith Coleman, Bob White, and Curly Lewis.

His achievements extended beyond recording and performing into marketing. He and longtime manager Jim Halsey pioneered the concept of corporate endorsements for music acts. Today's jeans-, tobacco-, and automotive-sponsored country tours began with Thompson's Falstaff Beer–sponsored tours in the 1950s. Still in college when he started booking Hank, the experience helped Halsey metamorphose into a super-manager of the 1970s and 1980s.

Interviewed in the mid-1990s and again in 2000, Hank Thompson revealed a keen intellect. Hank is articulate and well versed in country music heritage, proud and thoroughly aware of his achievements; his astute, incisive explanations of the ins and outs of his career distinguish him from many of his peers. He not only explained how and when things happened as they did, but also *why*.

The Brazos River figured prominently in the creation of Waco, Texas, named for the Huaco Indians, who lived along the Brazos River where the Texas Rangers built Fort Fisher in 1837. Waco grew up around it and in 1857 became a full-blown city, the county seat of McLennan County and the home of what became Baylor University. It remained a sleepy settlement until a new suspension bridge, one of the longest in the world at the time, spanned the Brazos in 1870. The railroad arrived a year later; another college sprung up in 1872. Even as Waco became a manufacturing center, farmland surrounded it.

The Koceks, Hank's paternal grandparents, emigrated from what's now the Czech Republic to Texas, where they farmed. At some point, they adopted the Anglo-Saxon name Thompson. Their son, Jule Thomas Thompson, grew up on a farm. After marrying Zexia Ida Wells, Jule Thompson became a railroad engineer. As automobiles proliferated across the Texas landscape, he wisely became a mechanic. "He realized that was gonna be a good thing so he got into that," Hank explained. "So although we lived kind of rurally, we did not farm."

The Thompsons had no musical background, and there was no reason to suspect that their son Henry William, born September 3, 1925, would be any different. Moving through childhood in the 1930s, with million-watt radio stations just south of the Texas border in Mexico, recorded country music sold well along with the patent medicine outfits who sponsored it. By the mid-1930s, Texas's diverse culture spawned the synthesis of vernacular styles later called western swing, epitomized by Milton Brown and His Musical Brownies and the Light Crust Doughboys. In the spring of 1933, Bob Wills and his Playboys, a mediocre band led by an ex–Light Crust Doughboy, settled in Waco. It moved on after a few months.

Henry William never noticed them. While he'd heard of the Doughboys and, later, W. Lee O'Daniel and His Hillbilly Boys, neither grabbed his attention the way southeastern hillbilly music did. The Carter Family, who worked the Mexican border radio stations in the late 1930s, and records by Jimmie Rodgers and Vernon Dalhart, became particular favorites. Every Saturday, the boy got his fix of westerns at the Waco Theater, drawn to Charles Starrett, Tom Mix, Buck Jones, and especially Gene Autry, who began his career as a Jimmie Rodgers disciple: "In his movies, [Autry] sang Jimmie Rodgers songs, and he played the guitar. I'd always been inspired by Jimmie Rodgers, but I never had seen him. So when I actually could see Gene Autry play that guitar and sing, I said, 'Well, heck, I could do that if I just had a guitar!'" He got a $4 Vernon brand guitar in 1934. His uncle and a friend of his mother taught him some chords: "If somebody knew something, I learned all I could from 'em. I'd go around singin' Jimmie Rodgers and Vernon Dalhart things. When I got the guitar, I really got into it because I could accompany myself with it. And Gene Autry was the inspiration for that."

Every Saturday night he faithfully absorbed the Opry:

> That was more hill country music, banjos and fiddles, whereas the music of the Southwest was a lot more uptempo and had more life to it. Also, you heard a lot of the cowboy songs, people singing songs of the Old West, "Little Joe the Wrangler," things like that. Of course, others were comin' along there in the mid- and late '30s [like] Jimmie Davis. On the Opry [was] Roy Acuff, people like that, so I got inspired quite a bit listenin' to them.

Attending high school, he found a local performing hero: Fort Worth's KGKO "Gold Chain Troubadour" Ernest Tubb, a founder of the honky-tonk style. He enjoyed novelty singer Peg Moreland: "He used to do a lot of the old things like 'When Father Hung the Paper on the Wall,' 'Everybody

Works At My House But My Old Man' and 'Big Rock Candy Mountain.'
I'd do a lot of those [songs] because kids like them." After school, he
jammed with a like-minded friend, budding steel guitarist Jimmy Gilliland.

Bent on enhancing Saturday matinee attendance, in 1941 the Waco Theater added a weekly *Kiddie's Matinee* amateur show, broadcast over WACO
radio. As with most amateur shows of the day, applause levels selected the
winners. At one show, a WACO announcer introduced Henry William on
the air as "Hank" Thompson. He sang Roy Acuff, Jimmie Rodgers, Vernon
Dalhart, Jimmie Davis, or Carson Robison tunes, throwing in a few favorites
by singer-songwriter Floyd Tillman, another pillar of the honky-tonk style,
renowned as the composer of "It Makes No Difference Now." Acuff's
"Wabash Cannonball" became Hank's signature tune.

Hank won the contest so often that Waco Theater officials scaled back
his appearances. WACO, impressed by his appeal, gave the teenager a
Monday–Friday 7:15 A.M. show. Christened "Hank the Hired Hand" by the
station, he performed each day before going to school. Saturday mornings,
he sang and strummed his fancy new Gibson J-200 acoustic guitar on Waco's
town square, signing publicity photos and mingling with the passersby. It
began a tradition that later became part of his live shows. Long interested
in electronics and ham radio, Hank was president of the school's Radio
Club. Since the military draft had grabbed so many local repairmen, he made
extra money fixing radios.

Hank's own military future loomed as his senior year wound down. His
parents signed papers allowing the 17-year-old to join the Navy after graduation in January 1943. After a final weekend at home, The Hired Hand
played his last broadcast Monday morning, boarded a streetcar and headed
for the Dallas induction center. From there, he took basic training in San
Diego and added training as a radio operator/technician, his planned voca-
tion after the war. To one so pragmatic, a musical career simply didn't seem
realistic: "I didn't really see the music business as being a career that you
could really pursue. It really wasn't a business like saying I'd like to play
major league baseball or I'd like to be a mechanic or an engineer. . . . There
were careers, but to say 'I'm gonna pick and sing on a guitar and make a
living,' not many people are able to do that."

The Navy stationed him on a ship in the Pacific. Off duty, he sang for his
shipmates. Returning stateside, he took officer training at Princeton University in New Jersey and continued his education at the University of Texas at
Austin. He earned the required "points" for discharge in March 1946.
Enrolled at Southern Methodist University in Dallas, he returned home,
assuming WACO would cheerfully welcome back Hank the Hired Hand.

Things didn't go quite as planned, he recalled:

They told all the service people when they left, "Don't you worry, son, go over there and fight 'em. When you come back, your job will be waitin' for you!" I came back assuming that would be the case. I went up there with my guitar and said, "When can you put me on?" and they said, "Well, tell you what. Give us your number and don't call us, we'll call you," the very polite brush-off.

Hank was walking downstairs, when a friend asked him when he'd be going back on the air. After Hank related the story, his friend told him about the new station in town: KWTX. Affiliated with the Mutual Broadcasting Network, the studios were under construction just around the corner. Hank found a more enthusiastic reception there, and landed a 12:15 P.M. slot between Cedric Foster's network news commentaries and the popular *Queen for a Day* quiz show.

The Hired Hand was history; on the air, he was now Hank Thompson, still singing alone with his guitar. As requests for personal appearances came in, he organized a band including boyhood friend Jimmy Gilliland on steel but stuck to the southeastern tunes he'd always played. Echoing the performing formats of the Southeast, he often performed at rural schoolhouses. He named the band by appropriating the name of the inactive Brazos Valley Boys, a local outfit. He'd already penned "Brazos Valley Rancho," which became the show's theme.

Garland DeLamar's Shelby Music Company was a Waco record store that serviced area jukeboxes with 78 discs. Hank hung out listening to the latest records, cadging new material for his on-air repertoire. He also asked DeLamar about recording. The businessman contacted Dallas record distributor Herb Rippa. Assuming that arranging a major-label contract would be tough, Rippa connected Hank with tiny, California-based Globe Records.

In August 1946, Hank went to Pappy Sellars's Dallas studio and recorded four originals: "California Women," the first song he ever wrote; "What Are We Gonna Do about the Moonlight"; and two tunes he wrote in the Navy, "Swing Wide Your Gate of Love" and "Whoa Sailor." Globe released "Whoa Sailor" and "Swing Wide" in September, the month Hank turned 21.

Dallas disc jockey Hal Horton liked Hank's new release and played it on his KRLD *Hillbilly Hit Parade* radio show. With KRLD's 50,000 watts, Horton's show had a national reach that afforded a new artist real exposure. He took listener feedback seriously, Hank remembered: "[Horton] played that thing and it went to number 1 [locally] and also he played the other side, 'Swing Wide Your Gate of Love' and IT went to number 1! When they tallied his mail, he'd box it up and send it to the various artists. I'd get a great big box of mail about once a week from everywhere, from Canada and Montana."

College suddenly went on the back burner. Hank's GI Bill allotment paid for flight instruction toward a commercial pilot's license. If he succeeded in music, he decided, he'd fly his own plane to shows. Then Rippa started his own Blue Bonnet label and issued "California Women" and "What Are We Gonna Do about the Moonlight" from that first session at Sellars's. Horton jumped on that one as well.

Herb Rippa may have been correct that arranging a major-label deal was difficult, but one was about to fall right into Hank's lap. Tex Ritter, long established as one of America's top singing cowboys, was Capitol Records' first country singer and at that time one of the nation's most popular country singers. During a Texas tour, Ritter, seeking to promote his records and his show, stopped by KRLD to visit Horton. Hearing that Ritter was set to appear in Waco, Horton suggested that Tex look up the talented kid at KWTX, piquing Ritter's interest. Capitol's Lee Gillette had suggested that Ritter scout potential talent for the label.

Alerted to Ritter's visit, Hank immediately realized the possibilities: "I was there to meet him and greet him, and we became immediate friends, and I had him up on my radio program and performed with him on the show when he was there in town." Hank had a new original, "Humpty Dumpty Heart." He'd recorded an acetate of it with a local swing band: the Lone Star Playboys; "I give it to Hal and, hell, the *acetate* went to number 1."

Gillette, contacted by both Ritter and Horton, signed Thompson to Capitol, and that fall, he and Cliffie Stone arrived in Waco to record Hank. Thompson turned on the charm, treating them to a Texas-style dinner of fried doves and gravy. On October 10, Hank and a group of local musicians including Lone Star Playboys' steel guitarist Ralph "Lefty" Nason assembled at WFAA in Dallas. A Capitol engineer arrived from L.A. lugging a Magnacord tape recorder. Up until then, records were cut onto acetate discs. Tape was a quantum leap because it could be rewound and recorded over again. Hank was among the first (if not the first) country singers to record on magnetic tape.

The plaintive, gentle "Humpty Dumpty Heart" hinted at the Thompson sound to come. The twin fiddlers and Nason's creative, ingenious steel guitar fills, which became fixtures of the Thompson sound, appeared on record for the first time. Why did he write a song based on a nursery rhyme? It happened while writing another song. As Hank's mind wandered, he drifted into the "Humpty Dumpty" idea:

> I kinda turned the paper over and wrote the song in I bet, 15 minutes, and turned the paper over and started workin' on the other one. It was one of the easiest songs that I ever wrote. It was coincidental it was a nursery

rhyme thing. I wasn't really makin' an effort to do that. . . . Of course when it became a hit, then naturally Lee Gillette said, "Hey, that nursery rhyme thing is a good lick for you."

Hank realized that Nason's voicings and embellishments set his records apart from anyone else's. "I never heard anybody play like that," he said. "That's what everybody said. He was working down in Austin the first time I heard of him, with [western swing bandleader] Jesse James. When I heard him, he came to Waco and I heard him play, and I said, 'That's it right there. The next recording session I do, I want him on it.' A lot of those things he did on that session became things that established my sound."

Texas music researcher Andrew Brown discovered Nason's surprisingly un-Texas heritage. Born Ralph Nazilian just outside Boston in Dedham, Massachusetts, in 1913, he was the son of Armenian immigrants who came to America to escape the genocidal wrath of the Turks. He grew up in Hartford, Connecticut. Still traumatized by the violence, fearing American prejudice against Armenians, Ralph's father anglicized the family name to "Nason."

Ralph began playing steel in the 1930s, later learned guitar and bass, and worked around Baltimore in the early 1940s as a pop instrumentalist. Playing bass for Zeke Clements inaugurated him into the country scene, and in 1946 Nason relocated to Texas. He lived first in San Angelo, then in Austin, where he joined Jesse James and appeared on James's Blue Bonnet recordings. By mid-1947, Nason had joined the Lone Star Playboys in Waco. His B-flat seventh tuning allowed him to create unique licks and "doo-wahs" so integral to the Thompson sound that all subsequent Brazos Valley Boys steel players were required to learn them.

Thompson knew exactly what he was getting:

He just did [the licks], and when I'd hear him, I'd say, "Hey, Lefty, remember that thing, right there that you do—use that lick more often." I'd hear the things that he did that I never heard anybody else do. I'd call his attention to it. The little chime thing, and crunchin' the bar, hittin' the bar on the strings, and the *Dut-Dut Do-Wha-aah*. And putting those identifying things [into records] was the tradition at the time.

Back then, you looked for a style, an identifying thing that was gonna make you sound different from somebody else. You could hear the intro and know who it was. Those things that he did on that particular record session, and later on [when] he worked as a regular member of my band, he developed a few other little old things that we used. Those became so identifiable, and nobody else had that sound, that it became known as the Hank Thompson sound, and we still use it today.

In mid-December of 1947, Hank began a tradition that lasted for the next 17 years. He made his pilgrimage to Hollywood to record again for Capitol. A sense of urgency prevailed. For the second time in six years, the American Federation of Musicians was about to strike U.S. record companies over a royalty dispute. The strike was scheduled to begin in January. With labels racing to stockpile enough material to wait out the strike, most L.A. studios ran 24 hours a day, as every company built a backlog. Capitol, lacking its own studio, used the company lounge as a studio, tied to a makeshift control room in the basement. That's where Hank recorded.

One hit emerged from the session: "The Green Light." Thompson recalled: "I wrote down the first things that came to my mind. I said, 'I've got it down, I'll come back later and polish it up.' Then I got the idea: why don't I do this little delay? 'I turned your whole cart (pause) upside down,' [I added] that little delay and that gave it a bit of a boost. That split bar really put zest to the song."

In April of 1948, Hank married Dorothy Jean Ray at Dallas's Arcadia Theater where Horton's live afternoon KRLD *Cornbread Matinee* took place. "Humpty Dumpty Heart" reached number 2 on the *Billboard* charts in 1948 and number 1 in many major regional southwestern markets. "Green Light" made the Top 10 in the fall of '48. A remake of "What Are We Gonna Do about the Moonlight" reached number 10 on *Billboard*'s Country Juke Box chart in early 1949, a year that brought mixed results.

Hank complained that though many of his early singles went to number 1 in regional markets in the Southwest, and sometimes did likewise in the Northeast, after *Billboard* "averaged" everything out nationwide, his records weren't placed as highly nationally. " 'Humpty Dumpty' was number 1 in all the other deals on the Hillbilly Hit Parade and a lot of stations," he said. "After Hal Horton, some other stations picked it up and started playing it. It was number 1 on all those."

Hank started the year in Waco, hosting a Saturday show over an 18-station Texas network. During a California tour, on March 12, he packed 2,783 people into the El Monte Legion Stadium by appearing at the dance following Cliffie Stone's new *Hometown Jamboree* TV and radio show. Mid-'49 brought an offer to join *Smoky Mountain Hayride*. Designed to compete with the Opry, WLAC, Nashville's other 50,000-watt station and a part of the Mutual Network, would host the show. Hank broke up the band and left for Nashville.

It wasn't surprising that, since even long-lived shows like the WLS *National Barn Dance* lost ground to the Opry, the *Smoky Mountain Hayride* was soon history. WLAC moved Hank to an early-morning show with a female singer, titling it "The Boy from Texas, the Girl from Tennessee" (a line from a 1948 Nat King Cole Trio hit). The show had little promise. When Hank met longtime hero Ernest Tubb, the Opry star bluntly told him, "Son, you need to be on the Opry. This is what your career needs. Stay two or three years, then do what you want."

Tubb approached the Opry's Jim Denny, and the next Saturday night, Hank debuted on the show he'd deified as a kid. The stars fell quickly from his eyes. Compared to the looser musical atmosphere in Texas, the Opry's conservatism and internal politics disillusioned him almost instantly. After handing in his notice and explaining it all to Hank Williams, Hank headed home. To fund the trip, Nashville promoter Oscar Davis booked him on a Birmingham, Alabama, show for $200. The money got him home with cash to spare. Later that year, a buoyant Capitol remake of "Whoa Sailor" paired with "Soft Lips" became Hank's first double-sided Top 10 single.

Back home, Hank reappraised his situation. Going back to playing schoolhouses wasn't an option. He'd done the math and realized real money was in playing clubs and dancehalls:

> You do some schoolhouse somewhere, and you couldn't go back for another year. If you'd play schoolhouses, we charged 50 cents for adults, and a quarter for kids, you'd have a house full of people and still didn't come out makin' a whole lot of money. At dances, they'd charge a dollar and 4 [hundred], 500 people for that and get 60 to 70 percent of the door—you'd come out with pretty good money.

Hank relocated to Dallas in late 1949 and reorganized the Brazos Valley Boys with Lefty Nason and singer Billy Walker. By fall, Hank came in at number 5 in *Billboard's* third annual Disc Jockey Poll, bested only by Eddy Arnold, Red Foley, Hank Williams, and Jimmy Wakely.

Nineteen fifty would be a pivotal year after Hank reinvented his sound for the dance halls by hiring guitarist Billy Gray to lead the Brazos Valley Boys. Born in Paris, Texas, in 1924, Gray, like Hank, began his career as a teenage radio star. Well versed in western swing, Gray reshaped the band's sound as Hank encouraged his musicians' ingenuity. "I tried to instill that in all the people that worked for me," he explained. "I said 'Use your imagination!' Like Lefty Nason. I'd tell the fiddle players, 'Play your thing!'":

> Gray was creative like that too, and liked to experiment and do a different sound. He was not by any means a good guitarist. He should've been a drummer, because he really had a good feel for tempos and rhythm. I used

to have him kick off the song because he knew more what tempo we should do a song than I did. . . . If I kicked off too fast or too slow, it wouldn't be right. But he had a sense of knowing the pace it should be.

In May 1950, Hank met a second crucial player in his blossoming organization. Twenty-year-old Jim Halsey of Independence, Kansas, was still attending Independence Junior College when he started booking shows at the local Memorial Hall. The kid's able handling of Hank's Kansas and Oklahoma tours impressed both Hank and Gray. Hank decided to keep in touch. Meanwhile, his hope that a newer sound would succeed for him soon hit a snag.

The problem had a precedent. In 1933, Bob Wills's original Playboys, a band so ragged that only Bob's personality put it across, faced a highly competitive atmosphere during its brief stay in Waco. Bob, noticing much of his fan mail came from Oklahoma, made history after moving the band to Tulsa in 1934. Hank faced an identical dilemma. Dallas and Fort Worth had too many similar acts with hard-wired followings. The farther from central Texas he traveled, the better the reception. He found Oklahoma audiences particularly enthused.

In 1949, after six years in California, Bob Wills relocated the Texas Playboys to Oklahoma City's Trianon Ballroom. In 1950, the band came to Dallas, where Bob had built a lavish ballroom. Although he left his younger brother Luke behind with a band, Oklahoma City was wide open. Since Hank played the Trianon even before Wills left, he made the ballroom his new base. With a ready-made audience, Hank and Gray bore down on reaching swing fans.

The move was smart on a couple levels. In 1950, western swing bands faced declining popularity as solo honky-tonk singers became dominant. None of that concerned Hank. For him, western swing was a means to an end:

I told Billy, if we're gonna go for this, let's shoot for the top. Let's be the best that there is, and get the best people we can, and make the best band. All your bands, Glenn Miller, Tommy Dorsey, Charlie Spivak, and Benny Goodman, Bob Wills, Spade Cooley, and Leon McAuliffe, they were the bandleader. The vocalist was like one of the instruments. I wanted to change that to . . . Hank Thompson the singer, with a good band that had the western swing flavor.

I wanted a different sound out of the fiddles than Bob Wills. Not the sophistication of Cooley, which sounded more like a symphony section. The thing I didn't like about Bob Wills was all the jazz backgrounds [being played] while the vocalist was singin'. In particular, the lead guitar. When

I'd be listenin' to Tommy Duncan sing, and I'd want to hear the lyrics, here'd be Junior Barnard or Cameron Hill or somebody playin' all this "butterfly" guitar in the background, and Bob hollerin' on top. Hell, I couldn't hear the words.

With a new sound, home base, and Texas booking agent who wouldn't relocate, Hank needed a manager and booker. He and Gray hadn't forgotten Halsey. On January 1, 1952, the young agent set up shop in Oklahoma City to handle Hank's bookings and business affairs. Just prior to his arrival, Hank had met his new Capitol producer: Ken Nelson, Lee Gillette's replacement.

Dorothy Thompson talked her husband into covering "The Wild Side of Life," recorded for Capitol by Texas honky-tonk artist Jimmy Heap and the Melody Masters. The song itself was no reach. Heap and his pianist, Arlie Carter, simply applied new lyrics to a melody shared by two country music classics, a melody Hank sang often as the Hired Hand:

She liked [the record] and said, "You ought to record that song." I said, "Oh, that's just that old melody of [Roy Acuff's] 'Great Speckled Bird' and (the Carter Family's) 'Thinking Tonight of My Blue Eyes' with new lyrics. I don't think it's anything original." She said, "Yeah, but you're [doing] honky-tonk music.... 'I didn't know God made honky-tonk angels'— that's a powerful line." I said, "Well, yeah!"

We always liked to rehearse new songs I'd written [or picked up], [work out] arrangements and put 'em on disc so we could play 'em and hear 'em back. I said, "Let's just do 'Wild Side of Life.'" It had three verses and the chorus, so it was a little long. [I decided] I'll use the first verse and the chorus, rewrite the second and third verse into one. We cut the dub.

Nelson insisted that he brought Hank the song, but both men were skeptical about the familiar melody. Hank convinced him by invoking Dorothy's argument about the "honky-tonk angels" line. But neither Nelson nor Hank saw "Wild Side" as anything more than the B-side to Hank's single "Cryin' in the Deep Blue Sea." That tune became a substantial regional hit with a first-rate vocal and outstanding soloing by the band's new steel guitarist, Curly Chalker. Within a couple of months of the single's release, fans and disc jockeys had noticed the B-side. By the spring of 1952, "Wild Side" was perched at number 1 for 15 weeks. It remained on *Billboard*'s charts 30 weeks: the biggest hit of his career. "I really was [surprised], 'cause I wasn't that impressed with the song. It was that hook line in it just did it. That melody, everybody's familiar with it, so it was just one of those things. I certainly never expected it to be any giant record."

Thompson's success inspired Louisiana songwriter J. D. Miller's answer song, "It Wasn't God Who Made Honky Tonk Angels." Recorded first by obscure female vocalist Al Montgomery, Decca producer Paul Cohen quickly grabbed the song for Kitty Wells, the wife of singer Johnny Wright of the duo Johnnie and Jack. At that point, Kitty's singing career was stalled to the point that she was ready to give up. When her single stayed at number 1 for six weeks in mid-'52, it not only launched her career but opened the gate for every other female country singer from Patsy Cline on.

Some of Kitty's newfound success rubbed off on Hank. He recalled: "Kitty's song made it a double barrel for me. Because mine came out and had kinda run its course and was fixin' to start slippin' down. And hers came out, and mine went right back up because [disc jockeys] would play mine, then hers. So I got a double shot at it because of the popularity of her recording." "Wild Side" proved the final step in Hank's graduation from regional favorite to national presence.

As 1952 brought change for Hank, it brought another type of change for Jim Halsey: a draft notice. Even during Army basic training, he kept handling Hank's career, assisted at home by his wife. It was characteristic of the man. Hank recalled the young Halsey as a man with a sense of infinite possibilities:

> He enjoyed doin' things that nobody else had done. He liked the challenge of sayin', "We ought to do this. Nobody else has ever done this." He was very innovative in that respect. He said, "We're going to play those big ballrooms up in the Midwest; we're going to play big fairs." He's the one that got me the endorsement deal with Falstaff Beer. I was probably one of the first artists in the country field to have a corporate endorsement. It was a big thing that lasted many years.

While Chalker's steel playing gave the band vibrancy, his temper gave Hank headaches (and later torpedoed a promising Nashville studio career). "The problem with Curly was he was not consistent. Lefty Nason played everything nicely and was consistent. Curly might play one song the best you ever heard, and [get] the next song all fouled up." Chalker's habit of slamming down his fretting bar and yelling "shit!" after an onstage mistake led Hank to have a talk with him:

> I'd say, "If you make a mistake, you're probably the only one that notices it, and also, you don't have to say 'shit' with all the people ganging around the bandstand." He was very inconsistent with his playing, but it seemed that when it was really important, he'd come through. On a record session, he'd play you some of the best stuff you ever heard, or some critical concert with a big audience, a lot of people on the show, he'd bear down

and play the best you ever saw. Next night, we'd be playin' some club somewhere and hell, every other song he'd mess it up.

Soon the Army requested Chalker's services. His replacement, Wayma K. "Pee Wee" Whitewing, was a Lefty Frizzell alumnus perfect for Hank's needs: "Pee Wee liked to sing, so he knew how the steel ought to sound behind a vocalist. He wasn't playin' for himself. He was playin' for you. Bob Wills mentioned to me one time, 'I don't know who that boy is you got playin' steel guitar, but I'm gonna tell you something, son. He lays it right in there for ya like it was served up on a platter.'" Whitewing proved his mettle on the December 1952 session that yielded another nursery rhyme ditty, "Rub-A-Dub-Dub," and one of the most eloquent of his early tunes, the divorce ballad "I'll Sign My Heart Away."

Hank's ideas about presentation caused a stir at the time. Wills and McAuliffe stayed onstage with their bands the entire night, an approach Hank disdained:

The problem I had was [in] the Southwest and Midwest ballrooms. They were accustomed to orchestras and big bands, where you had a band mainly for dancing. When you played back east, you were kind of a novelty anyhow. And if you played a club, most [people] didn't dance. They'd sit there and listen. You virtually played a concert in a club, which we do today.

In those ballrooms in the Midwest, where [pop] bandleaders stayed there in front of the band the whole night, I had an *extremely* difficult time tryin' to put this point across. [I'd say] I'm furnishing a band to play music. I will get up and perform as a featured act. I'm *not* gonna be up there countin' off these songs and sayin' 'a-one and a-two and here we go!'

In Oklahoma and Texas, bands would not take intermissions. You never had your whole band on the stage at one time. Somebody was already off takin' a break or going to the bathroom. I wanted to take breaks and get a chance to get off stage and talk to the people, sign autographs.

Hank's contracts decreed that the Brazos Valley Boys play onstage for four hours. Within that time, Hank played two hour-long sets and spent the remaining time mingling with the crowd as he had Saturday mornings in downtown Waco.

Club owners didn't buy it. They chided him for showing up late and complained about his circulating and chatting up fans offstage as the band played. Hank stood his ground: "I had so much difficulty. People would say, 'You're late!' I said, 'No, I'm *not* late! The band's gonna play the first hour, and then I'm gonna do my first show.' They'd say, 'Bob Wills don't do this.' I said, 'I don't care *what* Bob does! I'm not Bob Wills. I'm Hank Thompson. We're gonna do it this way. If Bob don't wanna take intermissions, that's up to him.'"

Other owners feared fights when the star wasn't on the stage. Hank had an answer for that as well: "They said, 'If you take a break, people'll start fightin'!' We've been on a break and a guy comes up and says, '*Start the music back! Start the music! They're fightin'!*' I'd say, 'Hell, if they would rather fight than dance, let 'em do it. Startin' the music don't have a damn thing to do with it!'"

For the hard-line club owners, Hank injected a fear factor. He warned, "'The (musicians) union requires we take 10-minute (breaks) every hour. If these musicians go back and report that I didn't let 'em take intermission, they'll fine me and put *you* on the blacklist.' I just used this as a bluff." Everyone eventually adapted, and the criticisms faded.

Except for "Wild Side," Hank largely avoided covering other artists' hits, especially for singles. Nonetheless, in 1953 he tackled the Carlisles' novelty hit "No Help Wanted," released by Mercury. Ken Nelson correctly suspected he could get Hank's version into areas were Mercury lacked distribution. Hank's single, while hardly a gem, peaked at number 9 nationally, largely due to the Capitol sales advantage.

When he heard teen singer Jean Shepard, an Oklahoma native, in a Hanford, California, club, Hank told Nelson about her as Ritter had told Gillette about him. Having passed on Kitty Wells before Decca signed her, Nelson signed Shepard in 1953 and she had a hit duet with Ferlin Husky on "A Dear John Letter." But Shepard's underage status required legal guardianship and red tape that soured Nelson on signing younger artists. That's why he initially passed on 15-year-old Wanda Jackson, whom Hank heard singing over Oklahoma City's KLPR. She and Gray signed solo deals with Decca, recording with the Brazos Valley Boys. Nelson finally changed his mind. At Capitol, she became one of rockabilly's few female stars before evolving into a solid country act.

Hank had three new songs: "A Fooler, A Faker," "Breakin' the Rules," and "Wake Up Irene," ready at Capitol's Melrose Avenue studios in June 1953. For the latter, he enlisted his buddy Merle Travis, whom he'd first met in California in 1948, to play Maybelle Carter-style guitar licks. Merle and Hank became so close that Merle called him "Brother." Hank even had Gibson custom-build him a Super 400 electric guitar duplicating one the company made for Merle a year earlier. Only the inlaid names on the fretboard differed. Except for a few sessions, Travis remained a fixture on Hank's records for nearly 20 years.

"Irene" earned Hank another Opry guest shot, one that reminded him why he'd left so quickly in '49. WSM program director Jack Stapp insisted Hank couldn't use his drummer, Paul McGhee, on the show. He parroted the fallacy that the show forced Bob Wills to perform with his drummer hidden by a curtain. Hank declined, suggesting he play a song that didn't need drums. Stapp wanted "Irene." To break the impasse, Stapp asked if the percussion was mostly snare drum. The Opry permitted snares. McGhee tapped on a snare.

On the *Kate Smith Hour,* which had featured Hank Williams and a Grand Ole Opry troupe a year earlier, the hostess presented Hank with *Cash Box*'s award as the year's number 1 country and western singer. While recording his *North of the Rio Grande* LP in 1954, Hank recorded the bouncy, catchy "Honky-Tonk Girl," a Top 10 single that became one of his signature tunes. He co-wrote it with Waco bandleader Chuck Harding, who worked on KWTX when Hank was there:

> He wrote good songs, and this particular one I really liked. I used to sing it all the time. Ray Price heard me do it, and he said, "Man, you ought to record that thing. That's a good song." I said, "I like it but I don't like it the way it is." So I kinda rewrote it. His lyrics weren't quite all rhyming properly and stuff like that. I didn't change the melody, but I did rewrite the lyrics quite a bit, and I wrote another verse to it.

His long-standing love of pop music surfaced at the same session when he recorded "Gloria," the 1948 pop hit. He didn't realize it came from his longtime pop music idols the Mills Brothers:

> The first time I ever heard that song, I heard Tommy Duncan sing it with Bob Wills. I thought boy, that's a pretty song.... Sometime after that I was in a restaurant in Dallas, that damn song was playin' on the juke box. It was the Mills Brothers. I said *that's* the song! So I went out and bought the record of it, learned the song and started singing it. So many of their things adapted real well to a country sound.

The Mills Brothers remain one of Thompson's favorite acts.

He recycled "Green Light" as "The New Green Light," in the fall of 1954. Peaking at number 3, it outdid the original. Hank's rationale was simple: "The fact we had the better sound, so they would know it was not the same recording, is why we called it 'The New Green Light.' People might have thought this is a reissue." He recorded another nursery rhyme hit in December: "Simple Simon" and an instrumental "Wildwood Flower," the 1928 Carter Family recording that established Maybelle Carter as a country guitar pioneer for her "drop-thumb" picking style. Unlike the Carter original, Hank did it as an instrumental built around Travis's guitar playing. The band recorded four takes. Ken Nelson created a flawless version by splicing the best solos from each take. It was the second hit instrumental featuring Travis's guitar prowess; Hank Penny's 1946 "Steel Guitar Stomp" was the first.

Billy Gray left Hank in 1955 to pursue his performing and recording career with his band, the Western Okies. Travis signed on as a featured stage act, performing solo with the band during its set, then backing Hank during his two sets. Both loved the arrangement. As he'd intended, Hank became one of the few artists in that era who flew themselves to shows. For him, it wasn't just love of flying. Time management also made it attractive: "Flying . . . afforded me the opportunity to get more utility for my time. Instead of havin' to be on that bus and drive all night and all the next day to get home, I could hop in that plane and in a couple or three hours, I'm back and I've got the whole day ahead of me." He didn't quit flying to shows until the 1980s, when airlines became more reliable and cheaper and maintaining a private plane became too expensive.

In December 1956, Hank and the band did their first session at the newly built Capitol Tower at Hollywood and Vine, which opened for recording earlier that year. The year had been a roller coaster for country and pop music as it marked Elvis Presley's explosion into the mass market. Hank wasn't fond of rock, but that didn't prevent him from joining his peers who tried to write rock songs.

Under his pseudonym of Orville Proctor, which he used for his ASCAP compositions (as opposed to the BMI songs he wrote under his own name), Hank penned "Rockin' in the Congo," an attempt to capitalize on the Elvis phenomenon, and Elvis's hit "I Was the First One." Thompson recalled, "I liked that thing Elvis Presley did called 'I Was the One.' I always liked that song and I wondered why it wasn't more popular than it was. So actually I copied [my song] after that song, changed all the ideas. I did it with a rock beat." He also did it with a technical aid that Nelson would use on a good bit of his material: the echo chamber at the Capitol Tower, which added a sparkling depth and resonance to all of Hank's Capitol recordings after 1956. The arrangement was outstanding, if a bit slick. The single didn't sell, yet Hank remembers that rock, which traumatized much of the country music industry, *enhanced* his popularity: "We really had a resurgence during the Elvis thing. . . . Our crowds increased because people would come out and say, 'By God, it's good to hear some good country music because you sure as hell can't hear it on the radio anymore.'"

Touring the nation, Hank viewed a major change in perceptions during the post-Presley years. "Honky-tonks were beginning to emerge as a big factor in our business," he said. "Before, they'd been kind of looked on as like, dives, and undesirable places. Then they were becoming fashionable, and honky-tonk then was taking on more of a complimentary or classic type of thing than the old connotation of the word had meant a decade before."

Billy Gray came back to the fold in 1958. That year, "Squaws Along the Yukon" spent four weeks at number 2. But Hank had an idea for a concept album bubbling in his brain. While he never lived the wilder end of the honky-tonk lifestyle, the themes appealed to him. He pondered recording Roy Hogsed's 1948 Capitol single "Cocaine Blues," with its explicit drug lyrics, as a single. Ken Nelson, who had been a new arrival at Capitol in 1947, remembered the controversy Hogsed's original generated. "He said, 'Hank, there's not a way in the world you'll ever get any airplay on that thing. We can do it in an album.' I said, 'If we can do it in an album, then there's probably several other songs that would fit. I do other things that are kind of raunchy like 'Deep Elem Blues' and 'Drunkard's Blues.' And he said, 'Well, okay, we'll do an album of songs with that theme.'" In the end, they decided to record an entire collection of such songs; they'd call it *Songs for Rounders*.

Recorded in December 1958, the album rollicked from the first note of Merle Travis's "Three Times Seven." With Hank in robust, playful form, they popped off a jovial rendition of Hank Williams's "I'll Be a Bachelor Till I Die," a volatile, rocking version of the Shelton Brothers' "Deep Elem Blues," and plaintive interpretations of "Left My Gal in the Mountains" and "May I Sleep in Your Barn Tonight Mister?" that took him back to his pre–honky-tonk roots. A relentless backbeat drove "Rovin' Gambler," and he successfully revived "Cocaine Blues" with lusty vocal and furious accompaniment, marred only by Nelson's ill-advised idea to pan Hank's vocals between left and right speakers on the stereo mix, an annoying effect common in those days when the medium was fairly new.

In November of 1959, Hank and the band leisurely performed their way through Texas and the Southwest, en route to Hollywood for a series of Capitol sessions set to begin on December 15. At a show in Wichita Falls, a sideman with another band approached him with an "original" song: "A Six Pack to Go." Hank recalled, "He said, 'What do you think of that?' I said, 'That's a hell of an idea! Give me a copy; I'm gonna be recording in a month or two. Did you write it?' He said, 'Yeah.' I said, 'Well, give it to me, and I'll do it!' He promised to send it."

By early December, they'd reached Arizona and played an American Legion hall in Holbrooke. After the show, Hank visited a nearby bar owned by a rodeo performer he'd met on the road. "He had a little old trio playin' up there in the corner, and it was about time to close. They were singin' 'Hey, mister bartender, please don't be so slow.' I said, 'Wait a minute. I want to hear that song!' And they played 'Six Pack to Go' the whole way through. They finished and said, 'Well, good night, folks. We'll see ya next week.'"

Hank introduced himself to the bandleader, Johnny Lowe, and asked him where they had gotten the song. "He said, 'I wrote it, along with a friend of mine, Dick Hart. We used to have a band back in Cairo, Illinois.' I told him about this old boy down in Wichita Falls. He said, 'Hell, he used to play in our band. That's where he heard the song. He didn't have anything to do with it. We wrote it.' I said, 'I'm on my way to California right now. Write that down and let me learn it and I'll record it.' His wife wrote out the lyrics, and I set there and learned the song."

In Hollywood, the band recorded its next LP, *This Broken Heart of Mine*. On the second day of recording, Hank played "Six Pack" for Nelson, who saw the potential immediately. With an aggressive arrangement and Travis's pulsing guitar, Capitol released the single in early 1959. Within the month, Hank and the band were back in Wichita Falls. There again was the song's "composer." Hank wryly noted, "This song's already up in the Top 10, and I said, 'Whatever happened to that damn song you was gonna send me, called 'Six Pack to Go'?"

The Brazos Valley Boys had surprisingly low turnover during Hank's peak years. With Halsey handling the business, Hank and Gray could worry about the band. Hank explained that "I tried to treat the guys right, never was a slave driver or ridin' guys, or criticizing or getting mad at them or things like that. I'd treat the guys like I'd like to be treated. I paid 'em as well as I could. I always was fair about that, givin' bonuses, and Christmas things and stuff to make 'em appreciate their jobs, and instill into 'em the pride that you're the best, so play like you're the best!" Nonetheless, money wasn't so loose in 1960, so Hank subcontracted the band through Gray.

The band received numerous awards as the best western swing band, the first around 1952 and the last in 1964. The awards came from publications, including *Cash Box*. In 1962, the band recorded their own instrumental album for Capitol. Few such bands remained by then; western swing became moribund by the late '50s or early '60s. Bob Wills and Leon McAuliffe were among the few still able to carry a band, and they worked mostly smaller Southwest venues. Many great swing sidemen had quit music. Only Thompson had the popularity to tour the nation.

The Brazos Valley Boys' new pedal steel guitarist was Dallas-born Bobby Garrett, hired away from Ernest Tubb's Texas Troubadours by Gray. Garrett had a high opinion of working with Gray, the man who hired him: "Billy, I think, was the best band manager and leader that I've ever worked with. He knew what Hank wanted. Billy was responsible for the Hank Thompson sound. He was the foundation of that band. He had the best imagination of creatin' new sounds than anybody I ever worked with. He was great at that."

In mid-December of 1960, while recording the *Old Love Affair* LP, Nelson prevailed on Hank to cover the Woody Guthrie composition "Oklahoma Hills." A 1945 hit for Jack Guthrie, Woody's cousin, Jack took credit for the song and, after some legal wrangling, he and Woody shared composer credit. It took 19 takes, according to Bobby Garrett. "We really weren't thinking of it as being a single release, but damn if [Ken Nelson] didn't put it out and it wasn't a big hit again," Hank explained. It peaked at number 7 in the summer of 1961.

Jim Halsey had an idea. In 1957, Capitol began recording singer-trumpeter Louis Prima and wife Keely Smith onstage in Vegas. Tennessee Ernie Ford recorded a live album at the Indiana State Fair in the summer of 1960, making him the first country singer to record a live LP. Country acts had faltered in Las Vegas when Hank Williams bombed during an engagement. But country was stronger there in recent years. Why not, thought Halsey, try a Prima-style live album with Hank? It was another Halsey groundbreaker.

Recording live in those days was a logistical nightmare. Unlike today's miniaturized, sturdy, and computerized gear, "portable" recording equipment of 1961 was heavy, fragile, and difficult to transport. Nonetheless, Capitol had sufficient experience recording Prima that Nelson agreed to give it a shot, arriving with Johnny Kraus to run the equipment.

Recorded with just enough real casino noise to provide ambiance, *Hank Thompson at the Golden Nugget* has long been considered the first live album by a solo country singer, a declaration made often in print (by myself as well). Ernie's album poses a problem, but only to a point. Most of the material on his Indiana Fair album wasn't remotely country. It was a mix of pop tunes and hymns with a country medley, along with "Sixteen Tons" and "Tennessee Waltz," typical of Ernie's concert repertoire. Hank's album qualifies as the first live album by a country singer made up totally of country material. Hair-splitting? Definitely. But it's an accurate conclusion.

On the *Golden Nugget* cover, a grinning Hank stood outside the Nugget's garish marquee looking prosperous, dressed in one of his trademark Nudie suits and holding a handful of silver dollars. The album captured Hank and the band at their absolute peak, tearing through a set of hits with precise fiddles, flawless rhythms, sparkling Travis guitar, and a whirlwind "Steel Guitar Rag" from Garrett. Hank recalled:

> We recorded Friday and Saturday when we knew we'd have the place jam-packed. After the show, Ken would go through and say, "This sounds pretty good," then we'd go back and listen and say, "Let's redo this one again, I think we can get a better cut on this one next time," so we'd go out. So we had 12 shots at it, getting all those songs and so then we'd do them until we were sure we had the 13 cuts that were the best cuts we could get.

Late that year, on his annual pilgrimage to Hollywood, Hank recorded a song that stands as a drastic departure from his norm. Though it didn't sell, it took him an entire three-hour session to nail down the bleak, haunting "I Cast a Lonesome Shadow." It is one of Thompson's best and most unusual recordings and, for him, a clear and satisfying departure from the usual beery honky-tonk:

> Lynn Russwurm, a Canadian boy, sent me that idea. It kinda reminded me of Edgar Allen's poem "The Raven": "When my soul from out that shadow/Lies floating on the floor/Shall be lifted never more." I liked the idea. It kinda had a real subtle implication, and so I was attracted by the idea of the title and the song. I principally wrote the tune. It was mainly his idea. He had a little bit of a lyric and some melody, but I pretty much wrote the song.

Meanwhile *Golden Nugget* sold well enough to justify two more live sets in 1962, one recorded at a Cheyenne rodeo, the other at the Texas State Fair. While the music was fine, achieving adequate sound for the recordings proved more problematic: "We had an awful lot of difficulty with those, technically. We had a lot of difficulty on that outdoor thing at the State Fair of Texas, and also we had problems with that damned old building up there in Cheyenne. The quality on those two was nowhere near as good as the Golden Nugget. The music was probably okay."

Travis, known for his booze and pill abuse, posed another problem. On one 1962 session, Hank planned to use him on the song "I Wasn't Even in the Running." Merle showed up late and so drunk he fell asleep, his guitar in lap. Someone took him home. Bobby Garrett faked Travis-style licks on the steel. A day later, Ken Nelson remembered, "Merle called me and said, 'Gee, Ken, I'm sorry I didn't make the session.' He didn't even know he was there!"

Garrett's 1963 departure from the band brought back a prodigal son. Curly Chalker, gone a decade and now a top voice among pedal steel players, returned, but didn't stay long. Whatever consistency problems existed in the '50s were clearly gone now. His playing on two songs particularly impressed Hank: "You listen to . . . 'Reaching for the Moon' and 'Just to Ease the Pain,' that's some of the prettiest steel guitar work you'll ever want to hear."

When Chalker moved on, Bert Rivera replaced him. Billy Gray also left to focus on his own career, with only limited success. By 1964, Hank and Halsey faced other realities. The Capitol Records that signed Hank in 1947 was a risk-taking, cutting-edge venture. Capitol's sale to British-owned EMI in the '50s had changed everything. His contract was set to expire in 1964, the hits were fewer, and the label that launched Nat King Cole and revived Sinatra's career was now known for the Beatles. Buck Owens was its country superstar of the moment.

EMI's corporate culture rankled Hank:

It used to be I could call Glenn Wallichs and get extra promo records or anything within reason. It got to where they'd say, "We'll have a meeting on this with EMI next week, and we'll bring this up." You couldn't get anything done anymore. Every time you wanted to do something, you got a run-around. They let our records lay, and were promoting the British acts. We felt we could negotiate a better contract with another record company.

Behind the scenes, Hank and Halsey decided that if Capitol wanted to renew, Capitol would have to agree to better terms. He recorded a singles session and Christmas album to fulfill the contract. Hank recalled, "I never really thought I had a real good deal with Capitol, moneywise. So we took the proposition to Ken, but he said Capitol wouldn't buy it." Moving to a new label became a necessity.

Unfortunately, like so much in the business end of music, perception and reality often part ways. Hank and Halsey approached Warner Brothers, where Mike Maitland, a former Capitol executive, held an executive position. Maitland gave Hank a good deal. The label needed a winner at that point. Aside from the Everly Brothers and comedy albums by Allan Sherman and Bill Cosby, Warners hadn't made much of a splash. Then, without warning, several Warners pop acts took off. Hank and Halsey, aware they'd been left in the lurch, negotiated an amicable separation.

They created their own production company, then signed with Dot Records in 1965, a deal that lasted until 1976. In 1968, Hank enjoyed his first Top 10 in seven years with "On Tap, in the Can, or in the Bottle," followed by "Smoky the Bar" in early '69. "We did the first Dot things at the Capitol Tower, but from that point on, we recorded in Nashville," Hank said. Working with producer Larry Butler brought singles like Hank's 1971 hit "I've Come Awful Close," recorded with standard Nashville Sound production values. Two 1974 singles, "The Older the Violin, the Sweeter the Music" and "Who Left the Door to Heaven Open" were his final Top 10s. While the renewed success was sweet, the satisfaction was minimal:

Although I had a bunch of Top 10 records out of the thing when I was with Dot, I could never produce the things I really wanted and get the sound I really wanted. I was never able to do that with Larry Butler. I'd play one of those Dot records and then drop one of those old Capitols on and my gosh, it was all the difference in the world in the presence and quality of the Capitols and what MCA put out. They were wantin' to get away from western swing, and do more of Nashville and I just never could get grooved into that type of sound. I was not comfortable with it. It was not the fun deal to do as it was havin' fiddles and the kickin' steel guitar and all that stuff.

When Dot folded into MCA, Hank recorded moderately successful singles in 1979 and 1980. Rights to the Dot masters reverted to him and Halsey. Now one of country music's top managers, Halsey relocated to Nashville and formed Churchill Records with Hank and Roy Clark, another of his top clients.

Even after divorcing Dorothy and marrying his second wife, Ann, Hank and Dorothy Thompson remained friends. When Dorothy married Merle Travis in the 1970s, Thompson referred to himself and Travis as "husbands-in-law." Billy Gray ran Ray Price's first post–Cherokee Cowboys band, and in the '70s, he filled that same role for Texas heartthrob Johnny Rodriguez. After a heart attack in 1975, he underwent successful triple bypass surgery but died of complications soon after.

In 1989, Hank Thompson became a member of the Country Music Hall of Fame. He worked more than 100 dates a year through the 1990s. As of 2002, he lives in Roanoke, Texas, where he oversees Thompson Enterprises. Halsey, who sold his management company to the William Morris Agency, is retired and living in New Mexico.

Hank's recording career had continued its ups and downs. Curb Records' 1998 album *Hank Thompson and Friends*, featuring duets with Lyle Lovett, Vince Gill, Brooks and Dunn, and Junior Brown, tried and failed to reintroduce him. Part of the problem was that Hank found himself acquiescing to Nashville's Music Row politics, as he had during his days at Dot. Personnel changes at Curb dampened enthusiasm for the project.

"We had to bend a lot of corners and do things for this and that reason," Hank admits. "Same with my old Dot and MCA things. Curb didn't really do much with it. That album seemed like it was jinxed. The music, of course, does not reflect that. I'm very proud of how those songs turned out and of Vince, Lyle, and Brooks and Dunn. They came in and worked and did these things, and I appreciate that. But it did not achieve what I hoped. I did not attract the Vince Gill and the Lyle Lovett fans."

In 2000, the year he turned 75, Hank recorded *Seven Decades* for the California roots label HighTone. Free to satisfy himself, he and producer Lloyd Maines, a Texas steel guitarist and the father of the Dixie Chicks' Natalie Maines, reverted to the Capitol sound and recorded in Dallas, where it all began in 1946. The album mixed old and new with a bit of pop thrown in. But the sound was quintessential Thompson, and it felt good. Interviewed after the album's release, he declared, "I feel better about this album than anything I've ever done since back in the old Capitol days." He said, "It's me, it's my sound, done the way I like it. Everybody on the session just had a good time. There was no pressure, no strain, no nothin'."

The question of whether Hank Thompson is a western swing or honky-tonk performer is moot. The success that George Strait, Tracy Byrd, and others had mixing barroom songs with a swing beat reaffirms Thompson's greatest musical contribution. Others replicated and improved on Halsey's innovative promotional ideas and commercial endorsements, all conceived outside of Nashville.

At this point, despite impaired vision in one eye, he pressed on, fully aware of his place in history: "I go pretty much back in the era not too far removed from Ernest Tubb and Eddy Arnold. I'm certainly a contemporary of Hank Williams." Asked if he was disappointed that he never became a mass-audience icon like George Strait, whose fusion of honky-tonk and swing echoed Hank's, his answer is direct. "No," he says. "I never even think about it. I have an awful lot of fans—I have people come out and have three generations there."

In the end, Hank Thompson fully understands every musical move he made and its ramifications. His ability to explain those moves is the mark of a true visionary, one who came far from the stage of the Waco Theater and, for that matter, from that one week on the Grand Ole Opry.

Adultery
Goes Mainstream

"Slipping Around"

"Slipping Around"
Recorded July 20, 1949, at Capitol Studios, Melrose Avenue, Los Angeles
Producer: Lee Gillette; Jimmy Wakely and Margaret Whiting, vocals; Fred Tavares, steel guitar; Cliffie Stone, bass; Eddie Kirk, rhythm guitar; Buddy Cole, piano and organ.

Floyd Tillman was several hundred miles from his Houston home for an engagement when, sitting in a diner, he overheard a woman he assumed to be married talking on the phone to someone he assumed was her boyfriend. She cautioned the caller on the other end to call her, but if a man answered, to hang up, a safe move in the days before Caller ID. That incident sparked a song idea. Tillman recorded a dignified, plaintive version of "Slipping Around" for Columbia in 1949. Unlike other songs on the subject, this one refused to judge. It contained nary a hint of moralizing or warnings of dire consequences for those who indulged in it.

Universal as it was, adultery was rarely discussed in polite American society, even in the 1940s. While everyone knew it went on, even in the White House, cheating was considered too egregious and embarrassing a moral failing to be appropriate fare for popular song. The closest thing to an acceptable country cheating song came in the fall of 1948, with western singer Jimmy Wakely's Capitol recording of Eddie Dean's "One Has My Name (The Other Has My Heart)," a married man's lament over his desire for another woman, a desire never acted upon. The harmony vocalist on "One Has My Name," according to legend, was California country singer Colleen Summers, better known as Mary Ford, guitarist Les Paul's wife and musical partner.

"Name" gave Wakely, up to then a modestly successful movie cowboy, his first big hit; it spent 11 weeks at number 1 in country and crossed over to the Pop Top 10. Wakely, born in Arkansas in 1914, had come far from mid-1940, when he came to Oklahoma as head of the Jimmy Wakely Trio with fellow musicians Johnny Bond and Dick Reinhart. Hooking up with Gene Autry, who'd heard them in Oklahoma and encouraged them to move west, they became regulars on his *Melody Ranch* radio show and appeared in Autry movies. Wakely had his own recording contract with Decca by 1943, his first and only hit with the label a cover of Elton Britt's "There's a Star-Spangled Banner Waving Somewhere." From 1944 through 1949, he did 28 westerns for Monogram Pictures, the results less than impressive because of Wakely's limited acting talent.

Floyd Tillman's Columbia recording of "Slipping Around" entered the *Billboard* charts on July 2, 1949, and wound up at number 5 nationally. Cliffie Stone recalls getting the single and playing it on his radio show. "I got the [Tillman] Columbia record and played it on the radio, and I got tremendous reaction to it. I called Wakely and I told him about it, and he took it to Lee Gillette, and next thing we're gonna do it. It was Gillette's idea to team him with Whiting."

Gillette organized a recording session so Wakely could cover the song with Whiting. Having Wakely cover it made sense for several reasons, not the least of which was his success with "One Has My Name." Also, Wakely had a hit single earlier that year with Tillman's ballad "I Love You So Much It Hurts." Gillette had good reason to bring Whiting into the mix. Born 10 years later than Wakely, in 1924, she was the daughter of composer Richard Whiting, who wrote such pop-music standards as "Till We Meet Again." She'd begun singing on big-band records at Capitol and by 1946 had her own pop hits. The biggest, "A Tree in the Meadow," came in 1948. She'd just had another hit duet with lyricist, singer, and Capitol Records co-founder Johnny Mercer on "Baby, It's Cold Outside" earlier in 1949.

Teaming the two singers was one thing; coming up with an acceptable arrangement was quite another. Tillman's original recording captured adultery's excitement and anxiety, with a fear of discovery never far below the surface. Such dark emotions wouldn't get the song wide airplay. To eliminate the forbidding edges, the musicians lightened the song for Wakely and Whiting. Using Cliffie on bass, Buddy Cole, a gifted studio musician and Capitol session regular, played both piano and organ. The steel guitarist, Freddie Tavares, was a Hawaiian native who worked in Southern California country bands. With *Hometown Jamboree* singer Eddie Kirk playing rhythm guitar, the arrangement differed 180 degrees from Tillman's.

Riding above the bouncy rhythm, Cole's organ playing was straight out of a roller-skating rink. According to Cliffie Stone, Cole played organ and piano simultaneously. "Buddy was terribly gifted," says Cliffie. "His kind of pop-sounding organ and piano pushed those records into the pop field." Whiting and Wakely sang it with enthusiasm, replacing the sobriety with an effervescence that turned it into an innocent love song, something that not only obscured the message but made the song irresistible to a wide audience. Even the flipside, the mournful Claude Boone ballad "Wedding Bells" (better known through Hank Williams's version), had a similar light touch.

Cliffie remembered the session well. An admirer of Wakely's crooning style, which he compared to Bing Crosby's, Stone was acutely aware of Wakely's ego. "[Wakely] knew all the harmonies, and could sing any part in tune," Cliffie remembered. "Get him off the mike, and he's counting the words Margaret Whiting is singing and got upset if she had one more [word to sing than him]. If she was singing harmony, he wanted to sing harmony." He adds that by appearing on "Slipping Around," "she was doing him a favor."

Actually, both Wakely and Whiting benefited. "Slipping Around" spent 17 weeks as a number 1 country record, and three weeks atop the pop charts. "Wedding Bells" went to number 6 in country and scored more modestly in the pop field. The record stirred surprisingly little controversy, and Wakely and Whiting followed up "Slipping Around" by recording Tillman's sequel to the song, "I'll Never Slip Around Again," which spent three weeks at number 2 on the country charts late in 1949 and made the pop Top 10. Over the next two years, Margaret Whiting and Jimmy Wakely continued to record together. They may not have been all that fond of one another personally, but nearly all their debut singles (until they quit recording together around 1951) were Top Five country hits that enjoyed pop success.

Cheating songs became a cliché long ago. With that in mind, it's worth remembering that over half a century ago, when few dared broach the subject in song, "Slipping Around" was a breakthrough number. Even with its bubbly musical sugarcoating, it helped country take a giant step toward reflecting the real world and the human frailties it continues to chronicle.

Harmony meets hillbilly: Ray Price, June Carter, Van Howard, circa 1956.
(Courtesy R. A. Andreas . . . and more bears)

8

I Can't Run Away from Myself

Ray Price

Grand Junction, Colorado, Late October 1953

Hank Williams's body had lain under Alabama soil nearly 10 full months when friend and protégé Ray Price, who now performed with Hank's old band the Drifting Cowboys, came to Grand Junction to play a dance. The group liked playing the Rockies that time of the year because they could mix performing with deer hunting at the start of hunting season.

Price and the band impressed everyone, and this night, one Hank fan was entranced by the music. Bubbling over with enthusiasm and admiration for the rising star and his late mentor, he approached Price to pay him the ultimate compliment.

"You sound just like ol' Hank!" the well-intentioned fan exclaimed.

Like most compliments received by stars, this one was certainly worthy of warm, polite thanks. But the remark made Price think, and think hard. He'd not yet found his own vocal style when he met Hank two years earlier. After meeting him, he consciously, slavishly followed Hank's raw phrasing. Now, a fan's plaudit forced him to confront a reality: in spite of his admiration for his benefactor and his friendship and respect for the Drifting Cowboys, if he didn't find his own way, he'd remain a Hank acolyte. Ray Price didn't want a career in *anyone's* shadow.

It didn't happen overnight, but eventually he quit touring with the Drifting Cowboys and began a quest for his own sound. In doing so, he saved his livelihood.

Ray Price in many ways symbolized the convergence and divergence of southwestern and southeastern music. His first vocal influences were southeastern; his earliest work foretold little of his true talent. Only after he found his true voice and blended it with the music of his native Texas did he find a style that not only clicked with the public but became a permanent part of country's musical lexicon. Nonetheless, his ambitions were always broader.

When musical wanderlust reared its head again in the mid-'60s, it took him in a direction light-years from his beginnings.

Hank Thompson was fairly new to stardom as he watched Price's rise and development. Reflecting on it years later, he said, "I think Ray Price makes a good model for somebody to say, 'If you say that it can't be done, look at Ray Price and by God, it *can* be done!' Here's a guy that did not have the natural talent but had the determination and stayed with it until finally he became what he thought he was all along." The late singer-guitarist Tommy Hill, the Cherokee Cowboys' first front man, echoes Thompson's view: "Price could not sing when he got in the business. I can play you some of my old records on Decca against Price's 'Talk To Your Heart,' and you'd have throwed him away. Price *learned* how to sing. He finally got a voice that could be identified and was commercial."

Commercial appeal was but one part of it. Price redefined himself as a vocalist of searing, even frightening power. The Texas-inspired "shuffle" rhythm and instrumental backing he created behind his voice became as recognizable as Bob Wills's holler or Bill Monroe's mandolin. Nearly 50 years after its creation, the shuffle remains one of country's most timeless styles, instantly evoking images of barrooms, neon signs, and dance halls.

His band, the Cherokee Cowboys, became legendary among country backup bands, able to satisfy sit-down concert audiences in the East and dance crowds west of the Mississippi. Some of the era's greatest instrumentalists passed through its ranks. His steel guitarists included Don Helms, Jimmy Day, and Buddy Emmons. The Hayes brothers (Big Red and Little Red), Wade Ray, and Keith Coleman occupied the fiddle chair. Singer Johnny Bush served an apprenticeship as the band's drummer. Price's front men, who opened his shows and sang harmonies behind him, included Roger Miller, Willie Nelson, Johnny Paycheck, Darrell McCall, and one unsung hero: Van Howard.

His zeal for self-determination was so overwhelming that once he'd made his mind up, he remained obstinate in the face of pressure. It was a godsend to mid-'50s country fans who despaired of the future amid the early rock and roll era. His decision to stick with fiddles and steel guitar made him a sequin-suited beacon of hope, earning him a loyal audience and solid stream of number 1 singles through the '50s and early '60s even while he made gradual stabs at changes in direction. Conversely, the musical 180 that Price did in 1966 by embracing the very smooth, urbane country-pop fare he had spurned nearly a decade earlier fueled a deep sense of betrayal among those same fans and within the industry. Again he stood firm.

Guitarist Harold Bradley, younger brother of Nashville Sound innovator Owen Bradley, began working recording sessions in 1946 before any real recording studio scene existed in Nashville. As a key member of the A-team, the Nashville session musicians who helped create so many classic records, he worked on Price's honky-tonk and pop material. It allowed him a unique vantage point. Bradley calls Price "the guy that brought us back out of the Elvis Presley stuff. We were all just doing rockabilly and all kinds of stuff, and he came back with that hard country stuff, the twin fiddles and all of that. He kind of turned it around."

Price the individual remains elusive. In published interviews, his recollections of dates, events, and places sometimes don't jibe with hard information such as session ledgers. Longtime associates describe Price as an immensely likable, good-natured friend, but also a guileless spinner of tall tales. Those who were there, who watched his rise, helped him create his sound, and worked with him through the decades, tell a fascinating tale of a complex man and his musical journey.

Reference works agree that Ray Noble Price was born in Perryville, Cherokee County, Texas, on January 12, 1926. He lived on his family's farm until his parents divorced in 1937. At that point, Ray moved to Dallas with his mother, Clara, whose new husband was in the clothing business. He spent fall and winter attending school in Dallas. During summer vacations, he lived with his dad on the farm. A 1942 graduate of Adamson High School in Dallas, he studied veterinary science at North Texas Agricultural College in Arlington until joining the Marines in 1943. Discharged in 1946, he returned to North Texas and his studies.

Singing quickly became an enjoyable pastime between classes. He hung out at Roy's House Café, a beer hall owned by an unsuccessful local singer. Price's friends, some of them musicians, kept pushing him to perform there. When he agreed, singing quickly became his calling. By 1948, he'd abandoned college to join *Hillbilly Circus* at KBRC in Abilene, Texas. After a year, he returned to Dallas, where the *Big D Jamboree* took root as the local counterpart to the Grand Ole Opry.

A friend, local songwriter Dick Gregory, wanted Price to record demos of some of his originals. Gregory took him to Jim Beck's studio on Ross Avenue in Dallas. Beck, a brilliant and visionary engineer, constructed much of his own recording gear. Former Bob Wills fiddler Johnny Gimble, who began working sessions there after leaving Wills, remembered Beck's as a facility with a high ceiling and knotty-pine walls. "I thought, 'Man, this can't have any sound at all,' because of echo and stuff. But [Beck] just recorded hit after hit. He had some sort of magic. . . . His control room was elevated. The windows you'd look out from were eight feet [off the floor]."

In 1949 or 1950, Beck recorded Price crooning two ballads: "Jealous Lies" and "Your Wedding Corsage," backed by the Frontiersmen, who appeared on *Big D*. He sold the masters to Nashville's Bullet Records, an independent Nashville country, pop, and R&B label. It's hardly surprising the record went nowhere as it had little going for it. Price tried—way too hard—on both sides to emulate Eddy Arnold's crooning. Texas music scholar Kevin Coffey, who interviewed accordionist Hi Busse, the leader of the Frontiersmen, in 1994, said that Busse, who recalled the session, also remembered an inexperienced Price asking him for advice on connecting with crowds. Busse counseled the young singer to go out between sets and talk to the audience.

Price learned plenty at Beck's. Buddy Griffin, who worked extensively around Dallas and also recorded in the late 1940s, became another early mentor. "Ray just hung around," he recalled. "I taught him to play guitar. He didn't even know how to play a guitar. And I taught him just enough to get by. He was livin' with his mother and stepfather, who owned a clothing manufacturer or something, here. I remember one time that in return for teachin' Ray guitar, they made me some shirts."

Art Satherley, the venerable Columbia Records A&R man who produced landmark records by Bob Wills, Roy Acuff, Gene Autry, Bill Monroe, and the Carter Family, used Beck's studio often. It was the launching pad for Lefty Frizzell in 1950. After Satherley's retirement in 1951, his successor and former assistant, British-born Don Law (who produced Delta bluesman Robert Johnson's seminal recordings, among others), continued to use Beck's. Price was supposedly present at Lefty's January 11, 1951, session, at which he ran one song short. Legend has it that 20 minutes later, Price came back with "Give Me More, More, More of Your Kisses." Though some details are in dispute, Price shared writer credit with Lefty and with Beck, who cut himself in on many songs he didn't write.

While at *Big D*, Price established a crucial contact with Troy Martin. Employed by Peer-Southern Music, Martin, with ties to both Don Law and to the Opry, urged Law to sign the young singer. Underwhelmed by what he'd heard on "Jealous Lies," Law declined. Martin kept the pressure on through late 1950 and early 1951. One day, the producer finally lost patience, insisting that Martin never again mention Price's name. A bit of reverse psychology did the trick. Martin uttered a sly and probably apocryphal warning: Decca would sign Price if Law didn't. Price signed a one-year contract with Columbia on March 15, 1951, hardly a resounding statement of faith in any singer's long-term success. His first sessions in March and May seemed destined to fulfill that destiny. The results confirmed Law's worst fears. At one session, he recorded Rex Griffin's ballad "Beyond the Last Mile." Singing it higher than his normal vocal range, Price at one point he approached Slim Whitman's mile-high falsetto. It reflected Price as an inexperienced singer still invoking others' styles.

Hank Thompson met Price when he came to Beck's to make transcription recordings for Mexican border radio stations. His opinion echoed Law's own skepticism: "He was not very good back then. He was trying to sing like Hank Williams, and he was a far cry from that. At times it was kind of embarrassing. I never did really think Ray would get anywhere because he just didn't have it. With Hank Snow and Lefty Frizzell, it was *there,* but with Ray, it wasn't. He was not born with a natural talent."

Since Price's Columbia contract designated Martin his personal representative, Martin continued pushing buttons in Nashville and at some point in the early fall of 1951 landed Price a guest shot on the Opry's *Friday Night Frolics.* When Price appeared at WSM's Studio C, Martin introduced him to Hank Williams.

The two clicked immediately. Hank was three years older, but may have seen some of his younger, hungrier self in the youthful Texan. He wrote "Weary Blues (From Waitin')" for Price (Drifting Cowboys fiddler Jerry Rivers recalls Hank and Price co-writing it), and took Price along to a Sunday show in Evansville, Indiana. There, Drifting Cowboys steel guitarist Don Helms remembered, "Ray went out and sung two or three songs and tore 'em up."

Price returned home and recorded "Weary Blues" at an October 1951 session. *Billboard* gave it a positive review, and the fact that a newcomer had landed a song from the biggest star in the business didn't hurt. A week before releasing "Weary Blues," Columbia released Lefty's "Give Me More, More, More." It went to number 1 for three weeks early in 1952. Almost simultaneously, Price was working around Kilgore, Texas, during January when Hank called. He'd used his clout to land Price an Opry guest appearance, all the excuse the young singer needed to relocate to Nashville and hit the road with Hank. "I'm not sure Ray was a regular member [of the Opry] until after Hank died," said Don Helms. "Mr. Vito [Pelletieri, the Opry stage manager] would put him on. Hank started puttin' Ray on some of his shows, and he took Ray on some short trips that we would make." Helms wasn't as skeptical of Price's talents as Thompson and others were. "I thought at the time he was very good," Helms continued. "At that time he was infatuated with the Hank Williams sound. He was emulating Hank quite a lot. . . . Ray watched Hank. He monitored what Hank was doing because he could see success at work. He influenced Ray a great, great deal. I saw a lot of promise in Ray Price."

Price didn't just accumulate performing experience on those tours. He had a front-row seat from which to view Hank's personal dissolution—his marital woes with his wife, Audrey; the pill-popping; the back trouble; the missed shows and pissed-off promoters; the rivers of booze and the endless, futile efforts to keep him sober. He got his feet wet with one now-legendary episode. Hank was booked for Richmond, Virginia, on January 29–30, 1952. Price accompanied Hank, Helms, and bassist-comedian Howard

Watts (a.k.a. Cedric Rainwater), who were augmented by local sidemen. Despite attempts to keep him away from booze, Hank cadged rubbing alcohol and tomato juice, which turned his gut inside out. Barely able to function, he went onstage and mangled two songs before being hustled off. With Hank indisposed, Price had to carry the show alone; Helms never forgot that night:

> Hank was out of it and couldn't play. So the promoter put Ray on because he knew Ray from having seen him on stage before. Ray went out to do 20 minutes or so, and the crowd just ate him up. They thought that was the greatest thing and wouldn't let him off, and they just kept applaudin' and stompin.'
>
> Finally the promoter said, "Go back and do more." So, Ray went out, did some more, and he tried to come off and they wouldn't quit applaudin.' Ray came back out on the stage and pulled his jacket off and hung it on the chair and as he walked by me, he said, "What should I do?" I said, "SING!" Instead of doing 25 minutes, he did 40 minutes, maybe more. Even at that time, when he finished and left the stage, the promoter went out and they were still applauding, and he finally got 'em quieted down and said, "Ladies and gentlemen, you have just met the *new owner* of Richmond, Virginia!"

Hank-isms erupted throughout Price's next session. One exception was the plaintive "Talk to Your Heart," which reached number 3 on *Billboard*'s charts. On it, Price consciously avoided parroting his mentor's Alabama twang. Jerry Rivers viewed that performance as a bellwether: "Ray didn't really push for a Hank [sound]. That song doesn't lend itself to that. I don't think Hank could've sung it well. Ray probably didn't know it, but that record was the first time Ray began to sound somewhat like Ray. He had [songs] where he tried to lay on Hank. But I think 'Talk to Your Heart' was the first record where Ray began to sound like Ray Price."

Rivers's view was substantially correct. The song's melody was a far cry from Hank's simpler originals that, "Lovesick Blues" notwithstanding, made up the heart of his repertoire. It wasn't the type of ballad that particularly suited Hank. In it, Price may have discovered the first seeds of his musical redemption.

Redemption of another type was part of Price's duties as a member of Hank's inner circle. He became yet another designated watchdog over Hank's bad habits only to find, as others had before, that keeping his boss away from intoxicants or any other substance containing alcohol was impossible. Another reality: Price was an added attraction on Hank's show, which meant that he relied on Hank, not show promoters, for his money. It became even more complicated after Hank separated from Audrey early in 1952 and moved into Price's rented house on Natchez Trace.

Pained over the imminent divorce, he caved in to Audrey's demands, and to ease the pain, he wallowed in debauchery, throwing parties that left Price's house looking as if a tornado had hit it. At one point, Price and Helms dragged Hank to a private psychiatric hospital in nearby Madison. He'd paid earlier visits, and attendants stuffed him into a tiny building with barred windows. Hank so dreaded the place, which he called "The Hut." Furious, Hank ordered Price to vacate his own rented house. Fed up by this time and not terribly concerned about future implications, Price went home and began packing. A hospital employee soon delivered home a contrite Hank, who apologized and begged his roommate to stay. Price declined as he loaded his belongings into a truck. Nonetheless, the two remained close. "Hank relied a lot on Ray, and when he was [drunk], he'd take advantage of Ray's good nature," Helms adds. "Ray just had a bellyful of it. I don't blame him."

By then, the Opry had had a bellyful of Hank as well. It suspended him in August 1952. He headed back to Shreveport and his original home base: *Louisiana Hayride*. Price and the Drifting Cowboys stuck together in Nashville. As Helms explained, "We kept playing with Ray, because Ray was starting to kick up some dust, and he drew more than [acts] who had much bigger records. He would do periodic appearances on the Opry and was getting to be a pretty well known artist."

On September 16, Price, the Drifting Cowboys, and local Dixieland pianist "Papa" John Gordy recorded what Helms recalled as a "rushed cover session to record 'Don't Let the Stars Get in Your Eyes.'" The Slim Willet composition was a hit single for both Willet and a number 1 record for Skeets McDonald on Capitol. Price's rollicking, animated version made it to number 4; Perry Como's cover version remained at number 1 on *Billboard*'s pop charts for five weeks.

Late that year, Price briefly encountered Hank when they were both in Dallas. It was the last encounter of a friendship that lasted roughly 16 months. On New Year's Eve, en route to Canton, Ohio, for a New Year's Day appearance, a lethal mixture of booze and drugs prescribed by bogus "doctor" Toby Marshall made the trip Hank's last. The Drifting Cowboys and Price continued performing and marveled at the transformation taking place. As Jerry Rivers explained, "He grew in stature and confidence every show. He deserves credit for that piece of a year with Hank. That's tough duty, and he had very little onstage experience except some regional honky-tonk experience. He had a lot of things to overcome in the beginning. Hank helped him establish a career but ... Ray had to sorta baby-sit him."

After Price's 1953 revelation that night in Grand Junction, he had time to think about what he wanted musically. He discovered what he wanted was close to home: Texas-flavored dance music mixed with a strong, assertive vocal style minus the Hankish twang. Yet even after Grand Junction, as he cut ties with the Hank phase of his career, he didn't yet cut ties with the Drifting Cowboys. Indeed, they would help him make the transition.

On December 28, 1953, Price, Helms, Rivers, and guitarist Sammy Pruett went into the studio. Joining them was ace studio guitarist Grady Martin, who became a key part of the Price studio team for the next 15 years. Also present was drummer Farris Coursey, a Nashville dance-band sideman and the first percussionist to show up regularly on Nashville country recordings. The Ray Price that emerged from that session radiated strength and confidence on his searing cover of Jimmy Heap's hit ballad "Release Me" and the flipside, the buoyant, joyous "I'll Be There (If You Ever Want Me)."

The Hank flavor had vanished. Price's pleading intensity on the first tune and unfettered elation on the latter were a far cry from "Weary Blues" or even "Don't Let the Stars Get in Your Eyes." Coursey's steady percussion added a strong dance beat. The guitar/steel guitar ensemble playing on "Release Me's" instrumental break came straight out of Bob Wills. "Release Me" spent two weeks at number 2 on the *Billboard* charts in 1954; "I'll Be There" got to number 6.

Some early skeptics reevaluated their views of Price, Hank Thompson among them. "I was wrong," he admitted. "He just kept hangin' in there, and the first thing you know, here he came and he flat learned to sing. It got better but by God . . . you could tell it was there."

In April of 1954, guitarist Sammy Pruett left to join Carl Smith's Tunesmiths. His replacement was 19-year-old Norfolk, Virginia, guitarist Herman Bland Wade, better known as Pete. "I was playing in a local band and [when] Ray and some of the Opry acts would come to Norfolk, we would open their shows with our band," recalled Pete. Wade's brother suggested he go to Nashville. Concerned their parents would object, the Wade boys concocted a tale that Pete had landed a job with Carl Smith; their parents bought it. Wade had one thing in his favor: he already knew Helms and Rivers, having met them when they appeared in Norfolk with Price. He arrived in Nashville on a Greyhound bus with $3.50 in his pocket. Unsure what to do, he called Rivers's home. The fiddler, just in from the road, picked up Wade at the bus station. Within a week he had become part of what was about to become Price's new band.

Around that same time, Price met singer Tommy Hill at a show in Freeport, Texas. A former *Louisiana Hayride* cast member and older brother of singer Goldie Hill, Tommy had written "Slowly," Webb Pierce's hit of the moment. He was working in Houston when he attended Price's Freeport show. "Ray talked to me, wanted to know what all I was doing," Hill remembered. "I told him, and he wanted to know if I'd come back to Nashville and work in his group. That's when he had Don and Jerry and all them workin' for him. I believe Pete Wade was also in that group at the time."

Price had a new manager: former Nashville fiddler J. Hal Smith, married to pioneer Nashville studio guitarist Velma Williams. For some reason, even with hit singles, money was tight, so for a time Price let his band scatter. Rivers briefly left music; Helms went with Ferlin Husky, who'd relocated to Nashville from California. For a few months, Price and Hill toured together, backed by house musicians at every place they played.

Late in the summer of '54, Price and Smith reversed course. "They wanted to put a band together . . . they could kick honky-tonks with," Hill said. Hill thought of a Texas band who'd previously backed Lefty Frizzell. "I said, 'I know a group in Texas; I don't believe they're workin' now . . . let me give 'em a call and see if they're interested.'" He phoned Houston and sounded out members of the Western Cherokees, led by singer Blackie Crawford, about joining Price. They were interested. He brought them to Nashville and by mixing the names of the Drifting Cowboys and Western Cherokees, they became the Cherokee Cowboys. The move to Nashville and new name were duly reported in the August 14, 1954, edition of *Pickin' and Singin' News*.

Their first appearance in Roanoke, Virginia, in the heart of the Appalachians, speaks volumes of the culture shock that southwestern music brought many country fans east of the Mississippi. Hill, who opened the show, never forgot it:

The first date we played with the two fiddles and the whole big band with the suits and western hats and so forth was Roanoke, and we had a packed house—some kind of an auditorium where they were gonna have a show and a dance. We had eight, nine pieces, and the band scared the hell out of [the audience]. They just sat and looked like we were monkeys in a cage.

Finally, about 45 minutes into it, I took a break. And of course, Price had come out and done some stuff, and he says, "What's wrong? They won't dance!" I said, "They're not used to this. Let's take our hats off, and take one fiddle and cut the band down to five pieces. Leave the piano out and see what happens." We went out there and by the second song, that dance floor was packed. It took time to educate the people on the swing stuff; when you got west of the Mississippi, it blowed 'em away.

The band's own repertoire included instrumentals for dancing. Some were western swing favorites, but not all. Hill said, "Instrumentals weren't just 'Steel Guitar Rag' or 'Put Your Little Foot.' It was 'Perdido' and 'In the Mood' and 'San Antonio Rose,' things like that." In true Texas western swing style, pianist Bernie Annett even used an electric pickup and a guitar amplifier to be heard over the guitars and drums. Pianist Millard Kelso had amplified his pianos while working with Bob Wills nearly a decade earlier.

The new sound was only one aspect of the new Price. He adopted a flashier image in line with Webb Pierce and Little Jimmy Dickens: Nudie suits in a stunning array of colors and adornments. Pete Wade never forgot the band's first outfits:

> He started ordering stuff from Nudie's in California. The Cherokee uniforms, I think were made in Fort Worth. They had the bibs, red bib and the blue, and we had a blue bib and red outfit. We had a couple of changes like that. The thing I hated was on part of the show, we had to wear full Indian headdress and [Ray] did too . . . a great big one. We hated those things. About halfway through the show or during the dance we'd change into our western hats.

Needing more income to support his family, Hill quit in the fall of 1954. Blackie Crawford briefly replaced him as front man before moving on himself. Price then turned to Clifton Howard Vandevender, whose stage name was Van Howard. A New Mexico native, Howard started singing on the *Louisiana Hayride* in 1951 while he worked a day job as a Shreveport bank teller. He spent nights and weekends performing with various *Hayride* acts and made his own records for Imperial. Howard was working in Tucson, Arizona, following a tour he and some other *Hayride* acts made with Lefty. A call from Frizzell's manager sent Howard to meet Price in San Antonio.

One night by happenstance, Howard discovered that he and his new boss had a magical vocal blend, one in many ways as riveting as the Louvin Brothers or even Buck Owens and Don Rich. He never forgot it: "I'd been on the road with him quite awhile before we tried the first duet. It kinda came about by accident. We were just sittin' around . . . singin' and playin'. He'd start singin' something and I'd join in with some harmony. He decided he liked it and then decided we would cut some records that were duets. So it was not anything intentionally done. He thought, 'This might sell, so we'll do it.'"

Price's awareness of the differences in audiences east of the Mississippi was something he'd dealt with since joining Hank. At this session, he decided for the first time in his career to record sacred material. One Price comment took former Texas Playboy Johnny Gimble, who fiddled on that session, aback. "He told Don Law after we'd recorded two or three tunes, 'I sure need to record a couple of gospel things. I really need 'em down through the South.' And I thought that was a funny way to treat the Gospel." It was Price's last session at Beck's. In 1956 while cleaning his tape equipment with chemicals, Beck failed to use proper ventilation and the poisonous fumes proved fatal.

In July 1955, Price recorded at Bradley Film and Recording Studio, a house that Owen and Harold Bradley had only recently converted into a studio. Those sessions introduced another vital component to the evolving Price sound: Thomas Lee "Tommy" Jackson. Formerly with Red Foley's Pleasant Valley Boys, Jackson had become a pioneer Nashville studio fiddler. The solitary "lonesome fiddle" that Jackson added to Price's sound involved Jackson spinning sympathetic counterpoints around Price's vocals.

What made Jackson's fiddling so distinctive? Part of it was his abiding admiration of Bob Wills's breakdown fiddling, as well as the improvisational styles of the various swing fiddlers in the Texas Playboys. (Wills, contrary to popular belief, played no swing improvisations himself.) "I think (Ray) wanted Tommy to sound a little bit like the Wills fiddle," said Don Helms. "Jackson was kind of a Wills type of fiddler. Jackson was one of the smoothest players in town."

Johnny Bush, Price's drummer from 1963 to 1966, became a student of Price's music and explained how Jackson obtained his unique sound:

Tommy would tune the fiddle up. He could tune up a half a step so he could play open strings. It would sound like "A," but [would] be a half-step higher. The open-string sound was the Price sound; Price made him a capo [a metal clamp used on guitars to permit key changes while playing basic open-string chords]. He took an old guitar capo and bent it, curved it where it would cover all the strings of the fiddle. Depending on key, Tommy would tune up or down from standard pitch or use that capo. That's why so many fiddle players could not emulate that sound. It sounded like trick recording, but back in those days, there were no tricks.

Price tried other new ideas as well. On one of these July sessions, as Helms whined away on steel and Jackson heavy-bowed thick double-stops, Earl Scruggs played his distinctive five-string banjo rolls, with tasty bent-note accents, on "I Can't Go Home Like This," a boozy, rollicking honky-tonk novelty akin to Hank Williams novelties like "Howlin' at the Moon" and one of the very few novelties Price ever recorded.

During 1955, Don Helms moved between Ferlin Husky and the Cherokee Cowboys. When he returned to Husky for good late that year, Price replaced him with former *Louisiana Hayride* steel player James Clayton "Jimmy" Day. An Alabama native, Day had a full-bodied, chord-oriented sound, clever modulations, and sensitive accompaniment that became a second crucial component in the Price sound. Inspired by Jerry Byrd's country steel playing and western swingers like Herb Remington, Day had worked with the best at the *Hayride*: Hank, Webb Pierce, Jim Reeves, Faron Young, and Elvis Presley.

Price and band had their first Elvis sighting at a 1955 Memphis show, and already knew more than they cared to. Van Howard never forgot how the Hillbilly Cat came on to play a couple songs. "He started that gyration, and I looked at Ray and said, 'Oh, Lord!' And he shook his head, too." Pete Wade picked up the story: "Tom Pritchard was playing upright bass with us. We took our intermission when Elvis got up and played. And while he was up there jumpin' around, he knocked Tom's bass over. Boy! It made Tom so mad he couldn't see. We wondered what was he tryin' to prove? Six months later, we knew."

By 1956, *everyone* knew. Elvis, fresh from Sun Records, freed from touring the country circuits of the Deep South, now heralded the first wave of rock and roll. Through the next year, country record sales flattened, concert attendance plummeted, and some country radio stations abandoned the format in favor of rock. Little Jimmy Dickens, Webb Pierce, and others tried recording for the teen market. Price scorned the new trends. He would not rock; he would not roll. Honky-tonk remained his stock in trade, hip-wiggling singers be damned. "Ray didn't care for rock," said Pete Wade. "We were kind of embedded in country and western swing." "Ray did not like (rock) at all," Van Howard added. His next session made that abundantly clear.

On the evening of March 1, 1956, in the Quonset Hut at Bradley's, also known as Studio B, Price recorded three songs. With him was guitarist Jack Pruett, brother of former Drifting Cowboys guitarist Sammy Pruett, Van Howard, and Pete Wade. Studio sideman Buddy Killen played bass, Tommy Jackson played solo fiddle, and Floyd Cramer played piano. Cramer, another *Hayride* veteran, only two months earlier played the spooky piano part on Elvis's "Heartbreak Hotel." They focused on a ballad written by Charles Seals and West Coast steel guitarist Ralph Mooney: "Crazy Arms." Price had heard an obscure recording of the song during a Florida tour. It caught his fancy, but he wanted a different beat: a 4/4 dance rhythm known as a "shuffle." In 1980 Price discussed it with writer John Morthland: "The sound they had going at the time in country was a 2/4 sound and a double-stop fiddle. I added drums to it, which had been done before, but not much, and a 4/4 bass and shuffle rhythm and the single-string fiddle. We came up with it right there on the session. I don't know why or where from; that's just what I wanted."

Jimmy Day confirmed Price's account. "Ray called in the guys [in the band] that had been doing the TV shows and Opry spots with him and told us he was looking for a new sound, and we came up with it. Ray had a lot of input on the records," Day added. "He would kinda tell them what he wanted them to play." During the session, Price also laid out Tommy Jackson's fiddle part. As for rhythm, Buddy Killen had been playing 2/4 tempo; he later remembered Don Law telling him to play it in 4/4.

Van Howard needed some help with harmonizing on "Crazy Arms": "I was havin' trouble hitting the first note. I couldn't get it for some reason or other. Floyd had to play it two or three times before I could come in on the first note. It was an odd note to start with, and after he played it two or three times, then it was natural. But just cold turkey, I had trouble findin' it."

But find it he did. With Price's galvanizing lead vocal, "Crazy Arms" was the culmination of the evolution that began in 1953, summarized in one moving performance, magnificent in its fervor, combining drama and passion with the new, insistent rhythm. "Ray was excited about it; I was excited about it because I thought it was great," said Howard. Day remembered a consensus in the studio that something special had emerged. "We all agreed it just had that 'hit feeling,'" he recalled.

"Crazy Arms" became Price's first number 1 single. It stayed there 20 weeks and spent a total of 45 weeks on *Billboard*'s country charts. Its vocal and instrumental combination set a standard for honky-tonk records that remains nearly half a century later. It pushed Texas-style dance music deeper into the country mainstream. While Hank Thompson pioneered that concept, Price's smaller band and the shuffle succeeded in a way that deepened the Southwest's influence on Nashville. "Ray Price was a whole sound back then," said Don Helms. "The high tenor singing, the big, heavy beat, and the Bob Wills–type single fiddle Tommy Jackson was playing by then. Pretty soon, there was country music and there was the Ray Price sound, and everybody was trying to get it." Tommy Hill, while out of the band, saw the same trend: "It really blossomed for Ray. The record got so big that people east of the Mississippi got into the rhythm-type thing."

Despite Don Law's presence in the control room, Price was usually the ultimate arbiter of material, a practice consistent with the freedom Law afforded his artists. There may have been another factor. Charlie Walker, whose early Columbia hits were produced by Law, recalled a tactic that many artists used that made Law even more passive: "We'd buy him a bottle of good scotch, take it out to the studio and give it to him, and he just watched the knobs. As far as arrangements, we did just whatever we wanted."

Price had established himself as a staunch keeper of the country flame, eschewing compromise with either rock or the pop-flavored Nashville Sound. Or so it seemed. Deep within, his musical wanderlust was already stirring. In March 1957, amid a series of honky-tonk sessions, he recorded Dave Burgess's "I'll Be There (When You Get Lonely)," a generic teen ballad that Elvis could have just as easily recorded, complete with pop-like piano triplets by Floyd Cramer and vocal harmonies (possibly the Jordanaires). With surprisingly little controversy, the single broke the Top 20.

In May, Price went a step further. He covered four best-sellers on a 45-rpm EP: *Four Hits by Ray Price*. While the musicians were those he regularly used, the session again included background vocalists. For the first time, Price anticipated his smoother vocal style of the late '60s by covering three hits that epitomized the new "Nashville Sound," conceived to sell country to pop-record buyers. He covered Ferlin Husky's 1956 "Gone," the first Nashville Sound hit; Jim Reeves's 1957 "Four Walls"; and Jimmy C. Newman's pop-oriented hit "A Fallen Star." The fourth song featured Price self-consciously tackling the Everly Brothers' rocker "Bye, Bye Love."

Whose idea was this? Was Don Law trying to sell another country star to pop fans? Not according to Jimmy Day, who was present at the session. He clearly remembered that "Price talked Don Law into that." Clearly, Price's dalliance with such material reflected early aspirations to branch out, even as he remained a stalwart of "hard country" in a changed musical world. His honky-tonk successes continued with Texas-bred shuffles like the Bob Wills–Lee Ross ballad "My Shoes Keep Walking Back to You."

While the Cherokee Cowboys launched several stars, Van Howard didn't find it a stepping-stone to fame. Price tried to help by persuading Don Law to record Howard. The released discs went nowhere; nor did a second Howard session with the Cherokee Cowboys for ABC/Paramount. Meanwhile, Howard came to detest the extended tours and left Price in 1958 after a show in Sioux City, Iowa. His new wife wanted him to find some steadier line of work, and he returned to banking. Price began overdubbing his harmonies on records.

Howard's replacement was Amarillo, Texas, firefighter and aspiring singer-songwriter Roger Dean Miller. Miller had been in Nashville once, recorded unsuccessfully for Mercury, and fiddled behind Minnie Pearl. Price heard him in Texas, and while Miller's fiddling didn't floor Price, his singing did. When Howard left, Price contacted Miller, who headed back to Nashville. It was a good move for Miller on several levels. He landed a songwriting contract with Tree Music. Then western singer Rex Allen picked up Miller's original ballad "Invitation to the Blues." Price loved the song and wanted to cover it.

Around that time, another song by newcomer Bill Anderson grabbed Price's attention. After graduating from the University of Georgia, Anderson worked as a disc jockey, newspaperman, and singer in tiny Commerce, Georgia, when he wrote "City Lights" one lonely night sitting atop a hotel roof. He recorded it for tiny TNT Records. During two sessions in May 1958, Price boosted the writing careers of both Anderson and Miller by recording "City Lights" and "Invitation to the Blues," and in the process created riveting, cathartic magic. Released on one single, "City Lights" remained at number 1 nearly three months; "Invitation" came in at number 3. Despite the song's success, Miller wasn't a Cherokee Cowboy for long; his unorthodox, loopy vocal approach simply didn't lend itself to the demands of harmonizing with the boss. Miller, who was on a compositional roll, would write other hits for other stars and find his first vocal success with RCA Victor in 1960.

On January 1, 1959, Price, Hal Smith, and Claude Caviness founded Pamper Music, a song publishing house that quickly attracted young, talented writers like Hank Cochran. At a January 29 session, Price threw in another Texas idea: twin basses. Harold Bradley played four-string electric bass guitar; veteran studio musician Joe Zinkan played upright acoustic bass. "Ray had some idea that Bob Wills used two basses at some point in his career," said Bradley. [Wills in fact did so at various times in the '40s and '50s.] "And he wanted to use my bass. Joe Zinkan and I played *exactly* the same notes. It was really like using an electric bass, when you match both of our tones. Joe and I were matching the same tone and the same notes on the hits, we had that clickin' sound."

He used twin basses on another incisive shuffle performance: Harlan Howard's magnificent "Heartaches by the Number." Price's plaintive, sublime phrasing, combined with Howard's concise lyrics, made the song a standard, its appeal broad enough that pop singer Guy Mitchell had a hit with it as well. That year, "Heartaches" won Price the *Cash Box* Triple Crown Award as well as awards for favorite male vocalist and country record of the year.

Price's first dalliance with arranged strings came in March 1960. Recording his sacred album *Faith*, he opted for conventional Nashville Sound mode with backup by the Anita Kerr Singers, members of Nashville's A-team, and a string section. With fans less inhibited about accepting such musical deviations for a gospel collection, no one questioned it. His searing version of Mel Tillis's "Heart over Mind" became his first Top 10 single of 1961.

Nineteen sixty-one also brought a new Cherokee Cowboys front man: Ohio-born Don Lytle (a.k.a. Donny Young, alias Johnny Paycheck), who doubled on electric bass. When Paycheck left after a few months, Jimmy Day brought in 28-year-old Willie Nelson. A songwriter on Pamper's payroll, Willie arrived in Nashville from Houston in late 1960. With a family to support, Willie needed steady work and inherited the front-man spot and the bass guitar. Even Faron Young's hit recording of Willie's "Hello Walls" didn't take him from the band right away. Willie and Price quickly became close friends, and, dazzled by his writer's royalties, Willie often threw parties on the road for the band.

Price's second hit of '61 had a co-producer: studio guitarist Grady Martin, who began playing an increasingly important behind-the-scenes role on Price's sessions and became the third pillar along with Jackson and Day. The moving "Soft Rain" was anomalous in that Price wrote it himself, inspired by the 1936 death of his beloved maternal grandfather and his memories of the sad, rain-soaked funeral.

It required just nine hours on September 25, 1961, for Price and the band to record *San Antonio Rose*, the first album-length Bob Wills tribute, a superbly executed collection of Wills favorites. Jimmy Day said that "Ray just decided to do a tribute to Bob Wills, and by this time Columbia let him do anything he wanted to do. We had been doing some of the songs on dance gigs already, so it was easy to do it in two sessions the same day." "Day and Jackson were at their peak on there," said Pete Wade. "We'd done those songs for years, but those arrangements were done right on the session. Ray'd say, 'Jackson, you take the intro. Day, take the turnaround . . .'" It remains one of Price's finest single albums.

As Don Law neared retirement age, the younger Frank Jones teamed with him in the control room. The first Price single Law and Jones jointly produced was the Willie Nelson-Price composition "I've Just Destroyed the World (I'm Living In)," a Top 20 single, and Price's snappy, upbeat Top 10 version of "Pride." Writing together seemed to come in the natural course of things for Price and Willie. Pete Wade explained that "they would always have these guitar pulls after the shows, back in the room . . . Day, Willie, Price, and all of us. We'd sing all these songs."

When drummer Steve Bess handed in his notice, Willie phoned his buddy Johnny Bush. The two had met in Texas in 1952 and played together on and off for years. Of all the Cowboys, Bush had perhaps the most remarkable recall of his days with the band. He recalled his first stint with the band in 1962 as brief, the second stretch much longer. When Willie left later in '62 to start his solo career, he took Day with him. Price hired Ray Sanders to replace Willie and turned to a known quantity to fill Day's boots: Buddy Gene Emmons.

Emmons, who'd been working with Ernest Tubb when he joined the Cowboys, got his first big break working with Little Jimmy Dickens in 1956. He and Shot Jackson had developed the Sho-Bud (a contraction of "Shot" and "Buddy") pedal steel guitar in the mid-'50s, and Jackson managed the company day to day as Emmons returned to touring. Shortly before joining Price, Emmons recorded the first-ever jazz album by a pedal steel guitarist. Being a Cherokee Cowboy delighted Emmons and made him the fourth pillar. Price, he said, "was good for me in the studios. He brought things out of me that I never knew existed, and we kind of had a rapport with each other, a silent rapport. . . . The better he sang, the better I played; the better I played, the better he sang. He told me that once."

After Ray Sanders left in the latter part of 1962, Emmons sold Price on Darrell McCall. A former front man for Faron Young, McCall had been a close friend of Paycheck's in their native Ohio; they moved to Nashville together. Price let Emmons and McCall run the band. The pair supervised rehearsals, worked out arrangements, and handled hirings and firings. Both had progressive tastes, but believed the status quo was Price's optimal format. "We were after more of the shuffle stuff, the 4/4 bass and stuff like that," McCall explained.

The "shuffle stuff" might have sustained Price, but his experimental side surfaced again on a September 1962 session. Along with the Cowboys, a string section made up of Nashville Symphony musicians [including classically trained western swing veteran Cecil Brower] stood by in the studio. In this case, the change was far less than it seemed. The section simply filled in the spots where Tommy Jackson would have played. Price's vocals were stellar on the single "Walk Me to the Door," which reached number 7. The B-side, "You Took Her off My Hands," came in at number 11. Being a minimal departure, the single was a success reflecting that Price's fans weren't worried about the strings—for the moment.

For Price, it began a period of musical conflict. While his honky-tonk credentials remained beyond criticism, he was restless, driven by his long-standing love of pop music, tempered by his love for the sound that had made him. Emmons saw the conundrum up close. "He was tryin' to cross over to kind of a lush kind of sound, which he finally wound up doin'. He would get into a mood of the lush sound, then he'd get on the bus the next day and say, 'Boys, I'm stickin' country.' It was back and forth." Pete Wade agreed. "Ray was gradually changing over, trying to get his feet wet and see how they [fans] would accept it. . . . Sometimes it worked, sometimes it didn't."

Sometimes, things wound up in the middle. In 1963 he covered Willie Nelson's intimate blues ballad "Night Life," a song Willie wrote in Houston around 1959. Price poured passion and humanity into his performance, exceeding his usual fervor and revealing a flair for blues that he should have explored further. Emmons and Grady Martin, who played a pivotal role in creating the band's arrangements in the studio, wrapped his vocal in some of the finest accompaniment the Cherokee Cowboys/A-team alliance ever created. Emmons's intimate, sophisticated steel guitar intro reflected his jazz consciousness. "There was one song I liked called 'Midnight Sun,'" he said. "Before it goes into the next verse, it had chords very similar. I thought, 'well, I've never heard it on an intro, and they're such beautiful chords, why wouldn't it work on an intro?'" As a single, "Night Life" was, like many of Willie's early records, simply too smart for the room; it barely broke the Top 30.

For McCall, life on the road with Price was "$15 a night and all you could pick and all the bus you could drive." On the bus, the musicians often jammed for hours. Given Price's extensive touring schedule, the bus coasted (sometimes precariously) through the Rockies, the Pacific Northwest, Canada, and the U.S. Northeast in the dead of winter. As before, the band played dances in the Southwest and Rocky Mountain states like Colorado, Idaho, and Montana. In the East, it was still mostly sit-down audiences.

Bush remembered Price's dead-on intuition: "One thing about Ray was his ability to read an audience. He could, by watchin' an audience, singin' a couple of songs, changin' the tempo . . . Say that one night, we'd do a song at a certain tempo and it would work, next night, he may slow it down or speed it up. Price would change that. He could feel an audience. . . . And I sat back there and I learned a lot from him."

Price again moved away from the shuffle beat at a June 1963 session with Hank Cochran's "Make the World Go Away," two years before Eddy Arnold revived it. Despite being a number 2 single, it wasn't one of Price's better moments musically. The strings that sounded so natural on "Walk Me to the Door" drenched Price's vocal in nauseating syrup. On "Burning Memories," recorded in December, Price's powerful vocal cut through a shrill, utterly overbearing string arrangement. The single stayed at number 2 on *Billboard*'s charts for four weeks in 1964.

These dalliances with "countrypolitan" caused some real sweating within Price's musical inner circle. Darrell McCall felt the problem started with "Night Life," which "got (Ray) over in that groove where he wanted to do 'Make the World Go Away' and all that, be more a Perry Como–type singer. Us boys really fought to keep it country at that point." The strings made it tough to re-create the recorded sound in performance. "We couldn't duplicate it onstage," McCall continued, "but I thought what was played onstage was better than the record because it was country."

The changes, McCall added, were even more glaring when the band toured Price's beloved Southwest. "The fans were definitely upset [with the pop-oriented songs] because they couldn't dance [to them]." Some of those fans expressed their displeasure to Price in no uncertain terms. McCall recalled Price as intractable: "He wouldn't listen to 'em, or pay any attention to 'em. He'd voice his opinion and walk off." It became clear to everyone that Price had made up his mind when, as McCall remembered, "He made us turn in our Cherokee Cowboy suits with the eagle feathers and rhinestones. He made us start wearin' black pants and a western shirt. Then he started wearing business suits, and it just really got me. There was something magic about the old Cherokee Cowboy uniforms and us boys walking out there and pickin' and Ray comin' out there with the eagle feathers on."

McCall finally left late in 1963. He'd recorded a hit single ("A Stranger

Was Here"), and Faron Young offered him his old job back. "I could see the direction Ray was goin', and it wasn't for me. I was more country than that," he explained. The Opry dropped Price from its roster in 1964 for the reason it usually dropped an act: failure to perform the then-required 26 shows a year.

It was no small paradox that as Price continued weighing changes in 1964, he hired two legendary swing fiddlers. Wade Ray had made his name on the West Coast as a bandleader and singer; Keith Coleman, one of the finest improvisers in western swing, had worked with both the Texas Play-boys and Hank Thompson's Brazos Valley Boys. Despite the changes, Price retained a steadfast pride in the Cowboys. With Ernest Tubb's Texas Trou-badours making their own records, Price talked Don Law into recording a Cowboys album with Grady Martin and Tommy Jackson present along with Harold Bradley.

At the first session for the *Western Strings* album in December of '64, this capable group of musicians, who'd worked together continually for years, were so nervous about recording on their own that, after 45 minutes of musical inhibition, a frustrated Price sent a studio handyman out to buy some Wild Turkey. He literally ordered everyone to get drunk to loosen them up; it worked. Emmons, Ray, and Coleman played brilliantly. "Grady and I ended up drunk, and a lot of the other guys were in good shape, too," Emmons laughed. "And when I heard [the songs played] back I couldn't believe how together it was for the condition we were in." Because record-ing costs came out of Price's royalties, the album included the original "Crazy Arms," and Price took credit for the arrangements to make back any money lost.

Wade Ray, perplexed by his boss's musical indecision, soon handed in his own notice. "Price was pretty hard to work for," he explained. "He didn't know what the hell he wants. One minute, we were ball-scratchin' hillbillies and the next minute, he was a pop guy. He could never make up his mind." Proof of that indecision came when he recorded "The Other Woman" in early 1965, a song penned by Don Rollins, composer of George Jones's hit "The Race Is On." This was solid honky-tonk, with no voices except Price's own, no strings but those on the guitars, steel, fiddles, and bass. The same applied to his 1966 hit "Touch My Heart," penned by Johnny Paycheck and Aubrey Mayhew. He recorded that in February.

A few days after that session, Price took his first shot at Fred Weatherly's 1913 ballad "Danny Boy." Adapted from the traditional Irish ballad "Lon-donderry Air," it had been a pop standard since 1918. Glenn Miller revived it as an instrumental hit in 1940. Price wasn't the first country singer to tackle it. Conway Twitty beat him to it in 1959, Jim Reeves in 1960, and Bill Monroe and his Blue Grass Boys in 1961.

Emmons remembered how Price, who recorded it three times before finding a satisfactory version, fell in love with the song: "I used to play 'Danny Boy' as an instrumental. Ray always loved that song, and he came in the studio one day and said, 'Let's cut "Danny Boy."'' I know we tried it two or three times." Harold Bradley remembered Price rejecting earlier versions because "he wasn't satisfied. There was something lacking, because we were just doing them with the country band. I don't remember doing it with the strings until we did it with the arrangement by Cam Mullins."

As Price wrestled with change, so did Columbia Nashville. Don Law was in his final year with the company before mandatory retirement kicked in, ending the label's final ties with the golden era of Wills, Acuff, Autry, Cooley, Monroe, and Lefty.

On November 8, 1966, Price finally got "Danny Boy" the way he wanted. He recorded it with a full-blown Mullins string arrangement. Viewed nearly 40 years later, it sounds less revolutionary than it did then. Although Mullins's arrangement jarred Price fans in that era, heard today, it reflects a subtle complexity that enhances the intimacy surrounding the vocal. Indeed, it's far more compelling and charismatic than some of Price's later, more successful pop efforts like "She's Got to Be a Saint." "Danny Boy's" Top 10 status validated Price's new direction. Nor was it the only standout performance from that session. With a brilliant orchestration from Mullins, Price recorded a remarkably compelling version of Willie Nelson's dark "I Let My Mind Wander," a song reflecting the blues influence that "Night Life" had.

After years of indecision, Price had finally, irrevocably committed himself to a new market of urbane, middle-aged folk who listened to Al Martino and Dean Martin (and Eddy Arnold). Harold Bradley understood Price's decision and praised Mullins: "Cam put more strings and movements into the arrangements that no one else at that time had ever come up with. And I think it really bowled Ray over. These were probably the best string arrangements to come out of Nashville up to then. And I think the impact of that really made Ray feel like that was the way to go. That's all he ever talked about, was Cam Mullins."

Price disbanded the Cherokee Cowboys in 1967, 13 years after forming the group. He created his new band the same way he'd created the original Cowboys: by hiring an intact group of Texas musicians, in this case headed by Hank Thompson's former bandleader Billy Gray. Three trained violinists replaced the fiddlers. Gray hired pianist Moises "Blondie" Calderon, an experienced jazz and Latino musician, to play xylophone. After Gray moved on, Blondie became to Price what Don Rich was to Buck Owens. Within six months, the beefy musician was Price's pianist, conductor, harmony singer, musical director, and later, his road manager. Price kept another steel guitarist but when he didn't work out, briefly rehired Emmons, who didn't stay long. "It wasn't Ray anymore, as far as I was concerned," he complained. "He was slowing things down onstage, dropping the volume. I was with him about two weeks and I left. There was no energy."

By the time of "Danny Boy," many fans had made up their minds about Price's sea change. Those who admired his refusal to blink in the face of rock and the Nashville Sound now perceived the cold chill of apostasy. As Price aimed at an audience who wouldn't have listened to 30 seconds of "Heartaches by the Number" or "City Lights," some stalwarts walked out of Price shows. In at least one case, a fan spat on him. In the days before consultants programmed country radio, some disc jockeys flatly refused to play the new Price records. One who did, Chris Lane, a deejay at Chicago's WJJD in the late '60s, remembered the "new" Price sound generating flak from angry listeners.

Outwardly, Price remained stoic. But beneath his tuxedo, the sensitive soul who penned "Soft Rain" was hurt and not a little bitter. A decade later, he told writer Tom Ayres: "In 1967 [sic] when I recorded 'Danny Boy' you would have thought I did something awful from all the criticism I got. Then 'Danny Boy' went gold and the first thing you know other performers were singing it on the Grand Ole Opry ..." Price had apparently forgotten the Twitty, Reeves, and Monroe versions; nor did his single earn an RIAA Gold Record. It went no higher than number 67 on the *Billboard* Hot 100 pop charts and didn't fare much better on *Cash Box* charts.

Johnny Bush attended one of Price's late '60s San Antonio concerts that included horns. He watched fans heckling the new sound and felt Price's pain as he watched his shaken, frustrated former boss trying to explain himself. "I liked what he was doing," Bush declared, "and I saw no reason why the fans should be like that. I heard a lot of heckling. I remember that the heckling got to the point that Ray said [to the hecklers], 'Listen! The horns are only doing what the voices [on the record] used to do!' Ray and the audience were both right. They wanted to hear 'Crazy Arms' and 'The Other Woman.' Price didn't want to sing it. So they were both right."

Bush understood Price's feelings: "I think basically he always wanted to be a pop singer. He wanted to be Tony Bennett. And there's nothing wrong in that if that's what he wanted to do. The only way I would see it would be wrong was if somebody didn't want to do it and just done it to make a buck. It *cost* him money to transfer over. It cost him his *career*, just about."

By 1968, Price faced other problems. With a failing marriage at home, an ill father in Texas, and continued hostility in Nashville, he relocated to Texas. As he refused to bend in Presley's presence, he pursued his new audience, going his own way while leaving his betrayed, embittered fans to go theirs. Other singers, including Johnny Bush and Mel Tillis, quickly filled the void with superb honky-tonk records continuing the classic Price shuffle beat.

Price eventually picked up Kris Kristofferson's "For the Good Times." With a lavish Mullins orchestration supporting his delivery of Kristofferson's sensitive, sensual love song, Price now grabbed adult pop fans, many of whom grew up on Elvis in their teens and couldn't stand contemporary rock. In 1970, "Good Times" became Price's first number 1 record since "City Lights," and reached number 11 on *Billboard*'s Hot 100 pop chart.

For six years, he prospered with his sound, though the orchestrations gradually became blander and predictable. "I Won't Mention It Again" came in 1971 and late 1972 brought "She's Got to Be a Saint." His mediocre cover of Gladys Knight and the Pips' hit "You're the Best Thing That Ever Happened to Me," reached number 1 in mid-1973. Things wound down rather quickly. In 1974, he left Columbia for the tiny, religious-oriented Myrrh label, a stopover until his 1975 deal with ABC/Dot Records. There, his biggest hit was a new version of Hank Williams's "Mansion on the Hill."

Jerry Rivers, who had returned to fiddle with a reunited Drifting Cowboys, also worked with Nashville-based Buddy Lee Attractions, which booked Price. Rivers saw firsthand how Price's musical requirements adversely affected his bookings. "It was tough to book him," Rivers said. "[Promoters] wanted him, but he would bring a core band and Blondie [Calderon]. Then the promoter had to provide 21 pieces. We just couldn't get anything going on him for that reason. It was too costly."

In 1977, Price, Blondie, and former Cherokee Cowboys Emmons, Pete Wade, Tommy Jackson, Harold Bradley, Buddy Harman, and Buddy Spicher assembled in a Nashville studio for the ABC album *Ray Price and the Cherokee Cowboys Reunion*. The results were flat, although one single, "Different Kind of Flower," broke the Top 30.

A second reunion fared far better. In 1980 Willie Nelson was one of the biggest stars in any musical genre. That year, he and Price teamed up for *San Antonio Rose*, a duet album that served to revisit Price's 1961 Bob Wills tribute (which Willie had played on as a member of the band) and to revive the classic Price shuffle sound. Price sounded comfortable in the re-created surroundings, the old sound masterfully conjured by Emmons, fiddler Johnny Gimble, and several of Willie's band members. Most significant, the collaboration shot Price back into the country Top Five with a duet on "Faded Love," giving the lie to views that the old sound wasn't viable for him any longer. A Price-Nelson remake of "Don't You Ever Get Tired of Hurting Me" just missed Top 10 status. The album may have forced Price to reexamine his direction. Eventually, he began doing what many thought he should have done from "Danny Boy" on: mix his old and new sounds onstage to please the entire spectrum of fans.

Afterword

Thank you; it's about time. I was beginnin' to feel like Susan Lucci.

The Country Music Hall of Fame inducted Ray Price in 1996. He was characteristically blunt in accepting the honor, minus the tears many newly minted Hall of Famers display (real and staged) during the public ceremony. The remark surprised no one who knew him. He'd said it backstage to Kris Kristofferson, who as composer of "For the Good Times" officiated as Price was inducted. Kris, no stranger to blunt talk, urged him to use the remark in his acceptance speech.

Though by then he was spending time raising horses on his Mount Pleasant, Texas, ranch, Price never quit the road. His tour bus continued rolling across the country. In the '90s, a few standbys returned, including Jimmy Day, who reoccupied the old pedal steel spot until his death in 1999. The polarization of 30 years earlier was history. In remarkably good voice, Price now combined the best of old and new in a way that left fans in both camps eminently satisfied. In March 1999, Price was arrested on marijuana possession charges near his ranch, charges that drew (and deserved) little more than a wrist-slap. Anyone who ran with Willie as long as Price did was clearly familiar with the stuff, and pot had been around the western swing scene six decades before that.

In 2000, Price was profiled in the mainstream music press as well as the new alternative country publications like *No Depression,* as the result of his new *Prisoner of Love* album. Produced by Texas music veteran Randall Jamail, Price walked the line between old and new with varying degrees of success. Flawless on "Prisoner of Love," he fell into predictability with the grossly over-recorded Louis Armstrong hit "What a Wonderful World," then totally overreached trying to swing out on a Sinatra-styled "Fly Me to the Moon."

Price made clear that he didn't intend to get off the road anytime soon, but that resolve was tested in October of 2000 when Blondie Calderon died unexpectedly after heart surgery. Given their 33-year partnership, the loss devastated Price. Yet he sucked it in and, with a new pianist, continued touring. In 2002, he returned to the studio to record *Time* for Nashville-based Audium Records.

It was, as the album blurb proclaimed it, a homecoming. Nashville producer Fred Foster, who'd founded Monument Records in the '50s, produced a record that Don Law could have produced in 1959. The studio band, too, was a reunion. Backing Price were former Cherokee Cowboys Emmons and Pete Wade along with Price studio fixtures Harold Bradley, Pete Wade, Bob Moore, and Buddy Harman, all surviving members of the legendary

Nashville A-team. Supplemented by a few newer Nashville studio pickers, Price sang a mixture of material by the late Harlan Howard and by contemporary honky-tonk writers like Max D. Barnes and Texas songwriter Cindy Walker. He revived Walker's ballad "The Next Voice You Hear," a 1955 Hank Snow hit. Approaching 77, Price's voice was huskier, yet still remarkably supple and smooth, in the furrowed, softened way of fine, aged leather. In 2003 Price reunited with Willie Nelson for another Audium album.

However, despite the changes and evolution of Ray Price's career and music, one thing is certain: In the end, he'll surely be defined by the shuffle records of his youth, records that represented another mass infusion of southwestern music into Nashville that became the next-to-last building block of honky-tonk idiom (the Bakersfield Sound being the capper).

In the end, Ray Price did it his way, relished the kudos and withstood the criticism. He did it all to and for himself. And he's serene about it all, having written the book on nonconformity while creating a style that will certainly outlive him.

IV
Flaming
Guitars

Jimmy hits the bigtime: Bob Wills and His Texas Playboys, late 1944. Left to right: Noel Boggs, Jack McElroy (announcer), Joe Holley, Joe Galbraith (bus driver), Louie Tierney, Billy Jack Wills, Rip Ramsey, Bob Wills, Millard Kelso, Jimmy Wyble, Laura Lee Owens, Cameron Hill, Tommy Duncan. Most members of this edition of the band appeared on the Grand Ole Opry stage in December. (Courtesy Glenn White)

9

Sears' Jubileers to *Ocean's Eleven*

Jimmy Wyble

"Everything that happened to me after Bob Wills was because of Bob Wills," James Otis Wyble declared. "As I child, I loved music, and I became influenced by people like Django Reinhardt and Charlie Christian, but [in the Texas Playboys] it was also sort of a party and an emotional high. When Bob hit the bandstand, we knew it was business. His words were 'Get it!' That meant play your heart out. And that's the most important thing and the most rewarding thing about being a musician."

It's safe to say that few western swing sidemen ever flew as far from the nest without losing their perspective as Jimmy Wyble. Over a 30-year span, the Texas native moved from Texas jazzman to western swing luminary to Hollywood's studios, jazz clubs, an appearance in the original *Ocean's Eleven* film, and, finally, to the status of a revered musical educator.

What's often overlooked is the scope of Wyble's impact during his days with Wills. While Wills's base of operations remained in the Southwest, the nationwide success of mid-1940s singles like "Hang Your Head In Shame" and "New Spanish Two-Step" gave Wyble's playing immense exposure. Country sidemen east of the Mississippi, particularly in Nashville, absorbed all the instrumental fire they could glean from Wills's (and Spade Cooley's) records. Western swing steel guitar, lead guitar, and fiddle solos were showing up on records made by southeastern and midwestern acts by the mid-1940s. In Alabama, Hank Williams, a Bob Wills fan, occasionally added drums to the Drifting Cowboys to play dance jobs.

Wyble's work with Wills had far-reaching repercussions. He was one of Hank Garland's first musical role models when the 16-year-old guitarist began working on the Opry with Paul Howard's Arkansas Cotton Pickers in 1946. Other guitarists there also took note of his work. Even Buck Owens, who played a simpler, more elemental style, took inspiration from his solos.

The names of those whom Wyble worked with onstage and in the studio speak for themselves: jazz greats Peck Kelly, Barney Kessel, Red Norvo,

Benny Goodman, and Anita O'Day, pop icons Dean Martin and Frank Sinatra. In western music, he worked with Bill Mounce, Wills, Cooley, and Hank Penny. He played sessions with Red Egner, T. Texas Tyler, and the Sons of the Pioneers. Over years of session work, he recorded with an even broader scope of artists, yet always kept his perspective: "I'm equally grateful for Hank Penny; I'm equally grateful to Bob Wills, to everyone that I worked for, including Spade Cooley."

Even in his western swing days, Wyble, slight and bespectacled, a shock of black hair swept back from his forehead, seemed more a hipster Clark Kent than a cowboy jazzman. He was part of the Texas-Oklahoma incubator that spawned amplified jazz guitar as we know it.

Black jazz guitar innovators Eddie Durham and Floyd Smith (who often played electric steel guitar in the 1930s) hailed from the Prairie states. So did Charlie Christian, the Texas native who absorbed inspiration from horn players and almost certainly heard pioneer western swing guitarists Bob Dunn, Jim Boyd, Leon McAuliffe, Zeke Campbell, and Eldon Shamblin. They weren't the only young jazz guitarists absorbing western swing on the radio. In Texas, Herb Ellis drew ideas from the western bands. So did Barney Kessel, who faithfully attended Bob Wills dances in his hometown of Muskogee, Oklahoma.

Pioneer musicians like the Light Crust Doughboys' Zeke Campbell recorded single-string guitar solos in the late 1930s, yet Wyble, who grew up in the same musically eclectic atmosphere as Christian, was surely the first in western swing to infuse Christian's innovative ideas into the idiom. He did it in Texas before World War II and in California during and after the war.

Wyble was born in Port Arthur, the refinery city along Texas's Gulf Coast, on January 5, 1922. "When I was a kid, six or seven," he remembered, "I spent a lot of time in a little country town outside of Port Arthur with an aunt of mine. And she had some Jimmie Rodgers records that I used to listen to and flip out over. It was shortly after that, that my folks bought me a little $7 Regal guitar."

An elderly lady in his neighborhood gave him his first guitar lessons; he took others from local machinist Raymond Jones. That informal instruction didn't sate his musical appetite. Wyble taught himself from Nick Lucas and Nick Manoloff instruction books and absorbed more from the groundbreaking jazz records by guitarist Eddie Lang and his partner, violinist Joe Venuti.

When Wyble bought his first record in the mid-1930s, he discovered his first jazz guitar hero: Belgian gypsy virtuoso Django Reinhardt. He never forgot that particular 78 disc: "It was Django's recording of 'Night and Day.' I tried very desperately to copy Django. I could only get three or four bars; his technique was so beyond me." As a teenager, he played informally around Port Arthur with his friend Tiny Moore, a fiddler/guitarist who later metamorphosed into an electric mandolinist and musical innovator in the postwar Texas Playboys.

After Tiny left to work in Louisiana, Jimmy joined Sears' Jubileers, a local band sponsored by the Port Arthur Sears store that evolved into a better-known western swing band called the Port Arthur Jubileers. Playing in clubs, he found inspiration listening to Bob Dunn, the groundbreaking electric steel guitarist renowned for his work with Milton Brown, Cliff Bruner, and Moon Mullican as well as for leading his own band, the Vagabonds.

In 1940, the year he turned 18, Wyble finally heard Charlie Christian. After joining the Benny Goodman Sextet in 1939, Christian revolutionized jazz guitar with his work on Goodman Sextet anthems "Flying Home" and "Seven Come Eleven" as well as "Solo Flight" with the full Goodman Orchestra. Christian used the primitive electric amplification of the day to create thick, saxophone-like tonalities as he played his solo lines; his advanced harmonic ideas pointed directly to bebop.

His records were a musical epiphany to many, Wyble among them. "[He had] a kind of energy that caused an immediate emotional response," he said. Jimmy's father upgraded his son's equipment to a Gibson ES-150, the first successful electric guitar, and a matching amp—identical to Christian's own equipment. When Wyble graduated from high school in 1941, his future was certain. He soon moved to Houston and joined the brilliant and reclusive jazz piano virtuoso Peck Kelly, whose obscurity and style inspired the 1940 pop hit "Beat Me Daddy, Eight to the Bar," with its tale of a pianist in "a little honky-tonk village in Texas."

Kelly left a deep impression: "He was a most remarkable pianist. He had an incredible harmonic sense that was *far* above any of [his sidemen]. He was such a strong player that even people who were not musicians were just absolutely fascinated by what he was doing. He was popularized by [the hit song], but Peck was much more than that. He was more like an Art Tatum–Oscar Peterson type of player."

Wyble didn't stay long with Kelly before gravitating to Houston's fertile western swing scene. For a time he played guitar with Bill Mounce and His Sons of the South, making his first recordings with that band for Bluebird in October 1941. He later moved over to Houston's popular Dickie McBride and His Village Boys, where he played guitar alongside guitarist Cameron Hill as a twin-guitar ensemble. Wyble played lead; Hill generally played rhythm.

World War II took a toll on Houston's musical scene, drawing away musicians to the military and defense jobs as it did everywhere else. Despite a slight build and poor vision, Wyble enlisted in the Army in September 1942 and spent a year stationed near San Antonio. Discharged in the fall of '43, he headed back to McBride and the Village Boys. The band now included pianist Millard Kelso, who'd briefly played with Bob Wills.

The band heard stories about the booming dance-hall scene in Los Angeles and wanted to get in on the high pay and enthusiastic audiences. In December of '43 several of McBride's musicians, including Wyble, Hill, and Kelso, headed to L.A. They landed at KTRH Radio. The station became Bob Wills's new home base after he relocated the Texas Playboys to Hollywood from Tulsa earlier in the fall. Aware of the tens of thousands of longtime fans newly landed in the L.A. basin, Wills wanted to tap that audience.

Kelso quickly regained his piano seat in the Playboys, then suggested that his buddies, Wyble and Hill, jam with the band. Wills listened and hired both guitarists on the spot. He also brought in the dynamic Oklahoma steel guitarist Noel Boggs, recently with Hank Penny. Wyble, Hill, and Boggs soon created an electric string ensemble similar to the one that Texas Playboys Leon McAuliffe and Eldon Shamblin invented in Tulsa. The three musicians played solo passages in harmony. It gave the band two voices: one of fiddles, the other of amplified guitars replacing the horn sections of the old Tulsa band. It differed totally from the old Tulsa ensembles. Boggs's tone was stronger and more biting than McAuliffe's smoother Hawaiian musings. Wyble and Hill played in close harmony, Wyble doing most of the soloing as Hill played the second harmony parts.

All those niceties were lost on Wills, a from-the-gut musician who got his start fiddling at West Texas house parties as a kid. That fall, the bandleader moved beyond his usual Southwest circuit by organizing a Vaudeville tour with the Music Corporation of America. He and a troupe would travel the Midwest, Southeast, and East Coast through the end of 1944 into 1945. Fastidious about visual as well as musician presentation, Wills realized the onstage impact the "twin guitars" had.

Jimmy and Cameron both played the Gibson ES-150 electrics that Charlie Christian (who'd died of tuberculosis in 1942) made famous. These instruments were utilitarian and unadorned. Wills wanted everything on the stage to project an image of elegance and class. To that end, he handed Jimmy and Cameron a check for $1,100 to buy fancier matching guitars. They each chose golden-blond Epiphone Emporer acoustic archtop models with pickups attached for amplification.

These were heady days for Jimmy Wyble. Wills paid the Playboys top dollar. Wyble recalled receiving $85 in 1944 dollars for three days of work, well above union scale at the time: "Bob paid—always—all of the hotel bills. He didn't buy the food we ate, but he paid all the hotel bills, all the transportation." During that tour, the Playboys made their infamous visit to the Grand Ole Opry, one of the few notable moments in a fatally flawed tour.

A show that mixed mundane stage performers with Wills's cowboy jazz, a style still exotic to the world east of the Mississippi, was doomed to fail.

"After this tour," said Wyble, "we came back to L.A., and we didn't go do our radio show and then everybody disperse. We went to a little place we had rented in the San Fernando Valley on Ventura Boulevard. We'd set up our instruments, go eat and play. We just played continually, just loving it. That was [the Village Boys'] routine before we ever left Houston."

In January 1945, Wyble made his most famous recordings as a Texas Playboy: Fred Rose's novelty tune "Roly Poly," sung by Tommy Duncan. Trumpeter Brashear, the Playboys' sole horn player, conceived the opening, where Wyble and Hill quoted the kiddie song "London Bridge is Falling Down." He wrote out the arrangement and Wyble, a reading musician, carefully taught non-reader Hill his part.

Although he normally took a laissez-faire approach with his soloists, for this number Wills asked Jimmy to play something specific on his solo: "The only direction Bob ever gave me was on 'Roly Poly.' We ran it down for a balance. And after the first run-down was over, he said, 'Jimmy—oftentimes when we're working a dance, you'll kind of walk up the guitar. You'll start down low, and you'll walk up.' And he conveyed to me in that way that he wanted me to play octaves. That's how I arrived at that little lick."

Wyble's aggressive, incandescent solo quoted the melody of the swing favorite "Them There Eyes." His left hand began "walking" the two-note octave phrases up the guitar's neck, as Bob asked. Never did he or Hill consider inserting any Charlie Christian licks. "We never felt it would be proper to steal his licks. We tried to play in that vein, but not quoting from it." His pride in working with Wills never diminished. "It was not just a band," he recalled wistfully. "It was family. It was pretty much party time all the time, but controlled. Nobody missed a gig." He also got ample solo space out on Wills's hit recording of "New Spanish Two-Step." During that era, those records left their mark on country guitarists everywhere.

Cameron Hill married Wills vocalist Laura Lee Owens and headed back to Houston in mid-1945. Wyble returned to Texas for a time, then headed back to California and joined Hank Penny's band along with Noel Boggs. That job ended following Penny's infamous fight with jazz-hating dance promoter Foreman Phillips.

The guitarist recorded what can only be called a white R&B session for King Records featuring former Texas Playboy fiddler Buddy Ray on vocals. Slated for release on King's Queen Records subsidiary, the session remained unissued until 2000. He hung around the L.A. studios, meeting such renowned guitarists as Al Hendrickson and George Van Eps. He also saw cross-genre prejudices among some players. "A lot of musicians in both fields, country and jazz, were closed," he said. "Like some of the country players that I worked with or listened to [who] weren't tuned in to that aspect of the music. But I swear Noel Boggs and a lot of the people like Hank Penny were wide open, and I think better musicians because of it."

He spent time in the studios playing on King western swing sessions with Penny, the Fiddlin' Linvilles, Jimmie Widener, Red Egner, and Tex Atchison through 1946. Cameron Hill returned to Los Angeles that year. By year's end, the pair had reunited the twin guitars as part of Spade Cooley's reorganized band, which featured full brass and reed sections. Wyble worked on and off with Cooley for the next six years. He, Hill, and Boggs made Cooley's first RCA recordings in 1947, particularly "Boggs Boogie" and "Texas Playboy Rag" (the best of Cooley's big-band efforts), which were nearly as stunning as their work with Wills.

Since Cooley largely remained on the West Coast, doing short tours in other Western states, Jimmy had ample time for studio work. He did some sessions with members of the Cooley band and backed Cooley vocalist Red Egner on his King recordings. Though he, Hill, and Boggs left in the fall of 1948 to join Tommy Duncan's new band, Wyble and Boggs eventually returned to Cooley when Duncan's career ran out of steam in 1949. Wyble stayed with Cooley and was a featured soloist on tunes like the neoclassical "Bach Boogie," until he left in 1953.

His departure allowed Wyble to become more involved with the Los Angeles jazz scene. He also led the band on Hank Penny's short-lived TV show and recorded his first solo album. The light, airy *Diane* featured swinging instrumentals backed by bass, accordion, and clarinet. That same year he played on a Clef Records session with Barney Kessel. He also indulged his desire to devote more serious study time to guitar. By 1955, he was working with Latin jazz virtuoso Laurindo Almeida when Red Norvo approached him.

One of the pioneers of jazz vibraharp, Norvo, the former husband of jazz singer Mildred Bailey, became renowned for an innovative swing orchestra he led in New York in the 1930s. Through his mid-1940s work with Charlie Parker and with Woody Herman's legendary, modernistic "First Herd" (and the smaller Herman combo, the Woodchoppers), Norvo became one of the few swing-era jazzmen to successfully transition to bebop, the style Charlie Christian, Parker, and Dizzy Gillespie coaxed from swing music.

In 1950, Norvo's drumless trio with guitarist Tal Farlow and bassist Charlie Mingus earned great renown. Jimmy's friend, guitarist Bill Dillard, had been Norvo's guitarist after Farlow's departure. When Dillard died in a fire, Norvo tapped Wyble to replace him. The guitarist jumped at the chance, only to soon find himself in a life-and-death battle of his own.

From the time he worked around Houston in 1941, Wyble adopted a jazzman's lifestyle that included plenty of pot, bennies, and booze. He was not alone; Cameron Hill even did a brief jail sentence after being nailed for pot possession in Texas. Wyble's demons were full-blown in the mid-1950s. "I drank a lot," he admitted. "I took a lot of pills. I smoked a lot of pot, and by the time I met Red, I was down on my hands and knees." Before an important job, he'd lay off and sober up. The job over, he went into the bottle head first. It was coming home to roost: "I got to the point where I was hemorrhaging, going to the doctor and the doctor's telling me, 'Well, you have to go to the hospital, and you're gonna die if you don't quit drinking.' And I'd sober up and start over." One afternoon, amid a punishing binge, he realized he had a job with Red that night and couldn't cut it. He called Red:

> I said, "I can't lie to you. I can't go to work because I'm too juiced and out of it to hit the guitar." And Red said to me, "Well, gee, did you ever think that you might have a problem?" He said, "If you can drive, you come to work tonight and hold your guitar. Sit on the bandstand, but come."
>
> I went. And Red was absolutely magnificent in the fact that he pretended to *ignore* all this. I bet I didn't play two notes all night. But after the job, he said, "Jim, I want you to drive me somewhere." I said, "Well of course, Red." And I was hung over from pills, booze and it was about 2 in the morning. We drove to this little house and a whole bunch of people were inside. He said, "You don't have to stay. This is an AA meeting. I'll get a ride home." And just instinctively, I said, "I'd better stay." And consequently, I sobered up and stayed with Red. That was 25 years ago.

As he fought his way back, Jimmy Wyble rededicated himself to his music. He toured constantly with Norvo, though he briefly rejoined the Texas Playboys in the mid-'50s before returning to Norvo. After Red renewed his friendship with Frank Sinatra, a vocalist with a jazzman's instinct, the singer took the small group on tour with dazzling results, including the now-legendary 1959 Melbourne, Australia, performance captured on tape and considered by many to be one of Sinatra's finest moments onstage. During the opening instrumental numbers, Wyble got ample solo space on the band's blazing version of "The Devil and the Deep Blue Sea."

In 1960, the Norvo quintet became the nucleus of Benny Goodman's touring band for a time in the late 1950s, part of the group Goodman took to Europe. There, they worked within the larger band and backed singer Anita O'Day. Sinatra brought the combo into *Ocean's Eleven*. Jimmy appears with Red and the band on one of the film's musical high points: backing Dean Martin on his invigorating performance of "Ain't That a Kick in the Head," a Martin ditty embraced in the 1990s by Gen-Xers who embraced the Vegas-style "lounge" ethos the film helped establish.

Jimmy himself relocated to Vegas after leaving Red in 1964, then tried unsuccessfully to carve a niche in jazz-conscious San Francisco in 1967, the year of the Summer of Love. Finally, he headed back to L.A., where he plunged into studio work. Along with others in the bustling studio scene there, he played on all types of sessions: country, rock, jazz, film sound-tracks, and TV shows. He recorded with the Sons of the Pioneers and Roy Rogers, and he spent 1978–80 as the guitarist for the L.A. run of the musical *Evita*.

When he wasn't recording, he wrote and taught. Among his better known, successful students are gifted traditional swing guitarist Howard Alden and Steve Lukather of the jazz-rock fusion band Toto. Jimmy realized that decades of accumulated experience afforded him another dimension. "I began looking inside myself," he reflected, "and examining my thoughts about what I would really like to play on the guitar if it's not involved with a group, with not anything but me and my guitar, what will emerge."

The Charlie Christian disciple, who built his reputation on single-string improvisational lines, now embraced fingerstyle jazz guitar, using his thumb and fingers instead of a pick, and multi-line "contrapuntal" improvisations that involved two single-string improvisational lines played in harmony, a sort of twin guitars concept played by one. He wrote two instruction books: *Classical/Country* and *The Art of Two-Line Improvisation*, still in print. He became part of his friend Tony Rizzi's recording band, the Five Guitars, which played arranged versions of Charlie Christian solos.

The western swing revival of the 1970s gave him surprisingly little chance to reprise his vital role in the field, except for a unique group of former Texas Playboys that Merle Haggard assembled for a TV special. He remained deeply flattered by the admiration shown him by longtime admirers like Asleep at the Wheel's Ray Benson, and retained his friendships with Hank Penny and other surviving western players from his past. In recent years, living again in San Francisco, he has focused almost exclusively on writing instruction books like *Concepts for the Classical and Jazz Guitar*.

Wyble, who turned 80 in 2002, explained his durability this way: "I learned to be myself. Not to be Tal Farlow, not to be Junior Barnard, but to be Jimmy Wyble. That's what I learned from Red Norvo. And I also learned that the only thing you can do and the best thing you can do is to be honest about your music, not to play a certain way, to be commercial or to impress somebody that's sitting in the audience but just to honestly play your instrument, and be yourself as a musician."

At *Hometown*: Flame one: Speedy and his Bigsby; Flame two: Bryant tears his Tele a new one.

10

Flippin' the Lid

Speedy West and Jimmy Bryant

Skid rows are the same everywhere. In Los Angeles, only balmier weather separates the slums there from the run-down, violent, unpredictable areas of New York or Chicago. In 1947–48, a skid row surrounded a section of Pico Boulevard, an area that had its share of shootings, stabbings, brawls, and an occasional murder. The Fargo Club was on Pico. Murphy's Bar, a tiny dive with an even tinier stage surrounded by somebody's idea of western fencing, was a block away. Speedy West played his homemade steel guitar there nightly when he wasn't working a day job to support his family.

One night, a lean, dark-haired man walked up and introduced himself. "Hey, cat," the man exclaimed in a Georgia accent crackling with self-confidence. "I like your pickin'. I'm playin' down the street at the Fargo Club. When you get off, come down and dig me."

Speedy went down to the Fargo, and dug—*really* dug—the playing of this cocksure guitarist. Decades later, as he remembered that first time he heard Jimmy Bryant play, the awe remained in his voice. "I just couldn't believe what I heard. He was playing great then." The two began jamming together. "I just knew that it was right, and he did, too," West said. He had no idea that Bryant had been playing guitar only a couple of years.

Their partnership teamed a fiddler-turned-guitarist with the man who first put pedal steel guitar into country music. Together, they created one of the most intuitive, daring, yet thoroughly musical instrumental teams of all time, whose records still delight and astound the uninitiated with a magic that time and technology can't diminish.

"You know what it was?" asked veteran jazz drummer Roy Harte of West and Bryant. "These guys had six ears. Most of us have only two. They could hear what was coming as well as what they were playing and what was past." Harte should know. He played alongside the pair on their own records, on Cliffie Stone's *Hometown Jamboree*, and on stage and countless recording sessions.

While West and Bryant's music incorporated western swing, it also epitomized the futuristic, progressive optimism that flourished in postwar Southern California even amid the Cold War, a time when TV, jet flight, and the atom bomb were new and unnerving, yet exhilarating. Their music reflected all that in ideas that flew hot and heavy from two fearless, audacious minds who followed the traditions of other instrumental teams: Charlie Parker and Dizzy Gillespie, Joe Venuti and Eddie Lang, Django Reinhardt and Stephane Grappelli, or Bix Beiderbecke and Frankie Trumbauer.

The pair built upon a western swing tradition that began in 1940 within Bob Wills's Texas Playboys when guitarist Eldon Shamblin's and steel guitarist Leon McAuliffe's experiments with playing solo lines in harmony created the amplified string ensemble. It generated landmark Wills instrumentals like "Twin Guitar Special" and "Takin' It Home." The amplified strings not only dominated Wills's postwar sound but profoundly influenced postwar Nashville music.

Owing to a longtime friendship with Bud Isaacs, who established the pedal steel guitar in Nashville with his groundbreaking work on Webb Pierce's 1953 hit "Slowly," Speedy never pushed the point of who was first. But unless researchers unearth an antecedent, it appears that he was indeed country's pedal steel pioneer, contrasting with non-pedal players like McAuliffe or Noel Boggs.

Listening to Speedy was like peering into a volcano. He performed a dizzying yet carefully crafted sequence of crazy, swooping runs and futuristic chords that he exploded like a bubble of molten lava. His left hand galloped the fretting bar up the neck, tightening his grip to make the strings chatter, then building to a crescendo that ended in a bouncing, crashing chord, always in tempo. Cutting edge as he was, his tasty, commercial versatility made him one of Hollywood's most popular session musicians in the '50s.

The steel guitar is a complex instrument. Playing it properly requires dead-on precision and impeccable timing. To that end, most steel players, whether playing electric or acoustic, pedal or non-pedal "lap" models, sit perfectly still, soberly contemplating the neck or necks as they play. Speedy broke those rules with his unprecedented onstage physicality. The few existing films of him and Bryant in action are a study in flamboyance. Even in the days of early TV, he played to the camera, grinning at the audience and at Bryant as he clowned, mugged, and swept his hands over the neck as if conjuring up a spirit.

Bryant, too, was a musical dervish who poured forth torrents of cleanly executed notes, clever slurs, glissandos, and advanced harmonic ideas. Feeding off each other, with split-second precision, he and Speedy often began in ensemble, flew solo for their respective breaks, then merged flawlessly to end a song. Today's fancy electronic effects boxes didn't yet exist. Bryant and

Speedy generated all their adventurous sounds with nothing more than nimble hands and fingers, picks, and fertile and creative minds.

Bryant's musical roots differed from Southwest-born country jazzers like Eldon Shamblin, Jimmy Wyble, Cameron Hill, and Junior Barnard, who drew inspirations from jazz guitar innovators Eddie Lang, Charlie Christian, and George Barnes. While echoes of Django Reinhardt, Bryant's primary influence, were seldom far away, bebop lines showed up in his solos alongside flashy string effects, frenzied chord melody passages, and dazzling technique. Yet he never lost his flair for hard country. He proved that in the '60s by writing "The Only Daddy That'll Walk The Line," a 1968 hit for Waylon Jennings that became one of the country superstar's signature tunes. One of the first musicians to play Fender's "Broadcaster" electric guitar (best known by its now-legendary name "Telecaster"), Bryant's use of the instrument realized Leo Fender's vision of a durable instrument with ample tonal color and sustain, achieved by anchoring the strings in the guitar's body like a steel guitar.

Billy Strange played rhythm guitar with the pair on their records, other artists' sessions, and on *Hometown Jamboree*. "Jimmy's facility was unbelievable, to say the least," he reflected. "It seemed to me, always, Jimmy's head was about a yard and a half ahead of where his hands came up." Strange found their mixture of both visual and musical excitement irresistible: "I think it was as much the showmanship as the playability of what they did. They got up there, and they knew how to sell what they were puttin' out."

Country-rock guitar innovator Albert Lee said in 1987 of Bryant: "I loved his technique, the incredible speed and definition in his playing, and his choice of notes. It was kind of country swing without being too far out. I just liked what he was doing with the guitar; I think it was more exciting than what else was going on at the time. He was getting this great sound out of his Telecaster when a lot of people playing that type of music would have been playing on a hollow-body Gibson."

Cliffie Stone, who gave both West and Bryant their breaks by putting them on *Hometown Jamboree* and by using them on Capitol recording sessions, never quit admiring them. Interviewed in 1996, he reflected that "Speedy was a trickster on the steel guitar. He had certain tricks that he could do, that would grab your ear, and Bryant was just playing his ass off on the guitar, and guitar players thought he was great."

For both men, that greatness began humbly.

Wesley Webb West was born January 25, 1924, in Springfield, Missouri, to Finley and Sue West. A linotype operator in a local gospel publishing house, Finley played guitar and also sang gospel in his off time. Wesley's neighbors, the Clines, provided another musical gateway. Each of the three Cline brothers played a string instrument—steel guitar, banjo, or guitar.

Their dad suggested that Wesley needed his own guitar, and Finley bought him a $12 Hawaiian guitar.

He played constantly, either with Finley or with the Clines, and like any kid enthralled by an instrument, he craved a top-of-the-line model. He soon saw a steel-bodied National resonator model at a local music store. For a family of the Wests' modest means, its $125 price tag put it out of reach. Wesley cried constantly over the instrument, stressed to the point he wound up sick in bed. Finley generously sold his own guitar to buy his son the National. Wesley practiced harder than ever and won a prize in a ninth-grade amateur contest. He listened to Leon McAuliffe's work with Bob Wills and His Texas Playboys in Tulsa but also appreciated Dobroists Clell Summey and Oswald Kirby who worked with Roy Acuff on the Grand Ole Opry.

In 1941, with World War II on the horizon, 17-year-old Wesley married his first wife, Opal Mae. They lived in St. Louis for a year while Wesley worked in an ammunition factory and jammed in his off hours with his friend Cleat Jones. Back in Springfield, Speedy's parents divorced. Finley's pious bosses at the gospel-publishing house disapproved and forced him to quit. When Finley's father died, leaving a 200-acre farm in Strafford, Missouri, Finley bought out his brother and sister and took it over. Wesley and Opal moved there in 1942. With farming as vital to the war effort as bullets, Wesley was draft-exempt. Sixteen-hour days in the fields were common.

After V-J Day, Wesley still farmed but had more time for music. An Opry tent show came to Springfield in the spring of 1946, starring Eddy Arnold and Minnie Pearl. When Wesley heard Little Roy Wiggins, Arnold's steel guitarist, playing his trademark "ting-a-ling" chimes behind the singer, he began thinking seriously about a musical career of his own. He'd played locally and on jam sessions broadcast over KWTO in Springfield, where local country personality Slim Wilson mistakenly introduced him on the air as "Speedy" West. The name stuck. Ready to go electric, he bought a homemade, hand-carved solid-body steel from a local cop, paying for it in installments.

A sailor passing through the area told Speedy of the expanded musical opportunities in Southern California. There, the serviceman explained, musicians earned a then-staggering $25 per night. Those prospects proved irresistible. On June 13, 1946, with $150 in his pocket, Speedy packed Opal, their son, Donnie, his steel, and their other possessions into a 1936 Lincoln Zephyr and left the farm. Despite several breakdowns, they arrived in L.A. three days later, having covered 1,675 miles.

Ivy J. Bryant, Jr. started life in Pavo, Georgia, south of Moultrie, on March 5, 1925, the first of 13 children. The growing family put a burden on Ivy Bryant, Sr., a fiddler and local sharecropper. Needing every penny to survive, Ivy taught "Junior" to play the fiddle in hopes it would bring in money.

The kid earned his first pair of shoes and overalls from the $5 in tips he made fiddling and dancing on downtown Moultrie's streets. The extra money helped the Bryants amid the grim realities of the Depression, but laid a heavy, traumatic burden on Junior. "My grandfather used to lock him in the room or beat him if he didn't practice the fiddle," said John Bryant, Jimmy's son.

That harsh life, combined with hardscrabble sharecropping, didn't exactly portend a bright future. As he grew, Junior occasionally ran away from home. Once he wound up in Panama City, Florida, fiddling behind teenage Alabama singer Hank Williams. Nearing adulthood, Junior knew one thing for sure: this life was a dead end. He needed a way out.

Like many in similar positions, World War II became that escape hatch. Junior joined the Army in 1943 when he turned 18. Assigned to a combat infantry unit, he was in Europe in 1945 as the Allies gained ground. As his outfit battled into Germany, an exploding grenade left him with head and hand wounds that earned him a Purple Heart. He later told Speedy that Army doctors had to insert a steel plate in his skull. Transferred to a Washington, D.C., military hospital to recover, the Army noted his fiddling skills and reassigned him to Special Services. When he arrived, he found his assigned unit didn't need a fiddler. With nothing to do, he had ample time on his hands.

Listening to jazz guitar, he decided to take up the instrument and cadged a cheap Stella acoustic guitar from the Red Cross. His knowledge of fiddling and quick ear gave him an edge. He listened to the right people. Django Reinhardt, the Belgian Gypsy jazz guitarist whose records were popular among jazz fans in the states even before the war, became his first guitar hero.

Discharged after the war's end, he remained in Washington and used his military separation pay to purchase an electric guitar and amp. "He was playing around Washington a lot," said John Bryant. "He was into jazz then, and he was going under the name Buddy Bryant." Apparently, he learned piano somewhere and played in a club where in 1946 he met the hostess, Gloria Davis. She became his first wife.

As Speedy acclimated himself to California, he quickly found that his sailor informant back in Missouri wasn't lying. The boom continued in postwar California. Many soldiers born elsewhere liked the climate and decided to remain along with the millions of civilians who moved there from the South and Midwest to work in defense plants. But Speedy still had to support Opal and Donnie. To that end, he landed full-time work at a local Martin's dry-cleaning plant that served various local stores in the chain. After work, he explored L.A.'s vibrant western swing scene and spent several months with the Missouri Wranglers, a group of part-time musicians who played the VFW Hall in Southgate.

He also found a new musical role model in Earl "Joaquin" Murphey, who came to prominence with Spade Cooley and joined Andy Parker and the Plainsmen in 1946. Murphey's abilities to combine complex chord work with remarkably fluid, expressive single-string soloing set him apart from any other steel guitarist in the country. In Cooley's band, Murphey distinguished himself with his original instrumental "Oklahoma Stomp." With the Plainsmen, he recorded scintillating versions of "Honeysuckle Rose" and "Sweet Georgia Brown" based on Django's recordings. Speedy also admired Cooley's new steel player Noel Boggs, formerly with Bob Wills and Hank Penny.

Leaving the Wranglers, Speedy wanted a place to rack up playing experience. He found the best venues were local bars. That's how he wound up at Murphy's. As his zeal to succeed continued, he heard that Joaquin, who'd rejoined many of his former Cooley bandmates in Tex Williams's band the Western Caravan, had subsequently left Williams. Still teaching himself Murphey's style, Speedy applied for the job. He didn't get it, but Tex, impressed by Speedy's drive and desire, encouraged him to sit in with the band.

Speedy hadn't been in L.A. long when he spied country guitarist Buddy Kelly's amplifier, made by Fullerton, California, radio shop owner Leo Fender. Fender, who designed and manufactured steel guitars and amps on a limited-edition basis at the time, was quickly becoming a favorite of local western musicians. Bob Wills used Fender amplifiers and steel guitars. Speedy ordered one of Fender's "Professional" Model amplifiers with an all-wood body and handle and three vertical chrome-strips as trim on the front grille.

Leo called Speedy's house one day in 1947 to let him know his amp was ready. So was another one that Fender built for guitarist Earl Smith, a friend of Speedy's. The two drove together to Fender's shop in Fullerton, in Orange County. Assuming their stay would be brief, they took their wives and three-year-old sons. When they arrived around 5 P.M., Fender had them wait in the office. It seemed that Fender and associate Ray Massie hadn't quite finished the amps. "Our wives like to divorced us," Speedy laughed. "They set in the car from five in the afternoon till one the next morning, and we would not leave until we could take those amps with us. Leo wouldn't release them until they were the very best they could be made." When Speedy took possession of his, the solder joints were still warm.

In 1946, Bryant took Gloria to visit his family in Georgia before the couple moved to California. There, he met actor Russell Hayden, who played Hopalong Cassidy's sidekick "Lucky." For the next several years, Hayden and singer Eddie Dean helped Bryant eke out a living in Dean's films. He worked as an extra or bit player in various western films while playing the Fargo Club and, occasionally, another club called the Four Aces.

Speedy's state-of-the-art amp made him painfully aware of the limitations of his homemade steel. Late in '47, he contacted Downey, California, inventor/innovator Paul "P. A." Bigsby, who had built Joaquin Murphey's three-neck, non-pedal model. An eccentric, temperamental pattern maker and motorcycle racer, Bigsby knew precision work. Speedy enlisted him to build a *pedal* steel guitar.

The pedal steel, or "console" guitar as it was sometimes known, took shape in 1939. Pop steel guitarist–orchestra leader Alvino Rey and machinist John Moore designed and introduced the first for Gibson Musical Instruments, which marketed it as the "Electraharp." Creating certain chords on non-pedal steels required slanting the bar, a tricky technique. Even then, some chords were impossible to voice. The Electraharp's mechanical system pulled on the strings to alter string pitches. It not only allowed a player to create different chords and voicings, but to modulate smoothly between them. Rey's radio and record exposure didn't help popularize the new instrument, which didn't catch on in pop or country music.

Speedy wanted three necks like Murphy's Bigsby instrument, plus four foot pedals to alter pitch. On February 8, 1948, Speedy took delivery of an exquisite console: three necks in a body of golden bird's-eye maple, sitting atop a solid chrome stand complete with caster wheels to allow easy movement. The four foot pedals sat side by side, a design that has influenced pedal steels ever since. Speedy created his own tunings. "Today, guys that want to flatten a note do it by pushin' a pedal," he said. "I did it by taking my foot *off* the pedal." Lugging the instrument around took some doing. Jim Loakes, who later ran the stage crew at the *Hometown Jamboree* TV show, helped Speedy haul it in and set it up. "It sure was heavy," he recalled. "That case must have been three feet wide and five feet long."

Speedy's first big break came that spring when he landed his first major job. Spade Cooley, by then fronting a 23-piece orchestra, hired him to replace Noel Boggs. Suddenly Speedy had weekly exposure on Cooley's Saturday night *Hoffman Hayride* TV variety series. He asked Cooley if he was doing well enough to quit the dry cleaning plant. Cooley said absolutely. The next night, caught up in one of Cooley's famous booze-fueled rants and mass firing sprees, Speedy was fired and had no backup job. As usual, a contrite Cooley called later, asking him to forget it and come back. A man of strong principles, Speedy declined but decided to stick with music.

He worked at the Riverside Rancho for a while with Cooley vocalist Red Egner's own band, the Shamrock Cowboys. Then, one night, pianist-accordionist Billy Liebert and fiddler Harold Hensley, sidemen with Cliffie Stone's KXLA *Dinner Bell Round-Up* radio show in Pasadena, heard Speedy with Egner. They recommended the guitarist to Stone. "I thought, 'He's doing some marvelous things I never heard on the steel. This kid is a comer,' and he was a quick study," Liebert recalled.

It was the right break for Speedy, because Cliffie assisted Capitol country A&R boss Lee Gillette in locating new acts and arranging for backup bands for recording. With the year-long Musicians Union recording ban ended in late 1948, on January 21, 1949, Speedy got a call for his first recording session. Gillette was recording *Dinner Bell* singer and rhythm guitarist Eddie Kirk, a smooth, polished vocalist. In the wake of Eddy Arnold's and George Morgan's successes with their smooth, crooning voices, Gillette had Kirk cover Morgan's debut hit "Candy Kisses."

Gillette didn't ask for much. He simply wanted Speedy to re-create the simple steel licks and "ting-a-ling" chimes that Billy Robinson played on Morgan's record and Wiggins played on Arnold's hits. Speedy had no interest in parroting Wiggins and his cornball clichés, however. He was determined to dazzle:

> I wanted to play all the notes I could play. I started to take off on [aping] Joaquin Murphey, all the stuff I knew of Joaquin's. Liebert and Hensley called me off to the side and said, "Hey, Speed, don't do that!" I said, "Don't do what?" They said, "They want you to play it commercial. We told 'em you would. Play like Little Roy Wiggins." I said, "I don't wanna play that 'twinkle fingers' shit!" I wanted to play every note I knew, get it on that one record in case I didn't make another one. They said, "Look, we told them you wouldn't be temperamental." So I was disappointed, but I played commercial, like Little Roy Wiggins.

Liebert had good reason for offering Speedy this reality check; he'd gotten one three years earlier after injecting some jazz accordion riffs into a 1946 Tex Ritter Capitol session. Not long afterward, Cliffie and Gillette had a few drinks at Liebert's home when, the musician recalled, "Cliffie said, 'You know your trouble? You play too goddamn good.'" Lee Gillette agreed. "You learn one thing, and you'll be so busy, you won't even be able to stand it," he told Liebert. "I said, 'What's that?' Lee said, 'Just play what the producer wants.'" Liebert had just passed that lesson on to Speedy.

Kirk's record reached number 9 nationally that spring. Giving Gillette what he wanted left Speedy in a good position. One day, Speedy gave himself a reality check, this one about his Joaquin fixation: "I thought, this is foolish. As much as I like Joaquin's playing, I could never build a name for myself bein' a carbon copy. So I never played another Joaquin lick. Not that I didn't enjoy him, but I threw it all out the door and started new. I wanted to make a style that people would recognize me by."

By early 1949, Speedy was working regularly with Hank Penny's Penny Serenaders and in that band he found a measure of freedom beyond anything he'd had before. The *last* thing that Penny ever wanted was any "twinkle fingers," as he loathed that sound even more than Speedy did. Speedy's playing on "Hillbilly Be-Bop" revealed the blossoming of his own distinct musical voice. "Speedy was brave," Hank said. "He had distinctive ideas of his own. . . . He was very good at tone and dynamics, young and full of vinegar. He would come in like a storm and did one hell of a job."

After Speedy spent a few months with Penny, Liebert and Hensley encouraged Cliffie to hire Speedy for his *Dinner Bell* show and for his Stone's band, which included Liebert, Hensley, lead guitarist Charlie Aldrich, Eddie Kirk, former Spade Cooley drummer Muddy Berry, and bassist Al Williams.

"Cliffie is the guy that probably opened more doors for me than anyone for recording and TV," Speedy reflected. "He wanted every person on that stage to be a star in their own right and have their own following. I owe him an awful lot." Merle Travis, a *Dinner Bell* cast member at the time, suggested that Speedy have Bigsby make a nameplate for his pedal steel to boost his name visibility. Bigsby crafted a bird's-eye maple panel that snapped onto the steel's front legs with Speedy's name inlaid on the front in ebony.

Bryant, meanwhile, was working at the Fargo Club, and as he jammed more with Speedy, they became close friends. In September 1949, Bryant did a record date he surely had to regret: a recording session for the local Modern label under his leadership ("Jimmy Bryant and the Sons of the Saddle"). The band included bassist Al Barker, Spade Cooley fiddler Cactus Soldi, and guitarist Sam Nichols, a competent enough band. Unfortunately, the vocals came from the thoroughly untalented vocalist Corky Carpenter and, on two unreleased tracks, the equally mediocre Hal Moore. It was hardly an auspicious debut.

With Cliffie's *Hometown Jamboree* TV show begun at year's end, Speedy recorded his first steel instrumental, "Steel Strike," at a January 10, 1950, Cliffie Stone recording session. Perhaps with the Kirk session in mind, Speedy was restrained and tasteful. The explosions would come soon enough.

By midyear, guitarist Charlie Aldrich had left Cliffie's band. Speedy and Liebert promoted Bryant to Cliffie, and Bryant soon got the call. He became "Jimmy" Bryant. On the TV show, West and Bryant drew on what they had learned from each other while jamming together. Their ensemble sound gave the band an entirely new texture. Billy Liebert said, "It worked right from the beginning. They both played so damn well."

A master showman, Cliffie saw their visual-musical confluence and made them an entity unto themselves by christening them "The Flaming Guitars." He went a step further, with production efforts that amazed Speedy: "They built a set, and we sat behind this frame. It had cut-out flames in front of it in different colors, and it looked like we was sittin' in a pit of fire. And they had one of those smoke machines and a wheel with a light and different color gels." On another occasion, Speedy took his flamboyance to new heights. At least once on a *Hometown* broadcast, he took the stops off the caster wheels of his Bigsby and literally rode it across the stage like a coaster wagon.

Cliffie, who began his career playing bass fiddle, understood the brilliance of their collaboration. "Speedy and Jimmy used lots of tricks onstage. And Bryant had probably the fastest action on the neck of a guitar that I've ever heard. I still don't think anybody's cut him," he said. "He had all the things you look for in a sideman. When he took a chorus, nobody could look at anyone else but him—he was a real showman. Jimmy was always there for me. He was never late on the job, and he was always onstage after inter-mission and always looked great—good lookin', handsome guy, clean, dressed, spic and span."

Capitol's country department changed leaders in 1950 when Lee Gillette's friend Ken Nelson, who'd previously worked for the label's transcription service, succeeded Gillette as head of Country A&R. Although he focused now on pop artists like Peggy Lee, Nat King Cole, and Dean Martin, Gillette continued producing Tennessee Ernie Ford. By midyear, he had paired Ernie with pop songstress Kay Starr on "I'll Never Be Free." Speedy and Jimmy were primed for the session. They stood out on both "Free" and the flip-side, the exuberant "Ain't Nobody's Business but My Own." Twinkle fin-gers? No way. He and Bryant's dazzling work made a great record a classic—and a double-sided smash. "Free" reached number 2 in country, number 3 in pop. "Nobody's Business" peaked at number 5 in country, number 22 in pop. Offers poured in for joint Ford-Starr personal appear-ances, including one from the Grand Ole Opry.

Set to appear on the show's Prince Albert Tobacco segment, broadcast nationwide over NBC and hosted by Red Foley, Ernie and Kay brought along only one sideman from the session—Speedy—to faithfully reproduce his part on the record. Things went well at the afternoon rehearsal at the Ryman Auditorium until a Nashville Musicians Union flunky strode in. He declared that because Speedy wasn't a member of the Nashville local, he couldn't play on the broadcast. Speedy never forgot the exchange.

"Look," Speedy said, pulling out his membership card from L.A.'s Local 47, "I'm in the biggest union in the United States, a lot bigger than you got here."

"That don't make any difference," the official snapped back. "You're not in this union, so you can't play the show!"

An incensed Red Foley jumped into the discussion, snarling, "If Speedy don't play the show, *none* of us play the show!"

The union enforcer backpedaled a bit. "Well, since he flew all the way back here, and he played on the record, we'll go ahead and let him play the show with Kay and Ernie, but," he cautioned Foley, "you're not to mention his name."

After the man left, Foley came over to Speedy. "Speedy, don't you worry about a thing. When we get on the air, they can't stop me. I can do any damn thing I want to."

And he did. "On the air," Speedy laughed, "you'd have thought it was my show and that Ernie and Kay come along for the ride, the way Foley just kept pluggin' me." Nashville guitarist Grady Martin, no stranger to country jazz, played Bryant's parts flawlessly as Ford, Starr, and Speedy performed both sides of the hit. "Grady played [the solos] note for note just like the record," Speedy remembered.

Two thousand miles away, *Hometown* aired. Jimmy was there, but the show lacked its star vocalist and steel player. Speedy heard what had transpired after he got back home. Cliffie called an intermission so the cast could listen to the Opry broadcast. Speedy recalled, "They had a radio backstage, and they [told me] when that came on and Grady played [Bryant's solo], Jimmy said, 'batshit!' It made him madder than hell!"

Bryant got his own outside date when Tex Williams asked him to play on an August 1950 session that produced "Wild Card," another of Tex's talking blues numbers. Since Tex's band no longer had guitarists Johnny Weis or Benny Garcia, Bryant was a smart choice. The record failed to score, yet Bryant's rapid-fire solo and juicy obbligatos behind Williams made it one of Tex's best later singles.

Leo Fender brought Bryant his new solid-body electric guitar sometime that year. He'd play other guitars, but the true Bryant sound came from Fender's instrument, originally named the Broadcaster. In early 1951, the Gretsch Company complained that the name encroached on its "Broadkaster" drums, on the market first. Fender switched to "Telecaster," and it became one of the most legendary electric guitars of all time. Jimmy's son John, a musician himself, recalled the memories of the night Leo walked into the Riverside Rancho with the new model: "My dad sat down at the edge of the stage and started playing it, and before you knew it, the band stopped playing, and everybody was sitting there watching him play this new guitar of Fender's."

Its strings anchored in the body exactly like a non-pedal steel guitar, the Telecaster possessed a remarkable level of sustain that gave it a bright, piercing tone, the diametric opposite of the thick tones characteristic of a hollow-bodied amplified guitar like a Gibson or Epiphone. Bryant not only used that tonality to his advantage, he often added grace notes or rapid-fire filigrees, slurred notes on a string that spiced up an instrumental.

West and Bryant recorded again with Ernie on the 1950 session that yielded another huge country and pop hit, "The Shot Gun Boogie." Speedy's remarkably restrained solo break, a flurry of strummed chords a la Alvino Rey, wasn't intentional: "I started to take a chorus and one of my fingerpicks flew off, so I just used my thumbpick and strummed, and grabbed the volume control. Notice there's no pickin' in it: just *Doo-wah!* It was one of the first takes, and that's the one they picked."

Speedy found new sounds by sheer ingenuity. To get the sound he used on "Shot Gun," he strummed the chord with his right hand, swooping the tone control with the same hand from bass to treble to get the *"Doo-wah!"* (the same principle used for guitarists' "wah-wah" pedals). He did it so often it became second nature to him.

His work on "I'll Never Be Free" landed him his own Capitol contract. In February 1951, he made his first solo records with the propulsive "Railroadin'" and "Stainless Steel," the first real West-Bryant instrumental duet. As the rhythm section of Kirk, Cliffie, and Berry cooked away, Speedy revealed both his individuality and his empathy with Bryant. Speedy urged Ken Nelson to sign Bryant as well.

Due to Ernie's hits, the pair—and much of the *Hometown* band—became first-call backup musicians for Capitol country sessions and for many country sessions on other labels. They played uncredited on Sheb Wooley's MGM recordings, Johnny Horton's earliest recordings for the tiny Cormac label, a session with musical satirist Red Ingle, with Roy Rogers, and singer Doye O'Dell's original recording of the trucker favorite "Diesel Smoke."

Speedy had no problem scheduling sessions. He had just one daily responsibility: Cliffie's *Dinner Bell Round-Up* show over KXLA from 11:30 A.M. through 12:30 P.M. Monday through Friday. Bryant, a *Hometown* regular, wasn't part of the *Dinner Bell* cast, but worked weekdays with Roy Rogers around 1951. He and West recorded with Rogers and Dale Evans in both 1951 and 1952.

One night after working several dates, a dead-tired Speedy leaned his guitar and amp next to the building that housed L.A.'s Radio Recorders studio, staggered into his car, and drove off. When he arrived for work at KXLA the next morning, Tennessee Ernie was on the air doing his morning *Bar Nothin' Ranch Time* disc jockey program. Speedy suddenly remembered what he'd left behind and panicked.

"Ernie was on his live morning radio show. I told him, 'You tell Cliffie that I'll be back but I gotta go check on my guitar, gotta see if I can find it, if no one stole it.'" Careening down the freeway toward Radio Recorders, his car radio tuned to KXLA, Speedy ("Speed," as Ernie called him) was startled to hear Ernie deliver a personal message: "Hey, Speed! Please slow down! Slow that car down, I know you're drivin' fast! Your guitar and amp's okay. Someone found them early this morning and took 'em inside the building!"

Jamming in an L.A. club.

Speedy's ubiquitous session work led Tex Ritter to quip, "You little curly-headed son of a bitch, I just heard a record a little while ago that you *weren't* on!" Ritter's joke had a basis in fact. Speedy's own handwritten logs indicated that between 1950 and 1955 he, with and without Bryant, played on more than 6,000 recordings with a total of 177 different artists.

Some of that notoriety came through his early pop-session experiences with Columbia Records A&R man Mitch Miller. History has been justifiably harsh in judging Miller's gimmicky, lowest-common-denominator productions with Frank Sinatra, Tony Bennett, and Rosemary Clooney. He undoubtedly saw gimmick value in Speedy's sound when he played on Frankie Laine and Jo Stafford's 1951 duet of Hank Williams's "Hey Good Lookin'" with Paul Weston's Orchestra. Speedy's trademark "gallop" lick, played as the duo sang "I got a hot rod Ford and a two-dollar bill," floored Miller.

The next day, Speedy's phone rang. "Mitch called me at the house, and he says, 'Speedy, when you get your check, it won't be a mistake, you'll get double money. From now on, everything you do at Columbia Records you'll get double money.'" Speedy advised Lee Gillette of the new arrangement. Gillette scoffed, and then called his friend Weston, who'd only recently left Capitol to join Columbia. After Weston confirmed the deal, Gillette doubled Speedy's pay, keeping it quiet to avoid upsetting the other musicians who worked sessions with him.

Pop producers and arrangers beyond Miller respected Speedy's talents. He recorded with the orchestras of Nelson Riddle and Billy May and backed pop singers from Sarah Vaughan, Dinah Shore, and Phil Harris to Frankie Laine, Jimmy Boyd, and Ella Mae Morse, as well as the duo of Bob Hope and Jimmy Wakely. In 1952, Spike Jones hired Speedy, Jimmy, Cliffie, and Eddie Kirk to record with some of his band for a series of RCA recordings issued as Spike Jones and His Country Cousins.

In November 1952 Speedy and Jimmy both recorded with Capitol recording artist Ferlin Husky, who at that point used the stage name Terry Preston. To come up with an appropriate introduction for "Undesired," a sympathetic tune about one tormented man's moves to suicide, Speedy rapped his steel bar and clicked his picks against the strings, an ingenious musical evocation of a dilapidated, detriorating mental state.

Speedy's schedule was intense during that time as he ran from studio to studio with and without Bryant. "At the time we cut these things, it didn't mean nothin' to us. We'd walk out on the sidewalk, and we'd be standin' out front and [if you'd] say, 'What'd you cut in there, Speedy?' If you give me a thousand dollars to tell me what songs you cut, I couldn't have done it to save my soul. I was on a lot of sessions that Jimmy wasn't on," he added.

In November 1953, Speedy joined the western group the Cass County Boys to accompany Bing Crosby on his cover of Arlie Duff's hit country recording of "Y'All Come." The song became a Top 20 hit single for Crosby in 1954. Speedy performed the song with Crosby on radio and TV. "I got paid for that session 15 times," he laughed. "The reason, at that time when that come out, Bing had a coast-to-coast radio show, and every time he played that record on there, the musicians on there, we'd get paid full session money. I'd go to the mailbox every three weeks, it seemed like, and I'd get another check."

Speedy was grateful for the work, but he stood his ground. One example involved Capitol western singer Jimmy Wakely. A smooth crooner with a number of hits under his belt, Wakely, though born in Arkansas, grew up in Oklahoma with Noel Boggs and preferred using his old friend on his sessions. When Speedy appeared in the studio, Wakely's attitude confounded him. The singer acted as if he was wary of Speedy's considerable skills. Confident in his ability, well aware of Wakely's fondness for Boggs, when Wakely phoned Speedy at the last minute to do another session, West had a quick, sharp response:

> I said, "Wait just a minute, Jimmy. I want to ask you something: Do you want me because you want Speedy West playing, or because Noel's not available?" He said, Why do you ask me that?" I said, "Every session I ever cut with you, you don't give me nothing to do," I said. "You're thinkin' I can't cut it, and I can play anything that you can sing." There was silence on the phone. He like to have died laughin'! He went all over the States when he was touring, telling people how I told his ass off.

At Capitol, Speedy got along with both Gillette and Nelson, crediting them with encouraging his and Jimmy's freewheeling approach to instrumentals: "Lee and Ken gave Jimmy and I an open door. We could write our own songs, which we liked to do because we got more royalties. We could use old country songs, old pop songs, anything we wanted to do was fine with them." On originals, if Speedy wrote it, his name came first on the label, above Bryant's. On Bryant compositions, the names were reversed.

How the pair created those performances is worth examining. Billy Liebert remembered how some songs jelled. "We'd walk in, there was nothing prepared," he said. "Sometimes it was a little complicated. I can just listen and write a chord sheet very quickly. Speedy would write the thing, but no one else had ever heard it until it was session time."

Billy Strange recalled:

> They were just things that Jimmy and Speedy would get together and dream up on their own. When we did them, everything was a head arrangement. Nobody wrote anything out. It was loose as a goose, but everything fell into place because those two guys were so damned inventive that you had to be inventive to keep up, even as part of the rhythm section.
>
> They would find noises electronically that they could replicate onstage. That was part and parcel of what made it fun, was the fact there was no kind of format. We had worked together as a live unit for so many years, that it was automatic. You didn't overplay your partner. You didn't try to "best" (outplay) the band, as it were. Those guys knew instinctively the right level to play at, and not only that, but the right notes to complement what the other guy was doing.

Speedy explained their creative process this way:

If it hit our minds, we'd try it right on the session. One of us might hum
a lick, and the other would start working out the twin guitar harmony to
it. If the lick didn't prove successful, we'd either put it out of our minds,
play it backwards, or hum another lick. I never did hear one of the songs
he wrote, and he never heard one of mine, until we got in the studio. We
did that on purpose, so we had a spontaneous sound; if we did ten takes,
we never played the same chorus twice.

    Sometimes Jimmy would stop and say, "What the hell's the matter with
you? Can't you think of something else?" I'd do him the same way. We did
this to get an exciting feel. We just let our minds run rampant. If we were
on a network television show, and a new thought struck us in the middle
of the dad-blamed show, we'd let loose and try to do it. It might be a *big,
bad mistake*, but it might be something real good, too, so we'd try it.

Roy Harte, who co-founded Pacific Jazz Records in 1952 and Nocturne
Records in 1954, had none of the snobbery some jazzmen had, especially
when it came to the West-Bryant sessions: "It was just like a jam session to
me. Bryant swung, he could swing. There are certain things on the records
when Speedy played something, what Jimmy did was repeat it on his guitar.
A lot of the things we hear, I smile at, because I know why they're there. It
didn't make any difference whether it worked out or not at the time. . . .
And then a couple of sessions later, one of them that didn't work out—
worked out!"

Among those that did was Speedy's 1952 composition "Pickin' the
Chicken," taken at a fast polka tempo that spotlighted Bryant's soloing on a
melody much like an old-time fiddle tune. Speedy came in, guns blazing,
throwing out slashing, high-register "ricochet" slurs. It's typical of the spon-
taneity of their recordings. Speedy's "Midnight Ramble" possessed a mus-
cular intensity featuring some of his most exciting work as he exploded
chords and furiously interacted with Jimmy. They reached a peak on the
white-hot "Comin' On," a number with energy to spare. On it, Bryant's fiery
fervor achieved a nearly sublime fluency. As Liebert and Speedy added licks
behind his solo, he leaped into a breathtaking bebop passage. During
Speedy's solo, Bryant switched to fiddle, returning with a fierce, swinging
break complete with stunning octave passage.

Bryant's syncopated, 1953 medium-tempo "Whistle Stop" had a harmonic and rhythmic feel similar to the big-band favorite "Tuxedo Junction,"
although Bryant added a few twists and turns of his own. Speedy added the
"whistling" effects with his steel bar. The furious, unrelenting "Speedin'

West" defined virtually Speedy's entire style in the space of one number. Bryant's "Hometown Polka" was another cleanly executed, commercial melody obviously named for the TV show.

With his broadcasting background qualifying him as an expert witness, Cliffie remembered that many Speedy-Jimmy recordings were "immediately accepted by many radio stations because they were hot instrumentals, there was no vocal, and a lot of the stations used them for themes, for opening a radio show, before the news, after the news. So they got a lot of exposure." Speedy agreed: "We got fan mail and performance royalties from all over the world."

Cliffie seldom played bass any longer because of his *Hometown* duties, yet he loved picking up the instrument again when Jimmy and Speedy did their sessions. He tried to play on as many as he could. Speedy recalled his friend paying a price: "Each session Cliffie played on, he said, 'I'll never record with you bastards again.' We actually saw blood run off his fingers, since we done so many uptempo things and his calluses [on his fingers] left him. I've seen him hold his left or right hand up, either one, and blood dripped off the end of his fingers."

One of the duo's most remarkable recordings wasn't an original. In 1952 they recorded a barn-burning rendition of the Rodgers and Hart pop standard "Lover," a 1948 instrumental hit for Les Paul on Capitol, the first to showcase Les's groundbreaking guitar-overdub techniques. West and Bryant reworked it into a torrid feature for Speedy, Bryant adding his own whirlwind solos live, without a single overdub. It remained in the vaults until 1997. Why? Speedy pointed the finger at Capitol and Les's clout with the company in the early '50s, when his hits with Mary Ford were flying high. Capitol didn't want to issue a tune that Les had already recorded.

A drive across the desert inspired Speedy's dreamy, waltz-tempo "Sunset" with sensitive accordion accompaniment (and a solo) from Liebert: "I was comin' across the desert, comin' home from Las Vegas. And I saw a beautiful sunset on the desert. I was hummin' that to myself. When I got home, I got my guitar out. I never took my guitar in the house, but I took it in and wrote that thing."

Given the low-tech recording processes of the mid-1950s, Bryant and Speedy's near-perfect audio balance was remarkable but achieved simply: "We had just one microphone between the two of us, and we controlled our own balance, which come out great because we done it ourselves, on our recordings. Sometimes, Jimmy'd sit in a plain old folding chair, but we always just used one microphone for both of our amps."

Most of their instrumentals had no title when recorded, save a generic temporary name like "Opus One." According to Jimmy's son John, coming up with titles often became a husband-wife collaboration: "He'd come home and say to my mom, 'We need 10 titles.' And they'd just sit there and think things up."

The only person who had some difficulty after sessions was Liebert, who was charged with translating their playing into musical notation. Liebert wrote the lead sheets needed by their publisher, Central Songs, the West Coast publishing company co-owned by Cliffie, Ken Nelson, and Lee Gillette. Liebert remembers: "All those damn notes, I wrote those things down. And I had to take a sheet and slow it down and make it an octave lower. I played some of those licks and they were correct as hell, but they weren't easy to do. It should have been put in a folio, although there aren't too many guitar players who could play that."

One good example would be their playful 1953 recording of "Jammin' with Jimmy." The Bryant original began with him and Speedy playing a catchy, riff-based melody in harmony, and Strange, Cliffie, and Harte bouncing the rhythm beneath. The two are playful, seemingly teasing and surprising each other with their swinging, witty improvisations. Bryant added a swinging fiddle break, humming and grunting in unison with the extraordinarily driving solo. Speedy teased him about it after they finished the take. He remembered Bryant's acerbic answer: "Aw, batshit!" "I was gettin' into it!"

At the same session, Speedy recorded his own "This Ain't the Blues," whose harmonic ideas, he said, came "from Woody Woodpecker's theme song." With an almost rolling feel in the beginning, Speedy added his "doo-wahs" and his "chattering bar" effect, which ended as he bounced the bar to explode a chord. He created the chatter with astonishing simplicity: "I tightened my left hand like you'd grab the rung of a chair and squeeze until your arm shakes and vibrates—that's the way I gripped the bar, until my arm started shakin.' This was done, of course, real quick, as I went up the neck."

In late 1953, the pair recorded their only actual album together: *Two Guitars Country Style,* which mixed West-Bryant originals, steel-guitar standards showcasing Speedy, and fiddle tunes Bryant played flawlessly on guitar.

Jimmy used a different guitar for part of his September 2, 1954, session: a prototype of the new double-neck Stratosphere Twin guitar. Although Bryant later claimed to own part of the company, the company's actual owner was Speedy's old Missouri jam-session friend Russell Deaver, and his brothers Fabor and Red. The instrument had both a standard six-string neck and a 12-string neck, its pairs of strings tuned in thirds so that melody lines seemed to be played in harmony. Bryant not only learned the instrument, he wrote songs around it for this session, including the slow, atmospheric "Deep Water," the instrument adding rich, full chords comparable to Speedy's chord melodies. "Stratosphere Boogie," one of their more popular tunes, took the instrument to new heights as Bryant pulled complex, high-velocity flurries of notes from an instrument he'd only recently acquired, much the way he mastered guitar in the years just after the war.

Aside from adapting fiddle tunes to guitar, Bryant was no slouch playing standard, garden-variety country fiddle. Speedy and most of the *Hometown* band appeared on a series of radio transcriptions featuring Tennessee Ernie Ford recorded for Missouri-based RadiOzark. These extraordinary transcriptions feature the band playing superbly behind Ernie, with Speedy and Hensley the dominant players. On occasion, Bryant joined the lineup, and on one such visit, he and Hensley played an extraordinary twin-fiddle version of "Arkansas Traveler." His polished playing demonstrated much about his understanding of the fiddle—and his skills at translating fiddle tunes to guitar.

Leo Fender continued relying on local musicians to refine his equipment. "We spent a lot of time out at the factory," Billy Strange remembered. "Speedy, Noel Boggs, Jimmy Bryant, and I—the four of us would go out there and just play around as much as we could and help them with the design, and tell them things that we wanted to see put on the instrument."

While the Bryant-West partnership was still going strong in the fall of 1954, Bryant's attitude and demeanor began changing for the worse. "I remember he wanted to sing and Ken said, 'Hell, you're not a singer. You're a great guitar player,'" said Speedy. Jimmy wanted to play bolder, more experimental music than even the music that his collaborations with Speedy engendered. Among the *Hometown* band's hard-drinking musicians, Bryant was first among equals, and, the more he drank, the worse his demeanor got. Even without the booze, he could lay on the attitude.

Capitol's tape machine preserved one example of Bryant's pique on September 2, 1954. They were recording Speedy's instrumental "Flippin' the Lid," based on the traditional "Fly Away, My Pretty Little Pink." As Bryant prepared to kick off the take, the following exchange took place between guitarist and producer.

NELSON: "Master, Twelve thousand, nine hundred and ninety-nine, take 12."

BRYANT (sings): *"Dee-dee-dee-dee-da-da da-da doo doo doo doo-do-do do do—doo-dah—do-dah!"*

NELSON (agitated): "We didn't come here to hear you *sing!* Would you *count it off* please?"

BRYANT: "FUCK YOU! I don't get to do enough goddamn record dates MYSELF to sing on! One—you ready? One, two, three . . ."

His tantrum in this case may well have contributed to an inspired, even kinetic final take. He aimed this bluster at anyone he felt would tolerate it, Speedy being a noteworthy exception. "I was the only one that could get along with Jimmy," he said:

> He was a dear friend of mine, and I loved him like a brother. I wouldn't take any nonsense off him. He'd cow down when I'd say, "Back off! Don't start that shit with me!" And he admired me so much because I wouldn't take nothing off of him. A lot of people cowed down to Jimmy. He wanted friends the worst way in the world, but he just didn't want to have to keep them. Sometimes he could be the nicest person you'd ever want to be around. At other times he could be a bastard.

Jimmie Rivers was one of Bryant's biggest fans. A country-jazz guitar virtuoso in his own right with his own reputation as a tough guy, Rivers worked around the San Francisco Bay area in the '50s. When he got a chance to meet his hero, Rivers quickly found he hadn't exactly stumbled upon Mr. Warmth. Recalling the meeting in 1995, he said: "Jimmy Bryant is one of the most marvelous players, a kind of a genius. He had an egotism problem. I met him one time, and I said, 'Jeez, I'm glad to meet you, man. I've admired you for so long, I just love the way you play. My name's Jim Rivers.' And he looked at me and said, 'So what?' When he said that, it just took something out of me. But it still can't take away from his playing."

Some of Bryant's woes involved money, and that led to problems with Fender. While he and Gloria had four daughters and two sons, stories of Jimmy's gambling were common. Speedy recalled Jimmy, short of cash in Vegas, hocking his Telecaster and amp. It happened more than once, not always after a Vegas excursion. "He'd go out to the factory, and Leo'd give him another new guitar and amp. And then it wouldn't be long that he'd need money for somethin' and he'd hock that, and this was about the fourth time this happened. Leo finally said, 'Jimmy, this is the last set we will be givin' you. We can't continue doing this.' It pissed Jimmy off."

That wasn't the only incident at Fender that pissed Jimmy off. He met his match with Forrest White, at the time Leo Fender's new, handpicked general manager. In his memoir *Fender: The Inside Story*, White wrote of Bryant driving his Cadillac through the side gate, ignoring the visitors entrance, and walking directly into an assembly building. In one hand he held a beer. That violated a rule of White's. White walked up, introduced himself, and was promptly rebuffed by Bryant. White then tried to explain the no-beer rule.

"He almost went through the ceiling," White wrote. "He said, 'Look, I'm Jimmy Bryant, and I have been playing your [expletive] Telecaster, but I don't have to play the [expletive] thing if I have to be told what I can or can't do when I come down here!'" White stood his ground, insisting he was glad Bryant played a Tele, but asserting that rules were rules, and that meant Bryant had to finish his brew in the visitors room. "He apologized, threw the beer away, and I can say that Jimmy Bryant and I were the best of friends from that day on," White concluded.

A dismayed Cliffie Stone soon found himself confronting Bryant's attitude problems during the Saturday night *Hometown Jamboree* broadcasts. A Bryant-West fan, Cliffie gave the band a wide envelope, one Bryant often pushed—hard. The memory still pained Cliffie nearly 30 years later. "Onstage, during our shows, I had to sit on the guy to get him to play commercial. He kept turning up and getting louder. Then Speedy would turn up; then Billy Strange would turn up. The first thing you know, it was killing us. You couldn't hear the drums, couldn't hear the bass, you couldn't hear anything."

In 1955, Cliffie remembered Bryant's problems on the show coming to a head.

> Bryant was a vain guy, and he always thought he should be featured a lot more on *Hometown*. Billy was playing electric guitar, too; Bryant didn't like that. I featured Bryant as much as I thought was proper, and I had some real stars there. And he eventually just walked out. He was drinking a lot, and he was a real pain in the ass, frankly. He had an old car, and the back seat, right up to the top of it, was beer cans. He'd drink a beer and just throw [the can] in the back seat. Unbelievable. But I think the drinking finally got to him.

Liebert felt that Bryant's angst at the time had a musical angle. "Jimmy was a bopper. And he wanted to play that style, and that was good on his own instrumentals. But you don't want to play that in back of a vocal. That's not fair to the people, or the guys working there. I'll sit in with anybody, but you don't [play] that unless you're in a jazz club."

Strange, an occasional target of Bryant's wrath, separated the man from the musician he admired: "He had a mouth that got in the way of his brain. I've known a lot of talented singers and musicians that have talked their way in and out of gigs in a matter of moments. Bryant had that facility. It's a real shame. Because he was one of the most talented musicians I have ever in my life been associated with, [but] when your ego gets bigger than your talent, you've got a problem."

While Jimmy still recorded with Speedy, Roy Lanham, who'd jammed often with Speedy at the Palomino in North Hollywood, filled Bryant's *Hometown* spot. His gentler chord melody style meshed surprisingly well with Speedy's style. Cliffie, relieved to be rid of Bryant but aware of the loss, never promoted the West-Lanham team as had West and Bryant.

Occasionally, Speedy's temper flared. While planning a 1956 session to focus on his steel playing, Speedy decided he wanted a sax section backing him. Nelson agreed to hire the saxes, then forgot about it. Speedy didn't. Billy Liebert hired the added musicians. At the August session at the new Capitol Tower at Hollywood and Vine, the normally temperate Nelson exploded when he saw four saxes sitting in the studio. Speedy and Nelson, who normally got on famously, were suddenly in each other's faces. As Nelson denied ever approving the saxes, Speedy snarled, "Well, you did . . . and I'll tell you what you can do. I'll pay for this session out of my pocket. I'll pay for all the musicians comin' down there, and you can take Capitol Records and shove it where the sun don't shine!" Cliffie Stone had to separate the two friends, but the dispute was forgotten as quickly as it began.

October 9, 1956, marked West and Bryant's final Capitol session together, and it focused on Bryant material. It yielded his final Capitol single: the reflective "The Rolling Sky" and the witty "The Night Rider," replete with bop-style flatted fifths. The unreleased "Hillcrest" came from a collaboration between Bryant and jam-session buddy Stuff Smith, who lived in L.A. Smith was the premiere black jazz violin innovator of the 1930s who made his name performing in clubs on New York's 52nd Street with his legendary Onyx Club Boys. His style influenced a generation of western swing fiddlers, including Jimmy. Sixteen days after this session, Smith recorded his own version for Verve.

Not yet aware that his Capitol contract wouldn't be renewed, Bryant was in rare form for the final song: a jam-session version of the 1920s jazz favorite "China Boy" that became a giant middle finger aimed straight at the control room where Nelson sat. Speedy remembered himself and the rhythm section struggling to keep up as Bryant blithely ignored repeated "cut" gestures from Nelson, who finally shut down the tape machine after six minutes and 10 seconds.

All that came home to roost when Jimmy's contract came up for renewal. Nelson passed on him, but renewed Speedy's. "Jimmy's records never did sell as much as mine," Speedy explained. "He got just a little too far out and over the people's heads with his melody lines." Maybe so, but that year, West and Bryant won *Country and Western Jamboree* magazine's award as "best instrumental group (less than six musicians)" in the magazine's annual disc jockey poll.

Sea changes reverberating throughout country music would have slowed the West-Bryant partnership in any case. Except for a handful of instrumentalists like Chet Atkins, few country instrumentals sold well. With rock and roll surging and changing the entire music industry, the cozy scene revolving around Capitol and *Hometown Jamboree* was fading. Speedy remained active on *Hometown* (playing a top-of-the-line Fender steel he helped the company design), but it was inevitable that interest in this type of music would fade. Bryant continued working sessions, but on the West Coast, except for Bakersfield artists, pedal steel fell out of favor in country music as it did in Nashville. Speedy recorded a Hawaiian LP for Capitol, *West of Hawaii,* in 1957 complete with Hawaiian orchestrations by Sam Koki and the Seven Seas Serenaders. Speedy remained with *Hometown* until KTLA canceled it in 1959.

Speedy, Billy Strange, country boogie singer-pianist Merrill Moore, the Black Sisters, and a teenage bassist and drummer started working the Nevada club circuit between Las Vegas, Reno, and Lake Tahoe as Billy and the Kids. The nature of Vegas audiences allowed them to play all kinds of music, but it was a bitter pill for Speedy. "My wages just took a helluva drop," he remembered. "All the record companies put their eggs in that rock and roll basket. . . . And it wasn't just Capitol, it was all of them."

Speedy had one more landmark country session in the cards. In the spring of 1960, he got a call asking him to go to a small studio on Cahuenga Boulevard. A singer-songwriter and her husband from Washington State specifically asked for Speedy to play on her debut record. He arrived and met Loretta and Mooney Lynn. He dismissed the pickup band she wanted to use and called in some ex-*Hometown* sidemen including Hensley and Lanham. They helped create Loretta's first hit: the Lynn original "I'm a Honky Tonk Girl."

Weary of hit-and-miss wages, Speedy realized he needed a career change and in September 1960, his friends at Fender gave him one. He was hired as manager of the company's new Tulsa, Oklahoma, warehouse/distribution center serving 37 states. Nine-to-five workdays took a bit of adjusting, but they allowed him to play as much as he wanted on the side. Trips back to California kept his hand in design, because Leo and his technicians still welcomed his input. On occasion, he fronted a western swing band at Leon McAuliffe's Cimarron Ballroom in Tulsa.

In 1960 Capitol released one LP each of instrumentals, one spotlighting Speedy's, the other, Jimmy's. Speedy's was titled *Steel Guitar*; Bryant's got the colorful and strangely appropriate title *Country Cabin Jazz*. Capitol used an old publicity shot on the back. It needed a new cover shot of Bryant, but Jimmy, still bitter over the company's dropping his contract, flatly refused. "You couldn't get him in to make a photo," Speedy, still in L.A. at the time, remembered. Billy Strange sat back to the camera for the color photo.

That year, Bryant's phone rang; it was Speedy. Ken Nelson wanted another album, and Speedy wanted Jimmy on guitar. Bryant agreed, and all seemed well—until everyone showed up for rehearsal at Billy Strange's home.

Jimmy demanded that Speedy intercede to get him back on Capitol's roster, or he wouldn't play on the album. Speedy called Ken Nelson, who refused. While it didn't rupture the West-Bryant friendship, Bryant walked as he had promised. Roy Lanham filled in on the *Guitar Spectacular* LP. A manufacturing glitch undermined the album's sales. The first run of albums featured side one on both sides of the disc. Meanwhile, Speedy and Opal divorced in 1964. In 1966, he married his second wife, Mary.

Bryant continued working in the L.A. studios. In 1963 he and a small band he led (featuring Harold Hensley, Junior Nichols, and Rue Barclay) appeared in the decidedly low-budget film *The Skydivers,* showing up in totally illogical places, playing "Stratosphere Boogie" and the strange instrumental "Ah-So," which they had recorded as a single in 1962. Bryant had a new major label deal with Imperial Records by the mid-'60s. Scotty Turner, Imperial's country producer, used Jimmy on sessions.

Bryant recorded six Imperial albums from the mid- to late '60s, one with L.A. pedal steel guitarist Red Rhodes in 1967 titled *Wingin' It with Norval and Ivy,* that failed to approach the magic of his work with Speedy. His strongest Imperial effort was *The Fastest Guitar in the Country,* released in '67, featuring dazzling performances of "Little Rock Getaway" and "Sugarfoot Rag." Bryant's rhythm sections were stellar, featuring jazz bassist Red Callender, guitarists Barney Kessel and Al Bruno, drummer Shelly Manne, and sax player Jim Horn. "When [*Fastest Guitar*] was released," Turner said, "a lot of disc jockeys thought it was [electronically] sped up. I brought the tracks to Nashville for the DJ convention. Jimmy sat in the [Imperial] suite that year and played the lead parts to the tracks. That ended that."

Jimmy also became an independent record producer. Ironically, he did some of his most memorable productions for Capitol, including the off-key comic vocals of elderly Mrs. Elva Miller. Having learned to read music, he persevered doing sessions with country and rock acts. Twice divorced, he married Patricia Murphy, daughter of a guitar maker, in 1970. They lived in Vegas by then, where Bryant was a partner in a local recording studio. Their daughter, Corrina, was born in 1971. After his partners bought him out, the Bryants returned to California. In 1973, Bryant, along with steel guitarist Noel Boggs and a rhythm section, recorded "Boodle Dee Beep," reuniting him with *Hometown* fiddler Harold Hensley. Only Jimmy still played with any semblance of his old fire. It was almost surely Boggs's swan song; he died a year later.

After CBS purchased Leo Fender's company, Speedy hung on in Tulsa until 1968, when new management closed Fender's Tulsa distribution center. He toured Japan as a musician, then, in that pre-Winnebago era, opened a recreational trailer dealership in Tulsa. The 1973 Arab oil embargo cut back long-distance driving, trailer sales tanked, and Speedy folded the business.

That turned out to be a blessing in disguise because it forced him back into music just as western swing was undergoing a renaissance in the wake of Merle Haggard's acclaimed 1970 Bob Wills tribute LP and revivalist bands like Asleep at the Wheel were gaining popularity. In the fall of 1973, Speedy formed a western swing band with former Bob Wills guitarist Eldon Shamblin (who co-created the guitar-steel ensemble) and other former Texas Playboys. They toured colleges and music festivals around the country.

Jimmy and Patty Bryant moved briefly to Thomasville, Georgia, in 1974. In September 1975, Speedy and Jimmy reunited for an LP produced by steel guitarist Pete Drake. "We went in cold turkey," said Speedy. "We didn't rehearse or nothin'. Went right to the studio, and I never heard any of his six tunes, and he never heard any of mine." Noticing Jimmy brought along his Gibson ES-355 electric, Speedy spied an unused Telecaster left in the studio and asked Drake if Jimmy could use it, to get "the sound we always had. We got the same feel we always had, and we hadn't worked together for 17 years."

The album, scheduled for release by Columbia, was delayed for various reasons and eventually shelved. It wasn't issued until 1990, two years after Drake's death, as *For the Last Time* on Nashville-based Step One Records. Less revolutionary than the Capitols and undeniably more contemporary, it bore out Speedy's opinion that the duo still generated fireworks. The surprise was Bryant's vocal on his original hymn "Jesus's Guitar Man," one of his rare forays into singing.

The Bryants moved to Nashville in November of 1975. If he was difficult in L.A., Bryant found himself up against a cliquish provincialism unlike anything he'd seen on the West Coast. His plainspoken nature didn't help; he openly defied unwritten Music Row etiquette by jamming in local bars— something frowned on. Recording-session work came infrequently, in part because Bryant bluntly rejected some offers. Billy Strange, who worked in Nashville song publishing, saw it happen: "Bryant made that mistake with everybody, particularly the guitar players. He put down everybody. You can just run down the list of guitar players in this town that he badmouthed."

But Jimmy faced a more catastrophic situation. He assumed that he'd contracted a bad case of the flu in mid-1977. Nonetheless, his gut instinct sensed something more ominous. He revealed it to Speedy when he visited town: "I was in Nashville, and Jimmy and I were down at the Hall of Fame Hotel one night to hear Curly Chalker. He just leaned over and said, 'Hey, Speed, I'm dyin'.' I said, 'What'd you say?' He said 'I'm dyin'. I don't know what it is, but I know I'm dyin'.' I said, 'Aw, bullshit, Jimmy. You been to the doctor to see what's wrong with you?' He said, 'No, but I'm dyin'.'"

Thirty years of playing smoky clubs, his own cigarettes close at hand, had taken its toll. Jimmy's instincts were, in this case, as acute as his musical ear.

The illness became full-blown pneumonia, a precursor to the grim reality Bryant predicted. He entered a Nashville VA hospital late in 1978 for exploratory surgery. Surgeons found a malignant tumor in one lung and discovered it had already metastasized. With time short, having trouble breathing and weakened by chemotherapy, he and Patty returned to his L.A. stomping grounds for several months. On August 27, 1979, friends organized a benefit concert for him at L.A.'s Palomino nightclub.

Speedy was inducted into the International Steel Guitar Hall of Fame in April 1980. That same month, the Bryants returned to Moultrie, Georgia, a place Jimmy hadn't lived in for more than 30 years. "He wanted to go home to die," Patty Bryant remembered. He entered the hospital for the last time that September, lovingly cared for by his sister Lorene, a registered nurse. His family standing by, Jimmy Bryant died on September 22, 1980. Buried in the family plot, his tombstone had a guitar motif and the slogan "Jesus's Guitar Man," based on the song he recorded in the 1975 session with Speedy.

Speedy faced his own mortality on April 14, 1981, when a stroke paralyzed his entire right side. The Tulsa hospital where he recuperated fielded nearly 300 phone calls and hundreds of cards and letters. His speech and memory unimpaired, he underwent risky surgery to bypass the clogged carotid arteries. While it restored movement in his right side, nerve damage left that side feeling constantly cold and painful, requiring substantial medication.

The stroke didn't erode that burning desire to perform. He took the stage at the International Steel Guitar Convention on Saturday afternoon, September 5, 1981. After a bit of comedy, he played a slow instrumental and a bit of "Woodchopper's Ball." The audience screamed for more. He tried to continue over the next few months, but playing was too taxing. He wore a huge mitten on his right arm to cushion any jolts or bumps and settled into retirement, traveling with Mary, enjoying their hobby of finding antiques.

Speedy kept his hand in music as a beloved regular at steel guitar conventions, an elder statesman filled with memories—most stunningly accurate—of his glory days in the studios with Ernie, Billy May, Bing Crosby, and, of course, Jimmy. Son Gary, who went by the name of "Speedy West, Jr.," became a talented steel guitarist and guitarist.

Only a few others seriously tried to emulate West and Bryant. On occasion someone actually exceeded their brilliance. At the 23 Club, a honky-tonk just south of San Francisco, longtime Bryant fan Jimmie Rivers and his band the Cherokees, featuring former Billy Jack and Bob Wills pedal-steel guitarist Vance Terry, carried on the tradition with dazzling results that would have surely elicited a cry of "batshit!" (or worse) from Bryant had he heard them. In Nashville, the most traditional of all bands, Ernest Tubb's

venerable Texas Troubadours, boasted a similar team in the '6os in steel guitarist Buddy Charleton and country-jazz guitarist Leon Rhodes, who
unleashed their synergy on personal appearances and four Decca LPs.

The millennium has come and gone. One thing, however, is certain: The
magnificent audacity of Speedy West and Jimmy Bryant, now more than half
a century old, sounds as crisp, fresh, and futuristic as it did the second it hit
the tapes at Capitol.

Plantation Roy with Hank Penny and the Plantation Boys, Cincinnati, 1943: Zed Tennis, Carl Stewart, Louis Innis, Roy Lanham, Hank Penny.

11

Neither Fish nor Fowl

Roy Lanham
and the Whippoorwills

In the early '50s, Donald "Dusty" Rhoads was in New York City working with the Whippoorwills at Madison Square Garden on a show with Roy Rogers and Dale Evans. Rhoads's sister wanted him to hear a combo that also played his "kind of music." When Rhoads got to the bar, he discovered it was jazz guitar virtuoso Johnny Smith's Trio. During a break, when Smith, who'd gotten his start playing country music, headed for the cigarette machine, Rhoads, a longtime fan, headed over to introduce himself:

> I walked over to the cigarette machine when he got off. I said, "Old buddy, good God, I can't believe I met you here. My sister had to drag me over here." Smith realized who he was talking to. "You don't look like you can ride a horse. Are you one of the Whippoorwills?" I said yeah. He said, "Jesus Christ, we been listening to you guys' transcriptions up here—the Standard Library stuff. You guys just knock our ass off!"

The Whippoorwills knocked a *lot* of people's asses off. Unfortunately, the majority of asses so affected belonged to fellow musicians, not the public as a whole. Despite having a wide audience through their extensive stage work with Roy Rogers and Dale Evans, they were taken for granted during their active years by all but the musically aware.

How to describe their sound? The dense harmonies floated almost cloud-like, with rich, undulating presence evoking such stellar '40s vocal groups as the Pied Pipers or Modernaires (or the latter-day Manhattan Transfer). Imagine that vocal blend supported by instrumental accompaniment not unlike that of Les Paul's classic records. Whether the Whips sang country, pop, or original numbers, their sound was joyous, rich, and life-affirming. Beneath and around the voices, Roy Lanham added rich chords and spicy lead phrases. Doug Dalton's playfully pungent electric mandolin took the lead, or darted in, out, and in between. At the bottom, Gene Monbeck played rock-steady, unshakable rhythm on his Stromberg arch-top guitar and

Rhoads held a steady bass. It seems terribly unjust that such a gifted group was so totally taken for granted in their time.

For that matter, the band's founder, Roy Lanham, also suffered from neglect. Despite his extraordinary work with the Whips, he earned far greater notice for his 25 years (1961–1986) as the Sons of the Pioneers' guitarist, successor to original Pioneers guitarist Karl Farr. Onstage, he comped behind Dale Warren, Hugh Perryman, Rome Johnson, and other members of the group on "Tumbling Tumbleweeds," "Cool Water," and the rest of their repertoire. Lanham's "solo spot" usually consisted of playing the schlock-pop standard "Somewhere My Love" or the theme from *Bonanza*. Surefire crowdpleasers? No doubt. Unfortunately, they revealed little of Lanham's true musical calling: country-jazz.

Lanham blazed a different trail from other country-jazz guitar exponents. Blazing single-string solo lines a la Jimmy Bryant or Jimmy Wyble weren't his specialty. Nor was he an intense be-bopper like Hank Garland or Lenny Breau. The harmonically rich Lanham style combined both single-note passages with luxuriant chord melodies played in the style of jazz masters or George Barnes or George Van Eps. The vibrant four-part harmonies that Lanham created for his chord solos were his own idea, based on the three-part harmonies in which Barnes specialized. His single-string improvisations, also influenced by Chicago guitar innovator Barnes, were more relaxed than Bryant's, yet still adventurous.

Merle Travis once said, "I get out a couple of Roy Lanham albums and play them. Then I listen to some of my recorded efforts and come up with this sort of remark: 'Dad-blame, buddy, that's awful!'" Travis, who popularized the popular western Kentucky fingerpicking style that bears his name, always minimized his own vast talents, but he wasn't exaggerating his estimate of Lanham's gifts. Hank Penny, Lanham's friend for decades, reveled in his versatility: "He could play single-string lead guitar, and play real funky on one chorus and play it in full chords on the next chorus. And he wouldn't have to stop and think and look down on his guitar neck."

Roy Howard Lanham was born in Corbin, in eastern Kentucky, in 1923. His interest in guitar came early, and one of his first influences was the obscure country player Harry C. Adams, who worked with the Brown County Revelers. "He was on WHAS in Louisville," Roy said of Adams. "He played acoustic and was a good, snappy, fast country guitar player, although he played some things like 'Sweet Georgia Brown.'" Roy learned the rudiments of playing on his brother Arvil's Stella guitar. "He was left-handed, and he saw I was going to learn, so he strung it up right-handed," Roy recounts. "I got my own guitar when I was about eight. It was a Cromwell, one of the first arch-bodies that they had."

In the fall of 1939, Roy met Grandpappy and His Gang from the popular *Mid-Day Merry-Go-Round* on WNOX Radio in Knoxville, Tennessee, who came to Corbin during a tour. "Grandpappy" was comic Archie Campbell, later famous on the Grand Ole Opry and as an original *Hee-Haw* cast member. When Campbell heard Lanham play, he asked Lanham to join the group and the guitarist began working on WNOX on October 19, 1939. Moving to a larger radio station broadened Roy's musical tastes, particularly when he met the Stringdusters, a WNOX pop/jazz quartet made up of guitarists Charlie Hagaman, Homer Haynes, mandolinist Jethro Burns, and his brother Aychie. Homer's and Jethro's skills as swing musicians clearly inspired by Django Reinhardt were clear to Roy from the start. "I would hear them on the air, and I loved what they played," said Roy. "They copied the Hot Club of France. I would go home and try to play as good as I could."

The Stringdusters disbanded when Haynes and Burns left to work as Homer and Jethro. Lanham formed his own Stringdusters-like group before moving to WDOD in Chattanooga. In the band were mandolinist Doug Dalton and guitarist Bynum Geouge. "I started out basically as a rhythm player, copying Homer," he explained. They called it the Fidgety Four, in anticipation of finding a bass player; in Chattanooga, bassist Red Wootten joined the group.

When veteran singer/composer Gene Austin heard the Fidgety Four, he added it to his troupe, which toured as a tent show. Austin still had star power in those days, renowned for his pop hit "My Blue Heaven." In tribute to that, his biggest hit, he changed the group's name to the Whippoorwills, an homage to "My Blue Heaven's" first stanza ("When whippoorwills call/And evening is nigh"). The group briefly returned to Chattanooga but rejoined Austin when he hired them to work in hotel ballrooms. Lanham modeled the Whips' four-part vocal harmonies after the pop group the Merry Macs. "They sang like the Pied Pipers, Hi-Los, and the Four Freshmen," he said. When the band worked in Cincinnati, Austin bought each member a new instrument. He paid $324 for Roy's blond Gibson L-5, his "first good guitar." By then Roy had been impressed by Charlie Christian and even more so by Barnes, among the first jazz guitarists to use an amplified instrument. "[Barnes] played jazz and country tunes," states Lanham. "I just liked Barnes's ideas. Anybody else who played the same notes would sound different, but I liked the sound he got out of his amplifier. He played with a lot of authority."

The Whippoorwills disbanded in October 1941. Lanham moved to Atlanta and joined Shades of Blue, a group built around a female pianist and blind steel guitarist Billy Galloway. "He played like George Barnes on a single-neck steel," marveled Roy. Lanham also learned from fiddler-guitarist Sheldon Bennett, who formerly played fiddle with Hank Penny's Radio Cowboys and went on to work with the western swing band the Hi-Flyers. Bennett piqued Roy's interest in playing chord melodies. "He played chord stuff in three parts," said Roy. "I added a fourth part. I play most of my songs in four-part harmony."

He met George Barnes during his Atlanta stay. Barnes had been drafted and stationed at Camp Wheeler, not far from Atlanta. Hank Penny, working in Atlanta at WSB, was present the night the two jammed together. He later remembered, "Barnes was so impressed with Roy's playing. Roy imitated him, and it just fascinated George that somebody could do his thing so well." In Atlanta, Penny introduced Lanham to singer Marianne LeGlise, whom he'd marry in 1946.

Roy returned to Cincinnati in 1943 and joined 50,000-watt WLW as a staff musician. He played guitar and bass with the station's country and pop acts, which included Merle Travis, Joe Maphis, and Grandpa Jones. His friendships with all three men lasted for decades. That same year Syd Nathan, a local used-record dealer, founded King Records. By then, Roy was part of Hank Penny's Plantation Boys. Over the next three years, Lanham worked as a studio musician on King sessions until he left Cincinnati. Some of his best studio work for King included Penny's late 1944 debut recordings for the label. A couple years later, his presence enhanced the Delmore Brothers' seminal country boogie recordings for King, recordings that laid the groundwork for the rockabilly of a decade later.

"On 'Freight Train Boogie,' it's me and Jethro Burns," Lanham said. That phenomenal solo features the two, Lanham on guitar and Jethro on mandolin, playing driving rhythms against one another, at one point quoting the famous riff from Woody Herman's big-band favorite "Woodchopper's Ball." "Jethro and I used those little licks me and Doug Dalton used with the Whippoorwills," Roy added. His guitar also graced such Delmore classics as "Hillbilly Boogie," "Steamboat Bill Boogie," and "Barnyard Boogie" and their more conventional country recordings. In 1946, after former WLW guitarist Chet Atkins joined Red Foley's band, Atkins made his first record, "Guitar Blues," for the Nashville-based Bullet Records. Lanham, who'd become friendly with Chet in Cincinnati, came to Nashville to play rhythm guitar.

Late in 1947, Lanham moved to Dayton, Ohio, to reorganize the Whippoorwills. Doug Dalton returned, and the band got three new members: rhythm guitarist Gene Monbeck, Dusty Rhoads, and singer Juanita Vastine, known professionally as "Sweet Georgia Brown." "When Georgia joined us," he remembered, "she sang the lead and we had four-part instrumental and five-part vocal."

Lanham realized full well that he had something special; he'd worked hard to create it. "What I thought was unique with the Whippoorwills, and nobody was doing this," he said, "was taking country tunes and putting jazz feeling behind them. There'd be no really bad country music today if all of the people who recorded played good chords. But they oversimplify it." Their repertoire featured songs like the pop standard "Lover." "We were doing that arrangement before Les Paul ever recorded that son of a gun," said Dusty Rhoads.

Through 1948 and '49 the group toured the Midwest and spent a year in Springfield, Missouri, at KWTO Radio, before being called to Los Angeles in 1950 to join the cast of western comedian Smiley Burnette's transcribed (pre-recorded) radio show for RadiOzark. Based in Springfield, Missouri, the company specialized in recording transcribed radio shows. It was owned by KWTO executive Si Siman, who in 1953 would found the *Ozark Jubilee* TV and stage show. He'd done similar transcribed shows with Maybelle and the Carter Sisters.

It seems remarkable that Georgia Brown wasn't enticed from the group, for her vocal poise, relaxed jazzy delivery, and clean phrasing had elements of June Christy or Anita O'Day. While the group's repertoire included showcase numbers like Lanham's perennial favorite, "Kerry Dance"; pop favorites ("Breezin' Along with the Breeze"); jazz standards (Woody Herman's beboppish instrumental "Lost Weekend"); and hipster fare like "Tabby the Cat," and Bob Wills's "Stay a Little Longer," much of its material was original. The group's harmonies indeed drew from the best of the Merry Macs, Pied Pipers, and Modernaires. Combined with the instrumental polish, it was a sound unique in its own day and any other.

On occasion, the group rechristened a jazz standard, as it did on "Elementary Canal," the Whipporwills' variation on the Count Basie favorite "Lester Leaps In." Dalton based "Mandolin King Rag" on the chord changes to the traditional Texas fiddle favorite "Beaumont Rag." Originals like "Blue Mood," penned by Lanham, Rhoads, and Monbeck, reflect a relaxed, 3 A.M. ambiance and possess an almost hypnotic quality even half a century later.

The group did dozens of the Standard transcriptions that so impressed Johnny Smith. For RadiOzark, the Whipporwills recorded hundreds of Burnette shows in Hollywood; in Springfield, they worked on George Morgan's transcribed shows for Robin Hood Flour. The Whipporwills' work backing Merle Travis on Capitol sessions in 1950 and 1951 for records like "El Reno" and "Trouble, Trouble" so impressed Lee Gillette that he signed the group to Capitol. The group toured theaters with Roy Rogers and Dale Evans after Rogers replaced the Sons of the Pioneers, backed Roy and Dale on their now-classic recording of "Happy Trails," and played behind Ferlin

Husky when he made his early Four Star recordings under the name "Terry Preston."

Through all the touring and studio work, though, the group never heard a word from Capitol. A year after Gillette signed them, said Rhoads, group members went back and asked why they weren't being recorded. "Little did we know that they [Capitol] got Les Paul [and Mary Ford] by now, and our sound was the same. We forced them to record us, and all they done was shelve it. In all due respect to Les, I guess they couldn't release anything that sounded like him." Apocryphal as this story might sound, Capitol also shelved a 1952 Jimmy Bryant–Speedy West version of Les's 1948 hit instrumental "Lover." The Whips had to find another record label. Finding a major label proved difficult.

Their musical similarities to Les and Mary came from their mandolin-guitar combination and the five-part vocal harmonies. Les had to speed up certain guitar parts to get a high-register feel. With the Whips' lineup, it had no trouble re-creating a Les-Mary sound without the overdubbing or technical trickery that became Les's trademark. Word of that got around. They were recording one set of Smiley Burnette shows at Radio Recorders in Hollywood when a representative of a company that produced cheap records for sale in five-and-dime stores approached the group. Impressed by their ability to nail the Les Paul sound live, the record man offered the Whips a shot covering four Les-Mary hits (including "Tiger Rag") for $500 a pop.

The Whips took him up on his offer, a decision that had repercussions many years later. Dusty Rhoads remembered that when Lanham was performing with the Pioneers in Tokyo, "he got with Les Paul over there, both of 'em drinkin' at the bar, and he [Paul] brought that up to Roy. He said, 'You know, a buncha sons of bitches copied our arrangement, Roy. They did about four tunes, cost us a lotta record sales on that ten-cent label.'" Lanham discreetly remained silent. Whether Les said it off the top of his head or knew that the Whips were responsible is open to speculation.

Though no major label seemed interested in the Whips in the early '50s, it recorded for Vita, a company owned by black Los Angeles recording maven Dootsie Williams. Rhoads remembered recording some of the Vita material in a garage in a black section of Los Angeles. The Vita single "Blue Raindrops" became a pop hit on the West Coast. When Monbeck left, Rhoads switched to guitar and brought in Red Wootten, formerly of the Stringdusters and a recent alumnus of Woody Herman's orchestra, to play bass.

When Lanham wasn't touring in the early '50s, he did a growing amount of recording-session work. He worked particularly closely with Fabor Robinson's Fabor and Abbott labels, including playing on Johnny Horton's and Jim Reeves's early Abbott sides. He played on the Reeves hits "Mexican Joe" and "Bimbo," and on Mitchell Torok's "Caribbean." Robinson used

Whippoorwills and friends. Back row: Dusty Rhoads, Roy Lanham, Sweet Georgia Brown (Juanita Vastine), Gene Monbeck, Doug Dalton. Front row: Roy Rogers, Dale Evans, Pat Brady without Nellybelle.

Lanham to handle arrangements. Finally in 1955, the mercurial guitar genius Jimmy Bryant stormed off the *Hometown Jamboree* TV show, where he and pedal steel pioneer Speedy West played in the show's house band. Founder and host Cliffie Stone hired Lanham to replace Bryant.

The Whippoorwills dissolved shortly after Lanham joined *Hometown*. The group's very diversity led to its ultimate undoing. That sophisticated, urbane, and smoothly delivered blend of jazz, pop, blues, country, and western swing couldn't adapt to the molds of the time. The Whips were simply too sophisticated for country audiences, but too country for the uptown types who should have appreciated the group. Its resemblance to the Les Paul–Mary Ford sound may have also hurt. In the end, the Whips never got beyond the status of supporting act. "I was trying to take good music and make it sell, and we just couldn't do it," Lanham concluded sadly.

On *Hometown*, Roy filled Bryant's place playing instrumental duets with Speedy West, though the pair never recorded together. Around that same time, Lanham, who'd first met Leo Fender in 1952, abandoned his amplified hollow-body Epiphone arch-top for solid-body Fenders when Leo gave him an early Stratocaster. That loyalty to Fender continued for the rest of

Lanham's life, when Fender, who'd sold his company to CBS in 1965, created the Music Man and, later, G&L.

He continued working in the studios during the late '50s, playing on Johnny Burnette's hit "Dreamin'" and his brother Dorsey Burnette's "Tall Oak Tree." His rock guitar instrumentals "Klondike" and the flipside, "Attitude," were issued on Fabor Robinson's Radio label. He accompanied various obscure rockabilly artists like Jimmy Patton. Some of Lanham's most notable studio work, however, was with the clean-teen vocal group the Fleetwoods, discovered by Abbott recording artist Bonnie Guitar, a Seattle native. She discovered the three Seattle high school students, who'd made an amateur recording of "Come Softly to Me" unaccompanied, using car keys to clang out rhythm.

Bonnie brought the tape to Lanham, who overdubbed additional guitar parts. Issued in 1959 by the L.A.-based Dolton Records, "Come Softly" became the Fleetwoods' first hit single. The next one was "Mr. Blue," also arranged by Lanham, with popular trombonist Si Zentner, a drummer, and Lanham playing the opening guitar arpeggios and fills. He even tuned the instrument down to overdub bass guitar parts for "Come Softly": "I tuned all *three* of the overdubs to their voices. 'Mr. Blue' was the next thing we followed up with, and I got Si Zentner to play trombone; we added a drummer, and I did the same thing with 'Mr. Blue.'"

Dolton offered Lanham the chance to record a solo LP: *The Most Exciting Guitar*. The 1959 sessions began at the home recording studio that Lanham had built at his home in Chatsworth, in the San Fernando Valley. A site for many impromptu jam sessions between Lanham, Rhoads, Thumbs Carlille, Jimmy Bryant, and even Les Paul, the studio used two Ampex tape recorders, with Marianne Lanham at the controls. He completed the album at Western Recorders in Los Angeles in 1959 with bassist Red Wootten and veteran R&B and rock drummer Earl Palmer. Dusty Rhoads played rhythm guitar on one track.

Lanham's late '50s session work included playing on western bandleader Spade Cooley's final LP *Fidoodlin'*, issued on Raynote Records. In 1960, summoned by Speedy West, Lanham played lead guitar on Loretta Lynn's first hit "I'm a Honky Tonk Girl," with Speedy producing. Around that same time, Lanham, Rhoads, and Dalton reunited for the Whippoorwills' NRC instrumental (no vocals) album *Sizzling Strings*. Veteran western swing singer-guitarist Jimmie Widener played rhythm guitar. This beautifully articulated collection revisited the band's virtuosity with easygoing, hip versions of such big-band favorites as "Summit Ridge Drive," an exquisite arrangement of "Sophisticated Swing," and new spins on such Lanham favorites as "Kerry Dance."

Rhoads had slightly different memories of the session: "The studio I wasn't happy with, and when you're used to workin' with [Gene] Monbeck, it was pretty hard when somebody else was tryin' to lay down a tight beat, but by and large, it came off all right. They recorded the bass a little hot." The album's songs were mostly longtime staples of the Whips' repertoire. The arrangement of the big-band favorite "Stompin' At the Savoy" began with an exaggerated faux-hillbilly introduction, then segued into hard-swinging jazz. In the mid-'90s, Rhoads played the album for a jazz saxophonist who snorted derisively at the cornball intro, only to be astounded when he heard the group suddenly switch into swing mode. "I thought that was unique," Rhoads said.

In the fall of 1961, Karl Farr, the Sons of the Pioneers' original guitarist, died during a performance. Farr, who often played Joe Venuti–Eddie Lang style jazz duets with his violinist brother, Hugh, was a charter member. Roy joined the Pioneers that September. He was not on unfamiliar ground. "Before I joined the Sons of the Pioneers, I [played on] their albums," he said. "That was me, Glen Campbell, Barney Kessel, and Jimmy Wyble. We used three or four guitars and played different rhythms. A couple of us would play single-note things, and some things we did ensemble."

In 1962, the year that he played on Ned Miller's hit single "From a Jack to a King" and on Speedy West's final album *Guitar Spectacular*, Lanham recorded *The Fantastic Roy Lanham* for Sims Records at Western Recorders, again mixing Dusty on rhythm guitar, former Spade Cooley drummer Muddy Berry on drums, and Red Wootten on bass. He spun lucid, swinging interpretations of country chestnuts like "Under the Double Eagle" and "Brown's Ferry Blues" with big-band standards like "In the Mood" and pop fare like "Holiday for Strings" and "Brazil." Roy contributed new originals like the boppish "Your Heart Darlin'" and "Roy's Blues."

Lanham's studio work earned him considerable respect from the West Coast jazz community, so much that one of the town's most stellar jazz guitarists once approached him for help with a technique: "Barney Kessel came out to our house in the early '60s," Lanham recalled. "He always told me, 'Take off your boots and hat, and you can be a great jazz player.' He wanted me to teach him the Travis-Atkins style, so I showed him the basics of the thumb and fingers. He felt he needed to know that to be a well-rounded guitar player."

Lanham remained with the Pioneers throughout the '60s and '70s. In the '60s he still did studio work, including sessions with the Monkees. Still, it's difficult to argue that while being a part of the Pioneers, long an American Institution, paid well and brought prestige, it was hardly the optimal outlet for one of Lanham's consummate virtuosity. Between tours with the Pioneers,

Lanham demonstrated Fender equipment, particularly at the NAMM (National Association of Music Merchants) shows in various cities, including Nashville, playing alongside musicians representing other companies. "I'd play for all the dealers," he recalled. "Barney Kessel would be there, and Chet Atkins would be there for Gretsch. Homer and Jethro and I would jam with Speedy West."

Roy Lanham stories have circulated in the business for years, like the time he and Marianne were driving their car down the circular driveway of a Burbank gas station when Marianne smelled smoke and noticed the car was on fire. Roy, known for his relaxed manner and unflappable personality, drove on while Marianne shouted for him to pull over and get his guitar from the trunk. Blissfully unaware of what was transpiring, he replied, "Aw, honey, I don't feel like playin' now."

Cardiac problems surfaced for Lanham in 1980, but he rebounded nicely from open-heart surgery. He continued with the Pioneers and played on Tex Williams's final LP. In 1986, Lanham was working in Branson, Missouri, with the Pioneers when I interviewed him for a *Guitar Player* magazine article, the only Lanham interview known to have focused on his guitar work and pre-Pioneers career.

He expressed a desire to do a straight jazz recording, fulfilling Barney Kessel's prophecy. "If I did (an album)," he said, "I'd put out some real good ballads, like Johnny Smith. I still like to play. I've thought of putting out a Duke Ellington album-composition like 'Prelude to a Kiss,' 'Caravan,' and things like that. And I'd like to do an album with Chet Atkins."

It wasn't to be. Shortly after the interview, Roy was diagnosed with bladder cancer. Though the surgery appeared successful, he suffered a stroke in the recovery room. He recovered sufficiently to return to playing, though not enough to rejoin the Pioneers. In 1989, he entered the hospital for an operation and this time the news was grimmer. Doctors discovered advanced prostate cancer. Roy Lanham died on February 14, 1991, and was given surprisingly few obituaries outside the western music field. Given the consistency of his work and the artistic (if not commercial) sense of his musical vision, he deserved better.

V

Against
the Grain

Ascot before bandana: RCA's new star. (Courtesy BMG Archives)

12

"One of These Days That'll Change"

Willie Nelson

"Dear RCA Artist . . ."

> —Willie's recollection of RCA's corporate form letters

Nobody admired him more than people in the business, but Willie was kind of ahead of his time. He was hot in Texas, and that was the only place we could sell him.

> —Chet Atkins, 1980

We couldn't record him as a hit artist here in Nashville.

> —Harold Bradley, 1981

Willie was never satisfied (with his RCA recordings), but he felt we had to do what the producer said. When Chet Atkins is your producer, you think . . . this is God. There's no way in hell a guy can produce that many artists and be successful with all of them.

> —Johnny Bush, 1997

You already made a mistake with that man, Hoss. Don't make the same mistake again.

> —Waylon Jennings, 1972, after spying a photo of the recently departed Willie during his own negotiations with RCA

Nineteen sixty-four through 1972 were eight unsettled years in Nashville. The pop-oriented "Nashville Sound" pioneered by Ken Nelson, Chet Atkins, and Owen Bradley was now the industry standard. It did its job admirably, setting the Nashville music industry back on track by broadening the country music audience by attracting pop fans. It made Don Gibson, Jim Reeves, and Patsy Cline bigger stars than they'd ever been when they previously sang hard country. Unfortunately, by 1964, its cutting edge gave way to pure formula. That year, Jim Reeves died when his private plane crashed near Nashville. A year earlier, a plane crash claimed Patsy. Eddy Arnold, whose decade-long string of hits tapered off in the late '50s, stood at the brink of a dramatic comeback that began in 1965 with elaborately orchestrated ballads like "What's He Doing in My World." By 1964, Ray Price had already wrapped a string quartet around the Cherokee Cowboys on selected recording sessions, manifested in hits like "Burning Memories" that sold well yet worried his longtime, hard-country fans.

Not even a southwestern honky-tonk giant of George Jones's stature was immune from Nashville Sound production values. While he still used fiddles and steel guitar onstage, in the studio, Nashville's A-team accompanied him, complete with vocal choruses. That sound began at United Artists and its use increased after Jones switched to Musicor Records. Though Jones never cared for this sound, there's little question that he acquiesced in using it; he maintained in a 2001 interview that in the studio, he and the session musicians, not longtime producer Pappy Daily, handled nuts-and-bolts production.

A few wild cards counteracted the syrupy side in 1964. As country's audience expanded, it divided. As Price slithered out of his rhinestone musical skin toward tuxedoes, Buck Owens's and Merle Haggard's stardom reflected many fans' belief that much of the Nashville Sound went too far afield. An alternative materialized closer to home, as Johnny Cash expanded his audience without the requisite compromises ("Ring of Fire's" Mariachi trumpets notwithstanding). Roger Miller, renowned as a hit songwriter, saw his languishing recording career catch fire after he recorded some goofy original novelty tunes for Smash Records. One, "Dang Me," topped the charts six weeks in mid-'64, followed by the Top Five hit "Chug-A-Lug."

Overseeing it all were the producers: Chet Atkins at RCA and Owen Bradley at Decca. Don Law at Columbia was about to retire, with Frank Jones his designated successor. Columbia's Epic subsidiary hired Billy Sherrill, a former R&B musician and engineer for Sun Records founder Sam Phillips, as a producer. His day would come, but in 1964, he was still recording lower-level acts. The Nashville Sound required that artists implicitly trust their producer's instincts, no matter what. That meant that unless a singer was a formidable songwriter like Roger Miller, producers picked material and offered "direction." In some cases, a producer wrote or co-wrote certain "recommended" songs, or perhaps owned an interest in publishing the material that they pushed at artists. Such conflicts of interest were routine on 16th Avenue South, the headquarters of Nashville's Music industry (now referred to as Music Row). Nor was it uncommon on the West Coast, where Capitol's Ken Nelson co-owned Central Songs with Lee Gillette and Cliffie Stone.

One problem that few producers of that time cared to address involved exceptions to the formula: artists whose styles simply weren't conducive to formula production. The major-label producers had convinced themselves that their one-size-fits-all approach was virtually infallible, that ooh-aah choruses and muted strings could sell anyone's records. The idea that it didn't— or couldn't—work for every artist seemed unthinkable, unspeakable.

Such was the world that Willie Nelson faced in 1964.

Abbott, Texas, south of Dallas but closer to Waco, is a tiny rural village bisected by railroad tracks. Old Highway 77, a country road and the main north-south street, is now Willie Nelson Road, named in honor of the town's favorite son. The town isn't much bigger than it was when Willie Hugh Nelson was born there on April 30, 1933, the second child of Ira and Myrle Nelson. They and Ira's parents arrived in Abbott from Searcy County, Arkansas, in 1929. Bobbie Lee, Ira and Myrle's daughter, was born in Abbott in 1931. The Nelsons were musical. Ira's parents taught singing; Ira, a mechanic by trade, played in local bands whenever he could. The young couple's marriage crumbled when Willie was six months old; Myrle left then, and Ira, giving in to his musical instincts, hit the road with a band before Willie was three. The kids stayed with his parents: William Nelson, a blacksmith, and his wife, Nancy. The kids called them "Mama" and "Daddy."

At age two, Willie got a toy metal mandolin from his cousins. Mama and Daddy took their Methodist religion—and gospel singing—seriously. Mama taught Bobbie to play piano and made sure both kids heard plenty of gospel and country. Willie's first public performance came at age four. Clad in a sailor suit, he recited a poem at a combination picnic and gospel sing in Abbott. A stray finger up one nostril quickly produced a nosebleed that soaked his outfit. Undeterred by the gore, he recited his poem anyway.

By 1938, when he was five, he wrote poetry and immersed himself in what comic books he could afford. A year later, Daddy Nelson started teaching him chords on a cheap Stella guitar he'd ordered his grandson from Sears. Those lessons ended soon afterward when Daddy Nelson caught a cold that led to pneumonia. The drugs given him may have aggravated a heart problem. His sudden death in 1939 devastated everyone and forced Mama Nelson to move the kids to a smaller, shabbier house with no indoor plumbing. With money tight, she took a job in the school cafeteria. Willie picked cotton.

Radio became Willie's window on the world beyond Abbott, and southwestern music made up a huge part of that world. He heard Bob Wills and his big-band version of the Texas Playboys from KVOO in Tulsa. From Nashville, he inhaled the Grand Ole Opry every Saturday night. He particularly enjoyed Ernest Tubb, the Texas honky-tonk singer whose entrance made electric guitars a permanent part of the Opry. Closer to home, he savored the music of a second honky-tonk pillar: singer-songwriter Floyd Tillman, whose unique vocal phrasing influenced Willie just as it did Lefty

Frizzell. From radio station WACO in Waco, he heard high school student Hank Thompson, known as "Hank the Hired Hand," singing cowboy songs and Opry-style country alone with his acoustic guitar every morning.

The airwaves transported Willie beyond the South and beyond country music to the world of big bands and pop music. He loved network broadcasts by the era's top big bands, particularly Benny Goodman and Tommy Dorsey, with his vocalist Frank Sinatra, whose relaxed vocal phrasing fascinated Willie. Those artists introduced him to the songs of George Gershwin, Johnny Mercer, Irving Berlin, Hoagy Carmichael, and Harold Arlen. Listening to their songs, Willie learned the value of a good lyric. In 1941, he wrote his own songs, putting each into his own homemade songbook.

Willie was 10 in 1943 when he landed his first musical job: playing guitar with John Raycjeck's local Bohemian Polka Band. Polka music, too, was part of Texas culture, because many German and Polish immigrants settled around the state. Each weekend, Willie traveled six miles from Abbott to the town of West, Texas, to meet the band, who played dance halls throughout the area. Mama Nelson's religious convictions made her uncomfortable with her grandson playing halls that sold liquor. The $8 a night he received quickly muted her concerns.

In March 1947, Bobbie Nelson met 22-year-old Bud Fletcher. They married a month later. Fletcher possessed no discernable musical talent, yet he formed a western swing band called the Texans. Bobbie played piano; Willie became their guitarist. The band's musical skills were debatable, but Fletcher's smooth talk got them local dance jobs that gave both Willie and Bobbie performing experience. They landed a regular radio show at nearby Hillsboro.

Willie's guitar playing improved as he found the right role models. He enjoyed the Bob Wills guitarists—Eldon Shamblin, Junior Barnard, and Jimmy Wyble—and idolized Belgian gypsy jazzman Django Reinhardt. Since Fletcher booked acts locally, Willie got a chance to see Wills and His Texas Playboys at a nearby dance hall. He gave Wills's every move his rapt attention, carefully observing the fiddler's intuitive skill at reading a crowd's mood to choose songs that kept them on the dance floor.

As a member of Abbott High's Class of '51, Willie faced a harsh reality: playing music couldn't earn him a living. Money was so tight that Bud Fletcher occasionally had to spring Willie's guitar out of hock. A tree-trimming job lasted only until Willie hurt his back in a fall. Classified 1-A by his draft board, he could be drafted at any time. With the Korean War raging, he joined the U.S. Air Force and wound up in basic training at Lackland Air Force Base in San Antonio. After nine months, the Air Force shipped him to Mississippi for radar training that lasted until some heavy lifting at the base medical infirmary aggravated his back injury. Given the options of surgery to correct the problem or an immediate medical discharge, Willie, a free spirit disillusioned by the military's insistence he follow orders to the letter, chose a discharge and headed home to Abbott.

Willie still had no prospects in early 1952 when he met local carhop Martha Jewel Matthews, who soon became his first wife. They moved to Oregon, where Willie's mother lived with her new husband, but didn't stay long. Back in Abbott, Willie hooked up with fiddler Cosett Holland. Looking for a place to play, Willie and Holland headed for San Antonio and showed up at a club just outside town one Sunday. The house band was playing. Their drummer was John Bush Shinn III, better known as Johnny Bush, who recalled those days in a 1997 interview:

> I was workin' with Dave Isbell and the Mission City Playboys, and we were working out on the old Laredo Highway, south of town in a place called Al's Country Club. [The name] sounds great, but it was a pure honky-tonk. One Sunday afternoon right after dark, a guitar player and fiddle player came in and wanted to sit in. It was a rule on Sunday: anybody who came in, you let 'em sit in. The fiddle player's name was Cosett Holland. He and Willie had come down from outside of Waco together and they set in. Dave hired 'em both.

Willie rented a house for Martha and their first child. Soon Holland, along with the Playboys' steel player and his wife, shared the house. Bush remembered the lively atmosphere: "Willie and Martha fought Custer's Last Stand; [they] fought constantly in the back of the house, and the steel player and his wife were fighting constantly in the front of the house. This poor guy [Holland] was in the middle."

Playing at Al's was hardly lucrative. Perpetually in need of money, Willie answered an ad for a disc jockey at KBOP in Pleasanton, 35 miles south of San Antonio. Bush went along for the ride. "The [station] owner was Doc Parker," said Bush. "He was a chiropractor, and the most educated man Willie and I had ever met. He was really a genius. He had Willie read some copy for him and hired him on the spot. Willie was a deejay, doin' the news, makin' commercials. In his spare time we would sell radio time for 45 to 50 dollars a week."

Parker also hired Bush for the loosely run operation. He, Willie, and the station engineer hosted 15-minute shows consecutively. Bush remembered the arrangement: "The engineer, Red Hilburn, would have me as his guest. And my show would come on after that, and I'd have Willie as [my guest], and Willie's show would come on, and he'd have Red as his guest. Each one of us got more time that way. In 45 minutes, we were on twice." Bush doubled as KBOP's weatherman. His meteorological skills involved standing outside the studio, observing the weather, then announcing what he saw. Off the air, he and Willie had a new band, playing clubs as "Johnny Bush and the Hillbilly Playboys." A band poster denoted Willie as Bush's "exclusive management."

None of it lasted. Parker finally canned Willie for chronic lateness. He and Bush moved to Houston, but in late 1954 Willie landed in Fort Worth, where he joined the staff of KCNC Radio and played clubs on the side. Their finances still precarious, the Nelsons moved to San Diego in 1956. Myrle and her husband now lived in Vancouver, Washington, across the river from Portland, Oregon. She persuaded Willie and Martha to relocate there.

Willie's radio experience landed him a deejay's position on KVAN in Vancouver, a job that afforded him the first real glimpse of what he might become. His 10 A.M. to 2 P.M. country music show was so popular it came in second only to Arthur Godfrey's overwhelmingly popular daily CBS morning radio program. Publicist Mae Boren Axton, the co-writer of Elvis's megahit "Heartbreak Hotel," met Willie when she stopped in the area to do advance publicity for a Hank Snow tour. Willie played her some of his original songs. Her encouragement kept him writing.

Willie had recorded demos and home recordings up till the fall of 1957, when he took his electric guitar and amp and a local steel guitar player into a converted Portland garage to tape his own composition "No Place for Me" and Leon Payne's composition "Lumberjack." Willie mailed the tape to Nashville-based Starday Records, and its pressing plant manufactured the 45-rpm single on the "Willie Nelson" label. Selling the records over KVAN for $1, listeners got both the disc and an autographed 8-by-10 photo of a pompadoured Willie, its caption depicting him as "Your Old Cotton Pickin'—Snuff Dippin'—Tobaccer Chewin'—Stump Jumpin'—Gravy Soppin'—Coffee Pot Dodgin'—Dumplin' Eatin'—Frog Giggin'—Hillbilly From Hill County." The first pressing of 500 discs sold out. Over time, Willie moved a total of 3,000 singles. Starday was cagey when it came to new singers. According to its pressing contract, the company reserved the right to release the record on Starday and publish the songs if no publisher existed. In Willie's case, it didn't exercise the option.

When Willie demanded a raise at KVAN, the station's manager balked. The Nelsons headed back to Texas. They stayed with Willie's dad for a time. Willie sold encyclopedias, then Kirby vacuum cleaners door to door, and played honky-tonks. Trying to put down roots, he joined a local Baptist congregation and taught Sunday school. When the minister heard that Willie sang in bars, he forced him to choose between that and teaching Sunday school. Infuriated by the minister's judgmental mind-set, Willie quit the church and soon moved his family to Houston.

Despite all the moves and day jobs, Willie's creative juices surged. He wrote a slew of new songs, including a ballad he titled "Crazy." With a growing family, he needed money and decided to sell his songs. He approached Houston bandleader Larry Butler and offered him a new original titled "Mr. Record Man." Shrewd enough to see the song's potential, compassionate enough to sense Willie's desperation, Butler declined the songs, loaned Willie $50, and hired him to play with his band.

After settling Martha and the kids into the Houston suburb of Pasadena, Willie became a Sunday morning deejay on KCRT in addition to playing Houston's Esquire Ballroom with Butler. On the side, he taught at the Paul Buskirk School of Guitar. The West Virginia–born Buskirk was a legendary guitarist-mandolinist who'd worked as a sideman for various acts, including Johnnie and Jack. Willie sold Buskirk, his business partner Walt Breeland, and singer Claude Gray one of his newer compositions: the gospel tune "Family Bible."

Willie's first real record deal came when he signed with Pappy Daily's Houston-based D Records in 1959. Daily was a veteran Texas music businessman. Known as a record wholesaler, he'd begun producing records and selling the masters in 1949. In 1952 he co-founded Starday Records with Jack Starnes. By 1957, he'd sold his interest in Starday to Starnes's successor, Don Pierce, and founded D Records. Willie's two D singles attracted little notice. Then in the spring of 1960, Claude Gray's D single of "Family Bible" became a Top 10 hit across the country. Selling the song meant Willie got no composer credit, but its success established his ability to write hits for others and sent his musical self-esteem soaring. He knew that if he could write one hit, he could write another.

Commuting to the Esquire one night, Willie conceived the blues-flavored ballad "Night Life." Given his perpetual cash-flow woes, he'd sold half the song to Buskirk and Breeland. Pappy Daily disliked the song. He felt it wasn't country, scorned the song's blues overtones, and refused to let Willie record it. Ignoring Daily's threats of a lawsuit, Willie booked first-rate local musicians, including steel guitarist Herb Remington and vibraphonist Dick Shannon, to record it and another blues piece. A small Houston label released both songs on a 45 under the pseudonym of Paul Buskirk and His Little Men featuring Hugh Nelson. The arrangement was relaxed, and more or less reflected the way Willie played the song for the rest of his career.

As 1960 came to a close, Willie Nelson came to two conclusions. One was obvious: Houston was a dead end for his musical career. Two, with a hit song under his belt, now was as propitious a moment as any to make his move on the big time. Late that year, he piled Martha and the kids into his 1950 Buick and drove them to Waco to stay with her family, then he headed for Nashville alone. The Buick, barely functioning all the while, finally died when he got into downtown Nashville.

Willie didn't arrive without contacts. He knew singer Billy Walker, who took him to Starday. Apparently no one there connected him with the old custom pressing from Vancouver. His talents impressed Starday producer Tommy Hill, a veteran recording artist and original front man in Ray Price's Cherokee Cowboys. Hill's boss, Starday owner Don Pierce, was far less impressed.

He soon sent for Martha and set her and the kids up in a local trailer park. Martha worked as a waitress while Willie struggled to get a foothold. Hanging at the legendary Tootsie's Orchid Lounge, across the alley from the rear of the Opry, Willie met Hank Cochran, a new and promising writer. When Cochran heard Willie's songs, he was so impressed that he took him to Pamper Music, the publishing company he wrote for.

Pamper was co-owned by Ray Price and his manager, former Opry fiddler Hal Smith. Both liked Willie's songs and signed him as a writer for $50 a week, money they'd orignally allotted as a raise for Cochran. He asked Price and Smith to give it to Willie instead. The stark surroundings in Pamper's writers' office led Willie to write "Hello Walls" in 10 minutes. He hadn't given up on selling songs to keep the family in food. One night at Tootsie's, he buttonholed Faron Young. Like Larry Butler, Faron refused. Alcoholic, short-fused, and foul-mouthed, Faron, renowned as (in his own words) the "softest touch in Nashville," lent Willie $500 instead and recorded "Hello Walls" for Capitol.

Willie had steady work by 1961 as bass guitarist and warm-up singer for Ray Price's Cherokee Cowboys. Like Tommy Hill and Van Howard before him, Willie sang a few songs at each show to warm up audiences before Price came out. Given Price's stardom and the high caliber of musicianship in the band, the Cowboys were a first-rate training ground for a new singer. Willie also played guitar on Price hits like "Soft Rain" and "Pride" and on Price's Bob Wills tribute LP *San Antonio Rose*.

To everyone's amazement, including Willie's, Faron's Capitol recording of "Hello Walls" stayed at number 1 for nine weeks in the spring of 1961. Lightning struck twice, and since Willie hadn't sold any part of the song, the writer's royalties were all his. Overwhelmed by his first $20,000 writer's royalty check, Willie strode into Tootsie's and French-kissed Faron. Even with a hit song, Willie continued playing the road with Price. The royalties from the hit allowed him to live higher than ever before. "All of a sudden, I was rich," Willie later remembered. "I would fly to all the gigs, stay in the penthouses, invite all the band up and use up room service, and have hellacious parties on 'Hello Walls.' "

Then Patsy Cline recorded "Crazy," the ballad Willie wrote in Houston. Her single became a Top 10 country and pop hit in 1962. By then it was clear that Willie, along with Hank Cochran, Mel Tillis, Roger Miller, and

Harlan Howard, represented a new generation of Nashville composers creating more true-to-life and honest music than any country songwriters before them except for Floyd Tillman, Lefty Frizzell, and Hank Williams. Cochran, whose own writing career was taking off (he wrote Patsy's "I Fall to Pieces"), played Liberty Records producer Joe Allison a tape of Willie's demo recordings. In the fall of 1961 Joe Allison signed Willie, who'd left the Cherokee Cowboys to start his own career.

Willie had a tougher row to hoe in the studio because the Nashville Sound best accommodated singers who sang on the beat like Faron, Patsy, and most others. Willie's vocal phrasing bore the stamps of two of his Texas role models, Floyd Tillman and Lefty Frizzell, whose penchant for holding a syllable for varying lengths for effect set them apart. Tillman's style bore the influence of pop singers; Lefty built his style on Tillman's. Such phrasing was common in pop. Willie's hero Frank Sinatra sang that way, as did western swing fiddler-singer Wade Ray. In the hands of a great vocalist, it enhanced a good lyric.

Proof that this line of thought didn't play in Nashville can be seen in an incident involving Tillman. In 1958, as Nashville Sound productions grew in popularity, RCA Victor released a newly recorded album of Tillman singing his greatest hits, including "Slipping Around." Jethro Burns, the mandolin-playing half of Homer and Jethro and a longtime Tillman fan who understood his vocal style, attended the sessions. Renowned for his country-jazz virtuosity, Jethro watched as Chet Atkins (Jethro's brother-in-law) gave the singer full-blown Nashville Sound production, with the Anita Kerr Singers doing background vocals. Overhearing the Kerr singers' derisive laughter at Tillman's phrasing behind the singer's back left Jethro outraged and disgusted.

Willie faced an identical dilemma. His style left many feeling that he sang "funny," in other words, out of meter. Wade Ray came to his defense in 1983 when he declared: "I've heard musicians say Willie sang out of meter. He did *not* sing out of meter; he phrased. He sang in front of the beat, behind the beat and just came out at the end." The phrasing problems materialized at Willie's first Liberty session, as Nashville's versatile studio musicians found it nearly impossible to follow him. Accustomed to listening closely to the singers they accompanied, they had to tune out his voice and focus only on playing their accompaniment. Nonetheless, he and Shirley Collie, wife of country disc jockey Biff Collie, sang a duet on "Willingly" that flew into *Billboard*'s country Top 10.

As his marriage to the hotheaded Martha deteriorated into a continuing flurry of violent fights, drinking sprees, and mutual infidelity, Willie took up with Shirley, a veteran performer who became his bass player. Late in 1961, Billy Walker took Willie's "Funny How Time Slips Away" into the Top 30.

Jimmy Elledge's late 1961 pop version demonstrated the appeal Willie's songs had beyond country.

Willie finally achieved Top 10 status with his original ballad "Touch Me" in the spring of '62. A steady, deliberate performance, it peaked at number 7 on *Billboard*'s country charts. Liberty issued his debut LP, ... *And Then I Wrote,* that year. He recorded half of it in Nashville, half in L.A. No follow-up hit materialized. In 1963, Liberty released his second and final LP for the label, *Here's Willie Nelson,* with liner notes by hero (and fellow Liberty artist) Bob Wills. That year, Ray Price's chilling version of "Night Life" reached the Top 20.

Shirley divorced Biff Collie; Willie and Martha also divorced; Willie married Shirley. He toured constantly as songwriting royalties continued flowing in. In November 1963, he and Shirley found their dream home, a brick ranch house on substantial acreage in Ridgetop, outside Nashville. With room for farming, Willie, unable to follow up "Touch Me," determined to raise hogs, write songs, and forget about touring. Soon Johnny Bush, drumming with Ray Price's Cherokee Cowboys, moved in near Willie's spread in Ridgetop. Across the road was Wade Ray, who'd moved to Nashville from Las Vegas.

In 1964, on one of his final Liberty recordings, Willie laid down an exquisite, intimate version of the classic pop ballad "Am I Blue" with lush and totally sympathetic strings by Hollywood jazz and pop arranger Ernie Freeman, who clearly had no trouble with Willie's phrasing. It had no truck with the Nashville Sound. Instead, it clearly anticipated his best-selling 1978 *Stardust* album of pop standards with strings. Thinking back to "Am I Blue" in 1993, Willie reflected on the cool reception such innovations got at the time. "To the powers that be, it wasn't an idea that was thought to be commercial at that time," he explained. "I think it would have been, had they put it out and promoted it as being not just a country song but across-the-board record. Once you put something out as country alone, as they tend to do these days, and they eliminate the rest of the music world, I think it's ... not good."

As his Liberty contract ended, Willie's failure to achieve consistent success on records frustrated him. Certain that he could turn things around if he signed with the right record label, he sought a new deal. Around mid-1964, he showed up at Johnny Bush's house:

> He come by one day and said, "I got a dilemma here." I said, "Whatcha got goin'?" He said, "I've got a choice of goin' with Monument or RCA." I said, "I know what decision I'd make." He said, "Which one?" I said, "RCA." He said, "I think I got a better deal with [Monument's] Fred [Foster]. We talked about this, and I just feel like this might be better with

me." He had lunch several times with Chet Atkins, and he's a very intelligent man, but Willie said, at some of those lunches, he [Atkins] wouldn't say a word. So, for some reason Willie went with Monument. He could have gone either way.

Willie made a few interesting records with Fred Foster at Monument in 1964, but Foster issued only one single: the dramatic "I Never Cared for You." It sank. Foster released nothing else and didn't try to hold Willie to his contract. But RCA was still interested. Atkins, who'd long admired Willie's writing, needed an off-the-wall singer in the wake of Roger Miller's successes; he had managed to record only one hit during Miller's brief stint with RCA. In 1965, Chet signed two other musical mavericks: Waylon Jennings and singer-songwriter John Hartford. Commenting for Willie's autobiography, Atkins explained his strategy at the time. "I said, 'Well, he sounds great in Texas. What we've got to do is spread him out of Texas.' So that was going to be our thing—promote the hell out of Willie and sell his records all over the country. But we didn't do it."

Willie joined the *Grand Ole Opry* cast on November 28, 1964. Around the same time, he joined Ernest Tubb's half-hour syndicated TV show, produced by Pamper co-owner Hal Smith's TV company. He appeared on the 100 Tubb shows along with Tubb's band, the Texas Troubadours, and Wade Ray. "Pamper put the money up for that and at that time, they had a booking agency. And they thought havin' a TV show would keep Ernest workin' and Willie workin'," said Johnny Bush.

The long-standing canon of Willie's career indicates that he was straitjacketed by Atkins and RCA. Over the years, that hype has grown, some portraying Atkins as a drawling corporate villain who forced, cajoled, and bullied Willie into conforming to the schlocky, string-ridden Nashville Sound. As is usually the case, the truth is far more complex. A look at the whole of Willie's RCA career shows clearly that Atkins wasn't locked into a single approach to recording Willie. Over Willie's eight years with the label, Chet tried nearly every format to move Willie into the mainstream. While some sessions featured boring strings and sugary vocal arrangements, other sessions surrounded him with hot or austere honky-tonk bands. It didn't matter. His early singles didn't chart or hit no higher than the Top 50. By August of 1965, Atkins, who'd begun hiring additional producers, brought Felton Jarvis on board. Initially, Chet and Jarvis co-produced Willie's material. On his first session with Willie, Jarvis emulated pop producer Phil Spector's "Wall of Sound" production with massed strings, without commercial success, though Nelson's gripping murder ballad "I Just Can't Let You Say Goodbye" emerged from this August session.

Appearing on Tubb's TV show, Willie worked closely with Tubb's band, the Texas Troubadours, one of the finest backup bands in the business. While onstage and in the studio, they dutifully gave their boss the austere melodic backing that his style required, and Tubb encouraged them to develop their own identity during their own sets at shows. That wasn't difficult. Country-jazz guitarist Leon Rhodes and pedal steel guitarist Buddy Charlton provided formidable instrumental voices. The band boasted two future star vocalists: guitarist Jack Greene and drummer Cal Smith. Bassist Jack Drake (brother of pedal steel wizard Pete Drake) ran the band. Tubb was so proud of the band's talents that he'd gotten them their own contract with Decca.

Willie suggested that he, the Troubadours, and Wade Ray record a straight-ahead Texas honky-tonk album. Chet readily agreed. Though the Troubadours' Decca contract prevented the band from being credited on the album, the result was an exhilarating collection of Texas material performed without compromise. Though Willie later commented, "I wasn't there to promote it or push it. Had it been Chet's or somebody's idea, they probably would have got it out," *Country Favorites Willie Nelson Style* made it to number 9 on *Billboard*'s Top Country Albums charts.

He may have wanted to avoid the road, but staying in Ridgetop got on Willie's nerves after a while. He wanted to tour again, albeit in a low-budget format with no band, only Wade Ray coming along to play bass. They'd pick up local musicians wherever they performed. Ray loved touring with him this way. "That was, to me, the thing that really let people know his versatility," Ray said in 1994. "It was like he was sittin' down in a chair and singing what he wanted to. That's the way Willie's at his best."

Maybe so, but that approach soon left Willie frustrated. The musical skills of sidemen varied from club to club. Some were excellent; others, barely amateur. One day Bush, who'd left the Cherokee Cowboys, stopped by: "I'd been cuttin' demos for a living to try to get something started on my own. I'd already left Ray, and Willie asked me if I'd do ten days in Texas and I said, 'Yeah, I need the money bad.' That's when he started workin' the road as a single, just carryin' Wade Ray."

Things improved a bit on the singles front. The somber, sarcastic "One in a Row" became Willie's biggest RCA single to date, peaking at number 18 in late 1966. "The Party's Over" followed early in '67, reaching number 24. Given the success of *Country Favorites,* Atkins, looking to enhance Willie's Texas sales, agreed to Willie's suggestion that they record a live album at Fort Worth's legendary Panther Hall, a hotbed of Willie popularity. Chet arranged for Felton Jarvis and engineer Al Pachuki to record Willie there. "Willie wanted to do a live album, and he was drawin' bigger crowds at Panther Hall than he was anywhere else," Bush said. "It was a great big room that would hold three or four thousand people. He was packin' it, and what better place to do a live album than the venue that you're really doin' great in? It was Willie, Wade, and I, the three of us straight through."

On the album, Willie demonstrated the eclecticism that marked his later, more successful years. He mixed strong renditions of his own songs, "Touch Me," "Night Life," and "I Never Cared For You" with the Beatles' "Yesterday," a bold choice for a country singer in that time. "Willie loved that song the first time he heard it," said Bush. "We rehearsed it at his house. We called [the harmonies], in those days, 'weird changes.'" Three numbers, Leon Payne's "I Love You Because," Willie's "I'm Still Not Over You," and Hank Williams's "There'll Be No Teardrops Tonight" were excised from the final release, most likely due to space problems. Reflecting on the live LP more than three decades later, Bush concluded, "That was a real great album because we didn't stop the tape, went through beginning to end. I don't think Willie went in to overdub. If he did, I didn't know about it." Willie didn't, but Jarvis later overdubbed studio rhythm guitarist Chip Young. Released late in 1966, *Live Country Music Concert* charted only briefly.

That year, Willie connected with a newcomer whose very existence stirred controversy. Willie met Charley Pride on a Texas tour headlined by Marty Robbins. Willie, a political liberal by Nashville standards, hadn't heard Pride but feared Deep South audiences upset by the ongoing turmoil over civil rights might become inflamed by a black country singer. The minute he heard Pride's undeniably country voice, Willie realized Pride's potential. While performing to a friendly crowd at Dallas's Longhorn Ballroom, a well-liquored Willie brought Pride onstage, introduced him, kissed him on the lips, and let him sing. Longhorn owner Dewey Groom, who'd insisted he could never risk booking Pride, stood stunned as Willie's fans listened and accepted.

A few Willie albums entered *Billboard*'s Top Country Albums charts, but singles were another matter. In mid-1967, his version of Red Lane's ballad "Blackjack County Chain," a tale of chain gang prisoners beating a sheriff to death, reached number 21. Bush knew the song's history; Willie recorded it after someone else wisely passed on it. "They wanted Charley Pride to do it," said Bush. "And Charley said, 'Man, there ain't no way I'm gonna beat a sheriff to death with chains. I'm lucky to get out of these (clubs) alive now!'"

After Wade Ray moved on, Willie expanded his band by hiring old Cherokee Cowboys bandmate Jimmy Day on pedal steel, adding drummer David Zettner, and using Bush on bass. Needing a band name, Bush recalled a TV commercial of the day for a remedy that could vanquish "the offenders" that caused halitosis. "The 'offenders' were onion, garlic, anything that made your breath offensive. I said, 'How 'bout [calling the band] "The Offenders?"' Willie said, 'Yeah, that's it, that's what we do: we offend everybody!'" Promoters and booking agents were also offended, so the band became "The Record Men," based on Willie's song "Mr. Record Man."

While Atkins can hardly be considered a villain in Willie's situation at RCA, he's not completely off the hook, either. Many of Willie's and Waylon's problems at RCA stemmed from the redefined roles of producers that began with Chet and Owen Bradley in the early days of the Nashville Sound. From the 1920s through the mid-1950s, producers generally helped the artist get his music on record, generally without active interference, with maybe one or two studio players at the most. The Nashville Sound began a trend that continues today: it put producers almost completely in the driver's seat, controlling every aspect of a record. Chet helped pioneer this style, and since his reach extended to both choice of songs and session musicians, it caused friction. Many artists felt more comfortable recording with musicians they toured with, who knew the sound they wanted and gave it to them onstage. Texas and West Coast artists particularly preferred that kind of autonomy. At Capitol, they got it from Ken Nelson, who only jumped in when he was needed.

Chet and other producers viewed things differently. To finish four songs in a three-hour session and come up with clever arrangements along the way, they needed musicians with whom they could communicate quickly and completely: players they knew who could take direction. While many great studio musicians began as touring sidemen, not all made the transition to studio work. Many road players found it hard to take direction and work with studio musicians. This issue of creative control became the true driving force behind the Outlaw movement.

In the studio, Chet and Willie had similar ends, but divergent views about the means. Willie had a Texan's urge to put together his sound as he liked it onstage. He had the band flowing exactly as he wanted. He knew what audiences wanted; Bush and Day gave him that sound. That didn't always fit Chet's criteria. A collision was inevitable. This situation left Bush, who'd resumed the drummer's role, caught in the middle:

We were workin' the road with Willie and were with him when he would write these songs. And we'd play 'em for audiences, and worked it out so [the arrangement] was what Willie wanted. When we'd get to Nashville, Chet didn't like it. He kept sayin' the drums weren't makin' it. If you hear some of Willie's recordings, he liked a little rhumba and a Bolero beat. That's what Willie wanted. Chet hated it. So here I am, wantin' to please Willie and Chet at the same time.

The situation came to a head for Bush on a mid-1967 session: "I knew what Willie wanted. I worked the road with Willie. He hired me because those house drummers [in clubs] were killin' him. So I went on the road with him because I knew exactly what he wanted. Well, I tried to do that in the studio, and it wasn't what Chet wanted. So I was confused, and Willie didn't say anything and Chet got mad."

After the session ended, Bush walked down the hall for his own record date (paid for by Willie) in RCA's Studio B. Many of the same musicians, who'd finished Willie's session and had witnessed the friction between Bush and Atkins, had been hired to back Bush on the session, among them Day, Jerry Reed on guitar, bassist Junior Husky, and pianist Jerry Smith. Bush remembered the boost he got: "After Reed heard me sing a couple of phrases of my first song, he said, 'Why don't you go over and tell Chet Atkins to kiss your ass!' I thought, 'What a compliment!'"

But Bush discovered he'd done his last RCA session with Willie. Soon afterward, Bush recalled, Willie flew to Texas:

> Jimmy Day and I picked Willie up at the airport, and Willie said, "John, I got some bad news for you." I said, "What's that?" He said, "Chet don't want you on my sessions anymore." I said, "I'll tell you what, Will. I'm relieved. I never wanted to be a session drummer. That's not my aim. I'm disappointed because I know what you want." And Willie said, "Well, I know. One of these days that'll change."
>
> And Jimmy Day just laughed like hell, saying, "John couldn't cut it! Chet Atkins fired him!"

It turned out that, after Willie's next session with Day in August 1967, Willie had to convey to Day, who'd had substantial studio experience, that Chet had vetoed *him* as well. As Bush concluded, "Chet had to have control, not Willie."

Chet undoubtedly felt he needed control in Willie's case, because by 1968, despite four years of patience, selling Willie Nelson to the public had proven no easier than finding a safety pin at the bottom of Old Hickory Lake. But his belief in Willie's talents led to another four-year contract. Willie continued trying new ideas. On one session that year, as the Vietnam War raged on, he recorded "Jimmy's Road," a song reflecting his strong antiwar sentiments. The song, released on a single, went unnoticed. Had he been a bigger star, the public backlash from conservative country pro-Vietnam fans could have done him in.

Oddly enough, 1968 brought Willie his biggest hit at RCA. Typically, it came out of left field. "Bring Me Sunshine" was a non-original pop tune, given a swinging, finger-snapping arrangement closer to something Bobby Darin or Buddy Greco might have attempted. It was catchy and different enough that early in 1969, it reached number 3 on the *Billboard* country charts.

With his own singing career taking hold, Bush gave Willie a year's notice, and Willie brought in drummer Paul English to apprentice. Bush explained why breaking in Paul took time: "Trying to teach someone to play behind Willie, you gotta feel what he's doing and you can't just count a tempo. You have to let Willie sing with you. It's not that complicated, but it takes awhile to feel him out. Willie doesn't break meter. Paul would watch me, and he did that for a year until my records hit." As Bush's singles for Stop Records (the first three written by Willie) began to chart, he was ready to move on. As the year ended, he remembered, "Willie said, 'After you introduce me, go onto the bus,' and he left Paul up there."

Meanwhile, things began deteriorating for Willie. At one 1968 session, Chet paired him with new producer Danny Davis (a.k.a. George Nowlan), a former big-band trumpeter renowned for his bland 1970s RCA instrumental recordings of country tunes with a studio band called the Nashville Brass, a lame variant on Herb Alpert's Tijuana Brass. With Willie, Davis took the lazy way out. In a typical Nashville Sound cliché, Davis indiscriminately slopped strings and voices all over Willie's *My Own Peculiar Way* album with all the flair and creativity of Lawrence Welk. Of all Willie's RCA producers, Davis came closest to fulfilling the conventional wisdom that Willie, the square peg, had been forced to fit himself into RCA's round holes.

Things weren't much better in Willie's personal life. Shirley was gone by late 1970. He'd wrecked five cars. His song royalties went down a black hole, subsidizing money-losing tours. He was in a relationship with Connie Koepke, a Texas woman who moved in after Shirley left and with whom he'd had a daughter. And all the while, he remained in the grip of the RCA machine. Even with Jarvis producing, the quality of his records vacillated. The syrupy *Willie Nelson and Family* rivaled *My Own Peculiar Way* for artistic inertia.

On the evening of December 23, 1970, while attending a party in Nashville, Willie got a message that fire was destroying his Ridgetop home. He later recalled flippantly suggesting someone "pull the car in the garage," then sped home to retrieve a special guitar case. He found it intact in the rubble and retrieved the case—filled with marijuana—before firefighters could find it.

In his mind, the fire became a bellwether, signaling the need for a major change. Shortly afterward, he moved his family to the Happy Valley Dude Ranch near Bandera, Texas. He'd had better luck with singles recently. "I'm a Memory" broke the Top 30 in early 1971. Divorced from Shirley, he married Connie in April 1971. Around that time, Felton Jarvis contacted him about sessions for his twelfth RCA album. Willie realized he had absolutely no material ready. Once he got to Nashville in early May, he furiously began writing. Combining new original numbers with older ones ("Family Bible"), Willie created his greatest artistic achievement at RCA: the concept album *Yesterday's Wine*. Recorded over two days, it chronicled one man's life beginning to end with the peaks and valleys in between. The album ends with "Goin' Home," as the protagonist watches his own funeral.

Concept albums were rare in country. Companies had released anthologies of the same style of music on multi-disc 78-rpm albums. In 1940, RCA issued the anthology *Smoky Mountain Ballads,* the first country reissue of early string-band material. Another early thematic effort came in 1947, when Capitol issued Merle Travis's newly recorded *Songs of the Coal Mines,* which featured Travis's "Sixteen Tons" and "Dark as a Dungeon." The first such LP came from another southwesterner: Oklahoma-bred Jean Shepard's 1956 *Songs of a Love Affair* took the listener through the end of a marriage from a woman's perspective, through stages of grief and recovery. Perhaps owing to his recent personal turmoil, Willie created a dramatic musical statement on *Yesterday's Wine,* one that attests to the way great art is sometimes assembled under terrific pressure.

In Texas, he formed a new band and started working honky-tonks, playing what he wanted for fans who knew and loved him. Even his lengthening hair, tame by rock standards, suspect by Nashville standards, didn't dissuade longtime fans in this time when Merle Haggard's "Okie From Muskogee" resonated with anti-hippie country fans. In the Lone Star state, prejudices against long hair on men remained strong. The fact that Willie's older friends like Ernest Tubb shared that view didn't faze him.

That mattered less to Willie than the new cultural convergence he sensed around the state capitol of Austin. The Austin of that day was not yet a high-tech center. It *was* home to the University of Texas, a place where Willie's older "redneck" fans and beer-drinking, long-haired, pot-smoking young people, united by their love of Willie's music, came together peacefully at the Armadillo World Headquarters, which booked both country and rock acts. Soon Willie implored Waylon Jennings to play there. He and Waylon were in the same boat: they both had recording careers that were only modestly successful, and they both laid the blame for that on RCA's control-freak mind-set.

While Nashville's core of intelligentsia saw *Yesterday's Wine* as the masterpiece it was, RCA saw only one more product not moving fast enough out of record store LP bins. Atkins was pulling away from day-to-day production work, the better to focus on administration and his own guitar instrumental records. In the fall of 1971, RCA released "Yesterday's Wine" and "Me and Paul" as a single; it squeaked into the Top 70. Writing in his autobiography years later, Willie said, "*Yesterday's Wine* was regarded as way too spooky and far out to waste promotion money on."

Although his contract hadn't expired, for all intents and purposes, Willie Nelson's RCA recording career was over. In his usual laid-back style, he simply bided his time until the last sessions. Early in 1972, the company released "The Words Don't Fit The Picture" as a single and it zoomed all the way to number 73. Clearly, he'd moved on in his mind. Proof of that came when he showed up at RCA on April 25 and 26, 1972, with drummer Paul English and his bassist Dan "Bee" Spears and an idea for a new concept album.

The first song, "Phases, Stages, Circles, Cycles and Scenes" and the songs following it—"Pretend I Never Happened," "Sister's Coming Home," "Down at the Corner Beer Joint," and "I'm Falling In Love Again"—expanded the concept Jean Shepard created: chronicling a broken marriage. Willie wanted to examine a broken marriage from both the husband's and wife's vantage points. RCA released only "Phases" as a single, along with a delightfully rough, funky rendition of "Mountain Dew," the famous Bascom Lamar Lunsford-Scotty Wiseman moonshine anthem that Grandpa Jones made a standard. After dangling for eight years in the abyss between non-seller and marginal artist, those last sessions ended Willie Nelson's relationship with RCA Victor.

Through 1972, RCA continued issuing material recorded at previous sessions. The LPs *The Willie Way*, released that summer, charted no higher than number 34; *The Words Don't Fit the Picture* didn't chart at all. No one on either side felt it worth the effort to try and renew his contract. The sales weren't there, nor was the company's enthusiasm. Willie was ready to move on. Disgusted, Waylon stayed and successfully battled RCA higher-ups to win creative control of his recordings.

Castigated by some for dropping Willie from the label, Chet Atkins, who died in 2001, denied he instigated the end of Willie's contract. Quoted in Willie's autobiography, Atkins's honesty was exemplified by a remark that showed clearly the guitarist as reluctant executive. "I was just about the worst at promotion and sales," he reflected. In 1980, he told me without prompting, that "I didn't drop Willie; someone else did." It was more a matter of an artist who was simply, in a term often used by performers, "too smart for the room." In fairness, RCA gave him eight years. Labels had been known to drop performers who'd sold far more records than Willie, in far less time.

One 1972 trip from Texas to Nashville became crucial to his future. During that trip, Willie attended a party at Harlan Howard's house. A guitar pull took place as singers swapped songs. Late that night, Willie took the chair and sang all the songs he'd written for *Phases*. Listening attentively was Atlantic Records vice-president Jerry Wexler. A former *Billboard* writer, "Wex" was responsible for the greatest R&B records of the era, from Clyde McPhatter and Ray Charles to Otis Redding and Aretha Franklin.

While it was a given that Wexler was well versed in blues, jazz, Tin Pan Alley pop, and, of course, R&B, many failed to realize the Atlantic executive was equally conversant in country, both mainstream and off-the-wall genres like Cajun and western swing. He knew Willie Nelson's work well. With Atlantic about to form a new country division, Wexler offered Willie a contract; Willie agreed, and Wexler allowed Willie greater control.

What followed was a marathon New York session that yielded the 1973 Atlantic album *Shotgun Willie* and the gospel album *The Troublemaker* (released by Columbia in 1976). *Shotgun* garnered acclaim and respect from the rock press. Though it charted only modestly in country, it still outsold any of his previous albums on RCA or Liberty. Wexler let him have at a full-blown *Phases and Stages,* mixing new versions of the material he recorded at RCA with other numbers creating a cohesive, profoundly moving whole. It resulted in still more acclaim, and while it only modestly grazed the country charts, the album nonetheless became a landmark. The label also recorded a number of live shows Willie did in Austin in 1974 that reflected his broad-based musical diversity. As he did on his RCA live album, he mixed his own songs with those by others, with rock tunes and classic country standards that satisfied both the old and young in his audience. Segments of these shows were released in 1995.

Atlantic folded their country division soon afterward. In Willie's case, the circumstances didn't produce massive sales, but public reaction, particularly among younger people, reinforced his idea that he could chart his own course.

Willie signed with Columbia. This time, his contract guaranteed him creative control. Using only his touring musicians, the very thing RCA had denied him, he created another concept LP, *Red Headed Stranger*, in 1975. He mixed older songs, including the title tune, to create a story of romance mixed with the violent side of the Old West. Recorded in a small Texas studio, the album's total cost was around $20,000. Columbia executives initially balked at the album's no-frills, underproduced sound, which to them, sounded like a demo (similar to the sound on the final RCA tracks). Nonetheless, Willie had the creative control, and they relented.

Any concerns evaporated after the album's breakout single, "Blue Eyes Crying In the Rain," a 30-year-old ballad penned by legendary songwriter Fred Rose, made it to number 1. It set Willie on a path to the success that had long eluded him, validating the visions he'd been denied at RCA. The album remained atop the charts for five weeks and eventually earned double platinum status, meaning over two million copies were sold.

Soon, with Waylon also enjoying substantial success as he controlled his recordings, RCA jumped on the Willie bandwagon. The pair had previously been tagged "Outlaws," based on a remark by Waylon's assistant Hazel Smith. The media seized on the term, often simplistically depicting it as the triumph of long-haired country singers over Nashville's old guard. There was a string of singles, and gold and platinum albums. (*Wanted! The Outlaws!*), featuring new and old RCA recordings by Willie, Waylon, his wife Jessi Colter, and Tompall Glaser, eventually became the first country LP to ever sell a million copies, earning a platinum record. All this set the stage for Willie's 1992 induction into the Country Music Hall of Fame.

In the years after Willie found stardom, RCA reissued numerous albums of older Willie material to grab the new audience. Many of these LPs substituted newly-shot photos depicting the shaggier current Willie, as opposed to the clean-cut singer of the years 1964 through 1972. Even more remarkably, RCA began releasing a steady stream of Willie singles from the old days. Suddenly RCA material like "Sweet Memories" and "If You Could Touch Her At All," virtually ignored in their time, reached the country Top 10.

Waylon's and Willie's successes allowed them to make music freed from the yoke of Nashville production values. Their contracts freed them to record what material they wanted with whom they chose and with any producer they chose, in any studio. Willie explained it to me in 1994 thusly: "Every guy needs a producer sometimes, but sometimes, he knows what he wants to do and he should have the freedom to go in and do it. I think a producer most of the time knows when an artist has the ability to do that, and a good producer will let him do it and then jump in there and take credit for it."

Revolutionary as all this sounds, it didn't change Music Row's fundamental complexion. Most artists lacked the self-confidence to follow Willie's lead unless strong sales gave them leverage. The dominance of producers forced to cater to the absurdly one-dimensional, consultant-driven country-radio formats remains a sorry fact of life in twenty-first-century Nashville, despite flattening record sales.

Would Willie have fared any better at any other major label from 1968 to 1972? That's doubtful. Had he recorded for Frank Jones at Columbia, Ken Nelson or Marvin Hughes at Capitol, Billy Sherrill at Epic, Owen Bradley at Decca, or Jerry Kennedy at Mercury, the results would likely have been the same. Perhaps Columbia's Bob Johnston, who produced Johnny Cash at Columbia, or Jack Clement, with a lifelong flair for the unconventional, could have succeeded with him. Perhaps. Was an independent label the answer? Hardly, given the non-results during his brief stay at Monument.

Atkins correctly characterized Willie as being "ahead of his time." True enough. During those eight years at RCA, he hadn't a chance in hell of being understood anywhere but Texas. Thirty years ago, the Lone Star musical eclecticism that underlies Willie's repertoire was a regional quirk few outsiders understood and most of Nashville couldn't fathom. Nashville could produce hits on Texas singers as long as they were malleable enough to fit the mold. The broader market that eventually embraced him wasn't yet ready.

America now embraced all the Texas idiosyncrasies that made him special: his deep roots, grab-bag musical eclecticism, ability to blend styles (his road band didn't use pedal steel, but former Texas Playboy Johnny Gimble was a frequent guest on fiddle), and even the phrasing that made so many in Nashville uneasy. By then, his RCA years were the subject of bad memories in interviews. Today, when Lyle Lovett and other musically quirky stars from that state like Jimmie Dale Gilmore enjoy broad acceptance, it's clear that Willie and Waylon, who died in 2001, blazed that trail.

Willie soared through the 1970s into the 1980s as he recorded a string of hit albums and singles, one of which, the pop album *Stardust,* gave him an audience far beyond country. Unaffected by his stardom, when he won the CMA's Entertainer of the Year Award in 1979, he spoke of others who he felt deserved the award, including his old friend Faron Young. Likewise, he recorded duet albums in the 1980s with friends, some megastars (Waylon, Ray Price, Merle Haggard, and Roger Miller), others heroes of an earlier time (Hank Snow and Webb Pierce). While the latter albums weren't big sellers, Willie's honorable intentions, to expose these legends to his new audience, reflected his continuing homage to the past. In the early years of a new century, he continues recording and performing in a variety of contexts.

Willie Nelson's early work at Liberty, Monument, and RCA proved amply frustrating. Despite that, his talents often allowed him to rise above the formulas to create quality music. It took longer than it should have to reach his goal, yet in its own way, the very Nashville that stymied him and Waylon for so long gave him the impetus to break free and leave a lasting mark.

"Move Those Things Out"

Bob Wills Invades the Grand Ole Opry: 1944

Bob Wills, the Playboys, and the "Goddamned upstart," early 1944. KMTR radio, Hollywood: Les Anderson, Louie Tierney, Rip Ramsey, Buddy Ray, Alex Brashear, unknown, Monte Mountjoy and his drums, Bob, Laura Lee Owens, Tommy Duncan, Millard Kelso, unknown announcer, Dick Hamilton, Everett Stover. (Courtesy Glenn White)

In November 1944, Bob Wills, the Texas Playboys, and Uncle John Wills, Bob's father and first fiddle teacher, left San Diego, California, in a Trailways Bus with their names emblazoned on the front and sides. A variety of novelty acts accompanied them, making up what MCA, Wills's booking agent, billed as Bob Wills and His Great Vaudeville Show. Beyond his usual milieu, the Southwest and West Coast, he hoped to play theaters all the way to the East Coast, a region he'd never played before. Bob's former Tulsa manager, O.W. Mayo, arranged for the Playboys to play the Grand Ole Opry December 30.

The Saturday evening of the 30th, their Trailways eased up the incline of Nashville's Fifth Avenue and pulled to a stop in front of the Ryman Auditorium, the Opry's home for the previous two years. The Opry would never be the same, and that night a legend began, one misstated and misinterpreted for more than a half-century.

Two basic misconceptions have circulated for years. First, the story that tradition-minded Opry officials, concerned with maintaining the show's integrity and its detachment from popular music or anything remotely "uptown," flatly denied Wills the use of his drummer and that Wills meekly complied. The second states that those officials agreed to allow Wills's drummer only if the drums remained behind a stage curtain to preserve the show's integrity. Opry officials repeated this tale for so many years that everyone took it as gospel. Such are the vagaries of history: a confusion of time frames, intermingling facts from various decades, creates something romantic or unbelievably vague. The truth lies in the remembrances of those who were there. When I interviewed them in 1981 and 1982, many were still alive, well, and actively performing.

Within an hour of Wills's arrival, the differences between him and the Opry came into undeniable focus. Musicians accustomed to working in the dance halls of Texas, Oklahoma, and now, California, were already out of their element playing midwestern theaters. Now they were playing the premiere radio barn dance show in the country, one that by then had surpassed Chicago's once-unrivaled WLS *National Barn Dance*. It was the land of "hillbilly" music, a style that few of the jazz-lovers in the Playboys cared much for.

Minnie Pearl, even then the Opry's star comedienne, wrote about Wills's appearance in her autobiography: "The people were awestruck. His men got off the bus dressed in an all-white western wardrobe—no sequins or fancy studs, just exquisitely tailored gabardine, cut in the Western style." Certain band members recalled renowned Hollywood western tailor Nudie Cohen making the suits they wore on that tour, but that was impossible. Three years would pass before Cohen jumped into the western wear business. The Playboys' outfits were almost surely designed by Nathan Turk, L.A.'s pioneer western tailor, who outfitted Gene Autry, Roy Rogers, and Spade Cooley's band. The outfits dazzled, but it was the instruments that caused the shit to hit the fan. The list reads like the chorus of the song "The Twelve Days of Christmas." There were:

> Fiddlers Wills and Joe Holley
> The twin bass fiddles of Ted Adams and Rip Ramsey
> Two electric guitars and amps (Jimmy Wyble and Cameron Hill)
> Electric steel guitar and amp (Noel Boggs)
> A trumpet (Alex Brashear)

Capping it all was a set of white pearl finish Slingerland drums, complete with cymbals and other accessories belonging to Monte Mountjoy, the former Dixieland drummer whom Bob had hired earlier that year. Mountjoy remembered that when an Opry employee saw his equipment, he directed the drummer to set up behind a backstage curtain. He gave no reason; Mountjoy was clueless.

The reason, of course, was the vision of Opry founder George D. Hay, the former Memphis newspaperman who had founded the *National Barn Dance* before coming to Nashville in 1925 to help WSM start its own similar show. Hay saw himself as a preservationist of old-time music in increasingly modern times, using the high-tech world of radio to bring the sounds of the southern mountains, farms, and hollers to the world at large.

It was, of course, never that simple. Historian Charles Wolfe's research has revealed that Hay fabricated much of the Opry's fanciful rural façade, even the colorful names that some string bands utilized. He photographed musicians in rural garb who normally wore suits and ties, and he routinely allowed pop-flavored vocal quartets on the Opry.

Nonetheless, Hay drew the line—sharply—at anything that smacked of mainstream popular music. That included horns of any kind, drums, and electric guitars. When pioneer Opry guitarist-banjoist Sam McGee, known for his work with Uncle Dave Macon and the Dixieliners, brought an amplified steel guitar to the show in the late 1930s, playing it several times, Hay gently admonished McGee: "I'd rather you not play that on the Grand Ole Opry. We want to hold it down to earth."

Try as he might, Hay, could not hold that rule firmly in place. Ernest Tubb's addition to the Opry lineup in 1942 required that he use the trademark lead guitar that graced his hit records, as well as electric steel guitar. Hay yielded on that one, but horns and drums remained verboten.

Though Hay, who had several nervous breakdowns, was no longer running the show alone as he had in the 1930s, WSM management nonetheless honored Hay's vision, and with the entrance of Bob Wills, irresistible force met immovable object. Someone on the Opry staff—it's unclear precisely whom; perhaps Harry Stone, Jack Stapp, or Hay himself—made it clear that the drummer had to play behind the curtain. Mountjoy heard about it after the fact. "Bob and the powers that be had it out. He said, 'My drummer either plays from out behind that curtain or we don't play!'"

While this confrontation went on, Mountjoy, setting up backstage, felt the undeniable discomfort of being watched, and not with benign interest. Opry regulars, versed in the musical etiquette of the show, were stunned to see the signature instrument of Gene Krupa and Buddy Rich at the Ryman. "I felt very self-conscious," Mountjoy remembered. "They looked at me like maybe my zipper was open."

When 74-year-old singer-banjoist-comedian Uncle Dave Macon, the Opry's true musical patriarch, came in and caught sight of Mountjoy's Slingerlands, the shit really hit the fan. "He about flipped his dipper," Mountjoy explained. "We were breakin' tradition and all that. He went by a couple of times mumblin' about 'Goddamn young upstarts'; and 'What they doin' with those drums here?' It was pointed at me, and I just went on settin' my drums up. I didn't pay any attention to it because it wasn't my place to say anything."

The Playboys were set for the 9:30 Prince Albert Tobacco segment. Although normally broadcast over NBC, this evening the network carried a half-hour of the WLS *National Barn Dance* instead. That effectively eliminated any chance this auspicious occasion would be preserved on transcription disc.

Opry management thought they'd struck a deal with Bob. Mountjoy set the drums behind a curtain, which of course, made no sense by Bob's standards. It was impossible for the drummer to play separated by heavy fabric, especially in a band where feel and non-verbal communications with the leader and with each other were paramount. Roy Acuff hosted the Prince Albert segment, normally playing a song or two with his Smoky Mountain Boys before presenting guests. The Playboys had assembled, tuned up, and were ready to go. Mountjoy's drums were still behind the curtain when Wills gave Mountjoy an order: "Move those things out on the stage." Joe Holley heard the order, but knew nothing of the backstage clash over the drums. Interviewed in 1981, he said:

> The [Ryman Auditorium] stage is pretty shallow, and there wasn't any place to put the
> drums out there with everything else goin' on. So we set Monte's drums up. In fact, I

helped carry 'em out. Everybody was there, a bunch of us, and the minute we was sup-posed to go, while they had a little announcement, we grabbed the drums and shoved them out from that curtain in the back and put them right out there where you could start playin', and I mean it was all done in a minute's time.

I had my fiddle in one hand, had it ready to go. We just grabbed some drums and headed out there. I mean, everybody had something to carry, a bunch of us, and we just set 'em out there and we was ready to go in nothin' flat.

Mountjoy, Joe Holley, and several other Playboys scurried to pull the Slingerlands not only in front of the curtain, but to *center stage*. It was the latest battle that Wills fought to maintain his musical integrity. Earlier he had battled his former boss, W. Lee O'Daniel, who tried to run him off Oklahoma radio in 1934. He'd faced down his producer Art Satherley, who tried to keep him from talking and hollering on his records at his first session. He'd outlasted Irving Berlin, who rewrote the lyrics to "San Antonio Rose" only to relent and restore Wills's original lyrics. Damned if he'd make an exception for the Opry's whining purists.

When Acuff finished the introduction, the Playboys snapped into "New San Anto-nio Rose," Mountjoy's drums and Brashear's trumpet clearly visible to the audience. Minnie Pearl and Eddy Arnold never forgot the moment. "They came on the Opry stage to tremendous applause," she wrote. "When Tommy stepped up to the micro-phone to sing 'San Antonio Rose' the crowd screamed and carried on the way they did over Elvis Presley years later."

Arnold, whose own solo career was just beginning after his departure from Pee Wee King's western swing band, understood and appreciated what the Playboys were doing. "They just stopped the show cold. They had a good, heavy dance beat. And in that old building, which had great acoustics, it was just overpowering," he said in 1981. From the stage, Holley, fiddling away, was dumbfounded. "They couldn't get the people to quit applauding; they just kept on and on and on. They kept tryin' to quiet the crowd down, and they wouldn't quiet down."

That kind of response usually justifies an encore. But Wills had remorselessly flouted Opry tradition, first by the act of bringing a drummer, then by defying their request that Mountjoy stay concealed. "The powers that be got pissed," Mountjoy remembered. There would be no encore. But no one forgot, either. The next April, when the Opry was preempted after Franklin Roosevelt's death, Pee Wee King fol-lowed an emotional rendering of taps by his trumpeter with his stage show, drums and all. Hay protested, but since the Opry had been canceled and Hay had asked for the stage show, Pee Wee gave it to him in all its percussive glory.

Wills found a different reception when he played the show as a guest in April of 1948. This time, drummer Billy Jack Wills went on without a problem. Nineteen fifty-four brought Buddy Harman of Carl Smith's Tunesmiths to the Opry stage. He became the show's first regular drummer, standing onstage with a snare. Eventually, the ban would relax. Bass players worked to get a drumlike sound, until the show relented enough to allow snare drums. Eventually, by the time the show moved from the Ryman to Opryland in 1974, full drum sets were there to stay.

INTERVIEWS

Chapter 1: Spade Cooley

Hank Penny, October 1976
Bobbie Bennett, October 1976
Tex Williams, October 1976
Smokey Rogers, October 1976
Johnny Bond, October 1976

Chapter 2: Hank Penny

Hank Penny, 1976–1987
Herb Remington, March 28, 2000
Benny Garcia, April 2000

Wade Ray

Wade Ray, October 29, 1994

Chapter 3: Tommy Duncan

Glynn Duncan, 1996
Acknowledgments: Kevin Coffey, Dave Samuelson, Glenn White

Luke Wills

Luke Wills, 1987
Acknowledgments: Kevin Coffey, Glenn White

Lee Gillette

Ken Nelson, October 1996
Cliffie Stone, 1996
Speedy West, 1996–1997
Jim Loakes, 1994–1996

Chapter 4: Ken Nelson

Ken Nelson, January 1992, October 1996
Buck Owens, January 1992

Smoke! Smoke! Smoke!

Cliffie Stone, 1995
Tex Williams, October 1976
Smokey Rogers, October 1976
Acknowledgments: Ken Griffis

Chapter 5: Cliffie Stone

Cliffie Stone, 1996
Speedy West, 1996–1997
Jim Loakes, 1994–1996

Chapter 6: Tennessee Ernie Ford

Speedy West, 1994
Jim Loakes, 1994
Jeffrey "Buck" Ford, 1994

Chapter 7: Hank Thompson

Hank Thompson, 1994–1996
Bobby Garrett, 1996
Acknowledgments: Dave Samuelson, D. D. Bray, Kevin Coffey,
    Andrew Brown, Cliffie Stone

Slipping Around

Cliffie Stone, 1996

Chapter 8: Ray Price

Harold Bradley, April 27, 1995
Johnny Bush, May 12, 1995
Jimmy Day, (written) June 1995
Buddy Emmons, March 17, 1995
Johnny Gimble, April 21, 1995
Buddy Griffin, May 22, 1995
Buddy Harman, May 23, 1995
Don Helms, March 24, 1995
Van Howard, March 30, 1995
Tommy Hill, May 5, 1995
Darrell McCall, April 7, 1995

Wade Ray, October 29, 1994
Jerry Rivers, March 22, 1995
Hank Thompson, May 1995
Pete Wade, March 13, 1995; August 4, 1995
Charlie Walker, April 21, 1995

Chapter 9: Jimmy Wyble

Jimmy Wyble, November 27, 1981; May 10, 1982

Chapter 10: Speedy West and Jimmy Bryant

Speedy West, 1981, 1984, 1985, 1987, 1994, 1995, 1996, 1997
Cliffie Stone, 1987, 1994, 1995, 1996, 1997
John Bryant, 1987
Jim Loakes, 1994, 1996
Albert Lee, 1987
Patricia Murphy Bryant, 1987
Ken Nelson, October 1995
Buck Owens, January 1992
Roy Harte, January 8, 1997
Billy Liebert, December 20, 1996
Jim Loakes, January 3, 1997
Billy Strange, January 20, 1997
Tennessee Ernie Ford, 1990

Chapter 11: Roy Lanham and the Whippoorwills

Roy Lanham, 1987
Dusty Rhoads, 1996

Chapter 12: Willie Nelson

Willie Nelson, summer 1993
Johnny Bush, late 1997

Bob Wills at the Grand Ole Opry

Ted Adams, December 5, 1981
Joe Holley, January 14, 1982
Monte Mountjoy, November 30, 1981
Jimmy Wyble, November 27, 1981; May 10, 1982
Eddy Arnold, December 18, 1981

BIBLIOGRAPHY

The Comprehensive Country Music Encyclopedia. New York: Times Books, 1994.

The Encyclopedia of Country Music. New York: Oxford University Press, 1998.

Ginell, Cary, with Roy Lee Brown: *Milton Brown and the Founding of Western Swing.* Champaign: University of Illinois Press, 1994.

Herman, Woody, and Stuart Troup. *The Woodchopper's Ball: The Autobiography of Woody Herman.* New York: Limelight, 1994.

Lynn, Loretta, with George Vecsey. *Coal Miner's Daughter.* New York: Da Capo, 2002.

Nelson, Willie, with Bud Shrake. *Willie: An Autobiography.* New York: Simon and Schuster, 1992.

Pearl, Minnie, with Joan Dew. *Minnie Pearl: An Autobiography.* New York: Simon and Schuster, 1980.

Smith, Richard R. *Fender: The Sound Heard 'Round The World.* Fullerton, Calif.: Garfish Press, 1995.

Whitburn, Joel. *Pop Memories: 1890–1954.* Menomonee Falls, Wis.: Record Research, 1986.

———. *Top Country Singles: 1944–1997.* Menomonee Falls, Wis.: Record Research, 1997.

Wolfe, Charles K. *A Good-Natured Riot: The Birth of the Grand Ole Opry.* Nashville, Tenn.: Country Music Foundation/Vanderbilt University Press, 1999.

DISCOGRAPHY

In the interest of full disclosure, records that I had a hand in compiling or annotating appear here with an asterisk after the title.

Spade Cooley

For years, nothing of Spade Cooley's substantial output was available on LP or CD. Some material from various transcriptions and live broadcasts appeared in the 1970s on the short-lived Club of Spade label, and Columbia's Historic Edition issued an LP compilation of Cooley Columbia material in the early 1980s. Bear Family's first venture into western swing, its Rompin' Stompin' Singin' Swingin' series, mixed Tex Williams and Cooley RCA recordings. The few Cooley titles included were not the best quality material.

Things have changed in recent years with a variety of CD releases, one of them official and the others consisting of rare live radio broadcast transcriptions and Armed Forces Radio material. These afford a far better, more balanced picture of Cooley's entire career with many numbers never recorded in a studio and some recorded numbers with looser, freer arrangements. At this writing, the Cooley RCA, Decca, and Raynote material remains reissued.

- *Spadella! The Essential Spade Cooley*, Sony Legacy, 1994, is a 20-track collection featuring the 1944–46 Columbia material. The recordings sound better than ever and are complete with false starts. The liner notes, however, incorrectly render Cooley a mystery. Not included is "Hari-Kiri, Hara-Kiri," a World War II anti-Japanese hate song.
- *Shame on You*, Bloodshot Revival, 2000, was conceived to reissue the Standard Transcriptions that so excited Johnny Bond, Hank Penny, and others. The one volume issued provides ample justification for that excitement on numbers like the jazz favorites "I Found a New Baby," and "Copenhagen," and the fiddle favorite "Silver Bell," though "Cow Bell Polka" and others reflect the band's schmaltzier side.

- Britain's Interstate Music has released several CDs of Cooley material from private collections of radio transcriptions, including some covering the 1944–46 Williams/Rogers/Murphey group of "Shame on You" fame. Packaging is acceptable but those with Kevin Coffey's annotations provide far more reliable background information. The sound is generally acceptable, even with the inevitable flaws of transcription discs.
- *Spade Cooley and His Western Dance Gang*, Country Routes, 1998, encompasses live broadcasts over nine weeks from August until early October of 1945. It gives a better measure of the band in performance, mixing some of its recorded material with the band's individualistic spins on traditional fare like "Fort Worth Jail" and "Night Train to Memphis" along with Bob Wills's "Miss Molly" (the latter considerably stiffer than Wills's original).
- *Spade Cooley: 1941–1947*, Country Routes, 2000, draws 34 tracks from a broader selection of material, beginning with an even dozen 1941 transcription performances featuring Spade and Tex Williams during their days with Cal Shrum and His Rhythm Rangers. Included are not only samples of Tex's early vocal prowess, but Cooley's hot fiddle interaction with guitarist Gene Haas in the style of the Farr Brothers. Following an additional sampling of 1945–1946 "classic" material by the Rogers-Williams band are 11 1947 performances by the early RCA band.
- *Spade Cooley: 1945–1946*, Country Routes, 2001, follows the same path as the 1998 release, featuring the classic band playing an early version of "Spadella" (which the band didn't record until June 1946). The variety of material also includes some utterly forgettable fare like "All That Glitters Is Not Gold," but it was, after all, a dance band.
- *A Western Swing Dance Date with Spade and Tex*, Jasmine (England), 2000, was drawn from transcriptions featuring Cooley's band and Tex's Western Caravan (essentially the 1944–46 Cooley band). The earliest Cooley material features Tex and Smokey Rogers on vocals. Post-1946 material includes the studio-recorded "Diggin' with Spade," one of Cooley's most progressive performances, featuring the stunning twin guitar team of Jimmy Wyble and Cameron Hill. The later transcribed Cooley material features the orchestral side with Red Egner's awful vocals and an abundance of odd material. One could live a long and satisfying life without ever hearing "Piggy Bank Polka."

    The Tex Williams transcriptions reflect the near-identical lineup to the original Cooley band, which largely left with Williams in 1946, including "Pale Moon," complete with flute soloist. No surprise in a group that included a harp and a vibes player.

- *Spade Cooley Big Band: 1950–1952*, Harlequin, 1999, excerpts material from Cooley radio shows. The music tends to support Hank Penny's criticism of that band's dullness, though Jimmy Wyble stands out on "Bach Boogie" and Noel Boggs on "Steel Guitar Rag." Vocals by Ginny Jackson and Freddie "Careless" Love are predictably mediocre. The Penny comic spots reveal Spade's skills at playing straight man to Hank's "Plain Ol' Country Boy" persona, much as they did on *Hoffman Hayride*.

Hank Penny

All of the ARC/Columbia recordings made by Hank Penny and his Radio Cowboys are currently out of print. *Tobacco State Swing*, Rambler Records, 1980, included 12 examples of the Cowboys' material.

- *Hollywood Western Swing*, Krazy Kat (England), 2000, assembles a good portion of the King recordings from 1944 to 1947, including much of the material from the Hollywood sessions.
- *Hillbilly Be-Bop*,* Westside Records (England), 2001, a collection that I compiled and annotated, focused on the 1949–1950 material with no duplication with the Krazy Kat collection. Since the collection was licensed through GML, the Nashville-based owner of the King-Starday catalog, it also included alternate takes and unissued material.
- *Rompin' Stompin' Singin' Swingin'*,* Bear Family, 1983, assembles a good portion of Penny's 1950–1952 RCA material on a LP now out of print.
- *Crazy Rhythm: The Standard Transcriptions*, Soundies, 2000, offers the complete 1951 Penny recordings in one place.

Wade Ray

Currently, none of Wade Ray's seminal RCA recordings are in print anywhere.

Tommy Duncan

Tommy Duncan's complete Capitol, Natural, Intro, and Fire material, both good and bad, were issued on two CDs: *Texas Moon* and *Beneath a Neon Star in a Honky Tonk*,* Bear Family, 1996.

Luke Wills

The four King recordings remain out of print. One LP of Luke's complete RCA recordings was released in 1988, but it too is now out of print: *High Voltage Gal*,* Bear Family (Germany).

Smoke! Smoke! Smoke!/Lee Gillette

The original version of the Tex Williams hit, along with a sampling of other material produced by Lee Gillette, is available on *Swing West! Volume 3* * (Razor and Tie), a collection of West Coast western swing material largely drawn from the Capitol vaults.

Ken Nelson

Representative examples of Ken Nelson's production work for Capitol can be heard on *Swing West! Volume 1* * (Razor and Tie), a collection that centers on material by Bakersfield-based Capitol artists from Ferlin Husky to Wynn Stewart, Rose Maddox, and Merle Haggard. In addition, any Capitol hits package by Buck Owens or Merle Haggard reflects Nelson's work.

Cliffie Stone and the *Hometown Jamboree*

Radio Transcriptions by Cliffie Stone, Country Routes (Britain), 1991, draws from the *Dinner Bell Round-Up* and *Hometown Jamboree* radio shows. It includes material by the regulars, including the Armstrong Twins, Tennessee Ernie, and Harold Hensley, and features Ernie's incredible performance of "Muleskinner Blues" along with material by Red Murrell, and guests like Jimmy Wakely, Fiddlin' Arthur Smith, and guitarist Jack Rivers.

Tennessee Ernie Ford

- *Sixteen Tons*, Bear Family, 1990, compiles 25 essential early Capitol tracks on one CD.
- *Masters: 1949–1976*,* Liberty, 1994, mixes secular hits, obscurities, and unreleased material in a three-CD box set compiled by Ernie's eldest son, Buck. The set has a heavy emphasis on the boogie material and the mid-'50s fare with Jack Fascinato, along with samplings of later material.
- *Vintage Collections*,* Capitol, 1997, is a mixture of secular material with an emphasis on material that didn't make the Masters set, including "Snow-Shoe Thompson" and the decidedly Hank Williams-ish "I Ain't Gonna Let It Happen No More."
- *Sixteen Tons*,* Capitol, is a 1995 CD reissue of the 1960 LP. It consists of Ernie's biggest hit surrounded by the prime early boogie material.
- *Ernie Sings and Glen Picks*, Capitol Nashville, originally issued 1960, reissued 1996, is truly Ernie's last great secular album for Capitol.
- *The Ultimate Tennessee Ernie Ford Collection*,* Razor and Tie, 1997,

mixes secular and gospel material, one of the rare times that has occurred.

- Ernie's gospel packages are evergreen items but beyond the scope of this book, but you can't go wrong with *All-Time Greatest Hymns*, Curb, 1990, and *How Great Thou Art*, 1998.
- *His Original and Greatest Hits*, Jasmine, 2001, includes versions of the Capitol recordings performed on the RadiOzark transcriptions.

Hank Thompson

- *Hank Thompson and His Brazos Valley Boys*,* Bear Family, 1996, consists of 12 CDs assembling his complete Globe and Blue Bonnet and Capitol output. It also includes rare photos and memorabilia from Hank's own collection.
- *Vintage Collections*,* Capitol, 1996, is still available though no longer in print.
- *Dance Ranch/Songs For Rounders*,* Koch, 1999, pairs both these classic Capitol LPs on one disc.
- *Seven Decades*, Hightone, 2000, is also still in print and well worth having.

Slipping Around

Floyd Tillman's groundbreaking original Columbia recording of his most famous song is available on *The Best of Floyd Tillman*, Collector's Choice, 1999. *Capitol Vintage Collections: Jimmy Wakely*,* Capitol, 1996, includes the Wakely-Whiting hit, solo Wakely material, and additional duets with Whiting.

Ray Price

- *The Honky Tonk Years 1950–1966*,* Bear Family, 1996, brings together on 10 CDs Price's 1950 bullet single and his complete 1951–1966 Columbia recordings except for a few lost Columbia masters. It also features the complete *Western Strings* LP by the Cherokee Cowboys.
- *Night Life*,* Koch, 1998, is a straight reissue of Price's 1963 LP.
- *The Essential Ray Price*, Sony Legacy, 1991, brings together 20 samples of Price's Columbia work from 1951 through 1962 and scrupulously avoids all the countrypolitan fare.
- *Time*, Audium, 2002, represents Ray Price in 2002, his voice still in excellent shape, reunited with several members of his old recording and touring groups and solidly back in the twin-fiddle shuffles of the '50s and early '60s.

Jimmy Wyble

In addition to the Spade Cooley material mentioned above, Jimmy Wyble's work with Bob Wills can be heard on *Bob Wills and His Texas Playboys: The Essential Bob Wills*,* Sony Legacy, 1992.

- *San Antonio Rose*,* Bear Family, 2000, features Wyble's complete Columbia recordings with Wills, as well as the "Roly Poly" outtakes.
- *Frank Sinatra with the Red Norvo Quintet Live in Australia*, Blue Note, 2000, features Wyble in an accompanist's role on Sinatra's most famous recorded live performance. Though Wyble generally remains in the background on the album, he throws off a couple of scintillating choruses on the quintet's warm-up instrumentals "Perdido" and "Between the Devil and the Deep Blue Sea."

Speedy West and Jimmy Bryant

- *Stratosphere Boogie* and *Swingin' on the Strings*,* Razor and Tie, 1995 and 1999 respectively, release a good portion of the duo's Capitol output at a reasonable price.
- *Flamin' Guitars*,* Bear Family (Germany), 1997, assembles their complete Capitol output along with selected tracks featuring West and Bryant, individually and together, backing other performers from Eddie Kirk to Bing Crosby, Spike Jones, and Tennessee Ernie Ford. It also includes both of Speedy's post-Bryant solo efforts for Capitol.
- *There's Gonna Be a Party*, Jasmine, 2000, consists of Speedy's solo performances culled from the Ernie Ford RadiOzark transcriptions, including six performances also featuring Jimmy Bryant, one of them a twin-fiddle version of "Arkansas Traveler" by Bryant and Hensley.

Roy Lanham and the Whippoorwills

- The Standard Transcriptions (Soundies) brings together selections from the group's extensive work for Standard Radio Transcription Service.
- *Sizzling Strings/Fabulous Guitar of Roy Lanham*,* Bear Family, 1996, offers on one disc both the early '60s, post–Georgia Brown NRC Whippoorwills instrumental LP and Lanham's 1963 solo LP on Sims.

Willie Nelson

- *Nite Life: Greatest Hits and Rare Tracks, 1959–1971*,* Rhino, 1990, is a sort of mini-digest of material from D, Liberty, and RCA including the original "Night Life" (spelled as it was on the original Rx release).

- *A Classic and Unreleased Collection*,* Rhino 1996, is a repackage of a set originally offered on QVC. It includes his first single on the Willie Nelson label, a sampling of his early '60s demos for Pamper Music, and material from both his 1973–74 Atlantic contract (some of it live concert material from Austin not previously issued) and from Willie's own files.
- *Nashville Was The Roughest*,* Bear Family, 1998, covers Willie's Monument and RCA recordings in their entirety on eight CDs.

INDEX